Readings in Marketing

CONTRIBUTORS

MILTON ALEXANDER
Fordham University

WILLIAM D. BARCLAY
Needham, Louis and Brorby, Inc.

WESLEY C. BENDER
University of Notre Dame

NEIL H. BORDEN
Harvard University

R. A. BORING
Kimberly-Clark Corporation

LOUIS P. BUCKLIN
University of California (Berkeley)

RICHARD C. CHRISTIAN
Marsteller Inc.

RICHARD P. COLEMAN
University of Oregon

RALPH L. DAY
Indiana University

ALLEN R. DODD, JR.
Schwerin Research Corporation

PHILIP A. DOHERTY
Cresap, Mc Cormick & Paget

ROBERT C. GARRETSON
Carling Brewing Company

M. H. GONSIOR
Hughes Aircraft Corporation

PAUL E. GREEN
University of Pennsylvania

MASON HAIRE
University of California (Berkeley)

HERTA HERZOG
McCann-Erickson, Inc.

STANLEY C. HOLLANDER
Michigan State University

CHRISTEN T. JONASSEN
The Ohio State University

RONALD J. R. KALLMAN
Philco Corporation

PATRICK J. KELLY
Schwerin Research Corporation

HERBERT E. KRUGMAN
Marplan

PHILIP KOTLER
Northwestern University

ALFRED A. KUEHN
Carnegie University

SIDNEY J. LEVY
Northwestern University

HARRY A. LIPSON
University of Alabama

FERDINAND F. MAUSER
Wayne State University

WILLIAM A. MINDAK
University of Minnesota

WILLIAM T. MORAN
Young & Rubicam, Inc.

LEON MORSE
Dun's Review and Modern Industry

BARDIN H. NELSON
Agriculture and Mining College
of Texas

JACK C. PAGE
Booz, Allen & Hamilton, Inc.

WILLIAM H. REYNOLDS
University of Southern California

HARRY V. ROBERTS
University of Chicago

LAWRENCE SALKIN
Associated Merchandising Corporation

STEVEN J. SHAW
University of South Carolina

MARTIN KENNETH STARR
Columbia University

JOHN F. STOLLE
Booz, Allen & Hamilton, Inc.

LAWRENCE X. TARPEY
University of Kentucky

D. S. TULL
Orange State College

DOYLE L. WEISS
University of Pittsburgh

CHARLES WINICK
J. Walter Thompson Company

DANIEL YANKELOVICH
Daniel Yankelovich, Inc.

edited by

Philip R. Cateora
University of Colorado

Lee Richardson
Louisiana State University

READINGS IN MARKETING:

The Qualitative and Quantitative Areas

NEW YORK
APPLETON-CENTURY-CROFTS
DIVISION OF MEREDITH PUBLISHING COMPANY

To Nancy and Doralee

PREFACE

Readings in Marketing is designed for use as a supplementary text in the principles course in marketing. Its purpose is to present to the student contributions to the field of marketing made by both the behavioral scientist and mathematician.

The introductory part establishes the relationship between other disciplines and marketing management. The articles were selected to illustrate the many facets of marketing that require not only varied knowledge but different analytical techniques and thought processes as well. Part II provides a sample of the vast literature in the quantitative and behavioral sciences that can be brought to bear on marketing problems. Within this potpourri are one or more analytical approaches to bodies of subject matter that the editors hope will stir curiosity and perhaps some independent inquiry.

Part III introduces the consumer and the market, the most important uncontrollable variables facing any marketing manager. It should be noted that while this section is not lengthy, many of the readings in other sections refer to consumer behavior patterns and methods of analysis while developing other ideas and topics. The market is the focal point of marketing management activity, so it is to be expected that many marketing strategies will be directly developed from observations of market patterns.

Part IV presents a number of new developments in the application of marketing's controllable variables. The determination of product, channel, promotion, and price policies and strategies appears to be a heterogeneous group of activities. This, of course, applies only to the individual techniques or methods of determination and not to the ultimate aim of these activities. The marketing manager must keep abreast of the bulk of new developments regardless of his personal evaluation of many of the myriad approaches.

Having seen something of the current trends in marketing, the reader's thoughts are directed to the future in Part V. Questions concerning the future must be thoroughly formulated if they are to be seriously considered; the concluding articles should aid the inquiring mind in attaining the proper focus. A few answers to some of the questions involving the future are becoming apparent from the results obtained by many of the new and often underdeveloped analytical tools and techniques covered in earlier readings.

We wish to thank the authors and publishers who granted us permission to include their articles in this book. In addition, we thank our colleagues for their advice and criticism and our students for their energetic response to the articles we have selected. We, of course, assume responsibility for the framework in which the individual selections have been placed.

P. R. C.

L. R.

CONTENTS

III. THE CONSUMER   171

IV. MARKETING MANAGEMENT   233

A. Product Policy

B. Place

C. Promotion

D. Price

V. MARKETING TOMORROW   433

Introduction

Introduction

Readings in Marketing has a primary objective of presenting to the student of marketing the recent developments in marketing management. In many respects marketing has come of age since World War II. It is recognized now not only as a profession but also as a field worthy of scholarly study. Recent years have seen the development of techniques and the establishment of certain principles in marketing. The market concept has evolved recognizing the fundamental nature of marketing management—service to the market at a profit to the business. Marketing scholars have continued to develop theories in marketing, pushing the discipline on to new heights. Marketing management has progressed from an area of concern with unrelated activities to recognition that marketing has certain unity. The new frontiers in marketing are still those of understanding marketing phenomena and developing guides for management decision making. The question now logically raised is where to look for direction.

Many systems have been suggested for the development of marketing, but much of the progress in marketing today is the result of systematic, selective borrowing from other sciences. In fact, the most important achievements in modern marketing management have been the application of techniques and concepts borrowed from other disciplines and evaluated by students of marketing in light of the needs of marketing management. The need for original or primary research and determination of the relative value of all new ideas and information, regardless of origin, must be considered.

Readings in Marketing illustrates the practical contributions of the many other disciplines to modern marketing. The organization of the materials presented is typical of several leading managerial marketing textbooks. Students should expect some readings to go beyond the apparent subject matter, thus defying any simplified classification system. This is inherent in the subject matter of marketing, where complex interrelationships among many variables is the rule rather than the exception.

This book incorporates two major sources of contributions into the

3

marketing management framework. The first source is made up of a variety of behavioral concepts developed originally in anthropology, sociology, social psychology, psychology, and related disciplines. Mathematical and statistical techniques, the second source, are similarly found useful for many tasks of marketing managers.

Marketing is only beginning to feel the impact of these developments. In fact, many of the readings have a pioneering sense of urgency that is not properly appreciated until the students see an application to a real dollars-and-cents situation. The new concepts in these readings promise continuing improvements in our understanding of the consumer, the competitive marketplace, and the strategies and tactics applied to achieve marketing objectives.

Students must be introduced to the changes occurring in marketing because change is a fundamental phenomenon for the marketing environment. The nature of change is unsettling and can be viewed either as new difficulty or as opportunity for progress and gain. Students may find themselves reaching both ways throughout the book, but the lesson is clearly demonstrated that marketing is a dynamic discipline that constantly forces decisions in response to change.

Certain of the readings will require concentration and study above and beyond the usual marketing fare. The difficulty of these articles should be viewed in the light of the objectives of marketing which include understanding and serving the wants of that most enigmatic animal, man.

I. Scientific Marketing Management

INTRODUCTION

Marketers and marketing students should be familiar with the nature and scope of their field. New approaches and developments are occurring that alter somewhat the concept of marketing management but leave the core of most activities the same. Professor Borden's article outlines the central elements of marketing management and discusses the interrelationships within marketing activities and their place in the business firm. It is within this setting that fresh ideas and new approaches are to be applied.

Management of the marketing mix has become increasingly sophisticated, often to such an extent that some scholars criticize the rapid pace of the change. While the precise state of the art or science of marketing is the subject of debate, marketing scholars definitely are moving away from the traditional management thinking toward a newer concept employing the overall methods of science more closely. In examining this movement, Professor Starr covers many developments in management and related areas and illustrates their uses in marketing. Marketing has only begun to notice the potential of some of these advances.

Professor Lipson has condensed such a spectrum of knowledge and disciplines in "Formal Reasoning and Marketing Strategy," that the immediate impression is that marketing cannot be large enough to encompass all the ideas presented. Further into the readings, however, specific examples of some of these areas will provide proof of the enlarging scope of marketing.

The variety in marketing problems is illustrated when some of the current business situations are examined as an indication of the tumult in marketing. Although fitting under the umbrella called marketing, the methods of facing new problems and opportunities do not require the same standard solutions. Even from a cursory examination of Mr. Morse's article we are obliged to admit to inadequate problem-solving devices and to incomplete understanding of our limited arsenal of solutions.

7

1. The concept of the marketing mix

NEIL H. BORDEN

I have always found it interesting to observe how an apt or colorful term may catch on, gain wide usage, and help to further understanding of a concept that has already been expressed in less appealing and communicative terms. Such has been true of the phrase "marketing mix," which I began to use in my teaching and writing some 15 years ago. In a relatively short time it has come to have wide usage. This note tells of the evolution of the marketing mix concept.

The phrase was suggested to me by a paragraph in a research bulletin on the management of marketing costs, written by my associate, Professor James Culliton. In this study of manufacturers' marketing costs he described the business executive as a

"decider," an "artist"—a "mixer of ingredients," who sometimes follows a recipe prepared by others, sometimes prepares his own recipe as he goes along, sometimes adapts a recipe to the ingredients immediately available, and sometimes experiments with or invents ingredients no one else has tried.[1]

I liked his idea of calling a marketing executive a "mixer of ingredients," one who is constantly engaged in fashioning creatively a mix of marketing procedures and policies in his efforts to produce a profitable enterprise.

For many years previous to Culliton's cost study, the wide variations in the procedures and policies employed by managements of manufacturing firms in their marketing programs and the correspondingly wide variation in the costs of these marketing functions, which Culliton aptly ascribed to the varied "mixing of ingredients," had become increasingly

Reprinted from the *Journal of Advertising Research,* June, 1964, pp. 2–7, by permission of the author and publisher. © Advertising Research Foundation, Inc., 1964.
[1] Culliton, James W., *The Management of Marketing Costs,* Boston: Division of Research, Graduate School of Business Administration, Harvard University, 1948.

evident as we had gathered marketing cases at the Harvard Business School. The marked differences in the patterns or formulae of the marketing programs not only were evident through facts disclosed in case histories, but also were reflected clearly in the figures of a cost study of food manufacturers made by the Harvard Bureau of Business Research in 1929. The primary objective of this study was to determine common figures of expenses for various marketing functions among food manufacturing companies, similar to the common cost figures which had been determined in previous years for various kinds of retail and wholesale businesses. In this manufacturer's study we were unable, however, with the data gathered to determine common expense figures that had much significance as standards by which to guide management, such as had been possible in the studies of retail and wholesale trades, where the methods of operation tended toward uniformity. Instead, among food manufacturers the ratios of sales devoted to the various functions of marketing such as advertising, personal selling, packaging, and so on, were found to be widely divergent, no matter how we grouped our respondents. Each respondent gave data that tended to uniqueness.

Culliton's study of marketing costs in 1947–48 was a second effort to find out, among other objectives, whether a bigger sample and a more careful classification of companies would produce evidence of operating uniformities that would give helpful common expense figures. But the result was the same as in our early study: there was wide diversity in cost ratios among any classifications of firms which were set up, and no common figures were found that had much value. This was true whether companies were grouped according to similarity in product lines, amount of sales, territorial extent of operations, or other bases of classification.

Relatively early in my study of advertising, it had become evident that understanding of advertising usage by manufacturers in any case had to come from an analysis of advertising's place as one element in the total marketing program of the firm. I came to realize that it is essential always to ask: what overall marketing strategy has been or might be employed to bring about a profitable operation in light of the circumstances faced by the management? What combination of marketing procedures and policies has been or might be adopted to bring about desired behavior of trade and consumers at costs that will permit a profit? Specifically, how can advertising, personal selling, pricing, packaging, channels, warehousing, and the other elements of a marketing program be manipulated and fitted together in a way that will give a profitable operation? In short, I saw that every advertising management case called for a consideration of the strategy to be adopted for the total marketing program, with advertising recognized as only one element whose form and extent depended on its careful adjustment to the other parts of the program.

The soundness of this viewpoint was supported by case histories throughout my volume, *The Economic Effects of Advertising*.[2] In the chapters devoted to the utilization of advertising by business, I had pointed out the innumerable combinations of marketing methods and policies that might be adopted by a manager in arriving at a marketing plan. For instance, in the area of branding, he might elect to adopt an individualized brand or a family brand. Or he might decide to sell his product unbranded or under private label. Any decision in the area of brand policy in turn has immediate implications that bear on his selection of channels of distribution, sales force methods, packaging, promotional procedure, and advertising. Throughout the volume the case materials cited show that the way in which any marketing function is designed and the burden placed upon the function are determined largely by the overall marketing strategy adopted by managements to meet the market conditions under which they operate. The forces met by different firms vary widely. Accordingly, the programs fashioned differ widely.

Regarding advertising, which was the function under focus in the economic effects volume, I said at one point:

In all the above illustrative situations it should be recognized that advertising is not an operating method to be considered as something apart, as something whose profit value is to be judged alone. An able management does not ask, "Shall we use or not use advertising?" without consideration of the product and of other management procedures to be employed. Rather the question is always one of finding a management formula giving advertising its due place in the combination of manufacturing methods, product form, pricing, promotion and selling methods, and distribution methods. As previously pointed out different formulae, i.e., different combinations of methods, may be profitably employed by competing manufacturers.

From the above it can be seen why Culliton's description of a marketing manager as a "mixer of ingredients" immediately appealed to me as an apt and easily understandable phrase, far better than my previous references to the marketing man as an empiricist seeking in any situation to devise a profitable "pattern" or "formula" of marketing operations from among the many procedures and policies that were open to him. If he was a "mixer of ingredients," what he designed was a "marketing mix."

It was logical to proceed from a realization of the existence of a variety of "marketing mixes" to the development of a concept that would comprehend not only this variety, but also the market forces that cause managements to produce a variety of mixes. It is the problems raised by these forces that lead marketing managers to exercise their wits in devising mixes or programs which they hope will give a profitable business operation.

[2] Borden, Neil H., *The Economic Effects of Advertising*, Homewood, Ill.: Richard D. Irwin, 1942.

To portray this broadened concept in a visual presentation requires merely:

1) a list of the important elements or ingredients that make up marketing programs:
2) a list of the forces that bear on the marketing operation of a firm and to which the marketing manager must adjust in his search for a mix or program that can be successful.

The list of elements of the marketing mix in such a visual presentation can be long or short, depending on how far one wishes to go in his classification and subclassification of the marketing procedures and policies with which marketing managements deal when devising marketing programs. The list of elements which I have employed in my teaching and consulting work covers the principal areas of marketing activities which call for management decisions as revealed by case histories. I realize others might build a different list. Mine is as follows:

ELEMENTS OF THE MARKETING MIX OF MANUFACTURERS

1. *Product Planning*—policies and procedures relating to:
   a) Product lines to be offered—qualities, design, etc.
   b) Markets to sell: whom, where, when, and in what quantity.
   c) New Product policy—research and development program.
2. *Pricing*—policies and procedures relating to:
   a) Price level to adopt.
   b) Specific prices to adopt (odd-even, etc.).
   c) Price policy, e.g., one-price or varying price, price maintenance, use of list prices, etc.
   d) Margins to adopt—for company; for the trade.
3. *Branding*—policies and procedures relating to:
   a) Selection of trade marks.
   b) Brand policy—individualized or family brand.
   c) Sale under private label or unbranded.
4. *Channels of Distribution*—policies and procedures relating to:
   a) Channels to use between plant and consumer.
   b) Degree of selectivity among wholesalers and retailers.
   c) Efforts to gain cooperation of the trade.
5. *Personal Selling*—policies and procedures relating to:
   a) Burden to be placed on personal selling and the methods to be employed in:
      1. Manufacturer's organization.
      2. Wholesale segment of the trade.
      3. Retail segment of the trade.
6. *Advertising*—policies and procedures relating to:
   a) Amount to spend—i.e., the burden to be placed on advertising.
   b) Copy platform to adopt:
      1. Product image desired.

    2. Corporate image desired.
  c) Mix of advertising: to the trade; through the trade; to consumers.
7. *Promotions*—policies and procedures relating to:
  a) Burden to place on special selling plans or devices directed at or through the trade.
  b) Form of these devices for consumer promotions, for trade promotions.
8. *Packaging*—policies and procedures relating to:
  a) Formulation of package and label.
9. *Display*—policies and procedures relating to:
  a) Burden to be put on display to help effect sale.
  b) Methods to adopt to secure display.
10. *Servicing*—policies and procedures relating to:
  a) Providing service needed.
11. *Physical Handling*—policies and procedures relating to:
  a) Warehousing.
  b) Transportation.
  c) Inventories.
12. *Fact Finding and Analysis*—policies and procedures relating to:
  a) Securing, analysis, and use of facts in marketing operations.

Also if one were to make a list of all the forces which managements weigh at one time or another when formulating their marketing mixes, it would be very long indeed, for the behavior of individuals and groups in all spheres of life have a bearing, first, on what goods and services are produced and consumed, and, second, on the procedures that may be employed in bringing about exchange of these goods and services. However, the important forces which bear on marketers, all arising from the behavior of individuals or groups, may readily be listed under four heads, namely the behavior of consumers, the trade, competitors, and government.

The outline below contains these four behavioral forces with notations of some of the important behavioral determinants within each force. These must be studied and understood by the marketer, if his marketing mix is to be successful. The great quest of marketing management is to understand the behavior of humans in response to the stimuli to which they are subjected. The skillful marketer is one who is a perceptive and practical psychologist and sociologist, who has keen insight into individual and group behavior, who can foresee changes in behavior that develop in a dynamic world, who has creative ability for building well-knit programs because he has the capacity to visualize the probable response of consumers, trade, and competitors to his moves. His skill in forecasting response to his marketing moves should well be supplemented by a further skill in devising and using tests and measurements to check consumer or trade response to his program or parts thereof, for no marketer has so much prescience that he can proceed without empirical check.

Below, then, is the suggested outline of forces which govern the mixing of marketing elements. This list and that of the elements taken together provide a visual presentation of the concept of the marketing mix.

MARKET FORCES BEARING ON THE MARKETING MIX

1. *Consumers' Buying Behavior,* as determined by their:
    a) Motivation in purchasing.
    b) Buying habits.
    c) Living habits.
    d) Environment (present and future, as revealed by trends, for environment influences consumers' attitudes toward products and their use of them).
    e) Buying power.
    f) Number (i.e., how many).
2. *The Trade's Behavior*—wholesalers' and retailers' behavior, as influenced by:
    a) Their motivation.
    b) Their structure, practices, and attitudes.
    c) Trends in structure and procedures that portend change.
3. *Competitors' Position and Behavior,* as influenced by:
    a) Industry structure and the firm's relation thereto.
        1. Size and strength of competitors.
        2. Number of competitors and degree of industry concentration.
        3. Indirect competition—i.e., from other products.
    b) Relation of supply to demand—oversupply or undersupply.
    c) Product choices offered consumers by the industry—i.e., quality, price, service.
    d) Degree to which competitors compete on price vs. nonprice bases.
    e) Competitors' motivations and attitudes—their likely response to the actions of other firms.
    f) Trends technological and social, portending change in supply and demand.
4. *Governmental Behavior—Controls over Marketing:*
    a) Regulations over products.
    b) Regulations over pricing.
    c) Regulations over competitive practices.
    d) Regulations over advertising and promotion.

When building a marketing program to fit the needs of his firm, the marketing manager has to weigh the behavioral forces and then juggle marketing elements in his mix with a keen eye on the resources with which he has to work. His firm is but one small organism in a large universe of complex forces. His firm is only a part of an industry that is competing with many other industries. What does the firm have in terms of money, product line, organization, and reputation with which to work? The manager must devise a mix of procedures that fit these resources. If his firm is small, he must judge the response of consumers, trade, and competition in light of his position and resources and the influence that he can exert in the market. He must look for special opportunities in product or method of operation. The small firm cannot employ the procedures of the big firm. Though he may sell the same kind of product as the big firm, his marketing strategy is likely to be widely different in many respects. Innumerable instances of this fact might be cited. For example, in the industrial goods field, small firms often seek to build sales on a limited and highly specialized line, whereas industry leaders seek patronage for full lines. Small firms often elect to go in for regional sales rather than attempt the national distribution practiced by larger companies. Again, the company of limited resources often elects to limit its production and sales to products whose potential is too small to attract the big fellows. Still again, companies with small resources in the cosmetic field not infrequently have set up introductory marketing programs employing aggressive personal selling and a "push" strategy with distribution limited to leading department stores. Their initially small advertising funds have been directed through these selected retail outlets, with the offering of the products and their story told over the signatures of the stores. The strategy has been to borrow kudos for their products from the leading stores' reputations and to gain a gradual radiation of distribution to smaller stores in all types of channels, such as often comes from the trade's follow-the-leader behavior. Only after resources have grown from mounting sales has a dense retail distribution been aggressively sought and a shift made to place the selling burden more and more on company-signed advertising.

The above strategy was employed for Toni products and Stoppette deodorant in their early marketing stages when the resources of their producers were limited (cf. case of Jules Montenier, Inc.).[3] In contrast, cosmetic manufacturers with large resources have generally followed a "pull" strategy for the introduction of new products, relying on heavy campaigns of advertising in a rapid succession of area introductions to induce a hoped-for, complete retail coverage from the start (cf. case of Bristol-Myers Company).[4] These introductory campaigns have been undertaken only after careful programs of product development and test marketing have given assurance that product and selling plans had high promise of success.

Many additional instances of the varying strategy employed by small versus large enterprises might be cited. But those given serve to illustrate the point that managements must fashion their mixes to fit their resources. Their objectives must be realistic.

[3] Borden, Neil H., and M. V. Marshall, *Advertising Management: Text and Cases,* Homewood, Ill.: Richard D. Irwin, 1959. Pp. 498–518.
[4] *Ibid.,* Pp. 519–533.

LONG VS. SHORT TERM ASPECTS OF MARKETING MIX

The marketing mix of a firm in large part is the product of the evolution that comes from day-to-day marketing. At any time the mix represents the program that a management has evolved to meet the problems with which it is constantly faced in an ever changing, ever challenging market. There are continuous tactical maneuvers: a new product, aggressive promotion, or price change initiated by a competitor must be considered and met; the failure of the trade to provide adequate market coverage or display must be remedied; a faltering sales force must be reorganized and stimulated; a decline in sales share must be diagnosed and remedied; an advertising approach that has lost effectiveness must be replaced; a general business decline must be countered. All such problems call for a management's maintaining effective channels of information relative to its own operations and to the day-to-day behavior of consumers, competitors, and the trade. Thus, we may observe that short range forces play a large part in the fashioning of the mix to be used at any time and in determining the allocation of expenditures among the various functional accounts of the operating statement.

But the overall strategy employed in a marketing mix is the product of longer range plans and procedures dictated in part by past empiricism and in part, if the management is a good one, by management foresight as to what needs to be done to keep the firm successful in a changing world. As the world has become more and more dynamic, blessed is that corporation which has managers who have foresight, who can study trends of all kinds—natural, economic, social, and technological—and, guided by these, devise long-range plans that give promise of keeping their corporations afloat and successful in the turbulent sea of market change. Accordingly, when we think of the marketing mix, we need to give particular heed today to devising a mix based on long-range planning that promises to fit the world of five or ten or more years hence. Provision for effective long-range planning in corporate organization and procedure has become more and more recognized as the earmark of good management in a world that has become increasingly subject to rapid change.

To cite an instance among American marketing organizations which has shown foresight in adjusting the marketing mix to meet social and economic change, I look upon Sears Roebuck and Company as an outstanding example. After building an unusually successful mail order business to meet the needs of a rural America, Sears management foresaw the need to depart from its marketing pattern as a mail order company catering primarily to farmers. The trend from a rural to an urban United States was going on apace. The automobile and good roads promised to make town and city stores increasingly available to those who continued to be farmers. Relatively early, Sears launched a chain of stores across the land, each easily accessible by highway to both farmer and city resident, and with adequate parking space for customers. In time there followed the remarkable telephone and mail order plan directed at urban residents to make buying easy for Americans when congested city streets and highways made shopping increasingly distasteful. Similarly, in the areas of planning products which would meet the desires of consumers in a fast changing world, of shaping its servicing to meet the needs of a wide variety of mechanical products, of pricing procedures to meet the challenging competition that came with the advent of discount retailers, the Sears organization has shown a foresight, adaptability, and creative ability worthy of emulation. The amazing growth and profitability of the company attest to the foresight and skill of its management. Its history shows the wisdom of careful attention to market forces and their impending change in devising marketing mixes that may assure growth.

USE OF THE MARKETING MIX CONCEPT

Like many concepts, the marketing mix concept seems relatively simple, once it has been expressed. I know that before they were ever tagged with the nomenclature of "concept," the ideas involved were widely understood among marketers as a result of the growing knowledge about marketing and marketing procedures that came during the preceding half century. But I have found for myself that once the ideas were reduced to a formal statement with an accompanying visual presentation, the concept of the mix has proved a helpful devise in teaching, in business problem solving, and, generally, as an aid to thinking about marketing. First of all, it is helpful in giving an answer to the question often raised as to "what is marketing?" A chart which shows the elements of the mix and the forces that bear on the mix helps to bring understanding of what marketing is. It helps to explan why in our dynamic world the thinking of management in all its functional areas must be oriented to the market.

In recent years I have kept an abbreviated chart showing the elements and the forces of the marketing mix in front of my classes at all times. In case discussion it has proved a handy device by which to raise queries as to whether the student has recognized the implications of any recommendation he might have made in the areas of the several elements of the mix. Or, referring to the forces, we can question whether all the pertinent market forces have been given due consideration. Continual reference to the mix chart leads me to feel that the students' understanding of "what marketing is" is strengthened. The constant presence and use of the chart leaves a deeper understanding that marketing is the devising of programs that successfully meet the forces of the market.

In problem solving the marketing mix chart is a constant reminder of:

1) The fact that a problem seemingly lying in one segment of the mix must be deliberated with constant thought regarding the effect of any change in that sector on the other areas of marketing operations. The necessity of integration in marketing thinking is ever present.
2) The need of careful study of the market forces as they might bear on problems in hand.

In short, the mix chart provides an ever ready checklist as to areas into which to guide thinking when considering marketing questions or dealing with marketing problems.

MARKETING: SCIENCE OR ART?

The quest for a "science of marketing" is hard upon us. If science is in part a systematic formulation and arrangement of facts in a way to help understanding, then the concept of the marketing mix may possibly be considered a small contribution in the search for a science of marketing. If we think of a marketing science as involving the observation and classification of facts and the establishment of verifiable laws that can be used by the marketer as a guide to action with assurance that predicted results will ensue, then we cannot be said to have gotten far toward establishing a science. The concept of the mix lays out the areas in which facts should be assembled, these to serve as a guide to management judgment in building marketing mixes. In the last few decades American marketers have made substantial progress in adopting the scientific method in assembling facts. They have sharpened the tools of fact finding—both those arising within the business and those external to it. Aided by these facts and by the skills developed through careful observation and experience, marketers are better fitted to practice the art of designing marketing mixes than would be the case had not the techniques of gathering facts been advanced as they have been in recent decades. Moreover, marketers have made progress in the use of the scientific method in designing tests whereby the results from mixes or parts of mixes can be measured. Thereby marketers have been learning how to subject the hypotheses of their mix artists to empirical check.

With continued improvement in the search for and the recording of facts pertinent to marketing, with further application of the controlled experiment, and with an extension and careful recording of case histories, we may hope for a gradual formulation of clearly defined and helpful marketing laws. Until then, and even then, marketing and the building of marketing mixes will largely lie in the realm of art.

2. Management science and marketing science

MARTIN KENNETH STARR [1]

1. INTRODUCTION

Marketing management problems have been receiving increasing attention from management scientists. In part, this is because the marketing complex poses an exciting challenge. It is also attributable to the fact that marketing management has *permitted* exploration by management scientists in its special preserve. But a fundamental question remains unanswered; namely: What can management science contribute to the marketing field?

In the April, 1956 issue of the Journal of The Institute of Management Sciences (Vol. 2, No. 3), Professor Melvin Anshen considered this question and its ramifications. The paper was entitled, "Management Science in Marketing: Status and Prospects." The article provided important perspective for management scientists who were then beginning to work in the field of marketing. It pointed to significant opportunities for achievement but little accomplishment as of that date.

Approximately seven years have passed since the publication of this paper, and it seems appropriate to resurvey what has been happening; where things stand at the present time; and where we are likely to be going in the future. As a convenient structure, this paper is divided into four parts: the environment for accomplishment, accomplishments to

Reprinted from *Management Science*, Volume 10, No. 3 (April, 1964), pp. 557–573, by permission of *Management Science* and Martin Kenneth Starr, Columbia University Graduate School of Business.
[1] I wish to thank Peter Langhoff and William Moran, of Young and Rubicam, Inc. and Sebastian Littauer, of Columbia University for their intrinsically helpful comments on an earlier draft.

date, the nature of marketing problems and the outlook for marketing science.

2. THE ENVIRONMENT FOR ACCOMPLISHMENT

Before jumping off into an accounting of the accomplishments of management scientists in the field of marketing, it is desirable to consider the background of *marketing* science and the environment in which it has developed.

Marketing science began with market research. That was about fifty years ago. Its objective then, as now, was to reduce uncertainty in the marketing process. As markets expanded so did competitive pressures resulting in ever greater penalties for uncertainty.

2.1 Disciplines Participating in the Development of Marketing Science

The variety of problems that existed attracted the attention of a number of disciplines. Basically, four different groups entered into the work of determining, in some formal or quantitative sense, factors that related to the transference of goods and services between a producer and consumers.

(a) One of the groups engaged in the development and collection of *descriptive statistics*. The core of the task was to categorize individuals by means of demographic-type variables. The fundamental intent was to define and identify *potential* customers in the population. As advertising became a force in the marketing process, the problem of matching media to marketing prospects gave great impetus to these efforts.

(b) Social scientists constituted another group. They were particularly attracted by the growth of advertising. Communications was a vital social phenomenon. Measuring the effectiveness of communications (its ability to instruct and persuade), was beset with intangibles that were at least familiar to these scientists. With the growth in importance of advertising research, the influx of behavioral scientists into market research has been rapid. Something of a high point was reached in the late 1940's when "motivational research" became a predominant technique in marketing analysis. Since then, this position of eminence has slipped away. It became quite clear that the behavioral scientist could not—by himself—provide a methodological basis for a science of marketing.

(c) Economists formed a third group. They attempted to provide effective forecasting techniques as well as an analytic base for predicting changes in the economy. They investigated the effects of price and the role of competition, but for the most part on a theoretical level. To a limited extent they studied the relationship of marketing variables to actual sales and profit. Although their results did not always find practical application, the econometricians can be credited with the first viable models in the field of marketing science. If any group broke the trail for management scientists, it was this one.

(d) The fourth group, composed of management scientists, began to work in marketing hardly a decade ago. Acknowledged model builders, this group held out the hope of identifying and synthesizing the variety of factors that are critical determinants of the marketing process. And, of course, the models were expected to have practical utility. Our comments throughout this paper deal with how well this group has fared.

2.2 Conflicts in the Marketing Field

Of importance is the fact that marketing science, defined by the operations of the four groups mentioned above, was found to be in fundamental conflict with the field of marketing which it had intended to serve. The conflict can be described as intuition and judgment used alone and opposed to the employment of scientific method for reaching decisions. We might call this—Art versus Science; but in fact it seems more reasonable to describe this conflict as Anti-science versus Science.

We should note at this point why a similar conflict has been less evident in the production field. Production technology is primarily a function of physical laws that are known; marketing technology is related to behavioral systems, whose laws, if any, are at present, unknown. Production technology develops in terms of equipment, materials and processes. Although not easily predictable, it is constrained and subject to a considerable set of impossibilities. Formal logic and mathematics were not antithetical to engineers and production personnel. On the contrary, they were a natural part of the production fabric. Consequently, when management science found its place within the field of production there was only minimal conflict between Anti-science and Science.

The essence of the conflict in the marketing field can be illuminated by the following quote from Karl Pearson:

In dealing with any natural phenomenon—especially one of a vital nature, with all the complexity of living organisms in type and habit—the mathematician has to simplify the conditions until they reach the attenuated character which lies within the power of his analysis.

Since a marketing man must deal with such living organisms it is understandable that the word "attenuated" could not be accepted by marketing executives and reconciled with the desire to achieve successful decisions. At the same time, none of these executives would describe their intuitive process for reaching decisions as being attenuated. Thus, they are forced into the position of being antiscientific because scientific and mathematical efforts to explain the marketing process tend to be superficial and attenuated—not practical and powerful.

2.3 The Problem of the Two Cultures

Particularly relevant is the C. P. Snow-F. R. Leavis debate. C. P. Snow, a Cambridge don, delivered the Rede lecture in 1959, which was later published.[2] Snow contended that Western society consists of two cultural groups. The first might be called the creative—being identified with literature and art; the second is the scientific. These groups, according to Snow, are totally intolerant of each other and have little or no understanding of the other's position. While Snow hopes that the gap can and will be bridged, he is clearly partisan in his belief that the scientific culture is superior for the destiny of man.

F. R. Leavis, who is identified by various sources as one of Britain's best-known literary critics, delivered the Richmond lecture in 1962. The following quote gives us a little of the flavor of Leavis' remarks:

The judgment I have to come out with is that not only is he (C. P. Snow) not a genius; he is intellectually as undistinguished as it is possible to be.

Lionel Trilling, writing in the June 1962 issue of *Commentary* provides us with a great deal of insight concerning this conflict. Trilling pointed out that eighty years ago the two-culture problem was argued by Matthew Arnold and T. H. Huxley. At that time Arnold delivered the Rede lecture in "Literature and Science." Huxley's lecture was entitled "Culture and Education." According to Trilling, Snow says nothing that is different from what Huxley had said and Leavis' argument parallels Matthew Arnold's.[3]

So we see that this conflict has existed for a long time. The basic nature of the antagonism is most aptly described as Anti-science versus Science and vice versa. The proponents of Anti-science can include any group that resists the characteristic approaches and results of scientific method. The conflict has not been resolved over these many years. And it still produces emotional outbursts from responsible, dedicated individuals. The relevance of this discussion to our topic is that the marketing field is particularly susceptible to such conflict. Through adaptation, research personnel have developed a non-antipathetic symbiotic relationship with the intuitive decision maker's culture.

2.4 Management Science's Degree of Acceptance

Management scientists are newcomers to marketing science. They should be aware of the conflict which has persisted in the field. Management scientists have had *a degree* of acceptance from marketing execu-

---

[2] Snow, C. P., *The Two Cultures and the Scientific Revolution*, New York: Cambridge University Press, 1961.

[3] Simpson, Mary S., "The Snow Affair," *Bulletin of the Atomic Scientist*, Vol. 19, No. 4 (April 1963), pp. 28–32.

tives. But we should not lose sight of the fact that three years passed before Leavis saw fit to answer Snow. Management scientists should not interpret incorrectly the degree of acceptance that they have achieved as being a permanent endowment on the part of the marketing field. Marketing men are sophisticated. Their attitude is: Let's wait and see. We need only consider the way in which the marketing field received the idea of "subliminal perception." The notion that effective communication might be carried on at a level of awareness below conscious perception was not immediately rebuked. The issues were carefully studied. "Wait-and-see" has been a marketing attitude even in the face of preposterous claims. The tradition of this restraint, albeit acceptance with hostility and skepticism, should be understood by those wishing to deal with the creative intuitive decision-making component of the marketing field.

What accounts for the degree of acceptance that management science has been accorded? Many factors can be listed, but briefly:

(a) Competition—the possibility that there is some value in an idea which might be exploited by a competitor prevents out-of-hand rejection.

(b) The profit squeeze—production efficiencies have already been tapped leaving the traditional practices of marketing to be examined.

(c) Short product life; sales volume begins to drop off a few years after the product's introduction—or the converse, which is a speeded-up consumer—requires haste in reaching decisions.

(d) New product failures—some estimates place this as high as 90 percent [4]—produce two kinds of penalties: sunk costs and foregone opportunity costs. (The latter, although seldom determined, may far outweigh the former.)

(e) Information inundation—the pressures, mentioned above, have led to the development and support of an increasing number of sources of information. The marketing manager cannot cope with the variety of data that is available to him.

(f) Public irritation with marketing practice—The Harris Committee, "Truth in Packaging" bills and other governmental efforts to investigate and control marketing practice are increasingly evident.

At the same time there are other good reasons why the marketing field would hand out a temporary pass to management scientists. Among these we can list:

(a) The reputation of management science—In effect, this amounts to "resting on one's laurels." Management science has a successful record of accomplishments in the production field.

(b) Shared boundary experiences are even more significant. There are areas where production and marketing have worked together with

---

[4] From an article appearing in *Advertising Age*, April 22, 1963. J. F. Merriman, Manager of Marketing Research of Campbell Soup Company, estimated that the new product failure rate was 92 percent.

management science. For example, distribution and warehouse location analysis, transportation analysis, inventory models for variable demand systems and product-mix solutions.

(c) The identification of management science with computer know-how—This might be called, "resting on one's computer," or "management science rides in on the back of the computer." Many marketing executives have been convinced that computers can be of substantial benefit. The gain that is expected is in speed, accuracy and scope, i.e., efficiency —not effectiveness. Management scientists are viewed by some marketing executives as computer specialists. The significance of model-building and issues of effectiveness are relegated to a secondary role. The computer is the primary force in such cases for whatever degree of acceptance is accorded to management science.

(d) The acknowledged accomplishments of management science in the field of marketing. (Discussed below.)

3. ACCOMPLISHMENTS TO DATE

The accomplishments of management science in the marketing field can be viewed in terms of four classes of effort. Many of the approaches that will be mentioned were in use long before The Institute of Management Sciences was formed. They have been expanded, modified and brought into sharper focus by management science practitioners.

3.1 Data Reduction

Masses of data must be reduced to a practical level if they are to be of use to the marketing decision maker. Management science has helped to increase the *validity* of such information by insisting upon the careful design of experiments. Frequently, data collection has preceded a knowledge of how the data were to be used. *Reliability* has been improved by paying careful attention to the sampling problems. Much effort has been expended in this direction. *Type I* and *Type II* errors have been recognized to a far greater degree than before. Marketing executives have been made increasingly aware of the problem of falsely accepting the hypothesis (the Type II error), in addition to the more conventional consideration of falsely rejecting the hypothesis (the Type I error).

3.2 Predictions

The ability to *predict* has been improved. Using *multiple correlation, autocorrelation, regression analysis* and new *smoothing* techniques, greater predictive strength has been developed. On the other hand, predictive techniques based on causal relations of variables have been essentially non-existent. Functional systems of marketing variables that are developed by means of correlation analysis seldom appear to hold over time. They are, therefore, only useful in explaining what has happened in the past—what was observed—but not what will happen in the future. It can be conjectured that the selected independent variables are not fundamental to the dependent variables. *Brand-switching analysis* has been applied to the prediction problem with some success. This model permits prediction and at the same time it presents a new way of looking at the marketing process.

3.3 Marketing System Models

The mechanics of marketing will only be understood when reasonable models of the marketing process are developed. The functional relationships that describe the way in which the system operates are required if such models are to be built. The brand switching model is a management science development that succeeds in describing certain aspects of *consumer behavior*. Simulation models are being used for the same purposes. They provide a reasonable way to explore consumer dynamics based on hypothetical functional relationships. At the present time, the major weakness is the lack of suitable hypotheses to be tested.

In another mechanical area—that of *competition*—game theory has great conceptual importance. For practical problem resolution, however, it has always been and it continues to be something of a toy. There are sufficient reasons to doubt the applicability of classical game theory. These include the fact that the payoff matrix is dynamic and that competitors have only bounded rationality. In addition, the analytical complexities of non-zero sum,[5] *n*-person games with special inter-player agreements has deterred even the hardiest marketing scientists in their enthusiasm to utilize the theorems that are available.

With respect to a third mechanical area—*communication channels*, a media model variant has been developed that is based on simulation. These models constitute a way of organizing great quantities of information which is vital to the media selection process. For this type of media model the individual specifies a number of media schedules which he considers both feasible and desirable. These alternatives are then tested and compared. Each schedule is measured or characterized in a number of different ways. The decision-maker is the final arbiter; he makes the selection.

3.4 Decision-Making Models

In this fourth area, decision-making (or optimum-seeking) models, there is a dearth of accomplishment. The only exception is in the media

---

[5] Because of utility considerations, a zero-sum game is a rare exception.

selection area. Here, we find both linear and dynamic programming systems being used. While these models qualify as optimum-seeking models, it must be pointed out that they are totally dependent on estimations of the critical marketing factors and these are derived by judgment. Furthermore, these models use operator intervention during the course of the solution. Therefore, these models are far from being "true" optimum-producing models. Instead, they produce an organized set of data upon which the decision-maker can operate from time to time, as he deems it necessary. Most of the media models are programmed on computers. The computations can be stopped from time to time to permit operator intervention. This sort of interaction provides an excellent example of man-machine interfaces.

3.5 Conclusion

Operations research and management scientists are strongly motivated to produce decision-making models where the objective is to find the optimal solution. Yet this type of achievement in the marketing field is almost negligible. In fact, although there have been some real accomplishments in marketing science, they have been quite different in nature from the kind of accomplishments that management science has achieved in other areas.

4. THE NATURE OF PROBLEMS IN MARKETING SCIENCE

We shall now discuss those difficulties and barriers which have been experienced by management science in the marketing field. Understanding the nature of these difficulties is an accomplishment in itself—since it can help point the way to a reasonable set of future activities.

To develop properly this part of our appraisal, we shall assume that the reader has some knowledge of decision theory. We shall, therefore, only briefly enumerate the elements of decision theory as they have been, more or less, successfully applied to the production field. This discussion we shall interlace with critical comments that apply to marketing science. A simple 3×4 decision matrix is shown below.

	P_1	P_2	P_3	P_4
	N_1	N_2	N_3	N_4
S_1	O_{11}	O_{12}	O_{13}	O_{14}
S_2	O_{21}	O_{22}	O_{23}	O_{24}
S_3	O_{31}	O_{32}	O_{33}	O_{34}

The $S_i, i = 1, 2, 3$, are the strategies. These are composed of independent variables that are entirely under the decision maker's control. The N_j, j

$= 1$, 2, 3, 4, are the states of nature. These are the uncontrollable or partially controlled independent variables in the system. The p_j's are predictions describing the likelihood of occurrence of the N_j's. The O_{ij}'s are the dependent variables, or outcomes. Each outcome describes the decision maker's utility for the result that comes when a specific strategy is used and a particular state of nature occurs. Control over the outcome is exercised by the choice of strategy. If the p_j's are believable then the decision criterion is to take the expected value for each S_i and choose that one which maximizes the degree of achievement of the objectives.

4.1 The Difficulty of Measuring Outcomes

Using the decision maker's objectives, the outcomes must be defined so that they are measurable. Frequently, sets of outcomes are required at each intersection for adequate definition of the objectives. In the production problem, the relevant outcomes can usually be defined and measured. In the marketing field it is generally impossible to observe the relevant outcomes such as sales volume and profit. As a result, marketing practitioners are accustomed to using sets of intermediate outcomes such as consumers' preference and other measures of consumers' attitudes and responses such as brand awareness, program ratings and print media noting scores. Under these circumstances, it is imperative that a reasonable hypothesis exist to connect intermediate outcomes with those outcomes that are a more "truthful" expression of the objectives. For example, high levels of awareness or strong measures of preference are assumed to reflect heavy sales volume, many customers, high re-purchase rates, large profit—any one of these or a combination of them.

In fact, the required intermediate hypotheses are rarely furnished. Is profit linearly related to preference? Does a high noting score or program rating indicate the attraction or the repulsion of many customers? Both are possible. If, "the familiar breeds contempt," or put in other terms, consumers can get bored, are high awareness measures preferable to low ones? Without getting too involved we have tried to illustrate the difficulty that arises when we cannot observe those outcomes that are directly related to objectives. It is always implicit in decision systems that the measured outcomes represent the decision maker's utilities for the observed results. But the outcomes traditionally observed in the marketing field are of a dubious nature. It is, presently, almost impossible to provide an adequate utility transformation.

4.2 The Difficulty of Separating the Relevant from the Irrelevant

Problem solving requires that all relevant variables be identified. In the normal course of a production problem the independent variables are of two kinds: controllable and uncontrollable. Both exist in the marketing field. However, in addition, the uncontrollable variables are of two types —those that are controlled by someone else, which shall be called C_k and those not under intelligent control, i.e., the N_j. The decision matrix below pictures this situation, with the supposition that only two competitive strategies, C_1 and C_2, are relevant.

	P_1		P_2		P_3		P_4	
	N_1C_1	N_1C_2	N_2C_1	N_2C_2	N_3C_1	N_3C_2	N_4C_1	N_4C_2
S_1	O_{111}	O_{112}	O_{121}	O_{122}	O_{131}	O_{132}	O_{141}	O_{142}
S_2	O_{211}	O_{212}	O_{221}	O_{222}	O_{231}	O_{232}	O_{241}	O_{242}
S_3	O_{311}	O_{312}	O_{321}	O_{322}	O_{331}	O_{332}	O_{341}	O_{342}

We see that the competitive variables create a degree of complexity which seldom applies to the production situation. Competition can usually be excluded from the resolution of production problems; whereas, it is a critical factor for marketing solutions.

Let us turn to another aspect of relevancy. Management science is relatively unfamiliar with situations where what appears to be relevant changes over time. This seems to occur in marketing. Undoubtedly, these phenomena can be attributed to the fact that we are not looking at the system properly. However, until a fundamental set of variables (equivalent in sense to such dimensions as mass, length and time, in physical systems), is discovered we can expect to observe that relevancy for both variables and functional relationships will require dynamic interpretation.

4.3 The Difficulty of Discovering What Is Relevant

Part of any decision problem requires that appropriate strategies be discovered and enumerated. In production and distribution problems this enumeration task is of a low order. Low order does not mean that the number of combinations is small. Rather, it signifies that the variables which enter into combination are reasonably apparent to the decision maker. Variables that might be overlooked are likely to contribute a negligible difference to the results. In marketing, on the other hand, the problem of strategy creation is recognized by both scientists and intuitionists to be critical. An overlooked variable is quite likely to be crucial. Its presence can frequently override all other considerations. A good part of the two-culture conflict is centered here. A few significant questions can be used to illustrate this.

Question 1: If we have x dollars, how much should be allocated to the creation of strategies? How much to choosing the best strategy from a set of alternatives?

Question 2: Does the probability of finding a strategy that will successfully achieve the marketing objectives increase as a function of the number of strategies that are developed?

Question 3: If a truly creative strategy is conceived, is it readily recognizable as such, or must formal testing procedures be used to identify it? (A creative strategy can be tentatively defined as a relatively unique strategy that is capable of producing a superior outcome.)

Question 4: Assuming that a creative strategy can be readily recognized, can management science assist in any way in the creation of such superior strategies?

This set of questions being far more appropriate to marketing than to production has received almost no attention from management scientists.

4.4 The Difficulty of Predicting What Competitors Believe To Be Relevant

The difficulties, previously mentioned in connection with the creation of strategies are even worse with respect to predicting *competitive* strategies. One must pretend to think like the competitors and to share their utilities. If optimal solutions are to be obtained it is necessary to determine what the competitors' strategies might be; whether or not these strategic alternatives affect our results; and if so, how. Even if it were clear how to develop strategies that competition would be likely to follow, the cost of doing this raises some interesting questions:

Question 1: How much should be spent in this way?

Question 2: For a given expenditure of time and effort, how likely are we to be right in anticipating competitive behaviors?

Question 3: How far wrong would we be if we assume that competitors think like we do?

Question 4: What effect does the number of competitors have and how do the respective sizes of competitors affect strategic formation?

4.5 The Prediction Difficulty in Behavioral Systems

Predictions of consumer behavior are fundamental to marketing operations. In decision theory we call these the p_j's. Such predictions are not likely to be stable for very long. The value system of the consumer is dynamic. There is ample evidence of the fact that the utilities of individuals change over time as a result of external stimulation, self-stimulation and interaction with each other. Studies, such as market surveys, based exclusively on the outputs of these relatively black box systems, are likely to be outdated before they can even be used. Production systems, on the other hand, are either stable to begin with or can usually be stabilized by appropriate use of statistical control methodology.

It is pertinent to point out that the behavioral problem also existed in production. It was never solved. It is no longer so important. Automation has been primarily responsible for this lucky state of affairs. Intensive analysis of workers' productivity has been conducted by such researchers as Littauer and Abruzzi. Their conclusions point up the difficulties of this work.[6] With increasing automation the uncertainty and variability of workers' behavior has been replaced by predictable risk factors and greatly reduced variability. But the effect of increasing automation for the marketing field has been, and will continue to be, emphasis and expansion of behavioral problems. The substantial investment required for automated lines coupled with a shorter payoff period, (the speeded-up consumer), necessitates intensive marketing effort within a short period of time. This spells greater involvement with consumer and competitor behaviors.

4.6 The Difficulty of Conducting Experiments and Building Theories

Outcomes can be derived in essentially three ways. The first method employs intuition to supply estimates. This approach has been commonplace in the marketing field and rare in the production area. The second method is to use observation and measurement. Paired comparison tests and test markets are a familiar part of the arsenal of market research. Laboratory experiments and pilot plants are the comparable experience in the production field. But, observation is generally costly. If we have to supply measurements for each intersection of the decision matrix it is apparent that only a limited number of strategies can be tested. Many times strategies are compared on a false basis. The marketing field is particularly vulnerable to the situation shown below.

	N_1	N_2	N_3	Comparison
S_1	x_1			x_1
S_2		x_2		x_2
S_3			x_3	x_3

What has happened here is that each strategy has been tested under different conditions which were not recognized as such. The direct comparison of the results is meaningless if the outcomes are sensitive to the

[6] Abruzzi, A., "Formulating a Theory of Work Measurement," *Management Science*, Vol. 2, No. 2 (January 1956), pp. 114–130; Littauer, S. B., "Technological Stability in Industrial Operations," *Transactions of the New York Academy of Sciences*, Series II, 13, No. 2 (1950), pp. 67–72; ———— and Abruzzi, A., "Experimental Criteria for Evaluating Workers and Operations," *Industrial Labor Relations Review*, July 1949. The investigations of Littauer and Abruzzi in the production field may be of fundamental importance for the development of a science of marketing.

N_j's. Good experimental design can help to avoid this pitfall. But the marketing field is so complex that it is possible to be unaware of all relevant, differentiating conditions. For production systems this problem is not likely to be crucial.

The third method is somewhat familiar to the production field. It is most closely associated with the aims of scientific method. Functional systems are hypothesized and equations are developed to explain the relationship between the O_{ij}, the S_i and the N_jC_k. Since only the most tentative theories are available to describe the marketing process this approach is almost non-existent in present-day marketing science. Until cogent steps are taken in this direction, *marketing science* will scarcely be raised from a pre-science stage.

4.7 The Difficulty of Distinguishing Resources

Restrictions arise in any non-trivial problem because of limited resources. Production resources being, for the most part, grossly physical are easily distinguished and cataloged. Marketing resources are almost exclusively intangibles. They consist of functional utility, form, shape, color, brand names, and so forth—and can be encapsulated by the significant term, "brand complex." Marketing strategies are derived from deep and insightful conceptions of the culture and sub-groups within the culture. We need only consider the importance of appearance design to the consumer to realize that production constraints and marketing constraints are of a different breed.

4.8 The Difficulty of Designing a Suitable Decision Criterion

The last point that we shall mention concerns the design of an acceptable decision rule. Problems that involve believable predictions, are resolved by means of the expected value criterion. But marketing problems are seldom associated with predictions having a high degree of believability. Therefore, the expected value criterion is frequently suspect.

As has been previously mentioned, classical game theory does not appear to be applicable for the resolution of real-life competitive decision problems because of the dynamic character of the payoff matrix, the fact that competitors are not entirely rational, and for other reasons as well. Because the production area has not been faced with such anomalies, classical decision critera sufficed. But for marketing some new, more appropriate rules must be found.

4.9 Conclusion

Although it has been sketchy, our appraisal of the nature of problems in marketing science leads us to conclude that "true" decision-making models are still non-existent in this area because marketing decision systems lie outside the present capabilities of management scientists to resolve them. A great deal of work will be required before such situations can be solved for optimal conditions.

5. THE OUTLOOK FOR MARKETING SCIENCE

Our intention is to appraise the prospects and frontiers of marketing science. The discussion will consist of four parts which highlight those areas that appear to hold the key to the resolution of marketing science problems. They are:

(a) The consumer and his value systems.
(b) Creativity, which deals with the way in which strategies are developed.
(c) Competition, with emphasis on the value systems of competitors and the derivation of meaningful decision rules for competitive systems.
(d) Optimization, which we have taken to be the fundamental objective of management science.

5.1 The Prospective Consumer

We must begin to define—in operational terms—the nature of a marketing prospect. Some organizations can describe the character of those individuals who are likely to be its customers. But many only think they can. When pressed, the definition breaks down. Frequently, it is taken for granted that the profile of present customers provides a satisfactory description of the kinds of people who are prospects. The understanding is implicit that if we could communicate with all such individuals, they would become customers. This notion can be shown to be faulty in many cases. If a company had never communicated with a particular segment of the population, this segment would have no representation in the customer profile. Yet, such a group might produce high volume purchases. The profile of a company's customers is a function of its prior marketing activities. Thus, the company structures the profile and the profile, in turn, reinforces the structure. This is not the way to determine a prospect.

An additional weakness of this approach is the Aristotelian notion that a prospect is either a customer or not a customer. Customers have different long-term values to the company. The point is neatly illuminated by an example, such as beer drinkers. Heavy users of the product account for a small percentage of all customers but contribute a major portion of the sales volume. The division of users that this suggests is not new to the marketing field. But it needs a great deal of further refinement including the concept of discounted life-time value. In many situations even the crude differentiation of prospects by purchase quantities, purchase frequencies, switching behavior and susceptibility to persuasion has not even begun.

5.2 The Consumers' Value System

An intensive investigation of the meaning of a prospect involves us directly with the value systems of consumers. We require hypotheses to explain—in a causal sense—why people act the way they do. Although the identification of causality is an objective common to all scientific effort, it is not an observable part of present-day marketing science. In the interest of pointing out that the stage for hypothesis development is not ten or twenty years off, let us set down a few examples of the kind of thinking that appears to be required. (These hypotheses are intended to be only representative of the sort of activity that skilled marketing practitioners could render meaningful.)

(a) Consumer decisions are based on a hedging strategy.[7]
(b) Consumer utilities are logarithmic transforms which take into account the individual's assets—including (discounted?) projections of his earning power.
(c) Consumer judgment of value is based upon a power law such as: $V_x = A_x{}^\alpha B_x{}^\beta C_x{}^\gamma$ . . . , where V_x is a relative measure of the consumer's value for brand x; A_x, B_x, C_x, etc., are the consumer's perceptions of the various characters that define the product class of x; α, β, γ, etc., are the exponential weighting factors used to indicate the relative importance of each characteristic to the individual. The trick here is to find out what numbers should be used for a specific case. An interesting aspect of this formulation is that it gets around another difficult definitional problem—namely, that of defining a *product class*.

Until meaningful hypotheses are developed, marketing science cannot furnish decision-making models. Predictions of the drift and movement of value systems will be limited to extrapolations based on observations of past processes and trends. This is the present state of the art for the brand switching model. We must now build into these systems the effects of such variables as price, quality and communication. Only in this way can we develop decision-making models. To convert this model from a purely predictive one, it is necessary to propose that the transition probabilities have the form

$$p_{ij} = f(S_i, N_j, O_{ijk}, C_k, t).$$

This takes into account the Chapman-Kolmogorov condition,[8] and even more general formulations of stochastic processes. We no longer assume

---

[7] The hedging strategy follows the Savage Regret Criterion; a decision criterion for problems under uncertainty; Miller, D. W. and Starr, M. K., *Executive Decisions and Operations Research*, Englewood Cliffs, N.J.: Prentice-Hall, Inc., 1960, pp. 88–90.

[8] Feller, William, An Introduction to Probability Theory and Its Applications, New York: John Wiley and Sons, Inc., 1952, pp. 386–391.

stationarity. If consumer value systems are stable, they must be dynamically so. Although such models may transcend mathematical analysis, in the sense of Karl Pearson, simulation techniques provide us with a powerful alternative.

5.3 Consumer Models

Further insights into the operation of the value system can be derived from sources that are still essentially untapped. For example, models from epidemiology would appear to possess many relevant characteristics. The words used to describe these systems are readily seen to parallel marketing experiences. Thus, we have the susceptibles, the diseased and the immune. We also have periods of contagion and periods of immunity. When immunity after illness is permanent and the conversion of susceptibles to diseased occurs in a short period of time the conditions describe a fad. Fads are associated with absorbing states in a stochastic process. A switching matrix is shown below for a fad-type marketing system.

		TO		
		NT	B_a	NTA
	NT	0.2	0.8	0
FROM	B_a	0	0.1	0.9
	NTA	0	0	1.0

NT = never tried
B_a = brand a
NTA = never tried again

Immunization can be related to consumer boredom or fatigue. A reduction in the period of immunization would be equivalent to an increase in re-purchase rate. A reduction in the length of the period of contagion would amount to the same thing. But in this case, the consumer's usage rate has been stepped-up.

Contagion models are not decision-making models. They are predictive. They might, however, supply the kinds of behavior for which functional relationships can be written. They introduce a number of elements that are presently missing from the conventional form of brand switching analysis.

Another point that should be emphasized when considering studies of consumer behavior is the fact that description of limiting states is far less rewarding than the description of trajectories. Limits are not particularly important because it is almost certain that conditions will have changed substantially by the time that such limits would apply. The use of expected values in our switching models can be quite misleading when our interest centers on trajectories instead of limits. We need only consider the following example:

	A	B
A	0.4	0.6
B	0.6	0.4

The limit of this system is easily derived as 0.5 since it is doubly stochastic. But what would occur if the probability of the transition AA is distributed as follows:

p_{ij}	Probability	
.10	0.5	$(i = j = A)$
.70	0.5	$\bar{p}_{ij} = OA$

A few moments of simulation will show that some weird trajectories occur. The situation is further complicated if thresholds are assumed. As an example of a threshold, assume that brand A is theoretically moving to 60 percent of the market when in fact it can only product 50 percent of all requirements. Consumer values change when the favorite brand is repeatedly missing from the shelves. Other interactions would also appear.

New directions are required. Simplifying assumptions, presently observed in the literature, are bogging us down. Even such difficulties as *what to observe* in a switching system must be threshed out in detail before we can expect substantial progress. Problems of how to lump, in a switching matrix, a number of competing brands within a given product class have arisen in actual marketing studies. In few cases are the complications understood.[9] We are even uncertain as to how to define a competitor. In what way do we affect our results and understanding if we choose, for example, to investigate the effect of competition between various brands of coffee as compared to studying the way in which these brands of coffee compete with tea, milk and perhaps soft drinks? The seeds for basic studies must be planted if we are going to develop a greater understanding of consumer behavior.

5.4 Creativity

Traditionally management science states that it is the executives' responsibility to develop strategies. But, in the marketing field this point

[9] Kemeny, J. G. and Snell, J. L., *Finite Markov Chains,* Princeton: D. Van Nostrand Company, Inc., 1960, pp. 123–145.

of view is hard to justify. The problems associated with creating strategies cannot be relegated by scientists to anti-scientists and intuitivists if understanding and respect are ultimately desired between these two cultures. Strategy development is far too fundamental to the marketing process to be by-passed by scientists.

In what ways can Management Science help here? Several approaches suggest themselves. First, we can attempt to identify all of the relevant variables that combine to produce strategic alternatives. The various combinations could then be obtained by random simulation. A set of rules would be required to filter out undesirable strategies. If the rules are improved by some learning process connected with judgment, fewer rejects would get through the net as time goes by. The process would be akin to a chess-learning program. A great deal might be discovered about creativity in this way. Furthermore, as the evaluation rules are tightened, exceptional strategies would begin to appear.

Random creation within the set of variables would be wasteful. Instead, an efficient creative system should be able to explore the logico-historical evolution of events. Each previous marketing effort can be viewed as a cluster of points in the n-dimensional space that scientists use to characterize it. Where gaps appear in these clusters, unique opportunities might exist. Although this discussion is quite abstract, it is easy enough to see how one might inventory the character of existing soft-drinks and determine that very tart, purple liquids in square bottles are rare. With some thought, this approach holds forth real promise.

Ideally, when we choose a strategy we would like it to blueprint our actions not only for the immediate present but over a reasonable period of time. In this way we would hope to avoid serious, in-time, sub-optimization. Such a strategy might appear in a tree-type form, e.g.,

Begin with S_1
- If O_{11} occurs, move to S_2
  - if O_{21} occurs, continue S_2
  - if O_{22} occurs, move to S_3
  - if O_{23} occurs, move to S_1
- If O_{12} occurs, move to S_3
  - if O_{31} occurs, continue S_3
  - if O_{32} occurs, continue S_3
  - if O_{33} occurs, move to S_1
- If O_{13} occurs, continue S_1
  - if O_{11} occurs, move to S_2
  - if O_{12} occurs, continue S_1
  - if O_{13} occurs, move to S_3

How should we describe such strategies? They are variable in a sequential sense. They are extensive, supra-strategies. They are far more complex strategies than present-day abilities can develop. Precisely because of this complexity, management science may be able to provide help in the formation of such strategies. Simulation techniques, rather than analysis, seem most promising in this endeavor. The computer will be a great ally of the management scientist in his efforts to help produce creative strategies.

It might be said that the inherent complexity of these operations is antithetical to the essence of scientific effort. A long-standing tradition that scientists have is that "truth" is simple, harmonious, elegant. The belief in a Principle of Parsimony dates back to the 14th Century. When it comes to the marketing area the Principle of Parsimony seems to have met its Waterloo. At least that appears to be the case for the moment. Perhaps in all behavioral problems we must first rid ourselves of the notion that only simple solutions will do—that only elegant mathematical formulations can be tolerated. To support the strong position that has been taken on this issue, we shall quote from Mario Bunge.[10]

All oversimplification should be avoided in science and in philosophy, except as a temporary methodological device enabling us to start work or to apply its results.

5.5 Competition

We must begin to analyze marketing problems in terms of the competitors' value systems; and to be able to identify those factors that trigger various competitive behaviors. The search for a reasonable decision criterion under conditions of competition leads us to recognize that although we seldom know what a competitor will do—if we can enumerate everything that he might do—we can then take steps to prepare ourselves for each and every eventuality. This is a system of "thrust and parry" which may well follow the lines of classical control theory. Simulation techniques may prove to be of considerable benefit in this area.

5.6 Decision Models and Optimization

If marketing management is to achieve "optimization" abilities, basic studies must begin now. The development and application of new techniques hinges on the establishment of a working rapport with behaviorists, economists, statisticians and people with marketing experience. The problem of conflicting cultures within the marketing management field cannot be resolved until all concerned recognize that one cannot proceed without the other. The consumer is forcing even further shrinkage of decision-time. There is insufficient time to allow intuition to work. Patterns are stable for only short periods of time. Intuitivists perceive that they are hard pressed. But science will not be accepted so long as elegance and simplicity are identified among its primary goals.

[10] Bunge, Mario, *The Myth of Simplicity; Problems of Scientific Philosophy*, Englewood Cliffs, N.J.: Prentice-Hall, Inc., 1963, p. vi.

Forcing marketing problems into production-type models cannot help but create, in the long run, a more serious breach than exists at present. In addition, we must become conscious of the cost of studying a problem. When it appears that a traditional approach is more rewarding it should be followed. There must be willingness to accept "improvement" instead of "optimization"—for the time being. This is realistic and necessary. But it should be explicit when "optimization" has not been achieved that this remains the goal of management science.

Using new techniques and approaches such as graph theory, information theory, mathematical topology and simulation techniques and by developing cybernetic models, epidemic models, prey-predator models, and addiction models, to name just a few possibilities, we may be able to move ahead. But this will only happen, if some support can be found for the pure research effort that is required.

On the other hand, perhaps management science does not wish to involve itself in these amorphous areas. Maybe it has no readiness to cross discipline lines. In that event, it does not seem likely that it can participate in the realization of a legitimate marketing science.

3. Formal reasoning and
marketing strategy

HARRY A. LIPSON

The past 15 years have seen the glorification of formal systems and their imposition where they have not been used before. The newer writings concerning decision-making processes should make marketers conscious of using formal systems to solve marketing problems. Several recent books have been specifically concerned with the application of formal systems to marketing.[1]

The search for formal models or conceptual structures of marketing stems from those who desire orderly, systematic, formal reasoning from which inferences can be applied to single instances. These persons believe that every investigation requires a model or theory to develop an optimal decision. The basic tool is not mathematics—it is formalizing.

It may seem that mathematics is the basic tool, but this is not the case. A theory is a set of mathematical formulas based upon a system of axioms, postulates, and definitions plus procedural rules from logic (formal reasoning).

Marketing men have been essentially empiricists rather than rationalists. They often start with data (from activities that are working reasonably well) and work through a series of intuitive leaps to generalizations. They sense that choice is not a mechanical but a creative act. They feel

Reprinted from the *Journal of Marketing*, Volume 26 (October, 1962), pp. 1–5, National Quarterly Publication of the American Marketing Association.

[1] Frank M. Bass, Robert D. Buzzell, Mark R. Greene, William Lazar, Edgar A. Pessemier, Donald L. Shawver, Abraham Shuchman, Chris A. Theodore, and George W. Wilson, *Mathematical Models and Methods in Marketing* (Homewood, Illinois: Richard D. Irwin, Inc., 1961); Harold Bierman, Jr., Lawrence E. Fouraker, and Robert K. Jaedicke, *Quantitative Analysis for Business Decisions* (Homewood, Illinois: Richard D. Irwin, Inc., 1961); and Robert Schlaifer, *Probability and Statistics for Business Decisions* (New York: McGraw-Hill Book Company, Inc., 1960).

that skilled executives may make many nonrational and/or unconscious decisions which are good decisions.

In the current formulation of marketing strategy, there are those who use formal models and those who do not. Those who build and/or use these formal models believe they have constructed a theoretical approach (or foundation) by means of which to make better marketing decisions. They believe that production has been rationalized; they suggest that distribution likewise may be rationalized.

The present article is a survey of the contribution of the formalists to the development of marketing strategy. The annotated footnotes provide a reference source for those persons wishing to investigate the application of formal thinking to marketing strategy.

THE FORMULATION OF MARKETING STRATEGY

In the context of formal thinking, strategy may be considered a sequence of decision rules which give a complete description of the marketing practices of a company, their order, and their timing.[2] These rules are formulated so as to provide for the best action in the event of any one of all possible happenings. The essence of strategy defined in this manner is that, in planning, the future is never known, so that the decision maker should provide in his plan for all eventualities.

Strategy implies that all dimensions of the marketing plan have been consciously integrated. The term "marketing mix" is frequently used to describe the state of these dimensions at any given point in time. Some believe that a marketing strategy consists of two parts: (1) operating objectives (called targets or goals), and (2) combination of instruments (called marketing mix or means).[3]

A great deal has been written and said about the sequence of steps involved in the development of recurrent and continuous market plans. There is some question as to the order of the first three steps because of their interdependence. Usually the steps are given in this order: (1) determination of goals or objectives, (2) market position audit, (3) generation of strategies, (4) design of the program, and (5) acceptance and installation.[4]

It is difficult to set up company objectives without knowledge of the situation of the company in its industry. Often the market-position audit

[2] John A. Howard, *Marketing Management* (Homewood, Illinois: Richard D. Irwin, Inc., 1957), pp. 36–40.

[3] Alfred R. Oxenfeldt, "The Formulation of a Market Strategy," in *Managerial Marketing*, edited by Edward J. Kelley and William Lazar (Homewood, Illinois: Richard D. Irwin, Inc., 1958), pp. 264–272, at p. 267.

[4] Edward S. McKay, "How To Plan and Set Up Your Marketing Program," Blueprint for an Effective Marketing Program, Marketing Series Number 91 (New York: American Management Association, 1954), pp. 14f; and "Theory and Practice of Market Planning," *Cost and Profit Outlook*, Vol. II (July–August, 1958), pp. 1–4.

must be taken before the goals or objectives can be identified and stated. Those experienced in market planning tend to regard alternative goals as hypotheses to be tested. They select the appropriate objective, and the action program designed to achieve the goal, by reviewing the alternative action plans or sequence of steps necessary for achievement of the goal. It is during these initial explorations in the planning process that strategy is significant.

It must be stressed that the initial phases of creating plans for marketing activities may be a circular process. The selection of the optimum alternatives is based upon the information fed back to the preceding phases. Feasibility, then, becomes the decision criterion by which the desired goal and the approach to achieve the goal are rationally selected.

THE GOALS OF MARKETING STRATEGY

There is a considerable division of opinion as to the role and goals of business enterprise in our economy. Survival, growth, profits, market position, size, degree of horizontal and vertical integration—and other goals of marketers—arouse vigorous debate. It must be recognized that there has been a shifting focus of objectives which characterize "the evolution of modern business—first, from a focus on profit for the owner to striving for market position and success against competition, and more recently to a focus on growth in which there is a continuing planned effort to enlarge the size of the market." [5]

As Joel Dean says, a business firm is designed to make profits. [6] John A. Howard hedges by saying that "strategy is designed to maximize long-term profits within the limits determined by top management's view of the company's basic objectives." [7] In his view this is the ideal toward which a firm strives.

The argument can be raised about maximum profits over what period of time and for whom? Herbert A. Simon argues that the notion of "satisficing" rather than maximization is significant. [8] Satisficing has long been of more interest to the psychologist than to the economist. In many psychological theories a motive to act is based upon a drive, and action ends when the drive is satisfied. Simon believes, like many others, that these models of satisficing are richer than models of maximizing behavior.

Economists have given us the assumptions of perfect knowledge and

[5] J. B. McKitterick, "What Is the Marketing Management Concept?" *The Frontiers of Marketing Thought and Science*, edited by Frank M. Bass (Chicago, Illinois: American Marketing Association, 1957), pp. 71–82, at p. 77.

[6] Joel Dean, *Managerial Economics* (New York: Prentice-Hall, Inc., 1951), p. 3.

[7] John A. Howard, same reference as above.

[8] Herbert A. Simon, "Theories of Decision-Making in Economics and Behavioral Science," *American Economic Review*, Vol. 49 (June, 1959), pp. 255–283, at p. 262f.

costless transactions. A real question for marketing men is the optimal method and cost of reducing the uncertainty from inadequate information. This is the aim of much research. The strategy to be followed by a marketer must come from a study of the firm itself, from study and analysis of competition, and from investigation of the market. How the marketer will solve his basic problems will depend upon the goals set for the business.

THE CONCEPTUALIZING OF MARKETING DECISIONS

The use of models in decision making should be familiar to those making marketing decisions and marketing plans. Models are used to show how the variables or factors in the particular operation will interact in the proposed solutions. These models, whether verbal, mathematical, mechanical, or physical, are a simplified framework of an operation, representing only those aspects which are of primary importance to the problem under study.

The empiricist tends to follow this sequence of steps in his research program: (1) probe, (2) look, (3) form the problem, (4) obtain data, and (5) develop a model. Using this method for developing marketing strategy involves less risk, but it is time-consuming. So much effort is spent in looking and relooking and reworking the material.

The rationalist notion of the scientific method of research is to: (1) formulate the problem, (2) develop the model, (3) obtain data, (4) draw the inferences—deductive conclusion from findings, and (5) recycle and rework the model.

Another way of looking at this sequence is to: (1) focus on one or more goals, (2) isolate the more obvious variables, (3) state the problem in its simplest terms, that is, by formulas using symbolic logic, (4) work out the solution using the formulas developed to have a *first approximation* to the answer, and (5) rework the problem after being alerted to the errors or variables found in reality which determine changes in the answer.

Those trained in the newer approaches to decision making are using the rationalist sequence of steps. Many disciplines converge on decision making. These include anthropology, business administration, economics, engineering, logic, mathematics, philosophy, political science, psychology, sociology, and statistics. All are interested in control processes.

The social scientist and the marketing planner have been criticized for never knowing when they have solved a problem in the optimal manner. Proponents of the rigorous models believe better and precise answers may be forthcoming in the future if marketers are informed in some of these areas—decision theory, organization theory, game theory, operations research, and linear programming.

Decisions and Uncertainty

Consumers and business managers must make many decisions or choices for many purposes. Decision theory (mathematical or physical models) concerns expressed preferences. The empirical study of individuals' choices has been relatively undeveloped and is only coming into prominence as a field of investigation.[9]

The books giving attention to analytical economic relationships between multiple markets, multiple plants, and multiple products are welcome additions to the literature.[10] Marketing managers looking for help in making decisions about market allocation and segmentation, price and product discrimination in buying and selling, and the problems of disequilibrium and dynamics in market behavior should be familiar with these tools.

There is a need for businessmen to recognize that marginal analysis may be used to make decisions under conditions of uncertainty based on anticipation of the future. The marginal productivity of inputs in relation to outputs may sharpen the thinking of executives about location, sales force, channels, promotion, and pricing problems. By focusing attention on incremental costs, improved decisions may be obtained in seeking the proper "marketing mix." These tools, pertinent to marketing, require further sharpening to reduce uncertainty. But such sharpening is not a job only for the pure theorists; they and marketing men must work together.

Quantitative analysis, including mathematics and statistics and parts of accounting, is receiving increasing recognition. A significant aspect of quantitative analysis, as it applies to marketing men, is statistical decision theory and hypotheses testing. Such tools of quantitative analysis are essential to a critical understanding and evaluation of many marketing problems, and constitute the analytical equipment necessary to measure the effects of alternative decisions in marketing.

Marketing men need to be familiar with the literature concerning decision processes and decision criteria.[11] They need to understand that

[9] An account covering the psychological and economic theories of riskless and risky decision-making is found in Ward Edwards, "Behavioral Decision Theory" (unpublished paper, Engineering Psychology Group, Willow Run Laboratories, University of Michigan). For a review article covering 1930–1954, see Ward Edwards, "The Theory of Decision-Making," *Psychological Bulletin*, Vol. 51 (September, 1954), pp. 380–417. A nonmathematical review is found in Kenneth J. Arrow, "Utilities, Attitudes, Choices: A Review Note," *Econometrica*, Vol. 26 (January, 1958), pp. 1–23.

[10] Dean, same reference as footnote 6; and for general numerical prediction techniques under uncertainty, see Milton H. Spencer and Louis Siegelman, *Managerial Economics* (Homewood, Illinois: Richard D. Irwin, Inc., 1959). A contribution to business management concerning marketing strategy is found in Robert A. Schlaifer, *Probability and Statistics For Business Decisions* (New York: McGraw-Hill Book Co., Inc., 1959).

[11] A number of books have been written in recent years about decision theory.

the decision criteria under certainty (game against nature) is an extremely special case. There is only a one-column matrix, for the decision maker knows the payout of each strategy. It is just necessary to scan the column for the highest payoff to make a choice. Under uncertainty, the decision criteria may be that of pessimism, optimism, minimax, least regret, or the rational approach of the highest payout.

Organization Theory

The individual decision premise becomes the smallest unit of description in the rational model approach to decision making. It is recognized that individuals live in an environment which limits choices. Here the economist and the social psychologist have a common ground for studying rational behavior and intuitive choice.[12]

Alderson emphasizes that consumer-buyers are essentially problem solvers in the face of uncertainty. He emphasizes that marketing behavior is primarily group behavior. It is his thesis that each individual acts as a member of an organized behavior system whose formation and persistence is explained by expectations. He goes on to say that a behavior system may be observed as a: (1) power system, (2) system of communications, (3) system of inputs and outputs, and (4) system of internal and external adjustments.

To develop good strategy, marketing men need to be familiar with the classical organization theories of Taylor, Gilbreth, Bernard, Mooney, Gulick, and Urwick, as well as recent literature. Marketers will not understand the Aldersonian notions without familiarity and understanding of the literature on adminstration.[13] Here they will come to grips with the fact that the model of the economic man and the model of the administrative man are not the same. Here they will find that the theory of the

---

For a simple introduction see Irwin D. F. Bross, *Design For Decision* (New York: The Macmillan Company, 1953). For a good annotated bibliography, see Paul Wasserman and Fred S. Silander, *Decision-Making: An Annotated Bibliography* (Ithaca, New York: Graduate School of Business and Public Administration, Cornell University, 1958).

[12] See Wroe Alderson, *Marketing Behavior and Executive Action* (Homewood, Illinois: Richard D. Irwin, Inc., 1957); C. Joseph Clawson, "Quantifying Motivation Research To Predict Consumer Behavior," *Advancing Marketing Efficiency*, edited by Lynn H. Stockman (Chicago, Illinois: American Marketing Association, 1959), pp. 54–70, at pp. 55ff; and Robert A. Dahl, Mason Haire, and Paul F. Lazarsfeld, *Social Science Research on Business: Product and Potential* (New York: Columbia University Press, 1959).

[13] See James G. March and Herbert A. Simon, *Organizations* (New York: John Wiley & Sons, Inc., 1958). An unusually good analysis of decision-making processes in administrative organizations is found in Herbert A. Simon, *Administrative Behavior*, 2nd ed. (New York: The Macmillan Company, 1957). Simon's essays from early journal articles are found in Herbert A. Simon, *Models of Man* (New York: John Wiley & Sons, Inc., 1957). A general book is Mason Haire, editor, *Modern Organization Theory* (New York: John Wiley & Sons, 1959).

firm and the theory of organization are not the same. The decision researcher considers this area of investigation an important influence upon strategy.

Game Theory and Simulation

Game theory deals with competitive situations in which two or more rivals have a common goal, such as that of obtaining a larger share of the market, and also have various strategies with attendant rewards in terms of increased or decreased share of the market.[14] By means of matrix algebra, an optimal strategy can be computed for each set of rivals. This optimal strategy has the unique property that it cannot be defeated even if it is known to the other contestant. Only a limited class of problems can be solved by this method, but one important type of problem that can often be solved by this method is that of plant investment.

Game theory is a formulation of optimal strategy. In the business world each of two or more rivals is trying to achieve maximum payoff for certain actions. A good strategy presumes that each firm wants to leave itself in the best possible position if the worst happens. This is similar to Alderson's "power principle," that each firm acts in such a way as to improve its position to act the next time.[15]

Strategic games are becoming increasingly popular as a method of training executives to make complex sets of decisions under pressure. While they may be overly simplified, not fully realistic, and controlled by rules not found in the business world, the person participating in the game has an opportunity to analyze the complex relationships, use accounting data, appreciate the fast computation of information, and discover the high cost of information acquired by experience. Attempts to solve the problems by rules of thumb based on experience or intuition may lead to costly decisions which do not bring about optimal achievement of the goals of the firm as stated by the participants before they begin to make decisions.

Business simulation is being used with a considerable degree of success to work out the next sequence of moves by a company in a particular situation. In this type of analysis the essential characteristics of a system are stated in a set of mathematical equations. The variables in the set of equations represent the various internal and external factors affecting the

---

[14] See Martin Shubek, *Strategy and Market Structure* (New York: John Wiley & Sons, 1959); R. Duncan Luce and Howard Raiffa, *Games and Decisions* (New York: John Wiley & Sons, Inc., 1957); and John McDonald, "Applications of Game Theory In Business and Industry" (paper read at Games Symposium of the American Association for the Advancement of Science, St. Louis, December 29, 1952). A simple book on game theory is John D. Williams, *The Compleat Strategist* (New York: McGraw-Hill Book Co., Inc., 1954).

[15] Alderson, same reference as footnote 12, p. 56.

operation of the system. Once it is constructed, the model is tested by inserting historical data as values in the variables, in order to determine how closely the answers agree with past performance of the system. A number of major firms are now working on simulators to look at policy choices. By means of these models, different operating conditions (such as change in price) can be simulated and the results determined without costly experimentation within the industry itself.

Operations Research and Linear Programming

Operations research endeavors to provide managers of organizations with a scientific basis for solving problems involving the interaction of components of the total organization or operating system.[16] The emphasis is on the word *research*. Operations research attempts to prescribe the best decisions for as large a portion of the total organization as possible.

In the narrow sense, operations research may be considered a formal, really mechanistic, quantitative model stating the situation. Some of the important models used by operations researchers in solving problems are the linear programming model, information theory, general system analysis, inventory models, waiting-line models, and sequencing or programming of resource allocation. The objective of the operations research group is to predict informed decisions. Both operations research and marketing research try to give all the information they can to the executive so he can make conscious choices. Operations research contributes to marketing strategy the systems concept, the model concept, and emphasis on experimentation.

Applications of linear programming, a computational procedure that will maximize or minimize a linear equation subject to linear restraints, may be used wherever there is a product-mix or input-mix problem with linear relationships among the variables.[17] Such problems can be solved to yield minimum expense or maximum profits by programming. Problems involving make or buy decisions, transportation movement or warehousing shipments, machine allocation, and problems requiring adjustment of production to a seasonal sales pattern are among those which have

[16] See C. West Churchman, Russell L. Ackoff, E. Leonard Arnoff, *Introduction to Operations Research* (New York: John Wiley & Sons, 1957); Charles D. Flagle, William H. Huggins, and Robert H. Roy, *Operations Research and Systems Engineering* (Baltimore: Johns Hopkins Press, 1960); Martin Kenneth Starr and David W. Miller, *Executive Decisions and Operations Research* (Englewood Cliffs, New Jersey: Prentice-Hall, 1960); and Maurice Sasieni, Arthur Yaspen, and Lawrence Friedman, *Operations Research Methods and Problems* (New York: John Wiley & Sons, 1959).

[17] For discussion of linear programming, see Harvey C. Bunke, *Linear Programming: A Primer*, Study No. 7 (Ames, Iowa: State University of Iowa, 1960); case on advertising strategy in John G. Kemeny, J. Laurie Snell, and Gerald L. Thompson, *Introduction to Finite Mathematics* (New York: Prentice-Hall, Inc., 1957); Robert Dorfman, Paul A. Samuelson, and Robert M. Solow, *Linear Programming and Economic Analysis* (New York: McGraw-Hill Book Co., Inc., 1958).

been solved by this technique. Nonlinear programming and dynamic programming involve mathematical concepts of a very esoteric nature.

One of the significant arguments occurring between those engaged in operations research is whether the scientist is obliged to study non-rational behavior or to include social morality within the scope of his activities. In the interest of prescribing the optimal (most efficient) decision, many scientists do not feel it necessary to consider the impact upon the people and society involved. Some leaders of the operations research movement argue that it will be possible to measure these important considerations.[18]

IMPLICATIONS

Marketing men can ignore the formal reasoning approach, or let others develop it, or learn the formal symbolic language so they can use it.

Those who are using these new techniques believe they may be able to develop improved marketing strategy, provided all of the variables are included and correctly stated in the new models. If the formal method is used, the marketing strategist may be able to make relatively better decisions, provided he has placed the proper values in his model.

[18] C. West Churchman, *Prediction and Optimal Decisions* (New York: Prentice-Hall, Inc., 1960); Thomas A. Cowan, "Experience And Experiment," *Philosophy of Science*, Vol. 26 (April, 1959), pp. 74–84.

4. New ways in marketing strategy

LEON MORSE

"Along with many other things in this world," pointed out marketing consultant Robert Bragarnick recently, "the modern customer is changing. He is no longer old-fashioned, conservative and relatively slow to accept new ideas." Bragarnick lists the big changes that the modern marketer is encountering on every hand: increasing youthfulness (by 1970, nearly 60 percent of the population will be under 35 years of age); greater education; higher income; a keener desire for quality; growing security; the rising relative spending power of Negroes and other minorities; and more people on the move.

With the market place in a state of flux, the modern marketing machine is itself undergoing a transition. To be sure, no brand-new, revolutionary techniques have appeared on the scene since computers were first summoned to the aid of the marketer in the mid-Fifties. A transformation is nonetheless under way. A new sophistication is sharpening and refining the traditional tools of the market place into sleek modern weapons.

The marketing battle, of course, is still being fought in the old arena of price determination, distribution, advertising and promotion and market research. And success, as always, demands effective use of such supporting strategies as a strong distributing system, an inventive marketing staff, an appraising eye on the demands of different income groups, the forging of strong brand names, constant checks on how a product is faring and precision in short- and long-term planning.

A NEW DIMENSION

One of the most apparent—and profound—of the new marketing refinements concerns pricing. Traditional theory, stripped to its essentials,

Reprinted from *Dun's Review & Modern Industry*, January 1964, pp. 43–44ff.

is based on the simplistic belief that the lower his price, the more of his goods the marketer will sell. Today that theory is being turned upside down by a handful of marketers who have grasped the full implications of the U.S.' new affluence, and this realization has enabled them to add a new dimension to pricing strategy.

The Alberto-Culver Co. is a case in point. "Most companies launch products at the most popular price and stay at that level," says President Leonard H. Lavin. "We've eliminated the lower dime-store prices. Thus we automatically increase the dollar value of the market and allow for greater promotional investment through greater dollar intake."

These higher prices, in other words, throw off greater sums to pour into advertising, which in turn produces more high-margin sales. This advertising leverage means that the higher priced product produces a fatter profit picture for Alberto-Culver than a bargain-priced item could be expected to provide.

One example of Alberto-Culver's tactics is the success of its VO5 hair spray. VO5 was introduced in early 1961 at a price of $1.50, well above the cost of the great majority of other sprays, which start as low as 79 cents. By October of that year, it was undisputed leader of the hair-spray market.

This pricing policy is the basis of the company's aggressive investment spending policies, which lift advertising use to new intensity. When VO5 was introduced, Alberto-Culver matched the budget of the then market leader, the Gillette Co.'s Toni division, dollar for dollar. For a short period, both were spending at the rate of $3.5 million dollars. "It took us only twelve months," recalls President Lavin, "to start breaking even on VO5. We had originally thought in terms of three years."

Only several months ago General Foods Corp. bowed to the same principle. It upgraded its frozen vegetable line by moving into the "boil-in-the-bag" field, and at the same time dropped its frozen dinners and its line of meat pies. If the new boil-in-the-bag line, known as Birds Eye Vacuum Sealed products, sells well, the company can count on higher margins of profit than the old lines produced.

General Foods vigorous marketing department has added polish to another traditional concept: decentralization of the selling process. One of its several categories of sales executive, the account manager, has been made the spearhead of a decentralized marketing effort. He has become, in effect, a territorial manager, spending two days each week working with large customers on various promotions. He is equipped to find the best solution for every kind of local problem. For example, he will organize programs for moving slow-selling items. He supplies ideas for reducing out-of-stock products and for tying promotions into local holidays and events.

Advertising costs continue to spiral. Between 1956 and 1962 maga-

vertising costs rose 19.5 percent, television advertising 19.4 per-
ad newspaper advertising 18.6 percent. But sales, of course, rarely
pace. Consequently, more and more package goods companies are
oiting a device to wring more out of each advertising dollar: the
. ad image is being made to assume larger and larger burdens. It is
being turned into an "umbrella" that covers a group of products with a
similar name.

For instance, Colgate-Palmolive Co.'s brand name *Ajax* throws off
the image of a product that performs heavy-duty work. Ajax cleanser
dates back to 1947. In 1961, the brand image really got a scrubbing,
when an Ajax liquid cleanser was introduced. In 1962 Ajax marketed an
Ajax floor and wall cleanser, and in 1964 it is going with an Ajax laundry
detergent.

Says Robert W. Young Jr., vice president and general manager of
the household products division of Colgate-Palmolive: "When you have
invested millions against a name with the American public, does that
name have more or less value on a new product? We have found to our
delight that it helps enormously." Colgate's delight is related to the
smaller amount of advertising needed for those products with the brand
name.

PROMOTIONAL DRUMBEAT

The increasing cost of advertising—and the need to get above the
noise of it—has also led to the more scientific use of another communications tool: promotion. Promotion has begun to play an intensive drum-
beat on the consumer's consciousness (see "Sales & Distribution," *Dun's
Review, September 1963*) and is being applied with increasing force and
flamboyance to the marketing drives of both very large and very small
firms. The Premium Advertising Association of America estimates that
well over $2.5 billion was spent in 1962 on promotion through premiums
alone.

Premiums are being used for new-product introduction, to open new
territories, to increase unit sales and the frequency of purchases, to improve off-season sales, to increase traffic, to build goodwill and to counter
price competition. The big-money sweepstakes promotions—Goodyear
Tire & Rubber Co. gave away $1 million in cash in 1962—create excite-
ment and attract large numbers of entries. The Coca-Cola Co., for example, received 8.8 million entries for its sweepstakes.

Self-liquidating premiums (where customers can buy the premium
at a cut rate) are less splashy but are being used equally effectively. Four
years ago, for example, Texaco started selling toy fire engines to gasoline
customers at wholesale price. This promotion is estimated to have captured 150,000 new regular customers in 1962 alone.

In soap and cosmetics, premiums promotions continue to multiply. The favorite marketing ploy in this field is the cents-off deal directed at the price-conscious shopper. A variation of this is the "cross ruff," which mates two related products. To illustrate, recently the Colgate-Palmolive Co. presented a small glass jar of its Lustre-Creme shampoo with the purchase of several bars of Palmolive soap. Another type of promotion is the "premium pack"; a Colgate-Palmolive promotion of this kind combined a free toy truck with several bars of Palmolive soap.

One marketing instrument that has become enormously more effective is market research. Before a new product is placed on the market, tests are set up for quality, distribution channels, packaging, pricing, point-of-sale, promotion, advertising, copy and media mix.

But above all, psychology in market research is being increasingly relied upon. Lysol, an old, serviceable product, was recently restored to life through the assistance of psychological research. After a period during which sales declined, the Lehn & Fink Products Corp. conducted a depth motivational study of the product. "We found that the bulk of our business was coming from a very few compulsive women who used Lysol to kill germs and to overcome some of their own psychological problems," declares Edgar W. Nelson, vice president of marketing at Lehn & Fink.

Nelson is referring to the fact that the product had an image as a great germ killer. It found favor with a relatively small number of housewives, who used it out of all proportion to their real need because they had a neurotic terror of germs. Many other prospective buyers were not being reached because of this rather stark product image. As Edgar Nelson asserts: "This meant the more we advertised in the old way, the more we kept driving logical users away."

Advertising was halted and a completely new program to remarket the product was instituted. It was decided to push the product for day-to-day homemaking problems. Research identified young mothers as the primary market, and Negroes as a secondary market because of their generally inferior living conditions where the battle against dirt is an endless struggle. Lysol has increased its market share 33 percent since it has started its new marketing program.

Psychology in market research is also becoming more complex. "We've been able to identify consumers we call carriers," declares Warren S. Seulowitz, senior staff member of product marketing at Arthur D. Little. "These are influential people who build product acceptance through word-of-mouth comments. We believe they can be particularly useful in the first phase of product introduction, specifically for prestige goods. Though the Wilkinson stainless-steel blade introduction was not a managed campaign, it was nevertheless a good example of the carrier concept at work—which is, in essence, the creation of desire without advertising."

SHOPPING AT HOME

Many consumers today are reacting adversely to shopping conditions in many discount or high-volume stores, where service is minimal and shoppers are buffeted by the horde as they fight their way through the store. Many simply stay at home, and alert merchants are capitalizing on the trend: at-home shopping is on the increase. Among the several forms of at-home shopping are catalog sales, telephone sales, mail order and door-to-door sales. According to Solomon Dutka, president of Audits & Surveys Co., a leading research firm that conducts an annual census of retailing, every one of these methods is becoming more important to the marketer. One fact bears him out: more than one-quarter of the volume of Sears, Roebuck & Co. is done through its catalog.

Nevertheless, marketers are only beginning to come to grips with this buying pattern. E. J. Korvette, the department store, and Helene Curtis Industries, a cosmetic firm, made an early start in setting up door-to-door subsidiaries. Singer Sewing Machine Co. is still testing catalog-selling at 800 of its stores, and the Mobil Oil Co. is marketing small appliances by mail.

In consumer marketing, of course, innovation is vital to continuing health. Some of the big marketers are using new and drastic measures to obtain it. If creativity lags, for example, a big marketer may wrench new ideas out of its people. "I set up matched teams of marketing people, chemists, market researchers and later some agency people and sent them off packing to invention sessions lasting three or four days," says Robert W. Young Jr. of Colgate-Palmolive. From such brainstorming came the plastic premium package for a Colgate-Palmolive children's bubble bath.

A more systematic approach to invention is taken by General Mills. It has set up an elaborate system for constantly charting and analyzing the sales of 32 different product categories. Such charting has produced six new convenience casserole mixes in one year.

As companies grow larger, flexibility becomes a vital requirement. "In marketing programs, the ultimate in flexibility is frequently required," maintains Chairman Thomas B. McCabe of Scott Paper Co. "Unanticipated competitive moves can outdate a plan overnight. We do not look askance at the marketing manager who says 'forget the plan I recommended six weeks ago.' We discarded almost all of a plan recently after it had been many months in preparation, because it was clear that a major change in conditions had precluded successful implementation."

An example of extreme flexibility is provided by Alberto-Culver. After watching Procter & Gamble Co. test Head & Shoulders, a dandruff shampoo, for a year in four markets, it decided to "beat them to the marketplace," in the words of President Lavin. "We created a name,

Subdue," he declares. "We created a package. Then a marketing plan came alive. We produced an extremely effective commercial. But we still didn't have the product." Needless to say the product was created. Subdue is now selling strongly. "Procter & Gamble had to knock Subdue off the limb rather than vice versa," claims Lavin.

Directly related to flexibility is another factor of significance: timing. "A difference of six weeks in the timing of a new product launch, we have found, can make the difference between success and failure," observes Scott Paper's Tom McCabe. "A difference of two weeks in the length of a new product promotion can have a similar effect. Taking the time to place extra salesmen in the market at the critical point of sell-in can make an enormous difference in sales success."

McCabe cites a recent experience of Scott: "With one consumer product currently in test, we realized from earlier experience that five individual timing factors were out of whack. What we look for is the most propitious timing considering a balance of factors."

One of the most important of these is the readiness of the market for a new or improved product. Marketers must be able to judge how great the demand is: Is it rising, leveling off or declining? For a mass marketer engaged in launching a new product, timing means widespread coordination. Literally hundreds of factors must be coordinated in manufacturing distribution, advertising, packaging and promotion. The logistical problems alone are staggering. Rarely does everything come off on schedule.

"One of the most difficult challenges faced by a marketing organization," declares Tom McCabe, "is auditing its own performance on a continuing basis. The quarterly audits made by product managers at Scott answer, in essence, three questions: Where do I stand? Why do I stand there? And what am I going to do to overcome an unexpected problem or take advantage of an unexpected opportunity?" This is done by a continual appraisal of plans and objectives versus results.

Because of the complex nature of marketing, most experts agree that it will always be an art. But there is one tool that can add to its precision and move it further in the direction of becoming a science. It is the computer.

General Mills' new $1.5-million data-processing and communications center is making important contribution to its marketing operations. This installation uses information retrieval to interconnect financial, production and marketing operations. Among the functions that bear more directly on marketing, it has been of greatest assistance as an audit to play back quickly the action in the market place.

A constant flow of information from every point, put in terms that everyone knows and uses, goes out to General Mills marketing executives.

It includes contribution to profit by brand, division, plant, salesman and sales territory. Computer operations research charts performance-goal ratios of brand, sales, production and competition.

Most of the data fed into the computer is generated internally. The next step for General Mills is to gather accurate external data that relates to marketing and can be fed into its data-processing installation. This mixture of internal and external data will create a total information system on which marketing strategy can be based.

When that occurs, the age of electronic marketing will commence. Meanwhile, the U.S.' big—and a handful of not so big—consumer goods manufacturers are rapidly honing their traditional weaponry into subtle and sophisticated selling machines.

II. Science in Marketing

INTRODUCTION

A veritable explosion in quantitative methods has occurred since World War II. Terms such as operations research, computers, Bayesian Statistics, simulation and others were mere curiosities or still untested ideas as little as twenty years ago. Any confusion in recognizing quantitative techniques as aids to marketing management might be understood within the time perspective. Application of many statistical and mathematical methods to marketing can be regarded as a current event since such practices did not get underway fully until almost 1960.

This section presents readings that emphasize the understanding of techniques and methods rather than managerial implications. However, it should not be considered an achievement to have understood only the nature of the techniques and not the potential worth to the real-world marketing man. Much of the confusion in this area is the result of treating these developments as solutions in search of problems. The fact that many of these techniques will have application should be kept in mind by the marketing department, and additional information must be sought from the particular specialists. The onset of such communication may come by sampling the quantitative readings, some of which cover broad areas of mathematics and statistics, and others which delve into some of the detail of particular techniques and methods.

The social sciences that have made major contributions to marketing include psychology, sociology, anthropology and social psychology along with political science and economics. The social sciences have provided the marketer with useful techniques as well as substantive findings that have direct application to marketing. This is most apparent in the area of consumer behavior, although organizational and personnel problems of marketing also have been successfully attacked with techniques from the social sciences. Major individual findings and analytical tools, as well as readings that survey whole areas of developments in the social sciences, are found in this section.

The neat cleavage of this section into behavioral science and the quantitative science leaves the impression that all major advances from outside marketing are either quantitative or behavioral in terms of content and origin. This is not the case, necessarily, in the behavioral sciences where applications of quantitative science are frequent, or in the quantitative areas such as operations research where large doses of behavioral science are found in formulating assumptions and in building techniques and models. Thus, in many problem situations, the marketer may rely upon a series of findings from several unrelated disciplines that together and only together provide the material from which better solutions are formulated.

A. Quantitative Applications

5. The computer and the marketing man

RICHARD C. CHRISTIAN

In less than ten years from now
. . . U.S. population will be almost 220,000,000.
. . . Gross national product will be close to a trillion dollars.
. . . Inflation will likely shrink our dollar another 20 percent or so.
. . . Individual incomes will be up nearly 50 percent.
. . . Automation and electronics will affect practically everything we do.

Industrial marketing will see many dramatic changes. The changes, wrought by the "black box" (electronic computer) will come from automation in nonmarketing functions as well as such marketing activities as personal selling, product design and development, marketing research, and communications.

SOME ELECTRONIC AGE PREDICTIONS

IBM predicts:
. . . Computers tied in with accounting and bookkeeping will simultaneously register a purchase in the credit office, inventory control department, production scheduling department, and the shipping office.
. . . Companies using computers to simulate business problems and analyze various alternatives for their solution will have top management free to concentrate on creative phases of their jobs.

Reprinted from the *Journal of Marketing*, Volume 26 (July, 1962), pp. 79–82, National Quarterly Publication of the American Marketing Association.

. . . Computer technology will enable the government to be far more scientific in planning roads, transportation, schools, and water needs. Tax records, birth and marriage records, deeds of sale, car registrations, criminal and public health records will all be stored in computers.

. . . Electronic data processing will give us complete health records for major segments of the country's population. And in hospitals, computers will help doctors to uncover secrets in body chemistry, the nervous system, genetics, and diagnosis.

Indeed, automation and electronics are already beginning to affect almost everything we do. Actually automation is not new. We have been "automating" since the wheel; but most of the significant progress in automation has been confined to production processes and manufacturing.

Only recently have automation methods been linked with marketing. And this has been confined largely to warehousing and transportation, order picking, and handling. Automatic vending and certain other functions in retailing are also being automated. These innovations speed up the distribution process and lower marketing costs. But what about the other important marketing functions: selling; new product development and testing; communications, including advertising, public relations, and publicity; packaging; and marketing research? These marketing functions are the economy's "dark continent." [1]

USING THE COMPUTER IN INDUSTRIAL MARKETING

Most sophisticated computer users, and certainly computer manufacturers, agree on one thing. We are just beginning to "scratch the surface" of electronic data processing applications in marketing. Any article or speech on the subject is almost out-of-date the day it is published. Innovations and potential possibilities are developed practically daily.

In *personal selling and sales analysis,* computers are helping industrial marketers to develop dramatic improvements in shaping alternative strategies and measuring performance against planned objectives. Faster and more detailed processing of sales data gives the industrial sales manager an opportunity to measure more quickly and scientifically individual salesman performance, sales-territory achievements, competitive records, and product-by-product performance.

Information on sales trends will be spotted automatically, and in time to give the sales management a chance to take immediate corrective action in many areas. Relative influence of multiple buying will be pinpointed. Weaknesses in certain territories can be eliminated in the early stages of a decreasing sales curve.

[1] Peter F. Drucker, "The Economy's Dark Continent," *Fortune* (April, 1962), pp. 103, 265, 266, 268, 270, at p. 103.

Data from computers will guide salesmen to the high potential, high profit customers. It will help interpret reasons for lost sales. The computer can be invaluable in providing direction to the management in allocating funds and time to the most profitable marketing mix. The computer helps to answer the fundamental question: how can we best apportion our marketing dollar to return us the highest profit percentage?

Marketing mathematical models are becoming as important tools to the industrial marketing manager as the more traditional tools of marketing. The predictive possibilities of the computer give the sales manager a tremendous head start in guiding his sales force to the right prospect, with the right product sales message, at the right time.

In *new product development and testing*, the industrial firm will increase its success odds greatly by applying computer technology. Almost all of the outstanding postwar industrial success stories are based on the successful development and introduction of new products. Most major industrial companies' sales records indicate that products not in existence ten years ago now account for between 25 percent and 50 percent of total sales. A company's survival depends on new product ideas.

But the development and eventual marketing of the new product out of twenty which achieves success is a very painful and profit-punishing corporate experience.

Alternative product factors, combinations of products, and the adding and dropping of products from the line will be basic marketing problems solved more quickly and effectively by electronic machines.

The coinventor of the electronic computer, J. Presper Eckert, predicts that the computer will revolutionize marketing in the future by pretesting products before they appear in the home, the store or factory. "There will be no miserable flops paraded before the public to tarnish a company's reputation," Mr. Eckert reports. "The computer will even have charted the times at which the product will reach its peak, will have matured, and when it will be dead." [2]

He goes on to say that computers should be used in analyzing alternative decisions using linear programing, for example, to tell management from which warehouse the product can be shipped most economically, in which plant it should be manufactured and how many maintenance technicians will be required to service it.

In *marketing research*, the computer gives the marketing man a tool which will drastically speed up processing and analyzing of data. It enables the researcher to provide his management facts and figures on a "before-the-fact" rather than the so common "after-the-fact" basis of today.

Aiding management decision-making are computer applications solving such problems as:

[2] *Chicago Daily News*, April 6, 1962, p. 41.

. . . Deciding where to locate a new plant or branch, based on an analysis of expected customer demand, transportation, distribution, and other factors contributing to costs and profits.

. . . Forecasting sales, using marketing research to determine sales probabilities in different geographical regions for different product lines.

. . . Inventory control analysis and warehousing methods, using operations research techniques.

An experimental laboratory for marketing management—simulation on a computer—is improving decision-making significantly. Computer simulation is a tool for discovering an improved mode of operation, one that stands somewhere between what you would have obtained by pure judgment and intuition alone, and the optimum policy which might be pursued.

Another forward advance in marketing is Information Retrieval. IR is the art of extracting from storage the information desired at a particular point in time, in response to specific requests. It is a process growing in importance. Retrieval of information as such is not new—we have had books, libraries, and reference librarians for years—but what is new is the application of mechanized methods for accomplishing the age-old tasks, and more recently the use of computers to assist in solving this universal problem.

IR involves all the aspects of information collection, selection, indexing, storage, retrieval and dissemination. The significance of IR to the industrial marketing research manager is obvious. The amount of duplication in terms of market measurement, buying practice studies, marketing trends, and market attitude and opinion research projects is staggering.

We are never sure we have all that is available; but worse than that, we are not sure that we have the most applicable information for our particular problem. Information Retrieval Systems, broadly available in trade associations and government agencies in addition to individual corporate IR systems, will materially improve the speed and effectiveness of industrial marketing research. Learning how to find out what we already know can bring major cost savings to industrial marketers.

In the *external communications programs* (advertising, sales promotion, and publicity) of industrial concerns, the computer is also making its presence felt.

In a very few short years computers will process the selection of media and much of the paperwork now necessary in analyzing the relationships between advertising and sales dollars.

Barnard, Inc., a Standard Rate & Data Service subsidiary, has developed an automated procedure for allocating advertising investments by sales territories, and then correlating these sales with advertising dollars while simultaneously effecting comparisons with year-ago figures.

Studies are well under way to explore the most satisfactory methods of converting business publication circulation data into machine language. Some publishing companies are already processing advertising inquiries on data processing equipment.

Standard Rate and Data Service sees a real possibility of integrating computers with its printing production to provide all of the data now in the directories on an instantaneously current basis. This would be accomplished through a high-speed communications linkage with transmission equipment located in the large advertising agencies, and available to smaller agencies from widely scattered but strategically located points throughout the country. A media buyer who wants to check rates would still refer to his printed directory to make media selections and gather basic comparative cost and coverage data; but once this was accomplished, he would turn to his transmitter linked by direct line to the SRDS computer and ask for a variety of specialized, derived figures— such as comparative cost per thousand figures for publications selected . . . or coverage by geographic or SIC industry breakdowns . . . or dollars to be invested in selected sales or market areas. His answers would come back across a distance of hundreds of miles in just a few seconds.

Before too long, business paper circulation numbers and audience characteristics will be reduced to standard machine language. It will be available in up-to-the-minute comparative form with the selection on this basis handled by computers.

We shall no longer worry about duplication of circulation and readership we are now buying in business papers. Statistical information will simply be fed into a data processing system big enough to store the information. Retrieval of pertinent duplication facts will then be readily available. Market data defined in the same terms used in the circulation and audience analyses, all in machine language, will provide an instantaneous matching of markets and media at different cost levels.

Scientific audience studies will be readily available from random access memory devices. Industrial advertisers and agencies will use computers to research the reading habits of every individual in a given industry or market. This information will be stored in a random access memory device which is easily updated from time to time.

Many people have ignored the fact that really high-capacity memory devices are now available. For example, for several years it has been possible to get an IBM RAMAC disk file which stores up to 10 million characters of information.

LIFE IN 1972

The publisher in 1972 will be building mathematical models of his magazine a year in advance of the issue date, just as the businessman will be looking at a simulated annual report a year ahead of time. Story details will be sped to the publication home offices by Tele-Processing; and computer-controlled printers operating at speeds in excess of two thousand lines a minute will print out story outlines. Output from high-speed printers will be photographed directly and become offset proofs for solid pages of text.

Reversing Tele-Processing input, publishers will be selling a new information service . . . providing punched card or magnetic tape marketing data to business and industry. Highly advanced information retrieval programs will turn publishing into an *information* business in which the publisher not only communicates general information in the form of magazines, but provides his audience with almost instantaneous, yet highly individual, information.

Money in the form of bank drafts will not be exchanged between the publisher, the advertiser, and the agency because the national banking system will almost instantly and automatically update corporate accounts from data fed from Tele-Processing units. For example, one signal from the agency's Tele-Processing unit will decrease the advertiser's account by a hundred dollars, increase the publisher's dollars. The same automatic updating of corporate accounts will be reflected in the updating of personal accounts so that payroll becomes a matter of communicating with the employee's bank rather than communicating through the form of a check with the employee himself.

Each morning, the editor and the publisher will meet to review a very brief statement on a single sheet of paper. On this paper will be an exception report of things they should worry about *that* day. The computer will be continually analyzing their business and telling them only the things that they have to worry about—the corporate officers then can work on the assumption that everything they do not know about is running smoothly.

Subscription fulfillment, which even now can be fully automated on high-speed computers, will be incredibly accurate. Change-of-address cards will be optically read by the computer and all subscription data updated in a millionth of a second—where a change of title occurs and it is obviously a promotion, the computer will also (as a byproduct) tell an electric typewriter to write a letter of congratulations over a facsimile signature of the president of the publishing company.

With the press of a button, the agency man will watch extremely detailed information fly out of a high speed printer—it will give him precise analysis of the publication's circulation, duplication, geographical breakdown by SIC codes by county, and by title; factors indicating renewal trends by SIC code over a 10-year period; terse comments on editorial evaluation from a 500-point mathematical profile; and rate trends over the past five years.

Four days after the publication has been mailed, all advertisers will receive an extremely accurate analysis of the readership of their advertisements—the information will be printed out for them at their Tele-Processing receiver.

Geared to its own employee profile requirements, a company will receive student profiles of college seniors who mathematically match the kind of person it wants to hire—the same service for experienced personnel will be provided by data centers specializing in personnel.

Many publications will become dailies, but will not even have a printing plant. The "issue" will be sent out on high-speed magnetic tape over Tele-Processing systems and type and halftones produced by facsimile machines at the subscriber's office. Just as we now have instant pie mix and instant coffee, there will be "instant news." The story on the hiring of a new president of a major U.S. corporation will appear in the publication *Business Minute* on the subscriber's desk within 20 minutes after the announcement has been made.

PARTNERS IN PROGRESS

The computer and the marketing man—partners in progress? It is no longer a question . . . it is a fact—today! Not when, or why, or how, or where . . . but how fast? The challenge and opportunity to industrial marketing is unlimited. The goal of "science in marketing" is closer than ever before, thanks to the computer.

But industrial marketing people must understand these facts first:

1. The computer does not replace judgment, common sense, or creativity. It can, however, replace guesses and "flying-the-seat-of-your-pants" business practices.
2. The computer is only as efficient as the facts and figures put into it. The programing and programers (the "software") must be equally as good as the computers (the "hardware").
3. There are few, if any, marketing functions which are not affected by electronic computer applications. The alert marketing man will explore electronic data processing for application in all marketing activities.
4. Size of company makes little difference in the possible uses of computer technology. With the rapid growth of computer service centers, a small company can rent computer services for a relatively small monthly investment.

6. A closer look at operations research

PHILIP A. DOHERTY

This article deals with three major features of Operations Research: the concept of the problem, the approach, and some techniques.

CONCEPTS OF OPERATIONS RESEARCH

Two principal factors have been responsible for the development of the OR (Operations Research) concept of the business problem: *growth* and *pace.*

As growth and diversification have progressed and the pace of doing business has accelerated, the manager's problems have become more complex, and he has less time in which to make decisions. The number of factors to be considered is constantly increasing; and the data now available, however voluminous, inadequately inform him on these factors.

The New Concept: Integration

Consider one action: the sale of a single item. This transaction will be processed through or affect every segment of the business. The item ordered will be removed from inventory and shipped. The accumulation of inventory depletions will initiate a replenishment order, which in turn will produce a manufacturing schedule and call for more raw materials. A succession of such manufacturing orders will require maintenance and ultimate replacement or expansion of facilities.

Product quality must be maintained, and products developed which will enable the firm to maintain or to improve its competitive position.

Each item shipped must be billed, and records of customer accounts receivable maintained. Inventories and facilities for shipment of orders

Reprinted from the *Journal of Marketing,* Volume 27 (April 1963), pp. 59–65, National Quarterly Publication of the American Marketing Association.

must be financed. These requirements are related to sales forecasts, which in part are based on histories of accumulations of customer orders, and in part on marketing research. Finally, the successful order immediately "signals" the marketing activity to take steps to generate more orders.

These expressed relationships demand an organizational concept which, in spite of lip service, has not yet been really accepted. That concept is *integration.*

Integration vs. Compartmentalization

The traditional concept of company organization is expressed in the form of the usual organization chart, which may itself have helped to perpetuate operation on a compartmentalized basis, with each manager concentrating primarily on his own segment of the problem.

Organizations often claim to have established horizontal lines of communication by committee or by management directive; but considerations of proprietorship, self-protection, empire building, and inadequate attempts to perform a single function without integration may reduce such "lines of communication" to ineffectiveness.

By contrast, the OR concept views the corporation as an organic whole, existing in an economic and sociological environment. It considers the problems of the corporation in the perspective of this environment, and implications posed by this environment in the solution of these problems. Within the corporation, Operations Research similarly studies the interactions of the various functions, quantifies them, and determines their effects on the solutions proposed.

Visually, we might represent the OR concept of the organization as a wheel—with management the policy-making hub, obtaining data from and providing direction to its established supporting functions through the spokes.

A Concrete Illustration

We may express this concept of functional interactions more tangibly by the problem of planning product inventories, illustrated in Figure 1.[1]

The exhibit shows only some of the factors involved. Obviously neither long-range nor short-range inventory planning decisions can be made until the corresponding sales forecasts have been provided, and until the actual demand, having a known reliability, has been estimated. Supporting these must be the functions of marketing research and line sales effort.

Once forecasts of demand and marketing plants are determined, policy and operating decisions may be made which encompass not only

[1] Based on the inventory planning model contained in John F. Magee, *Production Planning and Control* (New York: McGraw-Hill Book Co., Inc., 1958), Chapter 1.

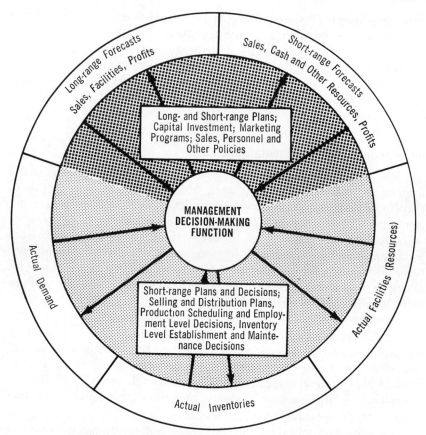

Figure 1. Schematic diagram, inventory management system

inventory planning but every other facet of the business as well—the use, acquisition, or disposition of manpower, money, machinery, materials, and methods.

Operations Research is thus more than an assortment of sophisticated, complex mathematical techniques for solving isolated, unrelated problems. Until its conceptual aspect is understood and applied, use of the available techniques will fall short of the full potential of this approach.

THE "OR" APPROACH

The OR approach to the solution of the business problem may be described as a series of sequential steps:

Identification and description of the problem and the objectives of the solution. *Representation of the problem in the form of a mathematical model.*

Quantification of the problem variables.
Reduction of the variables to a workable total, by elimination of those of little
significance or sensitivity.
Manipulation of the model under varying conditions, assumptions, and policy
restrictions.
Analysis and presentation of the sets of results obtained.
Evaluation of decisions based on these results.

Many persons consider the two italicized steps—involving the quantification of a problem within a model—the essence of OR.

It should be emphasized that the operations researcher is not the
decision-maker. He supplies management with analyses of the quantitative factors implicit in the problem; and he provides alternative solutions,
including evaluations of their costs and impacts. He thus makes it possible for management to assume its true role—the consideration of
families of decisions, by which many individual routine decisions may
be delegated, even mechanized.

Operations Research Defined

Operations Research has been defined in many different ways, but
one of the best definitions is: "Systematic inquiry into operating problems
for the purpose of predicting quantitatively the operating conditions
under which optimum results may be achieved, thereby developing
sound quantitative bases for management decisions." [2]

Since business problems may not on the surface appear to be susceptible to formal analysis, management may find it difficult to select and
measure the problem criteria and to assign relative values to intangible
problem variables. It is also difficult to determine the probability of risk
or degrees of uncertainty which must be included in the model, since
precise information on these matters seldom exists.

What makes the OR approach possible is the basic similarity of most
business problems—"the determination of the best (optimum) distribution
of a group of limited resources, among a group of competing requirements, within a common set of fixed limits." [3]

The Mathematical Model

OR frequently represents the business problem in terms of the
"mathematical model." This has been defined by many writers simply
as that system of equations which describes a business problem.

[2] Developed by W. H. Martin, Associate Professor of Management Engineering,
Rensselaer Polytechnic Institute, Troy, New York.
[3] Alexander Henderson and Robert Schlaifer, Mathematical Programming: Better
Information For Better Decision Making, *Harvard Business Review*, Vol. 32 (May–
June, 1954).

Although new to the solution of business problems, the use of models is certainly not new to industry. In the study of aircraft design, for example, extensive use is made of wind-tunnel models. In ship design, hull models are tested in tanks—mathematically formulated curves are constructed at each frame, from bow to stern, and lines of the hull are faired into these curves between frames. The model thus approximates, between stations, the formulated curves of these stations, and it is assumed that no more significantly accurate results could be obtained by solving for curves between stations.

Similarly, the business model need not duplicate every configuration of the real world which it represents, although it must *approximate* those conditions realistically. The problem solutions will then approximate the optimum closely enough to be valid.

Further, we do not always need actual data in the solution of a model. In many problems, simulated data (even random data) may provide the solutions sought.

While not all problems can be represented in model form, there are proved rules for those which can be so described. These rules permit us to know *positively* the degree of probability that we will reach the best solution, and it will be absolutely clear how this solution has been reached. Alternatively, by these rules we can identify the problems for which there is *no solution* or *no best solution*.

Specifically, our business model may take the form of a chart, graph, array, table of values, or a system of one or more equations. Each of these forms is derived from equations, or may be reduced to equations. An equation is the basic vehicle, manipulated by every OR technique, to resolve the problem described.

Two Sample Models

Our first example is a production planning model—basically a marketing problem based on a sales forecast.

An extreme simplification of a production planning system allows us to express a model in equation form:

$$P_Q = S_Q + (P_{Q\text{-}1} - S_Q) + (I_Q - I_{Q\text{-}1})$$

In this model, planned production is expressed as functions of forecast sales, previous excess or inadequate production, and anticipated inventory adjustments, since:

P_Q = production planned for the coming quarter

S_Q = sales forecast for the coming quarter

$P_{Q\text{-}1} - S_Q$ = last quarter's production related to coming quarter forecast sales

$I_Q - I_{Q-1}$ = coming quarter inventory compared with last quarter actual inventory.

In the model, all functional relationships are linear, although were it to be more fully developed these relationships might well become of second or higher order. The objective of optimization, although implied, is not conclusively proved.

Our second example is a better illustration of the process of optimization. This is an economic order quantity (EOQ) model, in the solution of which calculus may be used.

Differential calculus is an easy way to determine an optimum solution, since it allows us to reduce a function (the interrelation of two variables) to its first derivative, which by definition is the slope of the function at any point. Equating this function to zero (zero slope describes the horizontal) and solving, we find the value of the function at the point of horizontal slope, a maximum or minimum value, which represents the "optimum" solution.

This is shown by the economic order quantity model (Figure 2), representing a quadratic function (equation 1), the first derivative of which (equation 2) describes the most economic (minimum total cost per unit) lot to make or buy within the parameters of sales demand, setup cost, inventory cost, and acquisition cost.[4]

Not discussed fully here but of some interest is the rate-of-change model, frequently used to evaluate the effectiveness of advertising programs and salesmen's efforts. It is a quantitative model of customer activity, and provides a method for describing mathematically the anticipated switching of customers and noncustomers in a potential market. It further provides a means of evaluating the effects of imposed factors, such as advertising, on sales programs.[5]

SOME "OR" TECHNIQUES

The rapid development of OR and its extension to the business world has entailed the formalization of many techniques. These have been successfully applied to finite engineering problems (such as turbine design) and to product problems and process research problems, as well as to business problems. Some of the more important techniques are:

1. Mathematical statistics—including time series analysis and regression analysis.
2. Mathematical programming—including linear, nonlinear, and dynamic programming.

[4] Richard B. Maffei, "Mathematical Models, Values of Parameters, and the Sensitivity Analysis of Management Decision Rules," *Journal of Marketing*, Vol. 21 (April, 1957), pp. 419–427.
[5] John F. Magee, "Operations Research in Making Marketing Decisions," *Journal of Marketing*, Vol. 25 (October, 1960), pp. 18–23.

(1) $TVC = \dfrac{Q}{2} \cdot IC + \dfrac{Y}{Q} \cdot S$

(2) $EOQ = \sqrt{\dfrac{2YS}{IC}}$

WHERE:
Y = SALES DEMAND/PERIOD
S = FIXED COST/ORDER
I = INVENTORY CARRYING COST
C = COST/UNIT OF INVENTORY
Q = INVENTORY

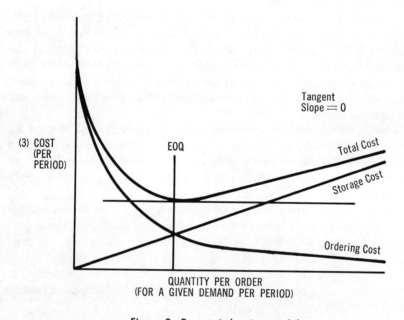

Figure 2. Economic lot size model

3. Simulation—including operational gaming or business games, and Monte Carlo analysis.
4. Network theory including program evaluation and review techniques (PERT), critical path method (CPM), and line of balance (LOB).
5. Queuing theory.
6. Game theory.
7. Electronic data processing (EDP).

Mathematical Statistics

The designs of experiments and investigations have long been based on mathematical statistics. In addition, the laws of probability, combination, distribution, and expected values have been used for years in quality control, market analysis and other business functions. The industrial engineer, for example, has developed statistical inferences based on assumed distribution probabilities, to prepare sampling plans for the continuing evaluation of product quality, thus substantially reducing product inspection required to ensure maintenance of desired outgoing quality levels. Later in this article, a description of a sales forecasting model discusses regression analysis, another form of mathematical statistics.[6]

Mathematical Programming

Mathematical programming is that method of optimizing, for a given objective (function), within established limits (parameters), any interacting set of conditions (interacting problem variables). It can require the use of matrix algebra and differential calculus. Programming can be:

Linear, in which all relationships can be expressed in directly proportional terms (for example, relationship of input to output would be a straight line if graphed).

Nonlinear, encompassing nonlinear (for example, $y = x^2$) problem variables and expressed graphically as a curve.

Dynamic, developing conditional optimum solutions for each phase of a problem, progressing in single steps, using the output from each step as the input to the next to arrive at a final optimum solution.

Simulation

Simulation is a trial-and-error technique of manipulating mathematical models to determine the effect of decisions in response to the conditions described by the model, over a given period of time.

Operational gaming, more frequently described as business gaming, is a simulation experiment in which the outcomes of strategies in interacting competitive situations, based on intuitive decisions, are developed. They are tested by including personnel as decision-makers during the running of the experiment.[7]

In *Monte Carlo* analysis, data are generated by use of a random number generator, according to some known pattern of randomness from the real world. It is the basis for formulating the inputs to many simulation experiments.

Network Theory

PERT is one of a number of forms of network theory. With CPM, LOB, and other techniques, it provides a means of maximizing the effectiveness

[6] Alexander McFarlane Wood, *Introduction to the Theory of Statistics*, (McGraw-Hill Book Co., Inc., 1950).

[7] Oliver B. Schenk, "Mathematical Models of Market Simulation," *Journal of Marketing*, Vol. 24 (April, 1960), pp. 69–74.

of project scheduling, evaluating the relationships of project functions, determining which are critical to project completion—hence, the development of the "Critical Path." It also provides a means of determining the effects on resources, such as manpower or money, of revising project schedules, and of alternative allocation of resources. Finally, it provides a means of evaluating project progress.[8]

Queuing Theory

Queuing theory, applicable to waiting lines, is the technique of establishing service priorities for units arriving at a given point, balancing the costs of waiting against the costs of providing the service required.

Game Theory

Game theory is the technique of determining the best strategy for one of two or more opponents in competitive situations where the outcomes of various strategies can be precisely predicted. It has assisted management successfully to determine the timing of advertising programs and the allocation of funds to competing types of advertising media.[9]

Electronic Data Processing

EDP is established as a separate category because it makes many OR solutions possible. This is not to say that OR cannot be used unless we have a computer; some problems do not require one, and service bureaus can handle others. However, it would be difficult to solve many of the integrated, complex business problems so appropriate to Operations Research without the ability of the computer to handle and process large amounts of data quickly.

CLASSIC "OR" MODELS

Some of these techniques have been used so frequently that "classical" models have been developed. Although named for their most common applications, these models are useful in many functions not specifically identified. For most, computer programs are available through equipment manufacturers and service bureaus. Some of these "classical" models are next described.

Sales Forecasting Model. Figure 3 illustrates a statistical sales forecasting model. If we have a time series analysis of the sales of a given

[8] George A. W. Boehm, "Helping the Executive to Make Up His Mind," *Fortune,* Vol. 55 (April, 1962), pp. 128–131, 218, 222, and 224.

[9] Cyril B. Herrman and John B. Stewart, "The Experimental Game," *Journal of Marketing,* Vol. 22 (July, 1957), pp. 12–20.

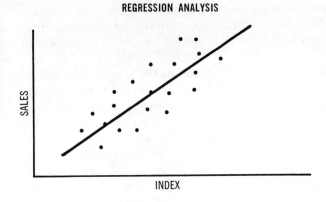

REGRESSION ANALYSIS

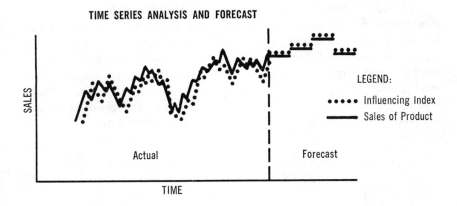

Figure 3. Sales forecasting model

product and the corresponding movement of an "influencing" index, we can determine the existence and degree of correlation between the two by means of regression analysis. Thence, we can develop a product sales forecast based on the forecast of the index.

A condition of uncertainty might call for Monte Carlo analysis in the manipulation of this model. If we did not have a product sales history by the required increments but did know the average historical sales and their probable distribution, we could generate data by use of some random number generator. This would provide a hypothetical sales pattern having the same statistical character as the actual experience, at less cost and less time than developing the actual data would require.[10]

Replacement Model. The replacement model is used to determine

---

[10] The application of Monte Carlo analysis to the sales forecasting model is described further in Werner F. Hirsch, "Decision Making in Industrial Marketing," *Journal of Marketing,* Vol. 24 (January, 1960), pp. 21–27.

replacement schedules for equipment to minimize costs of new equipment, maintenance of existing equipment, and equipment down time. Preventive maintenance scheduling is a special case of the replacement model.

Linear Allocation Model. The allocation model is generally defined as the most efficient allocation of limited resources to competing requirements. The problem can be represented geometrically if there are three or fewer competing requirements; beyond this it must be solved by the use of matrix algebra, frequently described as the "Simplex method." This is a procedure which through a series of repetitive operations (iterations) progressively approaches and ultimately reaches an optimum solution. It has been applied to a wide variety of allocation problems—including product mix determination, ingredient blending, capacity allocation, purchasing and evaluation of bids, and distribution.

Figure 4 illustrates the following distribution problem: Assign the production of three plants to fill the sales requirements of four warehouses at the minimum shipping costs.[11] Let us assume, as *known*, the requirements of each warehouse, the capacity of each plant, and the shipping cost from each plant to each warehouse. For simplification, total productive capacity is considered equal to total sales requirements. The map illustrates the relative locations of plants and warehouses, and the matrix developed in Table 1 shows all of the known data.

Problem: Assign production of three plants to fill sales requirements
of four warehouses at the minimum shipping cost.

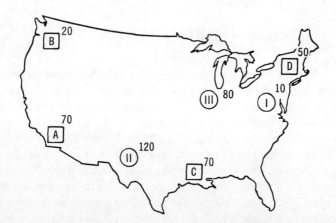

Figure 4. Resource Allocation Problem

[11] A similar but more complex distribution problem is developed by Edward H. Bowman and John B. Stewart in "A Model for Scale of Operations," *Journal of Marketing*, Vol. 20 (January, 1956), pp. 242–247.

Table 1
Freight Rates
Production = Demand = 210 Units

Factory →	I	II	III	Production
Warehouse	10	120	80	Demand
A	1.05	.90	2.00	70
B	2.30	1.40	1.40	20
C	1.80	1.00	1.20	70
D	1.00	1.75	1.10	50

The following steps (the Simplex method) lead to the solution of this problem, shown in Figure 5 and in Table 2:

1. Frame the problem, stating all requirements.
2. Determine an initial solution.
3. Evaluate the various choices.
4. Select the most favorable choice.
5. Determine the number and distribution of units reallocated.
6. Develop the new solution.
7. Repeat steps 3 through 6 until no possible favorable choices are available. At this point the procedure is complete. There can be no better solution.

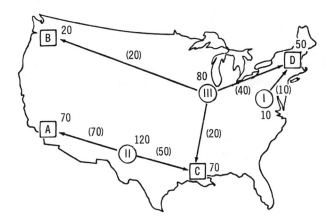

Figure 5. Solution to Resource Allocation Problem

Nonlinear Allocation Model. There is no single methodology for the solution of nonlinear allocation problems. Many lend themselves to simu-

Table 2
Optimum Production Distribution

Solution	I	II	III	Demand
A		70		70
B			20	20
C		50	20	70
D	10		40	50
Prod.	10	120	80	

lation, Monte Carlo analysis, or queuing theory. Some, however, can be solved by linear programming if they exhibit nonlinear relationships which can be approximated by straight lines (or planes), or nonlinear relationships which can be reduced to linearity.

Dynamic Allocation Model. As noted, dynamic allocation models frequently are solved by making optimum decisions for each step and proceeding from one stage to the next, integrating these interim solutions in following stages. A final optimum solution is achieved by summing each of the interim solutions.

PROVED APPLICATIONS

The number of business problems to which OR has been successfully applied is far greater than the marketing problems discussed, as the following list shows:

1. Selection of advertising media and expenditures
2. Revision of price and discount tables
3. Establishment of bonus and incentive plans
4. Strategy moves in view of competitive conditions
5. Sales forecasting
6. Sales (customer) service policies
7. Sales effort management
8. Product (inventory) distribution
9. Selection of warehouse location
10. Inventory policies
11. Formulation of new product plans
12. Research budget allocations
13. Determination of product mix
14. Transportation mix
15. Distribution scheduling

The principal objective of this article has been to create an awareness of a powerful new tool, its concepts, approaches to problem solving, and the techniques by which it translates ideas into decisions. Properly applied, OR will enable business to cope more effectively with its problems, and to meet the increasingly complex and demanding responsibilities with which it is faced.

7. What's the status of mathematical marketing?

It's 1965, or perhaps a little beyond. The scene is a special meeting of the marketing committee of the Bevatron Popcorn Co. The reason for the meeting: Bevatron, although in firm possession of 40 percent of the bagged popcorn market in the area, has just posted its third successive red-ink quarter. Worse, market intelligence shows that Bevatron's two competitors, Ajax and Atlas, are raking in profits hand over fist. Why? They charge more—one gives 11 ounces for 12 cents, the other, 15 ounces for 15 cents—and consequently receive a smaller share of the market. Bevatron's trouble is now clear; all efforts at cost reduction have failed, so the famous Bevatron 10-oz. bag for a dime must go.

Several alternatives are selected as holding the greatest promise: (1) raise the price a penny; (2) reduce the size of the bag to 9 ounces; (3) raise price 2 cents, up the bag size only 1 ounce; (4) "trade up" each sale by increasing both price and size of bag by 50 percent.

But plenty of disadvantages are evident, too, not the least being that it is impossible to say which plan would maximize profits while minimizing the damage to sales and industry position. Plan 1 is obviously the most flagrant price rise; it would undoubtedly irritate customers, and would certainly spell doom for the company's well-promoted advertising slant of "still only a dime." It would involve considerable public crow-eating, to be sure. But plan 2 would create the smallest bag of popcorn in industry history—one that might be too small for consumer tastes. And it just temporarily avoids the price-rise issue. Plans 3 and 4 mean matching competitors exactly. Both are active, responsive companies—and would be sure to retaliate. Even a price war is not out of the question. And these plans, while probably the soundest fiscally, would probably do most damage to Bevatron's industry position.

Today, there would be no way to get answers to the questions raised

Reprinted from *Sales Management,* July 1, 1960, pp. 25–27ff.

by our little fictional problem. But Bevatron, with 1960 a good five years behind, can use computerized mathematical analysis, or, as the company calls it, the "Predictron" system. By using these advanced techniques, it can get anwers to the questions, "What would happen if we did 1? . . . 2? . . . 3? . . . 4?" In each case, what would happen to sales? To industry position? What would competition do? With answers to those and other questions, the committee could meet again . . . decide which probable outcome best fits the company's long-range goals . . . and implement that plan quickly and confidently.

Right now, unfortunately, mathematical analysis is not so sophisticated. It is, in fact, largely a laboratory phenomenon—still quite untamed.

The brother-sister act of applied mathematics and the electronic computer is enough to scare the pants off of any sales or marketing executive. The long rows of hieroglyphic formulas . . . the strange, apparently untranslatable jargon of the trade . . . the intricate language understood only by machines and a select few mortals . . . indeed enough to put fear of the devil in the sales-trained marketer.

But woe to him who avoids that ice-cold duet of formula and machine. As 1965 heaves into view, it will be a major factor in marketing decision making. Indeed, some think it will be the most significant development yet in modern marketing. But it can't be brought into a company overnight.

It must be made very clear that no formula or machine will be making marketing decisions. Rather, the "decision systems" are tools—fabulous tools which allow the marketer to base his major decisions on reliable information, rather than on hunches and incomplete knowledge. In effect, it puts him in a class with the engineer whose theories assure him that his bridge will stand before the first girder falls into place.

To obtain a more exact picture of the role played by this new technology, it may be helpful to see how it fits into the over-all decision-making process.

This is how one expert describes it:

"It is useful to break the decision process into four distinct steps. First, we have *dissatisfaction* with existing operations, which leads to *nomination* of some alternative course of action. This is followed by *prediction* of what the effects of the alternative will be. This leads to *evaluation* of the predicted effects to determine whether or not the plan is satisfactory—if not, the process reverts to the first stage; if so, we take action. Our general hypothesis is that humans are far superior to computers in three of these components: dissatisfaction—sensing that something is wrong and that a change should be made; nomination—coming up with a totally new plan, and evaluation—comparing the expected outcomes of several different plans and deciding that one is best. We believe that in the prediction stage, however, computers and mathematical analysis may be far more effective than human intuition. The determination of the possible effects of a change in some aspect of a plan requires precisely the kind of detailed, exhaustive analysis in which computers and mathematics excel."

This is how it works: The computer simply predicts by quickly solving extremely long mathematical problems fed into it by operations researchers (operations research, applied mathematics, mathematical programming are, broadly, all names for the same activity). It is still up to the sharp marketing executive to wonder, "What would happen if we did 'A'? or 'B'? or 'C'?" and, when he finds out what would happen if he did any of the three, it is up to him to decide which path best leads to the fulfillment of his company's goals (also established by a person—not a machine), whether they be higher profits, more sales, more diversified line, de-emphasis of certain products, larger share of industry for others, and so on. The decision system of applied mathematics and computer has told him one thing: What would probably happen if he followed each of his proposed courses of action.

Incidentally, it is the ultimate wish of the operations researcher to eliminate himself as much as possible from the procedure. So long as he is between the executive and the machine, the process is limited to simple problems. By the time a complex problem is translated from executive language to operations researcher language to computer language and back again, the meaning and content is virtually destroyed. The problem is to enable the executive to communicate with the computer with as little interference as possible. The thought is not to make operations researchers out of marketing executives—but to make the computers more and more articulate and receptive. The ideal, of course, would be to have the executive address the machine simply, have the machine understand, translate and set up its own problem, solve it, translate its answer back to the executive in language he could understand easily.

Today, the average marketer has no definitive scientific predictions to help him. So he must make his own predictions. After he decides what might be done as an alternative to the present method, he begins to gather information. He succeeds in assembling vast amounts of data. But voluminous as it is, it is probably somewhat incomplete. He most certainly has only a superficial knowledge of the relative importance of each scrap of data, and has no way of knowing for sure exactly how each facet is interdependent with others. He often has no way of knowing what information will be obsolete by the time his alternative suggestion would be in use. He has only a sketchy idea of what new information is needed for an evaluation of a new procedure, or of how to obtain that information. In short, he has the super-human task of completing and exactly weighing mountains of information that is figuratively crawling with unknowns, obscure causes and effects and conflicts.

And he must go through this for each alternative that is to be studied. There is not a man alive who has the time or ability to fully and accurately make such a desirable set of exact predictions.

Fortunately, such major decisions are relatively rare in marketing. At least, decisions involving a free choice among several alternatives are rare. Major policy decisions are kept to a minimum by the expense of changeover and the loss of effectiveness that is often felt during the transition period. Then, too, many decisions, both in major strategy and minor policies, are not the results of free choice. They are, in fact, often dictated by internal policies or the competitive situation.

It is, of course, obvious that the mathematician's job of reducing the mountains of information needed for an accurate prediction into mathematical language that correctly assigns the right weight and the proper relationship to each tiny bit of data is almost impossible. And there are many tough nuts that remain to be cracked. But much progress has been made already, and work towards a more complete solution is advancing rapidly. This is about where it stands now:

Basically, it is now possible to use a mathematical prediction system on internal problems, especially those of a logistical nature. In addition, it is also possible to obtain incomplete but helpful predictions of the outcome of suggested external activities.

For example, the revision of a distribution network might make good fodder for the machines. Say, for instance, that over the years a shift in population has made a particular system of centrally located district distribution centers obsolete and costly. The biggest facilities are operated below capacity; others are overtaxed. Many are located too far from areas that have become the most important markets. A number of revisions might be suggested, analyzed mathematically, and the results studied to determine what moves would best accomplish the desired ends. This is a relatively simple procedure (compared to many now under study). At today's levels, it would still be incomplete as far as human factors would be concerned; such problems as the morale of workers, customer reaction, relocation of salesmen, etc., are still not subject to everyday quantitative analysis.

The more external in nature the problem becomes, the more incomplete is the prediction. A pricing problem might offer an example. Assume that a particular item that sells to distributors for $10 is selling badly this year. Its maker, Fritewigs, Inc., feels certain that next year will be a banner year. The problem is to get some of next year's business now. This can be done by lowering price on items purchased this fall (and paid for early next year). How far should the price be lowered to create a maximum incentive for the supplier to overstock during the special sale? How many items should be sold to give maximum benefit to the company this year and minimum damage next year? At what price can the company afford to sell what volume?

Again, mathematical analysis can predict what would happen at various prices. But at this time, some of the prediction would have to be filled in by the marketer. For example, a bold move by a competitor could really throw a monkey wrench into the works. The market for the product could suddenly drop, making next year a disaster. Right now, the inclusion of such outside influences in most cases creates a problem that is a little too sophisticated for mathematical prediction.

But it must be remembered that although a complete analysis is sometimes impossible in external problems, the portions that are workable are far superior to traditional by-guess-and-by-gosh methods. In other words, many problems of a more limited nature can be worked on quite satisfactorily by today's mathematical methods; for broader problems, applied mathematics can at least be of help.

For the researcher, the emphasis is very definitely on developing satisfactory techniques for predicting the outcome of problems that involve a competitive situation. It's not a pie-in-the-sky problem, either. For the most part, the mathematical techniques are known. Many of the cause-and-effect relationships needed for the equations are known; others need further research but experts are confident that answers exist, and time and study are all that are needed (an example of such a relationship: the effect of advertising on sales).

Great amounts of time and study are being devoted to the problem. Many large companies, such as General Electric, Sylvania, Du Pont have sizable research departments with their own computers for just such studies. The computer makers, such as IBM and Remington Rand are pouring research into applied mathematics in anticipation of fatter markets for their machines. Independent consultants are forging ahead, stimulated by the thought of providing smaller companies with a mathematical analysis service. Colleges and universities are spurred on by private grants. And the military, which was in large part responsible for many of the basic theories, continues its research programs.

The major reason for the top-drawer classification of these widespread research programs: The stakes are phenomenally high. The results of one organization's laboratory experiments give some idea of its importance.

For some time, this organization had been running "business game" sessions. In the business game, groups of executives are divided into competing "companies." They are given a product and a certain amount of money. They plan their "company" strategies (by quarters) for marketing, production, research, etc., and their plans are run through a computer. The results are announced, and the game is continued into the next quarter. (Needless to say, these exercises, while amazingly realistic, do not involve the complexities of real life.)

Note that the computer is used only for the purpose of showing the results of final decisions; it is not used to help the executives predict before they choose their courses of action. In all, this particular organization ran more than two dozen such sessions. Then, recently, one of the four competing teams was allowed to use the computer for prediction before it settled on a course of action. The other three teams proceeded to make decisions in the manner usually used.

The results were amazing. The team that was allowed to use the computer to predict, not only earned higher profits than the other teams (by a factor of five to one!), but earned the highest profits of any of the hundred or so teams which had previously done the exercise.

This is indeed stimulation enough; but there is one other factor that is responsible for the high degree of interest in the development of decision-aiding techniques. That reason is the computer itself. In the early fifties, owning an electronic computer was something of a high-level fad. Through no fault of the companies making them, the machines were somehow glamorized to the point of being "wonder brains." Many companies bought them, used them for a variety of drudge tasks (payroll, bookkeeping, etc.), and were frankly disappointed. In many cases, the machines cost the company as much to keep around as the corporate president; yet they gathered dust, unplugged, most of the time.

It was not long before they were given other, more important tasks to do. Sales data could be assembled on an up-to-the-minute basis. Inventory snarls could be ironed out by the fast-moving machines. But the emphasis was still on saving, rather than making, money—and it takes a lot of saving to keep hardware like a computer on the assets side of the ledger. Now, with prediction techniques, the computers will be put to use to make money. And it can't come any too soon for most companies.

To get a clear idea of how far the mathematicians have progressed, and what major obstacles they are encountering, it is necessary to have a basic understanding of just how a mathematical marketing prediction is made. The technique which is probably most widely used today, and which seems to hold the most promise for future development, is "systems simulation."

Simulation is mathematical model building. It is really just a logical expansion of the process of scientific market analysis. It is comparable to the theoretical, or formula, step in an engineering problem.

Look at it this way: The best way to see how something will work is to try it. For the engineer, this would mean building the airplane just to test a new idea—just on the hunch that it would work. Obviously, this is expensive and impractical. It is comparable to the marketer who plunges headlong into a full-scale marketing program simply on the basis of his experience—also frequently a costly procedure, but one that has to be followed all too often.

The next best thing for the engineer would be to construct a scale model and test it in a wind tunnel. But models are also expensive, and to be really sure he had the best possible design he would have to create a number of different ones. Again, he would not be likely to plunge head-long into this step. But this is where the marketer gets off; the creation of a small physical model (the test market) is just about as much removed from the real thing as he has been able to get.

But the engineer has a better way to begin: He can, with the aid of mathematics, create a "model" on paper, a series of equations that literally represent the physical airplane. And different figures and dimensions can be plugged into this "model" until the best combination is found. This is precisely what the operations researcher would like to be able to do with suggested marketing programs—to see if they would be able to get off the ground.

The big problem is immediately evident: putting marketing into mathematical form. Yet, this is not so impossible as it might seem at first glance. For example, what happens when the marketer himself studies a recommendation to see how it would work? Unconsciously, he does build a form of mental model. He tries to view the situation as a whole, in perspective as much as possible. He unconsciously assigns weights to various parts—knows that one thing is more or less important than another—to help himself judge a probable outcome. It is inexact, to be sure, but it does indicate that the assignment of numerical values to marketing problems is legitimate.

Perhaps the toughest part of the problems lies in discovering the correct relationships within the model. Virtually everything in marketing is an effect of one or more things, and is in whole, or part, the cause of something else. Every numerical value and relationship must be expressed as accurately as possible in equation form, if the model is to be a usable representation of marketing life.

This, by the way, is why operations researchers have been able to apply their prediction techniques and models to production and engineering problems with such success. For example, wonderful mathematical models have been built to simulate extremely elaborate oil refining systems—systems which are far too complex for the human mind to hold in their entirety. It can be done with models because all the chemical and engineering steps are known, and the interrelated processes are facts of science.

But again, the marketing problem is not all that impossible. Indeed, tremendous progress is being made. Of course, there will always be unknown factors in marketing. The problem is to reduce the number of unknowns as much as possible, then make estimates on the rest as accurately as possible. This is what Gerald B. Tallman, associate professor, School of Industrial Management, Massachusetts Institute of Technology, says about the construction of mathematical marketing models:

"We must represent each circumstance and action which is believed to have significant influence on the nature and working of the system. Each item must be assigned some quantitative expression of its influence and of the rate at which it may be expected to change under the influence of other things with which it is interdependent. In order to develop an operable model, all expressions of relationship of incidence and rates of change must be explicit. It is obviously desirable that, in so far as possible, the data introduced into the system model be drawn from real life experience; but, with the acceptance of certain risks, it is altogether feasible to substitute hypothesized estimates where real information is lacking."

A quick look at the four basic types of equations used in making marketing models gives a good indication of how accurate the models can be. These equation types are reported by Robert S. Weinberg, manager, Market Research for IBM, in the book, "An Analytical Approach to Advertising Expenditure Strategy," which was recently released by the Association of National Advertisers. Here are the four types of equations:

Definitional. These are completely reliable, because they express exact relationships, much like the laws of nature. The simplest might be "profits equals sales minus costs." Of course, many more highly intricate relationships have been discovered. (Here is one on profits, developed by the Market Research Corporation of America: "Profits of competitors, at competitive equilibrium, are proportional to the cube of their manufacturing margins, that is, the margin between manufacturing costs and price.")

Technological. These equations deal with the interaction of technological or physical processes. An example might be a shipping time or warehousing expense. These equations, too, can be completely accurate as long as the process described does not change.

Behavioral. The biggest fly in the ointment, this deals with how people will respond to a given stimulus. The people: customers, employees, competitors. This is the major reason why marketing models of competitive marketing situations are still in the laboratory stage. In the first place, such equations cannot be mathematically perfect, as human behavior is never totally predictable. It can be reasonably estimated, especially for the more stable behavior patterns, but much more work is needed along these lines.

It is the presence of competitors that really complicates things. It has been demonstrated that for a model to accurately predict the outcome of something, all the interactions must be expressed. Of course, how a competitor reacts to a company's marketing strategy is one of the most important relationships to be considered. Now, if a company has five competitors, and each could react in dozens of different ways, the complications are exhausting to think about. To include all these possibilities, the formula for the model would be yards and yards long and would take years to create.

Fortunately, a few ways out are under study. One is simply to use the best strategy that each competitor could come up with. But this, too, takes a lot of effort, and, since all competitors probably won't do the very best thing they could do, it might mean that the outcome predicted by the model would be too conservative. Another alternative is to select top executives within the company, have them act like competitors and play a regular computerized business "game" against the model. This, of course, assumes that the executives are as bright as those who work for the competition and would settle on solutions as effective as their counterparts'.

The institutional equation. Like the first two, this type of equation generally can be made to be quite accurate. This one involves company policy, the Government (laws, taxes, etc.) and other constraints on marketing. The equations can be accurate as long as these constraints do not change.

Incidentally, these equations point out one great value of the models besides their value as predictors: They show up, with great clarity, important gaps in information. Things that should be known to a company, but that, for some reason or other, seldom are fully known.

In any event, this is the situation: Right now, these methods of mathematical analysis are practical for internal or logistical problems, and for those phases of major competitive problems. In business the big companies are way ahead in the use of mathematical analysis. But the smaller companies are by no means left out; there are plenty of outside consultants available. Big company or small, it's still expensive. An outside consultant would program a logistical problem today for about $100,000, provided its customer is in possession of fairly complete and up-to-date information on itself. If the stakes amounted to about $1 million or more per year on a continuing basis, the job would be well worth it. The company need not even own its own computer; the model is the big thing, and once that is in hand, it can be run on a computer rented for a short while (or borrowed from a big company that is a major supplier of the company in need of it).

Five years from now the use of mathematical analysis for logistical predictions will be widespread. Much more will have been done on competitive problems. Indeed, it may be that some models will be complete enough to be extremely useful. Certainly, more factual data about marketing will be known, and will be used in everyday marketing decisions made by executives.

Maybe the executive will be able to work directly with the computer, without the operations researcher, in five years. He surely will in a decade.

Mathematically derived predictions will mean big things to marketing, in particular to those companies which are the first to employ the techniques. But, as previously stated, these techniques, even when refined, cannot be brought into a company overnight. Because much of the formula is based on history, preparations in the form of accurate and complete observations must begin now.

8. Who'll boss the computer?

Unless there's a big change, odds are it won't be the marketing chief who will control the computer, though many feel he should be the key man in directing a computer-based information system. Up to now, the machines have been largely under the control of financial or accounting executives, and this could pose a threat to marketing's dominance as business leans more heavily on the new techniques of management science.

Fast becoming a commonplace tool of business, the computer has already progressed well beyond the initial routine clerical functions assigned to it. The speedy, versatile machines are rapidly taking on new significance at the heart of companywide management information systems, and they are increasingly important as a factor in top level decision making.

Yet it seems that few marketing executives are making a real effort to marshal these tremendously promising computer capabilities in full support of the total marketing concept. And fewer still have managed to plant their thumbs firmly on the machine's control button. Even more disturbing is the attitude of many marketing men who appear only too happy to abandon responsibility for computer utilization to the comptroller, or accounting people, or to an internal systems and procedures expert.

This isn't meant to imply that computers have not been put to work on marketing tasks. They have, in a broad spectrum ranging from cumulative tabulations of sales performance to sophisticated market forecasts and projections. Unfortunately, however, most computer-produced information of value to the marketing department is simply a by-product of a billing operation, of order entry and accounting procedure, of inventory control, or other machine runs made for another purpose entirely.

In effect, marketing's information requirements must often play second fiddle where computer time is concerned. Right now, implemented at the instigation of other department heads, computer programs

Reprinted from *Sales Management*, October 16, 1964, p. 76.

are primarily aimed at maximizing efficiency of internal procedure. Computer runs are geared mainly to the insular demands of accountants or operating executives. Product sales statistics, for example, are broken out and accumulated almost as an afterthought to pre-billing and stock status updating and often in a form far more suitable for use by a bookkeeper than the average sales analyst.

The reason for this situation is not hard to understand. At the outset, data processing machines were job oriented, especially designed to handle run-of-the-mill paperwork. The machines fell into the domain of the accountants and bookkeepers.

However, modern computers bear little resemblance to their early predecessors. Today's sophisticated data processing systems are not job oriented, but management oriented. Their major contribution is fast, reliable information as a guide to running the business, and their influence reaches into the highest management echelons. Yet computer control remains largely in the hands of nonmarketing people, or in the hands of company committees notably lacking in marketing representation.

BELATED CONCERN

Evidently, a good many marketing and sales executives have become aware of this limitation and are worried about it. They feel it is unwise for marketing to continue shying away from control of a tool with so much marketing promise, but the majority are not yet certain how best to go about getting solidly into the act or are not yet ready to make an issue of the matter.

Some corporate marketing people who foresee a real threat to marketing's continued dominance in the overall activities of a business are working hard to bring computer programming and utilization under their control. A handful of others, perhaps a bit more perceptive and farsighted are already firmly established in the driver's seat.

In most companies, including veteran computer users and those just getting their feet wet in data processing, the marketing and sales heads seem unconcerned and uninterested. They might wake up some day to the painful realization that they've lost a golden opportunity by default.

9. Linear programming for marketing cost reduction

RONALD J. R. KALLMAN

For our purposes I wish to consider marketing as the function operating between the manufacturer and the consumer. Its area of concern is fourfold: merchandising, distribution, promotion and pricing. The first of these, perhaps, deserves some further clarification since the term has been used in many ways. My meaning is the concern with product planning from the market viewpoint. This implies selecting and identifying the product, structuring the price lines or package and paying close attention to the timing of any program of action.

Central to the idea of merchandising is the full identification of product. What exactly are we trying to market? If you will excuse me for using my own product line as an example, the Computer Division of Philco is marketing general purpose, digital computers; the very devices we have been discussing as an aid to effective marketing coordination. But this is not our product exactly. The hardware itself is only part of the package. Equally important is what has recently come to be known under the term "software," for want of a more descriptive title. Actually, we provide programs and systems to make effective use of the hardware. We provide training, guidance; and we maintain the equipment in top operating condition. In short, we are really providing a computer service. You might say we are moving the service bureau operation onto the customer's premises. This action provides certain financial benefits to the large user of this type service. He pays a lower use charge or rental when he installs his own equipment. He may use it whenever he wants. The service is more conveniently located on his premises than it would be at some distant service bureau.

Reprinted from *Proceedings*, American Marketing Association Conference, June, 1961 (Baker, editor). By permission of the American Marketing Association, pp. 554–560.

Lest I mislead you Philco is not the only firm offering a product of this nature: there are others. However, there are also firms in the field whose product is the so-called hardware only; and I have gone into this much detail merely to emphasize the need to be exact in identifying the product. If you are otherwise than exact, your marketing program may be, to say the least, inadequate.

But let me come back to the four basic concerns of marketing: merchandising, distribution, promotion and pricing. A little reflection shows costs intimately involved in each of these areas. Perhaps this is a pedantic way of saying the obvious—a marketing program does not come free; but the important point is that marketing costs really represent a significant part of the price of the product. Arguments can be made that the share is too high; and similarly, that it is too low. Regardless of the point of view, as responsible marketing individuals, we all want to reduce marketing expense. We are merely interested in getting a greater return for our marketing dollars.

The computer is a tool which can help us reduce marketing costs. In particular, computers make possible the solution of a pretty complicated type of problem called a linear program. This type of problem is of especial interest to marketing people because it deals basically with costs and available resources and finds application throughout our area of concern. Given certain conditions, a feasible linear program can be solved to minimize costs. A computer is not the only means of solving linear programs, but since there are usually hundreds, if not thousands, of conditions to be reckoned with, hand calculations, as a rule, are just not practical. The race is over before you have picked the horse you wish to bet on.

All sound management decisions are based on some information. In recent years, marketing people have grown more adept at obtaining vast quantities of information: so much so, in fact, that several of our salesmen are accusing us of taking lessons from the federal government, a pretty eminent information-gatherer. Such data come from special surveys, field reports, published statistics, test programs, and so forth. They are designed to provide a better basis for sound decision, but frequently overwhelm the decision-makers by sheer volume. An orderly analysis of such information is clearly required if decisions are to be well-founded. Linear programs frequently provide a means for digesting these facts and indicating some conclusions. It is still the manager's job, however, to develop the program and he bears full responsibility for appropriate decisions. Linear program solutions can only provide assistance in this task.

Having thus reassured everyone that marketing management is not being replaced by computers, let's consider a few cases; examples where linear programs can be and have been used in the four primary areas of marketing concern.

APPLICATIONS OF LINEAR PROGRAMMING

The first case selected illustrates an application in merchandising. Let's, for the moment, visualize a medium-sized company comprised primarily of engineering personnel and technicians. Certain buildings and sets of equipment are available for the use of this staff. The engineers, themselves, have definite capabilities based upon their training and experience. For example, they may have previously participated in the design and construction of radar sets, telemetering equipment, complex systems controls, and so forth. For such a group, today, there are many opportunities to bid on business. Hopefully there are many more opportunities to bid than the staff can possibly handle. A good question for the management of such an organization to answer is: which of the several possible opportunities for business should the company seek? It can be determined that success in some of these areas will bring higher reward than others. Perhaps there is a larger fee involved or greater skills will be brought into the organization. On the other hand, several of these programs may call upon the self-same people within the organization. The selection of these engineers for one of these programs thus rules out any consideration of the others. Just how do we go about directing our effort to maximize the profitability of this operation?

Here is a prime case where we are really trying to define the product of the operation. It will be seen that the product here is not necessarily nuts and bolts, or some consumer item; but rather, a service—an engineering capability of a rather technical nature. And yet, the way we define this capability will certainly determine the business in which we are interested. Such a problem situation can readily be formulated into a linear program for appropriate solution. While some of the numbers and data will be difficult to come by, it is certainly worth the effort to find them. Once the program has been set up and an initial solution obtained, it is then quite possible to alter some of the conditions. The manager can ask the question, based upon a preliminary finding: "what would happen if we ceased work on this one job, thus freeing our personnel for work in another area? What would happen if our customer should cancel further work in the other area? How would this affect our overall profitability? How would it alter our ability to compete with other firms in similar lines of endeavor?" The great value of a linear program solution in this area exists in the ability to change the original conditions once the problem has been formulated. In this fashion, in a very brief span of time, a manager can ask many, many questions and quickly obtain meaningful answers. Might not many of our aerospace companies, today, materially benefit from such a programmed approach to definition of their product; hence, greater capability in merchandising?

The second case I wish to describe for you is in the distribution area.

This is one, perhaps, where more of you have encountered the use of linear programs. During the war the armed forces were faced with rather substantial logistics problems. Should they stock-pile vast quantities of material at advance bases or at bases in the rear, relying upon airlift to meet emergency requirements for spares? This type of problem is the familiar distribution type of linear program and finds rather wide application in industry. The example today concerns a coal distribution company. The company has three warehouses serving a large metropolitan area. There is a fleet of trucks of varying capacities, a staff of drivers, garages with maintenance facilities, access to a source of inventory—coal cars are received at one edge of the city by the railroad's main line and subsequently routed to each of the three warehouses. Some warehouses have a higher delivered cost of coal than others because they represent a longer travel time for the coal cars.

You will observe there are many inter-acting elements of cost in this situation. Previously the problem has been handled by a very experienced driver knowing from experience when to send other drivers out to make delivery in order to meet the schedule and keep the total costs of delivery within some reasonable bounds. It is quite possible, however, to formulate this problem exactly and provide for a solution which generates the lowest cost in terms of overtime, rehandling, storage charges, delivery charges, lost customers, and so forth. In this situation the results are often quite surprising. The experienced truck driver is just not capable of handling all the variables involved for an optimum solution. He is, after all, only human. The situation becomes even worse when our friend is asked to consider what happens if we give him three more trucks and four more drivers? Can he do a better job at service? Well, the linear program solution will provide, within a matter of minutes, the effect of additional capacity for delivery in terms of equipment or people as well as giving a very clear idea of what happens if an exceptional number of trucks are laid up for want of spare parts, or because of difficulties with some segment of the driver-pool. I'm sure your imaginations will sketch out for you many horrible things that can occur, making the task of meeting delivery requirements to customers of this coal company overwhelming. Yet formulated as a linear program, solutions to changing conditions are fast, optimal and inexpensive.

For our third case, let's select one in the area of promotion. A well-known meat packer had been distributing his product for years and had developed quite a stock-pile of data on the value of colorful wrappings, counter displays, advertising in newspapers, magazines, radio, television, promotional visits from missionary salesmen, direct-mail campaigns to homes, and so forth. All of these items cost money. Let us further assume that the president has fixed the promotional budget. In this situation, therefore, we wish to maximize the sales from such an advertising and promotion campaign. A coordinated play of promotion can be developed, based upon the solution of this linear program. All these cost elements can be weighted in terms of historical data at various times, and their impact on a particular area for the sale of meat can readily be measured.

A question frequently asked in marketing managements these days, particularly with companies that appeal to the public, is: "can we afford to drop our television advertising?" Or the marketing manager may feel a small budget increase will bring large rewards. Well, the solution to this problem can be evaluated, again, in a matter of minutes, by changing some of the original conditions for this linear program model we have just described. At the same time, other combinations of promotional effort can readily be evaluated and the one providing the greatest volume can quickly be determined. As tastes change and reaction to various forms of advertising develop, it will be necessary to re-structure the model. Once it has been set up, however, subsequent changes are made quite readily and with a minimum additional investment in time and money from the marketing department.

The last case I wish to describe is in the pricing area. The company under discussion is a manufacturer of—let's say—razor blades. For simplicity, let's consider that there are three lines of blades; each selling for a different price, and each having a different quality. The company is obviously concerned with maximizing its profits. There are certain known restraints in this situation. For example, one man will presumably use only one razor blade at a time; some of the blades we are offering last longer than others, some cost more. If we sell more blades the manufacturing cost goes down; hence, our profitability should go up. But we only have so many buildings and so much manufacturing capacity at this point in time. If we raise our prices on some lines—say the higher priced ones—people may prefer our less expensive blades, or, worst of all, people may decide to change to "Brand X." The intentions of the consumer can be measured by surveys in this area and, consequently, we are able to structure a problem based upon price. We can, presumably, determine the optimum assortment of prices for our various lines of razor blades in such a way as to maximize our profit-potential. We can investigate what differences slight changes will have. In short, we can develop a program which is designed to handle our current pricing problems and yet smooth the way for perhaps the introduction of a new product a little later this year or next year, without disturbing our entire price structure.

In these examples we have tried to show some areas where the new tool of the computer can be used to save money in marketing with the use of linear program models. Anyone can take advantage of this method. One may use the computer that his controller has obtained to keep track of cost distributions, or go to a service bureau such as Philco's own Western Computing Center in Palo Alto. The marketing manager may do as much or as little with his own staff as he wishes. He may hire all elements of this problem formulation and solution done for him by various consultant firms, or he may develop his own staff to provide greater insight into the different alternatives of solution.

For those who might be giving thought to conducting the operation on their own premises, it's perhaps worthwhile to look at some of the characteristics of a computer which would be important for the efficient solution of linear programs. First of all, the computer should have fast internal speeds. Its arithmetic times should be in the microsecond range for there are many, many calculations to be formed in the solution of a linear program. Second, the computer system should have very high-speed magnetic tapes because there is much information which must be passed over again and again while zeroing in on a meaningful solution. The tapes should also be buffered from the computer so that computing is not interrupted while information is inputting or outputting. And then finally because of the method of solution of particularly the Simplex, it is desirable that the magnetic tape system have the capability of reading backward as well as forward. In the actual solution of a linear program, the data are analyzed in one direction and new information written out on another magnetic tape. At the end of a single pass, a whole new set of data is then created which is the next approximation to the solution. This becomes the latest case, is written on magnetic tape, and the procedure restarts in a backward direction. Computer systems which do not read magnetic tape backwards must provide two sets of records; one in the forward direction, and continually process both of these. This doubles the number of magnetic tapes necessary for a solution and materially increases the time required.

The program to obtain a solution to a linear program is usually provided by manufacturers of data processing equipment as part of their software. At least, such a program is part of the Philco Computer Division product line. All you have to do is provide the data unique to your company. The opportunity for marketing cost reductions through linear programming is barely tapped. A powerful new tool is waiting to help you develop better marketing programs.

10. Bayesian statistics in marketing

HARRY V. ROBERTS

The application of statistics to marketing has grown substantially in recent decades. Yet statistics has remained more of a "sideshow" than an integral part of the process of decision-making. Too often, consumer surveys and sales analyses have been carried out with little thought about their contribution to management problems.

This is hardly surprising, because it is only recently that statistical theorists themselves have seen the potential contribution of statistics to decision-making and have begun to evolve a formal structure of *decision theory* than can actually be applied. Although the structure is still incomplete, its promise is bright. This structure is called *Bayesian statistics*.

The adjective "Bayesian" comes from Bayes's theorem, an elementary result of probability theory traceable to the Rev. Thomas Bayes, an English clergyman of the 18th century. His theorem typically, although not necessarily, plays an essential part in a Bayesian statistical analysis. Strangely enough, the really distinctive feature of Bayesian statistics is not Bayes's theorem but rather the personalistic interpretation of probability. That is, it is legitimate to quantify our feelings about uncertainty in terms of subjectively assessed numerical probabilities, even when confronted by a single unique decision and when there is no extensive past history on which to base the assessment of probabilities.

Assessments are made of probabilities of events that determine the profitability of alternative actions open to a decision-maker. Assessments are also made of profit (more generally, utility) for each possible combination of action and event. For each possible action, expected profit can then be computed, that is, a weighted mean of the possible profits,

Reprinted from the *Journal of Marketing*, Volume 27 (January, 1963), pp. 1–4, National Quarterly Publication of the American Marketing Association.

the weights being the probabilities mentioned above. The action is chosen for which expected profit is highest. The dominating principle of decision, then, is maximization of expected profit (or utility).

AN EXAMPLE

Consider the following hypothetical, simplified, yet reasonably realistic marketing application.

A manufacturer of automobiles is testing a new direct mail approach B versus a standard approach A. An experiment is conducted in which each of the two approaches is tried out on random samples of size n (sample size $2n$ in total) from a large national mailing list. Suppose that $n = 100,000$, so that 200,000 is the total sample size of the experiment. During a three-month period, approach B has 761 sales and A has 753.

The problem is: should A or B be used on a national scale, or should a decision be deferred until more research has been done?

Suppose that additional evidence cannot be obtained and that a choice must be made between A and B. Many statisticians would suggest a test of significance. It turns out that the difference is not significant at any of the usual levels. What to conclude? One answer is that nothing can be decided from the experiment because A and B do not differ significantly. Another answer is that the standard method A should be continued because it is not significantly worse. Still another answer is that it does not matter whether A or B is used because they are not significantly different. The correct answer is that if all *other* considerations are evenly balanced, then the slight edge of B over A should be decisive.

While this common-sense answer can be given a justification of sorts by conventional statistical theory, it can be supported easily by a Bayesian analysis. Three assumptions about "all *other* considerations are evenly balanced" can be made explicit. First, it can be assumed that other evidence on the effectiveness of the two approaches is negligible by comparison with this statistical evidence. Second, it can be assumed that if the true effectiveness of each method were known, we would be willing to adopt the one with the higher effectiveness; that is, there are no differences in costs or side benefits: the "break-even" difference in true effectiveness is zero. Third, it can be assumed that the difference in effectiveness measured in sales rates per mailing is proportional to the difference in effectiveness measured in profit rates per mailing.

Under these assumptions a Bayesian analysis proceeds as follows. Compute a *posterior distribution* (posterior to the sample, that is) of the true difference of effectiveness between B and A. Under our present assumptions, Bayes's theorem shows that the posterior distribution of the true difference in sales rates per mailing can be approximated by a normal distribution with a mean of

$$\frac{761}{100,000} - \frac{753}{100,000} = \frac{8}{100,000} = .00008$$

and a standard deviation of

$$\sqrt{\frac{(.00761)\,(1 - .00761)}{100,000} + \frac{(.00753)\,(1 - .00753)}{100,000}}$$

$$= \sqrt{\frac{.00756}{100,000} + \frac{.00748}{100,000}}$$

$$= \sqrt{.0000001504}$$

$$= .00039,$$

where familiar classical formulas, $p_1 - p_2$ and

$\sqrt{\dfrac{p_1 q_1}{n_1} + \dfrac{p_2 q_2}{n_2}}$ are used in the calculation.

What does this mean? It means that we are attaching probabilities to the thing we are uncertain about, namely, the true difference in effectiveness between B and A, and that these probabilities are summarized approximately by a normal distribution with the stated mean and standard deviation. Once we attach probabilities to the things we are uncertain about, we can implement the rule of decision: Choose that action for which expected profit is highest.

In our present example, it can be shown that this rule tells us to compare the mean of the posterior distribution, .00008, with the break-even point of true differential effectiveness, or 0. Since .00008 exceeds 0, we should choose appeal B.

Reasonably realistic numerical assumptions show that the expected superiority of B over A is $2,000,000. The assumptions are that the balance of the national mailing list has 50,000,000 names, and that the incremental profit per car sold is $500. Under these assumptions, 8 added cars per 100,000 names implies an expected differential profit of (.00008) (50,000,000) ($500) = $2,000,000. It is hardly a matter of indifference which approach is chosen.

The decision to choose B could, of course, be reached by unaided common sense. Even if the economic break-even point were different than zero, unaided common sense would still work. Suppose that it was judged that because of certain changeover costs, B would have to be at least .00020 units more effective than A to warrant its adoption. Then we would compare .00008 with .00020 and conclude that A should be retained, since .00008 is less than .00020.

THE ROLE OF JUDGMENT

Suppose, however, that other evidence is not negligible compared to the statistical evidence. For example, suppose that prior to the experiment management had felt that on balance A was better than B, but that the chances that they were wrong were enough to warrant the experiment.

More quantitatively, suppose that it had been judged that the odds were even that the true effectiveness of B over A did not exceed —.00010, but also that the odds were only even that the true effectiveness was within —.00026 of .00010. Note that .00010 is about 1.3 percent of the sales rate for A, and that .00026 is about 3.5 percent of it.

Moreover, management assumed that the normal distribution fitting these requirements, which will have a mean of —.00010 and a standard deviation of .00039, can be taken to be the *prior distribution* of the true difference in effectiveness. "Prior" simply means prior by comparison with the statistical evidence contemplated, which in this example was the experiment already described. Bayes's theorem again tells how this prior distribution should be revised in the face of sample evidence to arrive at a posterior distribution. It turns out to be approximately a normal distribution with mean

$$\frac{-.00010 + .00008}{2} = -.00001,$$

so that the decision would now go *against* approach B.

In order to make this calculation, the standard error of the sample difference, .00039, had to be used. It is an accident of this particular illustration that the reconciliation of judgment and sample evidence is achieved by a simple average; in general, the two would not be weighted equally. While the details of operation of Bayes's theorem will not be developed here, the important thing is that the theorem gives a formal reconciliation between managerial judgment, expressed quantitatively in the prior distribution, and the statistical evidence of the experiment. This reconciliation might be much harder to arrive at by common sense alone.

Incidentally, managerial judgment is not, as assumed at the outset, likely to be given negligible weight by comparison with the experiment evidence. There is likely to be good reason to believe that the differential sales effectiveness of A and B is rather small, as in this last illustration, because the direct mailing itself has a relatively small influence on total sales.

THE PROBLEM OF SAMPLE SIZE

Turn now to a more difficult question, that of deciding whether additional evidence should be sought, and if so, how much. This question is really the problem of sample size.

To give a concrete illustration of how it is solved, let us revert to the situation in which prior evidence was negligible compared to that of a sample, so that the posterior distribution is normal with mean .00008 and standard error .00039. This posterior distribution now can be regarded as a *prior* distribution with respect to additional experimental information that might be obtained.

In addition to this prior distribution, an assessment must be made of four key economic quantities: (1) the incremental profit to the company (assumed constant) of an added car sold; (2) the size of the national mailing list; (3) the fixed cost of an experiment; (4) the incremental cost per name (assumed constant) on an experimental mailing list.

For illustration, take $500, 50,000,000, $10,000, and $0.25 for these quantities. The result of a numerical calculation is that a further experiment involving about 500,000 names for each approach—1,000,000 in total—should be run, and then a final decision between A and B should be made based on the mean of the posterior distribution after that experiment. (The added or lost sales attributable to B during the experiment was not accounted for in this approximate calculation. The details of this calculation would be meaningless without a great deal more background than can be developed in a short exposition.[1])

POTENTIAL CONTRIBUTIONS

There are three potential contributions of Bayesian statistics illustrated by the example above:

1. How to choose between marketing alternatives on the basis of sample evidence when virtually no weight is to be given to managerial judgment.

2. How to choose between marketing alternatives on the basis of sample evidence when substantial weight is to be given to managerial judgment.

3. How to decide on how much research, if any, should be done before a final choice is made.

For completeness, there is a fourth potential contribution not indicated in the example above:

4. How to choose between marketing alternatives when no sample evidence is available: judgments would be expressed as a prior distribution, and the mean of this distribution would be compared with the break-even point.

IMPLICATIONS

Consider the importance of each of these contributions. The fourth, how to make a choice in the absence of sample evidence, is simply a

---

[1] Robert Schlaifer, *Probability and Statistics in Business Decisions*, corrected impression (New York: McGraw-Hill Book Co., Inc., 1959), especially pp. 544–546.

way of formalizing what would otherwise be done informally and intuitively. It is like having a checklist to assure that nothing will be forgotten or given distorted importance.

The first, how to make a choice when the evidence is almost wholly statistical, can be made by common sense without Bayesian statistics. On the other hand, the Bayesian approach helps greatly to avoid errors that are common in practice, and especially those due to serious yet natural misunderstandings of traditional statistical methods.

The second, how to reconcile strong judgments with statistical evidence, is very difficult to do by common sense alone. The formal Bayesian apparatus is a great help.

The third, how to choose the best sample size, is not obvious at all to common sense. On no other problem are the recommendations of different statisticians likely to differ so much. The Bayesian calculation illustrated is the only defensible way to give an answer. Traditional statistical theory tells how to choose a sample size that will meet a specification for precision. It does not tell how much precision should be specified, except to give informal advice that the benefits of added precision must be balanced against the costs of attaining it. Such informal advice is not an adequate guide.

Not all marketing problems can be answered as easily as the one given in this example. However, a substantial fraction of marketing problems are of this type, although perhaps more complicated, as where a choice must be made between three approaches, A, B, and C, where C might be no direct mailing at all. The Bayesian apparatus has been worked out for these problems. Moreover, the apparatus has been extended to certain other kinds of problems.

There was not sufficient realism in this example to make it completely convincing. One defect is that an experiment of this kind would have to be carried out in selected markets rather than in a random sample of a national mailing list. There is uncertainty as to how the differential effectiveness of A and B in Denver, for example, might compare with differential effectiveness in the rest of the country. A formal Bayesian apparatus exists for dealing with such problems.

Of course, much needs to be done to work out Bayesian solutions for common marketing problems. But much has already been done, and important problems can be solved now.[2]

The real difficulty in applying statistics to marketing is that until recently no theoretical bridge existed between "statistics" and "business judgment." For the first time we now know how to fit both these elements into the process of decision-making. In particular, no statistical analysis

[2] Schlaifer, same reference as footnote 1. Also, Robert Schlaifer and Howard Raiffa, *Applied Statistical Decision Theory* (Boston, Division of Research, Harvard Graduate School of Business Administration, 1961).

is complete unless "business judgment" is incorporated into it. It *does* matter, for example, what management thinks about the comparative effectiveness of A and B before statistical evidence on the question can be intelligently sought or analyzed.

Marketing statisticians cannot pursue the illusory goal of trying to provide "definitive answers" in the sense that scientific research is sometimes supposed to do. "Definitive answers" might require exorbitant sample sizes, and even then the answers might not turn out to be really definitive.

Likewise, marketing executives cannot leave statistics solely to the statisticians. They must communicate the essence of their judgment about marketing problems before statisticians can make a fully satisfactory technical contribution; and they must understand the underlying rationale of decision theory.

B. Behavioral Applications

11. Contributions of sociology
to marketing

CHRISTEN T. JONASSEN

A sociologist is a social scientist who undertakes to isolate, define, and describe human behavior in groups and social settings. He seeks to formulate valid laws and generalizations about human nature, social interaction, social organization, and culture.

Anyone who engages in such activities, seeks such ends, and who in the eyes of other sociologists contributes to these functions is practicing sociology. Therefore, a *sociological contribution* to marketing is anything done by a recognized sociologist that leads to a better understanding of the nature, functions, and processes of marketing.

In what areas and in what ways have sociologists developed materials significant for marketing? And what impact has this knowledge had on marketing, and through what channels has this impact been transmitted? This article gives some of the answers.

NATURE OF MARKETING

We have come a long way from the mechanistic, self-regulating approach of the *laissez-faire* economic theorists. They viewed the market in terms of an equilibrium of forces and general, universalistic, immutable, physical-like laws. The classical economist saw the consumer as an "economic man," a creature who exercised free individual choice in a market which seemed to operate in a cultural and social vacuum. This view looked on individual wants and desires as motivating forces, and on individuals as the acting agents.

Reprinted from the *Journal of Marketing*, Volume 24 (January, 1960), pp. 15–19, National Quarterly Publication of the American Marketing Association.

Sociological influences are most apparent in the modern institutional approach, which sees economic processes as part of an organic whole of the total society. This approach means that marketing activities are not looked on as the individualistic acts of atomistic man, but rather as *functions* operating through various marketing structures which are part of the total social organization.

It views marketing processes as the *activities* of groups of people: buyers, sellers, and marketing functionaries, who are motivated by group pressures as well as individual predilections. It recognizes the influence of culture, custom, heritage, and mores in determining the final outcome.

Its emphasis throughout is not on the individual, but on the *group* . . . not on mechanistic, self-regulating, universalistic forces, but on particularistic *social* and cultural forces . . . not on "rational economic" man, but on men as members of *social* groups susceptible to irrationality and sentiment, as well as social values and pressures generated within such groups. Duddy and Revzan, for example, say that "what the producer is finally confronted with is the forecasting of human behavior," and that "in our modern dynamic society the individual, whether consciously or unconsciously, more often acts as a member of a group." [1]

Such terms as "institution," "group," "society," "mass," "culture," "structure," and "structure-function," are found in the institutional approach. These are terms constantly in use by sociologists, and they have had considerable influence on people in other disciplines. Fundamental changes in viewpoint about the nature of man and his marketing behavior have been due largely to the impact of sociological thought and research on economics, psychology, and marketing.

SOCIOLOGICAL CONTRIBUTIONS

Population Studies

The statement, "Markets are people with money to spend—and the desire to spend it" [2] points to two additional areas of sociological contribution: *population studies* and *consumer motivation.*

For a long time population studies have been a branch of sociology. In most universities the subject is taught in the department of sociology, and sociological journals contain numerous articles on this subject. Precise knowledge of population factors enables the marketing man to determine how many and what kinds of people there are and where they are. This enables him to predict future populations and thus gives him lead time which helps to adjust the distribution system to future requirements. This is an obvious necessity for a scientific approach to marketing.

[1] Edward A. Duddy and David A. Revzan, *Marketing* (New York: McGraw-Hill Book Co., Inc., 1953), pp. 124 and 125.

[2] Duddy and Revzan, same reference, p. 8.

Thompson and Whelpton,[3] Hauser, Ogburn, Margaret Hagood, Hawley, Kingsley Davis, Paul Hatt, Kiser, Duncan, Bogue, and Schmid are a few of the sociologists who have made contributions to our knowledge and understanding of populations, processes, and problems. Their publications in this area are so numerous that each would require a bibliography too long to cite here.

Consumer Motivation

In some of the early marketing texts motivation is discussed in terms of the now-discarded instinct theories, emphasizing the individual and largely ignoring the group. But marketing men today are aware that men do not possess "instincts," and that if they have such desires or motives they are the products of group life. This evolution of thought owes much to sociological influences. Knowledge significant for understanding motivation has emerged from sociological research on class, voluntary association, leisure-time activities, and attitude measurement.

Numerous studies of social class—such as those of the Lynds,[4] Davis,[5] Dollard,[6] Hollingshead,[7] Warner,[8] and Kahl[9]—have focused attention on the implications of class and status, and have described differential motivational patterns and styles of life in different classes. Understanding of motivation is also aided by findings from research on participation in voluntary association such as that of Kamarovsky,[10] and by studies of leisure and recreation such as the one made by Alfred Clarke.[11]

Men like Bogardus[12] and many of the sociologists discussed below in the section on measurement and scaling were among the first to devise valid and reliable instruments and scales for the measurement of atti-

[3] Warren S. Thompson and P. K. Whelpton, *Population Trends in the United States* (New York: McGraw-Hill Book Co., Inc. 1933); Warren S. Thompson, *Population Problems* (New York: McGraw-Hill Book Co., Inc., 1953).

[4] Robert S. Lynd and Helen M. Lynd, *Middletown* (New York: Harcourt, Brace & Co., Inc., 1929); *Middletown in Transition* (New York: Harcourt, Brace & Co., Inc., 1937).

[5] Allison Davis, Burleigh Gardner, and Mary Gardner, *Deep South* (Chicago: University of Chicago Press, 1941).

[6] John Dollard, *Caste and Class in a Southern Town* (New Haven: Yale University Press, 1954).

[7] August B. Hollingshead, *Elmtown's Youth* (New York: John Wiley and Sons, Inc., 1949).

[8] Lloyd Warner and Paul S. Lunt, *The Social Life of a Modern Community* (New Haven: Yale University Press, 1941).

[9] Joseph A. Kahl, *The American Class Structure* (New York: Rinehart and Co., Inc., 1953).

[10] Mirra Kamarovsky, "The Voluntary Association of Urban Dwellers" *American Sociological Review*, Vol. 11 (December, 1946), pp. 686–699.

[11] Alfred C. Clarke, "The Use of Leisure and Its Relation to Levels of Occupational Prestige," *American Sociological Review*, Vol. 21 (June, 1956), pp. 301–307.

[12] Emory S. Bogardus, "Measuring Social Distance," *Journal of Applied Sociology*, Vol. 9 (March–April, 1925), pp. 299–308.

tudes. Sociologists also have been a healthy counterbalance to the more extreme claims of Freudians and some of their anthropological followers. Rigorous research like that of Sewell, Mussen, and Harris [13] has shown that there is little evidence for many of the theoretical pronouncements regarding the effects of early child-rearing on the personality.

Human Ecology

Another area where sociologists have made a considerable contribution is in human ecology which analyzes the processes involved in the spatial and temporal adaptation and distribution of human beings and their institutions. Those aspects of marketing which can most directly profit from a knowledge of ecology are: transportation and storage, and the whole area concerned with market-area structures.

In all approaches to marketing, the *area* is an important variable and factor. Sociologists have been concerned with spatial systems for over forty years—in 1915 Galpin [14] brought out *The Social Anatomy of an Agricultural Community*, and in 1916 Robert E. Park [15] published his article "The City" in the *American Journal of Sociology*. Galpin's pioneering study introduced a technique of marketing research which has been widely used since, with certain modifications.

Since then the contributions of sociologists to the description, delineation, and analysis of the dynamics of spatial and temporal systems has been continuous and constitutes a vast amount of research too great to analyze here. There should be mentioned, however, the contributions of Odum and Moore,[16] Murkerjee,[17] and Mangus [18] to the study of regional systems; of R. D. McKenzie,[19] Hawely,[20] and Bogue [21] to the

[13] William H. Sewell, Paul H. Mussen, and Chester W. Harris, "Relationships Among Child Training Practices," *American Sociological Review*, Vol. 20 (April, 1955), pp. 137–148.

[14] C. J. Galpin, *The Social Anatomy of an Agricultural Community* (Madison: Agricultural Experiment Station of the University of Wisconsin, May, 1951), Research Bulletin 34.

[15] Robert E. Park, "The City," *American Journal of Sociology*, Vol. 20 (March, 1916), pp. 577–612.

[16] Howard W. Odum and Harry E. Moore, *American Regionalism* (New York: Henry Holt and Company, 1938).

[17] Radhakamal Mukerjee, "Social Ecology of River Valley," *Sociology and Social Research*, Vol. 12 (March, 1928), pp. 341–347.

[18] A. R. Mangus, *Rural Regions of the United States* (Washington, D.C.: U.S. Government Printing Office, 1940).

[19] Roderick D. McKenzie, *The Metropolitan Community* (New York: McGraw-Hill Book Company, Inc., 1933).

[20] Amos H. Hawley, "An Ecological Study of Urban Service Institutions," *American Sociological Review*, Vol. 6 (October, 1941), pp. 629–639; also *Human Ecology* (New York: The Ronald Press Company, 1950).

[21] Don J. Bogue, *The Structure of the Metropolitan Community: A Study of Dominance and Subdominance* (Ann Arbor: Horace H. Rackham School of Graduate Studies, University of Michigan, 1949); see also the numerous population studies by the same author published by the Scripps Foundation, Miami University, Oxford, Ohio.

analysis of metropolitan community systems; of Park, Burgess, and Mc-Kenzie,[22] Schmid,[23] Firey,[24] Wirth,[25] Duncan and Reiss,[26] and Quinn [27] to the analysis of urban systems; and of Galpin,[28] Kolb and Polson,[29] and Brunner [30] to investigation of rural systems.

Most marketing people are familiar with Reilly's [31] law, and equations of retail gravitation. Those interested in the mathematical-model approach to spatial systems would be rewarded by a study of Stouffer's [32] theory of intervening opportunities, of Zipf's [33] equations and hypothesis on intercity movement of persons, and of Dodd's [34] equations describing message diffusion.

Collective Behavior

The realization of distribution specialists that they are dealing with interacting groups, masses, and publics, and the fact that our nation and the world are developing more characteristics of the mass society make the area which sociologists call "collective behavior" ever more important and relevant for marketing. The contributions of sociologists to this area of human behavior have been fairly continuous since Durkheim's [35]

[22] R. E. Park, E. W. Burgess, and R. D. McKenzie, *The City* (Chicago: University of Chicago Press, 1925): E. W. Burgess, "The Growth of the City: An Introduction to a Research Project," *Publications of the American Sociological Society*, Vol. 18 (1924), pp. 85–97.

[23] Calvin F. Schmid, *Social Saga of Two Cities* (Minneapolis: Minneapolis Council of Social Agencies, 1937); *Social Trends in Seattle* (Seattle: University of Washington Press, 1944).

[24] Walter Firey, *Land Use in Central Boston* (Cambridge: Harvard University Press, 1947).

[25] Louis Wirth, *The Ghetto* (Chicago: The University of Chicago Press) 1928; "Urbanism as a Way of Life," *American Journal of Sociology*, Vol. 44 (July, 1938), pp. 1–24.

[26] Otis Dudley Duncan and Albert J. Reiss, Jr., *Social Characteristics of Urban and Rural Communities*, 1950 (New York: John Wiley and Sons, Inc., 1956).

[27] James A. Quinn, *Human Ecology* (New York: Prentice-Hall, Inc., 1950).

[28] Galpin, same reference as footnote 14.

[29] J. H. Kolb and R. A. Polson, *Trends in Town-Country Relations*, Research Bulletin 117, Agricultural Experiment Station, University of Wisconsin, (September, 1933).

[30] Edmund de S. Brunner, "Village Growth and Decline, 1930–1940," *Rural Sociology*, Vol. 9 (June, 1944), pp. 103–115; "Village Growth 1940–1950," *Rural Sociology*, Vol. 16 (June, 1951), pp. 111–118.

[31] William J. Reilly, *The Law of Retail Gravitation* (New York: W. J. Reilly, Inc., 1931).

[32] Samuel A. Stouffer, "Intervening Opportunities: A Theory Relating Mobility and Distance," *American Sociological Review*, Vol. 5 (December, 1940), pp. 845–867.

[33] George Kingsley Zipf, "The Pl. P2/D Hypothesis: On the Intercity Movement of Persons," *American Sociological Review*, Vol. 11 (December, 1946), pp. 677–686.

[34] Stuart Carter Dodd, "Diffusion Is Predictable: Testing Probability Models for Laws of Interaction," *American Sociological Review*, Vol. 20 (August, 1955), pp. 392–401.

[35] Émile Durkheim, *Les Formes élémentaires de la vie religieuse, le système totémique en Australie* (Paris: F. Alcan, 1912). Translated by Joseph Ward Swain, *The Elementary Forms of Religious Life: A Study of Religious Sociology* (London: George Allen and Unwin, Ltd., 1915; also Glencoe, Ill.: The Free Press, 1947).

early work. Another pioneer in this area was LeBon.[36] Recent contributors are Albig,[37] LaPiere,[38] Lazarsfeld,[39] Merton,[40] Raper,[41] Lee,[42] and Blumer.[43] *An Experiment in Mass Communication* by Otto Larsen and Melvin L. DeFleur [44] contributes to the understanding of the phenomena indicated by the title.

Measurement and Scaling

Another contribution to marketing research made by sociologists is in methodology, measurement, scaling, and prediction. Chapin,[45] Sletto,[46] Bogardus,[47] and Guttman [48] have made basic contributions to scale construction; Burgess,[49] Hornell Hart,[50] Monachesi,[51] and Stuckert [52] to the science of prediction; Chapin [53] and McCormick [54] to the development of

[36] Gustave LeBon, *The Crowd* (London: Unwin, 1899).

[37] William Albig, *Public Opinion* (New York: McGraw-Hill Book Co., Inc., 1939).

[38] Richard T. LaPiere, *Collective Behavior* (New York: McGraw-Hill Book Co., Inc., 1938).

[39] Paul F. Lazarsfeld, Bernard Berelson, and Hazel Gaudet, *The People's Choice* (New York: Duell, Sloan and Pearce, 1944).

[40] Robert K. Merton, *Mass Persuasion: The Social Psychology of a War Bond Drive* (New York: Harper and Brothers, 1946).

[41] Arthur F. Raper, *The Tragedy of Lynching* (Chapel Hill: University of North Carolina Press, 1933).

[42] Alfred McClung Lee, *The Daily Newspaper in America* (New York: Macmillan, 1937).

[43] Herbert Blumer, "Collective Behavior," Part IV of *An Outline of the Principles of Sociology*, Robert E. Park, Editor (New York: Barnes and Noble, 1939).

[44] Otto Larsen and Melvin L. DeFleur, *An Experiment in Mass Communication* (New York: Harper and Brothers, 1958).

[45] Stuart F. Chapin, "Preliminary Standardization of a Social Insight Scale," *American Sociological Review*, Vol. 7 (April, 1942), pp. 214–224.

[46] Raymond F. Sletto and E. A. Rundquist, *Personality and the Depression* (Minneapolis: University of Minnesota Press, 1936); Sletto, *Construction of Personality Scales by the Criterion of Internal Consistency* (Hanover: The Sociological Press, 1937).

[47] Bogardus, same reference as footnote 12.

[48] Louis Guttman, "A Basis for Scaling Qualitative Data," *American Sociological Review*, Vol. 9 (April, 1944), pp. 139–150.

[49] E. W. Burgess, "Factors Determining Success or Failure on Parole," in A. A. Bruce, E. W. Burgess, and A. T. Harno, *The Workings of the Indeterminate Sentence Law and the Parole System in Illinois* (Springfield: The State of Illinois, 1928).

[50] Hornell Hart, "Predicting Parole Success," *Journal of the American Institute of Criminal Law and Criminology*, Vol. 14 (Nov. 1923), pp. 405–413.

[51] Elio D. Monachesi, *Prediction Factors in Probation* (Hanover: The Sociological Press, 1932).

[52] Robert Paton Stuckert, *A Configurational Approach to Social Prediction*, unpublished Ph.D. Dissertation, The Ohio State University, 1956; "A Configurational Approach to Prediction," *Sociometry*, Vol. 21 (September, 1958), pp. 225–237.

[53] S. F. Chapin, *Experimental Designs in Sociological Research* (New York: Harper and Brothers, 1947); *Design of Social Experiments* (New York: Harper and Brothers, 2nd ed., 1956).

[54] Thomas C. McCormick, *Elementary Social Statistics* (New York: McGraw-Hill Book Co., Inc., 1941); Thomas C. McCormick and Roy G. Francis, *Methods of Research in the Behavioral Sciences* (New York: Harper and Brothers, 1958).

models and research design; Parten [55] to sampling; Sletto [56] to the use of control groups in social research; Bowers [57] to methods of studying paths of diffusion in the use of new products; Galpin [58] and Schmid [59] to techniques for mapping quantitative social data; Lazarsfeld [60] and Stouffer [61] to the use of quantitative methods in the study of many areas of human behavior; and Moreno [62] and Lundberg [63] to sociometry.

IMPACT OF SOCIOLOGISTS ON MARKETING

How much impact, if any, have sociological contributions had on marketing? This is difficult to determine. But inferences may be drawn from marketing literature, from an examination of activities of sociologists in the marketing field, and from a look at the structures and processes through which sociological knowledge diffuses into the marketing area.

Publications

Normally one should expect academic channels and textbooks to be an important means of diffusion, but they appear not to be in this instance. Writers of marketing textbooks, while showing evidence of some of the substance of sociology, rarely mention sociology or sociologists. It would require considerable research to determine definitively what emphasis if any is given to sociology in undergraduate courses; but if textbooks are a guide it would seem to be rather negligible. On the graduate level, however, there seems to be more attention given to this subject matter; *The Shopping Center Versus Downtown*,[64] for example,

[55] Mildred B. Parten, "Leadership Among Pre-school Children," *Journal of Abnormal and Social Psychology*, Vol. 27 (January–March, 1933), pp. 430–440; *Surveys, Polls and Samples* (New York: Harper and Brothers, 1950).

[56] Raymond F. Sletto, "Sibling Position and Juvenile Delinquency," *American Journal of Sociology*, Vol. 34 (March, 1934), pp. 657–669.

[57] Raymond B. Bowers, "The Direction of Intra-Societal Diffusion," *American Sociological Review*, Vol. 2 (December, 1937), pp. 826–836.

[58] Galpin, same reference as footnote 14.

[59] Schmid, same reference as footnote 23; also *Handbook of Graphic Presentation* (New York: The Ronald Press Co., 1954).

[60] Paul F. Lazarsfeld, *et al.*, *Mathematical Thinking in the Social Sciences* (Glencoe, Ill.: The Free Press, 1954).

[61] Samuel A. Stouffer, *et al.*, *The American Soldier: Adjustment During Army Life*, Vol. 1 (Princeton: Princeton University Press, 1949).

[62] J. L. Moreno, *Who Shall Survive?* (Washington, D.C.: Nervous and Mental Disease Publishing Co., 1934).

[63] George A. Lundberg and Mary Steele, "Social Attraction Patterns in a Village," *Sociometry*, Vol. 1 (April, 1938), pp. 375–419.

[64] Christen T. Jonassen, *The Shopping Center versus Downtown: A Motivation Research on Shopping Habits and Attitudes in Three Cities* (Columbus: The Ohio State University Bureau of Business Research, 1955); also published as *Shopper Attitudes*, Special Report 11-A (Washington, D.C.: Highway Research Board, National Research Council, 1955).

is being used in graduate marketing training programs of some universities.

In marketing and business publications, on the other hand, evidence of sociological influence is more evident. Bartels, for example, in an article in the *Journal of Marketing* in 1951 considers certain aspects of sociology, economics, and some other disciplines, to be part of the area of marketing.[65] *Business Week* of March 29, 1958, reporting on a marketing conference, featured the remarks of sociologist David Riesman.[66] *The Shopping Center Versus Downtown* mentioned above has been reviewed extensively by marketing and business publications. *Consumer Behavior,*[67] published in 1955, has an article by Nelson N. Foote on "The Autonomy of the Consumer," and another by Frederick L. Strodtback on "Recent Developments in Attitude Research." An article entitled "A Commercial Application of Guttman Attitude Scaling Techniques"[68] appeared in the *Journal of Marketing* in 1957.

Climate of Ideas

Much sociological influence on marketing, of course, is exerted indirectly through the medium of the general culture and climate of ideas. Another means is through the effect of sociology on other disciplines such as psychology and economics, which in turn produces similar reactions in marketing.

Sociological contributions to the general evolution of thought about the nature and dynamics of man as a consumer and of the market as a social institution and structure have already been discussed. But much sociological material reaches marketing men second-hand, very late, and sometimes in garbled fashion.

Participation of Sociologists in Marketing

Another path of diffusion of sociological knowledge is through direct participation of sociologists in the marketing process as researchers, consultants, and participants in marketing seminars and conventions. The participation of David Riesman in the *Life* sponsored regional roundtable in Chicago has already been mentioned. Packard would have us believe that there may be sociologists behind the so-called "hidden persuaders," and states that Likert and Stouffer participated in a public-rela-

[65] Robert Bartels, "Can Marketing Be a Science?" *Journal of Marketing,* Vol. 15 (January, 1951), pp. 319–328, at p. 323.

[66] "The Riddle of Consumer Behavior," *Business Week* (March 29, 1958), p. 95.

[67] Committee for Research on Consumer Attitudes and Behavior, *Consumer Behavior,* Lincoln H. Clark, editor (New York: New York University Press, 1955).

[68] Elizabeth A. Richards, "A Commercial Application of Guttman Attitude Scaling Techniques," *Journal of Marketing,* Vol. 22 (October, 1957), pp. 166–173.

tions conference at Columbia University.[69] Some sociologists are now found in marketing-research organizations and on the staffs of advertising agencies.

Evidence of direct and indirect influence of sociologists is furnished by the results of some recent marketing research. For example, one of the most ambitious pieces of marketing research of recent years, the *Life Study of Consumer Expenditures*,[70] conducted by Alfred Politz Research, Inc., offers much internal evidence of sociological influence in research design, sampling, questionnaire construction, and selection of essential categories of analysis. The "wave" technique of intermittent interviewing of the same households, for example, is very similar to the technique developed by Lazarsfeld in his study of voting behavior.

The study is not of individuals, but of groups, families, and households living in the United States. These families and households are studied by socio-economic status; education of head of family; stage of "life cycle"; age of household head; and by regions, urban, rural, and different-sized communities.

One category which appears in the *Life* research that is not common in previous marketing studies is "Household's Stage in the Life Cycle." The study credits the development of this concept to the Survey Research Center of the University of Michigan; [71] but the concept of stages in family life cycle has been common coin in sociology for a long time. In their *Systematic Source Book in Rural Sociology*,[72] Sorokin, Zimmerman, and Galpin discussed four stages of family life cycle as early as 1931; and E. L. Kirkpatrick in 1934 wrote an article entitled "The Life Cycle of the Farm Family in Relation to Its Standard of Living." [73] The concept appears in a book of Waller's [74] in 1938; and it is the organizing theme of Duvall's *Family Development*.[75] Thus, what appeared originally as a concept in sociological literature appears about a generation later in a marketing study as an important category in terms of which data are gathered and analyzed.

Similarly, the use of such categories as "metropolitan" and "non-metropolitan" owes much to McKenzie, whose writings on the metropolitan region appeared as early as 1924 and 1926, and whose *The*

[69] Vance Packard, *The Hidden Persuaders* (New York: David McKay Co., 1957), pp. 220, 221.

[70] Time, Inc., LIFE *Study of Consumer Expenditures*, 1957, Vol. 1.

[71] Same reference, p. 13.

[72] Pitirim Sorokin, Carl C. Zimmerman, and C. J. Galpin, *Systematic Source Book in Rural Sociology* (Minneapolis: University of Minnesota Press, 1931). Vol. 2, p. 31.

[73] E. L. Kirkpatrick, *et al.*, "*The Life Cycle of the Farm Family in Relation to its Standard of Living*," Research Bulletin No. 121 (Madison, Wisconsin: Agricultural Experiment Station, University of Wisconsin, 1934).

[74] Willard Waller, *The Family: A Dynamic Interpretation* (New York: The Cordon Co., 1938).

[75] Evelyn Millis Duvall, *Family Development* (New York: J. B. Lippincott Co., 1957).

Metropolitan Community was published in 1933.[76] Bogue's *The Structure of the Metropolitan Community* appeared in 1949; [77] and this research monograph as well as the earlier work of McKenzie, Hawley, and other sociologists probably contributed heavily to the decision of the U.S. Bureau of the Census to order its data in terms of Standard Metropolitan Areas.

In Conclusion

Lack of space has made it necessary to omit names of other sociologists and also some relevant work of the sociologists who are mentioned. Many sociologists have made significant contributions to marketing by their impact on the general climate of ideas concerning the nature of man and society and the relations of economic institutions to society. They have also carried out important studies on population, communication, collective behavior, motivation, stratification, methodology, research design, measurement, prediction, human ecology, and the family. Sociological knowledge and methods have diffused into marketing through marketing publications, through participation of sociologists as consultants and researchers, and to a lesser extent through academic channels.

The participants in the *Life* marketing conferences mentioned earlier stressed the necessity of developing basic theories and facts to explain buying behavior. The present article has pointed to some aspects of sociological activity and to some materials that might aid in the solution of this problem.

[76] McKenzie, same reference as footnote 19.
[77] Bogue, same reference as footnote 21.

12. Simulation for decision making in marketing

DOYLE L. WEISS

The development of the modern computer and its problem-oriented languages has made simulation a feasible technique to apply to the complex problem situations faced by researchers and policy makers in marketing.

Problem-oriented languages allow researchers to instruct the computer with terms and symbols which are most meaningful to the problem being studied. The result is that the computer with its language systems provides researchers with a flexibility for model construction that has never before been available.

Before the arrival of the computer most marketing theories which attempted precisely to relate the decision variables, initial conditions, and parameters (constants specific to the problem being studied) to observations of actual business operations were restricted in form to linear models.[1] This restriction was necessary because large systems of nonlinear equations representing a theory cannot for the most part be solved by standard analytic techniques to yield solutions for their decision variables.

The result of this constraint has been a failure by researchers in following up on the development of models with enough detail to describe adequately the phenomena being observed.[2] The extreme computation speed and programing flexibility of modern computers allows

Reprinted from *Journal of Marketing*, Volume 28 (July, 1964), pp. 45–50, National Quarterly Publication of the American Marketing Association.

[1] A. T. Steele, "Why Daily Department Store Sales Fluctuate" in Robert Ferber and Hugh G. Wales, Editors, *Motivation and Market Behavior* (Homewood, Illinois: Richard D. Irwin, Inc., 1958), pp. 381–388.

[2] A good example of too much abstraction is Reilly's Law of Retail Gravitation. A version of this model may be found in C. H. McGregor, *Retail Management Problems* (Homewood, Illinois: R. D. Irwin, Inc., 1962), p. 27.

the researcher to build as complicated a theory as he desires, and still be confident that its overall implications may be computed for any given set of parameters and initial conditions.

However, optimal solutions are not guaranteed by computer simulation models, as they are when linear and quadratic programing or calculus can properly be applied to the problem being investigated. When linear or quadratic programing models can be used, the structure of rules for performing their calculations (or algorithms, as they are usually referred to) is such that optimal solutions *are guaranteed.* The test for using one of these techniques as an alternative to simulation, though, must be made in terms of the amount and kind of abstraction from the "real-world" situation made necessary by the rigid form of their structure.

Such difficulties are well illustrated by the researcher who encounters advertising-effectiveness problems after an initial exposure to statistical methods. His usual response to the problem is to build a simple regression model, relating sales to advertising expenditures. This he finds appealing because he knows he can apply standard statistical techniques and generate a correlation coefficient which will allow him to "predict" the sales response to a firm's advertising expenditures. The results of this model's predictions, however, will usually be poor enough to convince him that the model is much too simple (abstract) to handle his problem adequately.

If he persists in his search for an explanation of advertising phenomena, his next theory is likely to be expressed as a multiple regression model, with such additional independent variables as income levels, retail availability, and price considered along with advertising expenditures. Unfortunately the results are still unlikely to be satisfactory; and this model, as the first one, will lack sufficient predictive power.

The problem is that the variables in the system tend to influence each other *simultaneously;* and simple models are unlikely to predict or explain the underlying processes adequately.

For useful results to be achieved, this means that models rich in essential details must be constructed. Such detailed models are quite unlikely to fit the computational form demanded for analytic solution, and so must be studied by an application of simulation techniques.

SIMULATION PROCEDURE

The role of the computer in simulation is as a computational device. Actually it does nothing more than could be done by a human being with a desk calculator, a pad of paper as a memory aid, and a *few years of spare time.*

The important aspect of both the computer and the human desk-calculator system is the quality of their operating instructions. Neither the computer nor simulation is a substitute for sound theory construction. This must precede *any* use of the computer, although the process of programing the model for the computer is a step-by-step logical process which may in fact aid in theory development by forcing every aspect of the model to be specified completely.[3]

What the computer does is to allow the model to be evaluated repeatedly when initial conditions, parameters, and current values for the variables have been supplied. Time paths for years of operation can be produced by a fast computer in only a few minutes!

One researcher has described a single evaluation of a simulation model as an experiment performed upon the model.[4] In the experiment the model has been operated for one cycle after all conditions affecting the outcome have been completely specified. By examining the results of many such experiments the response characteristics of the model can be discovered.

Such experimentation with the model may expose a time path which is completely at variance with the time path of the "real-world" system being simulated. Turning points may be overlooked; or perhaps the response characteristics of the model are unstable, with the result that the time path produced by the model is quite erratic. When this occurs, it may mean that the theory must be revised or even abandoned.

Only a small number of simulation studies have been attempted that are of interest to people in marketing. A few of these will be described.

DEPARTMENT STORE PRICING MODEL

One of the earliest and more interesting of these was a simulation of a specific department of a major department store, in which the internal pricing and ordering decision rules of the department were modeled.[5] This model hypothesizes two general goals which serve as performance evaluation criteria. These are a sales goal and a markup goal. Decision making by the department takes place in response to problems associated with one or the other of these goals.

Nonfulfillment of these goals causes the department to search for methods of reducing the variance between the goal and the actual performance. Search takes place within the context of a well-defined list of

---

[3] A description of how this process was conducted for one problem may be found in Alfred A. Kuehn and Ralph L. Day, "Simulation and Operational Gaming" in *Marketing and the Computer*, Wroe Alderson and Stanley J. Shapiro, Editors (Englewood Cliffs, N.J.: Prentice-Hall, 1963), pp. 234–247.

[4] Guy H. Orcutt, "Simulation of Economic Systems," *The American Economic Review*, Vol. 50 (December, 1960), pp. 893–907.

[5] Richard M. Cyert, James G. March, and Chadwick G. Moore, "A Model of Retail Ordering and Pricing in a Department Store" in Ronald E. Frank, Alfred A. Kuehn, and William F. Massy, Editors, *Quantitative Techniques in Marketing Analysis* (Homewood, Illinois: Richard D. Irwin, Inc., 1962), pp. 502–522.

alternatives, and continues until some means have been discovered for reducing the observed variance. Among the alternatives for variance reduction examined by the search precedure are markdown promotions directed toward stimulating sales, introduction of new merchandise to help sales or relieve pressure on markdowns, or even re-evaluations of the original goals.

Parts of the model were tested, and with encouraging results. In estimation of monthly sales, the model was able to predict 95 percent of such sales within 5 percent. The model was able to predict prices from a sample of invoices to the penny in 95.4 percent of the cases tried.

An interesting feature of this model is that it is not expressed mathematically, but consists mostly of fairly elaborate "switching rules" based on logical tests. Furthermore, the model is descriptive rather than normative in that it attempts to describe what is actually happening within the department rather than what should happen. Such a model affords a very good point of departure for any research aimed at improving the department's performance generally.

A MODEL FOR RETAIL CREDIT APPLICATIONS

A credit-card application rejection rate considered to be high in relation to the industry's average rejection rate caused the Gulf Oil Corporation to develop a probability model which simulates the decision criteria of their human credit appraisers.[6]

The initial concern was to discover the importance imputed by credit appraisers to characteristics on application forms and credit reports (such as importance attached to age and occupation). As a means of finding which characteristics best classified the applicant as an acceptable or unacceptable credit risk, a sequential least squares analysis was used—random samples of 500 accepted applicants and 500 applicants who were rejected were taken to develop the decision model.

The statistical procedure used sequentially adds the various characteristics to the least squares model, and tests them to see if they have added any significant predictive power to the model being constructed. The result of the analysis is a list of characteristics, and attendant weights, which allows the applicant to be labeled acceptable or unacceptable.

The resulting model was tested under two different conditions. It was used to process 191 applications in which the credit appraisers had decided that Credit Bureau reports were not necessary as additional information. Of the 191 applications, the model disagreed with the human

    [6] Robert H. Nelson, Coordinator of Statistical Sampling, and Robert J. A. Pratt, Graduate School of Business, University of Pittsburgh and Consultant to Gulf Oil Corporation, "Problems in Retail Credit," internal publication by the Domestic Marketing Department, Gulf Oil Corporation.

appraiser on only 6 individuals. It rejected 4 applications that the appraiser had accepted, and it accepted 2 that he had rejected.

For 834 applications on which the additional information from Credit Bureau reports was used, the model did not do quite as well. It rejected 34 applications which were accepted by the human, and accepted 59 which the human had rejected. Its error rates, as compared with the human appraiser, were 3 percent and 11 percent respectively in the two tests.

The researchers then extended their model to a 2-stage process.

Stage I classified the applicants three ways: accepted, rejected, or Credit Bureau report needed before a classification can be determined.

Stage II then determined the final acceptance or rejection of the remaining applications, using the credit report as additional information. This 2-step model produced the results shown in the accompanying table:

Results from 2-Step Model

(1,474 applications)

Credit appraiser		Model decision (Stage I and II combined)	
Decision	Applicants	Acceptance	Rejections
Acceptance	968	887	81[a]
Rejection	506	87[a]	419
Total	1,474	974	500

[a]A total error rate of 11.4%.

A low acceptance criterion was established intentionally, in order to produce a bias toward accepting more of the human appraiser's rejections. By providing an objective criterion for acceptance, the model allows the proportion of acceptances to be raised or lowered by including the marginal applicant; that is, if expansion is desired, only the best of what would have been rejections are accepted. This bias was placed in the model to reduce what was considered to be a high rejection rate by the human appraisers.

Work with the model has led to solutions of several problems associated with retail credit applications. It is now possible to begin to relate the relative emphasis on certain characteristics (such as age) with the present value of an applicant's expected total revenue. Losses from bad accounts can also be investigated as a function of the sales expected to be lost as a result of an overall acceptance rate of only 63 percent. In addition, Stage I of the model has cut the use of Credit Bureau reports and resulted in immediate and direct cost savings. (The Credit Bureau report is used as an additional decision variable for 72 percent of the applications processed by the Credit Department.)

An extension of the model to include the process by which the Gulf Oil Corporation loses credit-card holders is being planned. The inclusion of this process will allow the simulation model to define the long-term distribution of credit-card holders (and the profits associated with such a distribution) for a number of different acceptance criteria. Comparisons among these distributions will allow the credit standards to be defined in terms of some long-run profit criteria.

A MODEL OF THE DETERGENT MARKET

The author is also experimenting with a simulation model of the detergent market.[7] The complicated nonlinear model attempts to consider most of the effects and interactions of the merchandising variables in the detergent industry controlled by competing detergent manufacturers.

Consumer Choice Structure

The consumer choice of brands in the model is based on the brand shifting model first developed by Alfred A. Kuehn.[8] In this model, sales for a brand are produced by two kinds of consumer purchasing behavior.

In the first of these, the consumer is treated as repurchasing the same brand he purchased last period because of habit. This demand, termed habitual demand, may be thought of as the core of a brand's sales, consisting of purchases by the brand's established customers. Although each consumer has a unique probability of making this habitual buying response, determined by his recent purchase history and the length of time between purchases, the simulation model uses an average probability as a parameter representative of all the consumers in the market.

If the consumer is not making a habitual purchasing decision, he is a potential brand shifter for the current period. That is to say, the consumer considers all of the marketed brands as feasible alternatives. As a result, he is subject to competing influences from the marketing activities of all the available brands, although he may in fact repurchase the brand he purchased in the last period. The process underlying this kind of a decision to repurchase a brand is quite different from the one for habitual repurchases.

[7] Doyle L. Weiss, "Simulation of the Detergent Industry," in *Marketing Precision and Executive Action*, Charles H. Hindersman, Editor (Chicago: American Marketing Association, 1962), pp. 152–161.

[8] Alfred A. Kuehn, "A Model for Budgeting Advertising," in *Mathematical Models and Methods in Marketing*, Frank M. Bass, Mark R. Greene, Edgar A. Pessemier, Abraham Shuchman, Robert D. Buzzell, William Lazar, Donald L. Shawner, Chris A. Theodore, and George W. Wilson, Editors (Homewood, Illinois: Richard D. Irwin, Inc., 1960), pp. 315–348.

Market Structure

Because the model is dealing with products which retain brand identity and have distinct product characteristics, its demand function is unlike the market-clearing mechanism of pure competition. The actual industry demand function used in the model is the following:

$$Q_t = Q_o \cdot \left(\frac{p_t}{p_o}\right)^{\eta\,p} \cdot \left(\frac{E_t}{E_o}\right)^{\eta\,E} \cdot \left(\frac{Y_t}{Y_o}\right)^{\eta\,Y} \cdot K^t$$

where: o   is a subscript implying a base or normal industry value for the subscripted value,

Q = demand in units

p = average industry price weighted by market share

E = total promotional expenditures by the industry

K = growth term for period to period trend effects

Y = disposable income (exogenous to this model)

η = elasticity constant determining the responsiveness of demand to changes in the variables

t = time period

However, total industry demand is a function of several industry parameters, including price elasticity. For instance, total demand for the industry will expand (but not necessarily at the same rate) with an expansion of industry advertising and promotional expenditures. Industry demand in the model is also responsive to the price of the individual brands (actually an average price in which each brand's price is weighted by market share) and the level of consumer disposable income. A trend term is included in the industry demand function, to allow the effects of a growing, dying, or stable industry to be simulated and studied.

Marketers have long recognized that the end use for which a product is purchased will influence what the consumer prefers in terms of product characteristics. For example, the products of the detergent industry competing in the dishwashing submarket (detergents for automatic dishwashing equipment are not considered) usually are promoted for their high-sudsing characteristics and their gentleness. By contrast, much of the promotional emphasis on products produced for the home laundry market seems to be on low sudsiness and a high washing power characteristic.

These differential effects of product characteristics on demand are handled in the simulation model as distinct submarkets. This does not mean that a consumer who is buying a detergent for dishwashing purposes cannot buy a brand generally thought to be more suitable for home laundry uses. It does mean, however, that a brand's physical product characteristics will have their greatest impact on those consumers making up the submarket for which it is most suitable.

Interbrand Competitive Aspects of the Model

Marketing researchers recognize more clearly than ever that the effects of the marketing variables such as price, advertising, retail availability, and the physical product characteristics interact together. In most cases they cannot effectively be "compartmentalized" and studied independently of each other.[9]

Each of these variables can be expected to influence both the sales position of the brands and the effectiveness of the other variables to such an extent that only poor predictions of the outcome of a promotion can be made in terms of the advertising budget and price alone.

Also, the timing of the sales force's efforts in providing shelf space and in-store promotional activities for the brand—along with advertising expenditures, pricing policy, and physical characteristics of the product —are important in sales outcome. It is in this complex area of interdependency that computer simulation models should make the greatest contribution to understanding the complete system of these interrelationships.

The model of the detergent industry attempts to explain how these interactions take place, and the effects they have on sales in a specific market. It relates the interdependent variables in what is believed to be a realistic and rational manner, so that the combined effects of the variables on sales may be observed and studied.

The manner in which the physical product characteristics are handled by the model provides a good example of its theoretical detail. The model considers three physical product characteristics: sudsiness, washing power, and gentleness. With washing power and gentleness, consumer reactions are fairly straightforward; that is, the more washing power and gentleness possessed by a brand, the more desirable that brand is for most consumers. However, gentleness is relatively more important in the dishwashing submarket, and washing power more important in the automatic-washer and general-purpose submarkets.

As to sudsing characteristics, though, this is not true. For certain uses such as dishwashing, suds are desired by the consumer, while for other purposes such as home laundry, an excess of suds may be thought of as interfering with the "cleaning action" and resulting in damage to the laundry equipment.

This means that we can consider consumer preferences to be distributed across a scale of sudsiness values, ranging from zero to some upper

[9] Alfred A. Kuehn, "How Advertising Performance Depends on Other Marketing Factors," *Journal of Advertising Research*, Vol. 2 (March, 1962), pp. 2–10.

limit where demand is zero. Concentrations of demand will appear along the distribution as peaks occurring at values of the product characteristics most preferred for particular end uses. If other effects were equal, and if consumers were considered to purchase the brand nearest in sudsiness value to their preferences, then the relative effect of sudsiness for a brand would depend on its position on the sudsiness scale with respect to the position of competing brands, and the distribution of consumer preferences representing the various end uses.

The fact that consumers are not able to tell with perfect accuracy when the characteristics of the product they are considering represent their exact preferences was taken into consideration in developing the model. As the characteristics of the product being considered move farther away from the levels of the consumer's exact preferences, the probability of the consumer recognizing this difference is treated as increasing in a fashion which is consistent with empirical blind-product preference test data.[10]

In addition to the usual variables of price and advertising expenditures, inputs of sales-force size and a retail allowance are provided. The management may hire or fire salesmen and direct the allocation of their effort among brands; also, management may offer a retail allowance of $X per case of product sold. The computer model treats the allowance as if it were given to the retailer by the detergent manufacturer. The retailer passes on part of this price concession to the consumer in the form of a deal which serves to stimulate retail sales. If the manufacturer offers retail allowances too frequently, the promotional price effect is lost.

The interaction of a brand's advertising expenditure, retail allowance, allocation of sales-force effort, and market share determine the relative measure of a brand's retail availability. This measure attempts to simulate the effect of retail distribution, the allocation of shelf space, and in-store special display promotions on the brand's sales. Once these interaction mechanisms are tested and developed to the point where they are reasonably correct determinants of sales effectiveness, guidance can be provided to marketing executives in proper allocation of resources to these variables.

Research with the Model

The model is capable of simulating any number of firms which have one or more brands. In practice, the only limitations to the number of brands and firms that can be simulated are the speed and capacity of the computing system being utilized.

With minor changes in the parameters and structure, the model will

---

[10] Also see Alfred A. Kuehn and Ralph L. Day, "Strategy of Product Quality," *Harvard Business Review*, Vol. 40 (November–December, 1962), pp. 100–110.

simulate a wide range of market conditions, including those of imperfect markets as well as the less complex market structures of perfect competition, monopoly, and oligopoly.

Research is being undertaken to discover the relationships underlying the market variables of advertising, price, retail availability, and product characteristics at competitive equilibrium for a variety of market structures. In particular, the effects of variable costs, the number of brands in the market, and the distribution of brands among firms are being studied. By varying these values and then searching the model directly with the aid of a computer for the attendant equilibrium positions, the nature of the effects can be isolated.

This research is expected to yield answers to questions of market strategy for products whose characteristics are quite different from those of competing products. Problems connected with the allocation of resources among brands competing in different submarkets are expected to be partially solved. In addition, the question of how a new product should be introduced with respect to timing and the promotional variables controlled by the firm is being analyzed.

The model has also been programed in the form of a marketing game as well as a market simulation.[11] This allows experimentation with alternative strategies to be done in the "synthetic" market instead of the real one, and without danger of large sums of money being lost.

Provisions have been made in the game to enable the players to purchase research reports. These are estimates of various aspects of competitive marketing activities, such as price, advertising expenditures, market share, retail stockout, and distribution. There are additional provisions to permit the firms to develop and improve new products, to copy competitor's products, and to conduct blind-product paired-comparison preference tests.

The usual claims made for the educational value of business games can be made for this one.[12] However, since it is a relatively realistic game, the participant not only gains experience in operating in a dynamic world of business, but also discovers some institutional facts about marketing interrelationships.

IMPLICATIONS

It would be both foolish and presumptuous to predict that simulation will solve completely all of marketing's problems. Indeed, if it is very

[11] Alfred A. Kuehn and Doyle L. Weiss, "CIT Marketing Game," Research in Marketing Project Paper No. 4, Graduate School of Industrial Administration, Carnegie Institute of Technology.

[12] William R. Dill, James R. Jackson, and James W. Sweeney, Proceedings of the Conference on Business Games as Teaching Devices (New Orleans: Tulane University), 1961.

successful it may even be instrumental in exposing new problems which are now unformulated, because the current state of theory is not well enough developed to recognize them.

However, by making more realistic systems of marketing variables amenable to analysis, simulation techniques allow marketing people to move even closer to a practical theory of marketing.

13. Marketing research and behavioral science

LAWRENCE X. TARPEY

The purpose of this brief article is to explore the relationship between marketing research and behavioral science. To do this it will be necessary to analyze both of these concepts. It is this writer's contention that the orthodox approach to marketing research is too narrow and, hence, too restrictive. An attempt will be made to argue, by means of example, that marketing research must not merely borrow from the behavioral sciences but must merge with them whenever necessary.

Marketing research, in essence, combines insight and intuition with the scientific method to solve the many problems that confront marketing management. These problems center around the four ingredients of the marketing mix—product, place, price, and promotion.[1] However, if defined broadly enough, marketing research includes the study of *any* aspect of human behavior that might have a significant effect on the distribution, sale, and consumption of goods or services.[2] Given this broadened definition, the philosophical scope of marketing research is enlarged to include studies which have as their central focus not only the *what* or the *how* of consumption, but the *why* as well. Substantively speaking, there will be a necessary spillover into the fields of psychology, sociology, anthropology, political science, semantics, and so forth.

Reprinted from *Business Topics*, Winter, 1965, pp. 61–67, by permission of the publisher.

[1] E. Jerome McCarthy, *Basic Marketing: A Managerial Approach* (rev. ed.; Homewood, Illinois: Richard D. Irwin, Inc., 1964), p. 73.

[2] A standard definition of marketing research says it is "the systematic gathering, recording, and analyzing of data about problems relating to the marketing of goods and services." This definition emphasizes the *process* of research rather than the substance.

126

To understand the consumer, it is necessary to know something of his economic, psychological, sociological, and physiological make-up; and the proper development of marketing strategies demands an *in-depth* understanding of the customer and his modes of behavior. In order to provide the marketing manager with these necessary human insights, one must look to behavioral science. Before this is possible, however, it is important to know the answers to two questions. First, what is meant by behavioral science? Second, in what unique ways can behavioral science contribute to the marketing researcher's knowledge and measurement of consumer behavior?

A NEW CONCEPT

The concept of a "behavioral science" is relatively new, so that today scientific inquiry can be subdivided into the physical, the biological, and the behavioral. Like most new disciplines, however, it is impossible to define it to everyone's satisfaction.[3] For example, some writers want to restrict the term "behavioral science" to the social sciences, while others want the term to include all sciences as they relate to human behavior. The following is offered as a working definition: "Behavioral science is a combined endeavor of many fields investigating all aspects of behavior leading to understanding of human beings as individuals and in social relations."[4]

The above definition should be a meaningful one to most marketing researchers. First of all it is a person-centered definition and marketing is a discipline whose primary concern centers on the individual consumer. Secondly, marketing research has been a multi-disciplinary endeavor whenever necessary. Motivation research is clearly a case in point. Finally, the marketing researcher, like the behavioral scientist, is also interested in understanding human nature because without this understanding so much product planning, sales promotion, packaging, store engineering, would result in wasted time and money.

MARKETING RESEARCH

Traditionally, marketing research has been employed to provide businessmen with concrete answers to specific questions in a few selected decision areas. According to studies made by Richard Crisp for the Ameri-

[3] One of the most recent texts in marketing research devotes an entire chapter to "the behavioral sciences." The authors do not attempt to define behavioral science; they merely give an intelligent discussion of how marketing and marketing research have "borrowed" from psychology, social psychology, sociology, and cultural anthropology. See R. Ferber, F. Blankertz and S. Hollander, Jr., *Marketing Research* (New York: The Ronald Press, 1964), ch. iv.

[4] Behavioral Research Council, "A Current Appraisal of the Behavioral Sciences," *Bulletin* (Great Barrington, Mass.: Behavioral Research Council, 1963), p. 5.

can Management Association, the marketing research activities performed by the largest proportion of the firms surveyed were as follows:

Determining the competitive position of company products.
Analysis of the size of the market for specific products.
Analysis of territorial potential.
Variations in territorial yield, market share, etc.
Determining consumer acceptance of new products.
Preparing estimates of demand for new products.
Determining market characteristics for both new and old products.[5]

On the basis of what has just been said, one can reasonably conclude that most marketing research effort has three operational characteristics. First, it is extremely pragmatic in that the sponsoring firms expect the research to provide the decision maker with specific data or answers to very practical questions. Second, heavy emphasis is placed on learning or estimating the *what* and the *how* of market phenomena; the question

Table 1
Some Contributions to Marketing Research from Behavioral Science

Sociology	Psychology	Social Psychology
a. Content Analysis	a. Learning Theory	a. Cartoon Tests
b. Sociometric Ratings	b. Cue Theory	b. Picture Tests
c. Human Ecology	c. Eye Camera	c. Propaganda
d. Samples and Polls	d. Recall	d. TAT
e. Scaling Techniques	e. Semantic Differential	e. Error Choice
f. Ranking	f. Galvanic Skin Response	f. Forced Choice
g. Interviewing	g. Personnel Tests	g. Subliminal Perception
h. Group Theory	h. Depth Interviewing	h. Need Theory
i. Social Status	i. Habitual Behavior	i. Taboos
		j. Attitudes

of *why* is usually given secondary attention. Finally, most marketing research studies have a short-run viewpoint because the information from the studies is generally used to make decisions that will affect the firm's profit or competitive situation for the next few accounting periods.

BEHAVIORAL RESEARCH

The above comments should not be construed as criticisms. They are merely observations that can be useful in trying to give the reader a framework for understanding the relationship between marketing research and behavioral science. Research in the behavioral sciences tends to be highly theoretical. A great deal of attention is given to the question

[5] Richard D. Crisp, *Marketing Research* (New York: McGraw-Hill Book Company, Inc., 1957), ch. iii, esp. pp. 65–67.

of why people act as they do. Much of it is sponsored by institutions of higher learning or by foundations; consequently, the behavioral scientist is under no strong pressure to generate either quick or useful answers to practical problems. Also, the behavioral scientist does not have to justify his expenditure of the research funds in terms of profits or market share; all that is usually required is some type of manuscript such as a report, a journal article, or a monograph.

It will be very useful at this juncture to explain the character and the precise dimensions of the interrelationship between marketing research and behavioral science. At the beginning of this article it was suggested that marketing research, if defined broadly enough, would encompass behavioral science. However, up to this point the entire discussion has been limited to an analysis of the meaning of these two concepts. The next step will be an attempt to demonstrate, by means of example, the validity of this hypothesis.

APPLIED SOCIAL SCIENCE

If marketing research is intimately concerned with the substance of behavioral science, then it follows that marketing research might be viewed as an applied social science. This would be logical because an applied social science is above all concerned with the prediction and production of change in both social and personal behavior.[6] Broadly conceived, shopping, spending, and much of consumption is social behavior. Manufacturers, for example, want to be able to foresee changes in living patterns or spending habits in order to stay ahead of the market. Likewise, business firms, in introducing new products, want to be able to control or modify consumer behavior in order to have their innovations accepted by the masses. Thus the social change referred to here is limited to change in marketable behavior.[7]

The marketing researcher, as an applied social scientist, borrows concepts, ideas, hypotheses, principles, theories, and models from the behavioral sciences. Table 1 is a brief list of some of the tools and concepts which have been borrowed from behavioral science.

What is borrowed becomes part of the marketing researcher's technology. This point is well illustrated in the field of social stratification. Two sociologists, W. Lloyd Warner and Paul Lunt, developed a six-cate-

[6] Alvin W. Gouldner, "Explorations in Applied Social Science," *Marketing and Behavioral Sciences*, ed. Perry Bliss (Boston: Allyn and Bacon, Inc. 1963), p. 9.

[7] Over the past few years there have been several very interesting behavioral science studies dealing with this type of marketing problem. See for example, L. A. Fallers, "A Note on the Trickle Effect," *Public Opinion Quarterly* (Fall 1954); Saxon Graham, "Class and Conservatism in the Adoption of Innovation," *Human Relations,* IX: 1 (1956); Kurt Lewin, "Forces Behind Food Habits and Methods of Change," *The Problem of Changing Food Habits,* National Research Council Bulletin 108, Washington, D.C., October 1943.

gory social class framework, which they have used to analyze different communities.[8] This classification scheme has proved to be a very useful tool not only for other sociologists but for marketing researchers as well. A classic example of this can be found in the studies conducted by Pierre Martineau for the *Chicago Tribune*.[9] Using the Warnerian social class system, he studied the effects of social status, education, source of income, family background, and housing on consumer behavior.

It is no easy task to determine the value of such research for the marketing manager. The research findings of Pierre Martineau and others like him would probably not have been possible without help from the sociologist. Nevertheless, in a very practical sense manufacturers and retailers are now better able to understand the consumer and thereby anticipate his needs. Thus, for example, product research now has a sociological and psychological dimension it lacked when marketers used income as the primary index to family consumption.[10]

Group Theory

One area where behavioral science has made a significant contribution to marketing research is "group theory," particularly small group behavior. Sociologists and social psychologists, as opposed to clinical psychologists, tend to study individuals as group members. They have developed a classification scheme for studying groups just as Warner and Lunt did for analyzing society at large. Some of the more useful types of group concepts are: primary groups, reference groups, experimental groups, natural groups, and secondary groups.[11]

For the purposes of marketing research, primary groups and reference groups are perhaps the most important.

Wroe Alderson has argued that to understand market behavior the marketing man must come to grips with the organized behavior system. He says that "market behavior is primarily group behavior" because "individual action in the market is most characteristically action on behalf of some group in which the individual holds membership." [12] If Alderson

[8] Gregory P. Stone, "City Shoppers and Urban Identification: Observations of the Social Psychology of City Life," *American Journal of Sociology*, LX: 1 (1954), 36–45.

[9] See P. Martineau, "Social Classes and Spending Behavior," *Journal of Marketing*, October 1958, and *Motivation in Advertising* (New York: McGraw-Hill Book Company, Inc., 1957). See also Richard P. Coleman, "The Significance of Social Stratification in Selling," in Bliss, *op. cit.*, pp. 156–71.

[10] On this point see Sidney H. Levy's classic article, "Symbols for Sale," *Advancing Efficiency in Marketing*, ed. L. H. Stockman (Proceedings of the American Marketing Association, 1959), pp. 409–16.

[11] W. J. H. Sprott, *Human Groups* (Baltimore: Penguin Books, 1958).

[12] Wroe Alderson, "The Analytical Framework for Marketing," in Bliss, *op. cit.*, p. 32. See also Alderson, *Marketing Behavior and Executive Action* (Illinois: Richard D. Irwin, Inc., 1957), ch. vi.

is correct, then it is imperative that marketing research take into account the effect of group membership on spending and consumption. The anthropologist also deals with groups. One beer manufacturer wished to extend his market share among Negroes living in northern cities. An experienced anthropologist was consulted who pointed to the proven effects of Negroes' race membership on their purchasing behavior. The ambiguity of their role has led many Negroes to be sensitive to merchandise that has status connotations and sensitive to whether a brand symbolizes racial progress. On the recommendation of the anthropologist, the beer manufacturer began to support major social events related to the arts in Negro communities and began to identify the product with successful Negro personalities.

Household and Shopping Behavior

A clearer understanding of the utility of small group theory for marketing research can be derived from a close examination of certain studies which have been made on household behavior. Households, strictly speaking, are not families but have many of the same characteristics. The social psychologist would probably classify a household as a primary group; [13] if the household also happened to be a family it could function as a membership group, which is a specific type of reference group.[14] The economist, on the other hand, tends to view the household as a decision-making organization engaged in much the same activities as a business firm.[15] Certain types of expenditures (e.g., consumer durables), it has been found, are primarily group decisions.[16] The research also shows that households tend to budget expenditures differently depending on such things as social class, neighborhood, income expectations, status, and need.[17]

Once it has been determined that identification with a group can have a significant effect on shopping and spending behavior, the prudent marketing researcher must take this fact into account. He must become

[13] Relatively small number of people in face-to-face relationship.

[14] There are several important kinds of reference groups. Reference groups may be *categories* to which an individual automatically belongs by virtue of age, sex, etc. Interestingly enough there are negative or dissociative reference groups which the individual seeks to avoid.

[15] Robert Ferber, "Research on Household Behavior," *The American Economic Review*, March 1962, p. 49. It should be noted that the social psychologist has, along with the economist, been interested in the economic aspects of family life. See M. Young, "Income Within the Family," *British Journal of Sociology*, III (1962), 318.

[16] E. A. Wilkening, "Joint Decision-Making in Farm Families as a Function of Status and Role," *American Sociological Review*, XXIII (1958). Aiderson, *Marketing Behavior and Executive Action, loc. cit.*

[17] W. Lloyd Warner and Paul Lunt, *The Social Life of a Modern Community* (New Haven: Yale University Press, 1940): W. Lloyd Warner, Marchia Meeker, Kenneth Fells, *Social Class in America* (Chicago: Science Research Associates, 1949).

an applied social scientist by not only integrating these new research findings into his own models but also by pioneering some behavioral research on his own. To illustrate, social psychologists have discovered that in the absence of objective standards or accepted authority, an individual will turn to other people for judgments and evaluations.[18] For the marketing manager this may mean that a buyer is more inclined to seek others' advice in purchasing a new product; however, the commercial value of this research finding will largely depend on the subsequent research efforts of marketing people.[19]

Shopping behavior has always been an important marketing problem. Surveys to discover why shoppers patronize particular retailers or certain shopping centers have limited predictive utility. Behavioral science has recently found that it is possible to discover some basic sociopsychological attributes of shoppers, which can be useful to marketers. An intensive field study by a sociologist yielded a useful four category classification scheme of shoppers.[20] Dr. Stone discovered that women shoppers patronized stores on the basis of their personality. He classified them according to whether they were: (a) economic consumers, (b) personalizing consumers, (c) ethical consumers, or (d) apathetic consumers. For example, economic consumers are primarily motivated by low prices while at the other extreme the apathetic consumer shops wherever it is most convenient.

Consumer Behavior

Orthodox marketing research studies generally reveal little about *why* consumers act as they do. In this sense, statistics do lie. A cereal manufacturer may want to know his market share, tonnage shipped, sales increase or decrease; but he should also want to know whether his cereal is eaten because of habit, impulse, price, or for other reasons. Behavioral science can help because superimposed across the entire gamut of consumer knowledge and motivation is the character of the product itself. Some products have the capacity to get consumers ego-involved to a high degree—others do not.

Psychologists have developed a product classification scheme totally different from any found in marketing texts. This classification is based

[18] M. Sherif, "Group Influences Upon the Formation of Norms and Attitudes," *Readings in Social Psychology,* eds. E. E. Maccoby, T. M. Newcomb, and E. C. Hartley (3rd ed.; New York: Holt, Rinehart and Winston, Inc., 1958).

[19] In other words, the consumer's membership in or identification with certain groups affects his perception of the real world, his aspiration levels, his contentment, his desire to conform, and so forth. Behavioral scientists have not been able to refine many of their preliminary findings. It is to be hoped that tomorrow's marketing researcher will be able to add substantially to these findings.

[20] Stone, *op. cit.*

on the types of psychological demands the products have on consumers: [21]

Demands of ego-involvement in the external symbols which the product conveys. ("All executive wives wear mink.")
Hedonic demand. ("It's such a pretty hat, I must buy it.")
Functional demands. ("Give me the 19¢ aspirin.")

The first group above can be further broken down into four subclasses of product where ego-involvement is at issue: (1) prestige products (Rolls Royce), (2) maturity products (cigarettes for young people), (3) status products (color TV), (4) anxiety products (mouth wash). This behavioral type product classification scheme can be very useful to the marketer in planning a promotional campaign where the strategy of market segmentation is to be used.

CONCLUSION

Marketing research is growing up and is today, in many respects, close to maturity. Part of its continued growth process will be the recognition and acceptance of the value of behavioral science for marketing research. This point of view is well expressed by John A. Howard in his book, *Marketing: Executive and Buyer Behavior*. He says: "The contribution of market research to decision in practice has sometimes been less than it ought to be. Another weakness . . . has been the tendency to ignore the need for generalized knowledge—a theory—of human behavior in a buying context." [22] This broad social science view of marketing research is consistent with the new "marketing concept" of business management.

The purpose of this article has not been to survey the entire field of behavioral science attempting to delineate its commercial value potential. This article is merely an attempt to argue the proposition that marketing research should be defined more broadly to include the concepts, tools, definitions, and models of behavioral science. The limited evidence or examples were introduced, not to conclusively prove the point, but rather to dramatize the need for this new attitude towards marketing research.

[21] Walter Woods, "Psychological Dimensions of Consumer Decision," *Journal of Marketing*, XXIV: 3 (January 1960), 15–19.
[22] John A. Howard, *Marketing: Executive and Buyer Behavior* (New York: Columbia University Press, 1963), p. 7.

14. Anthropology's contributions to marketing

CHARLES WINICK

The relative slowness of anthropologists and marketers in finding common ground is surprising.[1] Anthropologists have served as colonial administrators, in foreign-aid programs, and in other situations requiring a special sensitivity to foreign cultures. They have also developed sales-training procedures which involve the analysis of the rate of speech of salesmen with potential customers, through devices which measure the rate of interaction between people talking.[2] Another specialized industrial situation in which anthropologists have worked involves the application of their knowledge of the field of anthropometry or measurement of the body, in the design of products like chairs and knobs.[3]

Other anthropologists have worked in applied fields such as: reactions to disaster, the operation of internment and relocation centers, mental health, medical care, labor-management relations,[4] the culture of a factory,[5] community organization, social work,[6] military government, the

Reprinted from the *Journal of Marketing*, Volume 25 (July, 1961), pp. 53–60, National Quarterly Publication of the American Marketing Association.

[1] John Gillin, "The Application of Anthropological Knowledge to Modern Mass Society," *Human Organization*, Vol. 15 (Winter, 1957), pp. 24–30.

[2] Eliot D. Chapple, "The Interaction Chronograph," *Personnel*, Vol. 25 (January, 1949), pp. 295–307.

[3] Earnest A. Hooton, *A Survey in Seating* (Cambridge: Harvard Department of Anthropology, 1945).

[4] Charles R. Walker, *The Man on the Assembly Line* (Cambridge: Harvard University Press, 1952).

[5] Eliot Jaques, *The Changing Culture of a Factory* (New York: Dryden Press, 1953).

[6] Franklin K. Patterson, Irving Lukoff, and Charles Winick, "Is Society the Patient," *Journal of Educational Sociology*, Vol. 30 (October, 1956), pp. 106–112.

cultural change associated with economic development,[7] contact between cultures, the nature of small-town life, behavior in extreme situations, the study of culture at a distance,[8] the reconstruction of the themes of a culture, relations among minority groups, the social structure of a hospital,[9] American national character,[10] and television.[11]

Although anthropologists have published their findings on America in very accessible formats,[12] there has been little discussion of how their findings could be applied to marketing problems.[13] One advertising publication has published an article on the possibility of using anthropology in advertising.[14] The journal of applied anthropology, formerly called *Applied Anthropology* and now called *Human Organization*, almost never carries any material on marketing; and the national journal, *American Anthropologist*, also ignores the subject.

ANTHROPOLOGY, SOCIOLOGY, AND PSYCHOLOGY

Anthropology is usually defined as the study of man. Such a definition is so all-inclusive that the field is generally divided into four subfields: archeology, cultural anthropology, linguistics, and physical anthropology. Archeology is concerned with the historical reconstruction of cultures which no longer exist. Cultural anthropology examines all the behaviors of man which have been learned, including social, linguistic, technical, and familiar behaviors; often it is defined as the study of man and his works. Linguistics is the comparative study of the structure, interrelationships, and development of languages. Physical anthropology is concerned with human biology and the development of the human organism, with special interest in race differences.

When anthropology is employed in marketing, it is usually cultural anthropology which is relevant. Cultural anthropology began with the

[7] Almost every issue of *Economic Development and Cultural Change* carries relevant articles.

[8] Margaret Mead and Rhoda Metraux, *The Study of Culture at a Distance* (Chicago: University of Chicago Press, 1952).

[9] Charles Winick, "The Hospital as a Social System," *New York State Nurse,* Vol. 26 (January, 1954), pp. 9–13.

[10] David M. Potter, *People of Plenty* (Chicago: University of Chicago Press, 1954).

[11] Charles Winick, *Taste and the Censor in Television* (New York: Fund for the Republic, 1959).

[12] Margaret Lantis, editor, "The U.S.A. as Anthropologists See It," *American Anthropologist,* Vol. 57 (December, 1955), pp. 1113–1380.

[13] Richard C. Sheldon, "How the Anthropologist Can Help the Marketing Practitioner" in W. David Robbins, editor, *Successful Marketing at Home and Abroad* (Chicago: American Marketing Association, 1958), pp. 209–304.

[14] Alan S. Marcus, "How Agencies Can Use Anthropology in Advertising," *Advertising Agency,* Vol. 49 (September 14, 1956), pp. 87–91.

study of primitive cultures, and its comparative analyses documented the different ways in which cultures have solved their problems of living.

Cultural anthropology has much in common with psychology and sociology. All three are concerned with the examination of man in his cultural setting. They differ in the emphases which they place on different elements of the relationship between a person and his environment. It can be said that all human behavior essentially is a function of the interrelations of personality, the social system, and culture.

Oversimplifying, psychology is concerned with personality, sociology addresses itself to the social system, and anthropology explores the culture. The interdisciplinary field of social psychology may draw on all three of these fields, and there are integrated social psychology texts which do so.[15]

A sharper focus on the differences among these three social sciences may be obtained by speculating on how each of the three might look at a family.

The psychologist would be interested in the personal adjustment and emotional health of each member of the family. He would want to examine their attitudes, mutual perceptions, and motivational systems. Their happiness or lack of it would interest him.

The sociologist would be concerned primarily with the dimensions of role and status within the family and with the number of different kinds of families. He would examine how the social structure created various kinds of internal arrangements which made it possible for the family to exist. He would be interested in the norms of behavior and the stresses and strains shown by the deviations from the norm and resulting from role conflict. He would study class membership as well as the rates of various kinds of behavior, such as the birth rate.

The cultural anthropologist would examine the technological level which the culture had reached and the interrelations of technology with culture. He would scrutinize the procedures for inheritance of property and how kinship was reckoned and described, and how the spouses got to know each other. He would study the family's food and housing. He would be interested in the language level and dialects and in who talked to whom. He would be concerned with how the age of different members of the family affected their behavior, and with trends in illnesses. He would study how the culture "rubbed off" on the family unit. The anthropologist thus does not have information which it would be impossible for the sociologist or psychologist to obtain, but he has a special sensitivity to certain facets of social life.

The sociologist and psychologist bring a powerful and varied arsenal

[15] Steuart Henderson Britt, *Social Psychology of Modern Life* (New York: Rinehart & Company, 1949 revised edition). S. Stanfeld Sargent and Robert C. Williamson, *Social Psychology* (New York: The Ronald Press Company, 1958).

of concepts and approaches to the study of social life. In what ways is the anthropologist able to contribute insights and experience toward the science of "marketology," and to what extent may they not be immediately accessible, for example, to the sociologist? [16] The anthropologist is especially trained to have empathy with groups other than his own and to "tune in" on their patterns of culture. Inasmuch as his training has exposed him to a wide variety of cultures, he can take a global view of a situation and see it in the context of a larger background. His training makes him sensitive to cross-cultural differences which may be of crucial importance in many different situations, because his entire training is geared toward awareness of such differences.

Anthropology has less of the factionalism which characterizes psychology and sociology. This is not to suggest that all is serene in anthropology or that it has never been troubled by theoretical or methodological issues. However, even though anthropologists may disagree on something like the exact value of the contribution of a particular anthropologist, they would generally agree on what the cultural anthropologist looks for, and there are standardized check lists on how to view a culture.[17] In contrast, a psychologist's allegiance to the Gestalt, behaviorist, psychoanalytic, learning-theory, or perception schools is likely to influence what he does with a given problem. A sociologist's commitment to the structure-function, historical, ecological, "middle range," environmental-determinism, or demographic schools would largely determine the emphases of his approach to a problem. Since such divergent schools are less likely to exist in cultural anthropology, it is probable that anthropological guidance on a given marketing problem woud be relatively consistent.

WHAT THE ANTHROPOLOGIST KNOWS

The anthropologist is specifically trained to study national character, or the differences which distinguish one national group from another. He should be able to provide measures for distinguishing the subtle differences among a Swede, a Dane, and a Norwegian; or between a Frenchman and an Englishman; or a Brazilian and an Argentinian; or between a typical resident of Montreal and one of Toronto. The anthropologist is also a specialist in the study of subcultures. He would be able, in a city like New York, to differentiate the patterns of living of such disparate but rapidly homogenizing groups as Puerto Ricans, Negroes, Italo-Americans, Jews, Polish-Americans, and Irish-Americans.

[16] Robert Bartels, "Sociologists and Marketologists," *Journal of Marketing*, Vol. 24 (October, 1959), pp. 37–40; Christen T. Jonassen, "Contributions of Sociology to Marketing," *Journal of Marketing*, Vol. 24 (October, 1959), pp. 29–35.

[17] Royal Anthropological Institute, *Notes and Queries on Anthropology* (London: The Institute, 1956).

Because almost any large community consists of a variety of sub-cultures, this awareness of subcultural trends can be especially useful. A more subtle area of special interest to anthropologists is the silent language of gesture, posture, food and drink preferences, and other non-verbal cues to behavior.[18]

Related to this is the anthropologist's professional interest in languages and symbols. He might, for example, be especially concerned about why a particular shape has special significance as a symbol in a society, or how the structure of a language or a regional speech pattern was related to how people think.[19]

Another area of concern to the anthropologist, because of its symbolic meanings, has to do with "rites de passage" or the central points in a person's life at which he may ritually be helped to go from one status to another, for example, birth, puberty, or marriage.[20]

Taboos represent a continuing area of interest to the anthropologist.[21] Every culture has taboos or prohibitions about various things, such as the use of a given color, or of a given phrase or symbol. The anthropologist is aware of the larger values of a culture, which represent the substratum of custom which is taken for granted and the violation of which represents a taboo.

The anthropologist's method is primarily the exposure of his highly developed sensitivity to the area in which he is working, via observation and extended interviews with informants. Projective tests have also been widely used in anthropological studies. The anthropologist can bring a wealth of insight to marketing situations.

USE OF ANTHROPOLOGY IN MARKETING

There are at least three kinds of situations in which the knowledge of the anthropologist has been employed in marketing: specific knowledge; awareness of themes of a culture; sensitivity to taboos.

Specific Knowledge

Here are a few cases in which the specific knowledge of an anthropologist was applied to marketing situations.

A manufacturer of central heating equipment was planning to introduce central heating to an area which previously had used other heating. Since people generally grow up to accept a certain approach to heating which they take for granted, introduction of the new central heating

[18] Edward T. Hall, *The Silent Language* (New York: Doubleday & Co., 1959).
[19] Benjamin Lee Whorf, *Collected Papers on Metalinguistics* (Washington: Department of State Foreign Service Institute, 1952).
[20] Jan Wit, *Rites De Passage* (Amsterdam: De Windroos, 1959).
[21] Franz Steiner, *Taboo* (London: Cohen and West, Ltd., 1957).

posed marketing problems in coping with deeply imbedded consumer resistance to what would be a major innovation. An anthropologist was able to draw on his knowledge of the folklore and symbolism of heat and fire in order to suggest methods of presenting the new system, so as to make it as consonant as possible with the connotations of heat, even though the nature of the heating method had changed radically. There was considerable consumer resistance to the central heating, but it decreased substantially after the first year.

In addition to a marketing problem, the introduction of central heating also posed problems of public policy which the manufacturer had to overcome before he could obtain approval for the introduction of the heating equipment. The area was one which suffered from a declining birth rate, and officials were concerned about the extent to which central heating might cause the birth rate to decline further, because of their belief that heated bedrooms would cause a decline in sexual activity and ultimately in births.

The anthropologist was able to point to some cultures in which the birth rate had declined and some in which it had not done so after the introduction of central heating. The anthropologist's data made it possible for the manufacturer of the central-heating equipment to discuss its probable effects realistically with the appropriate officials.

Another field in which the anthropologist has specific knowledge that other social scientists are not likely to have is that of clothing and fashion. The only empirical study of the fashion cycle in woman's clothing which has successfully been used for predictive purposes by clothing manufacturers was conducted by anthropologists.[22] In marketing situations, the anthropologist has often been able to combine his special knowledge of the needs of the body for clothing of various kinds at different ages, his sensitivity to what technology makes possible and his awareness of fashion.

For example, an anthropologist was consulted by a leading manufacturer of overalls for young children, a product which had remained unchanged for decades. He examined the product in the light of the special needs of children who wear overalls, the growing use of washing machines to launder the overalls, their relative frequency of laundering, and contemporary technology. He suggested that the overall straps have a series of sets of metal grippers instead of buttons, thus making it possible to use different sets of grippers as the child grew instead of tying or knotting the straps. Noting that the straps often fall off the shoulders when children played, he suggested that the shirts which children wore under the overalls have either a loop for the straps to pass through or a synthetic fastener which faced matching material on the strap, so that

[22] Jane Richardson and Alfred L. Kroeber, *Three Centuries of Women's Dress Fashions* (Berkeley: University of California Press, 1940).

the shoulder of the shirt could be pressed against the strap and remain attached to it until shoulder strap and shirt were pulled apart.

He also recommended that the seams of the overalls, previously single stitched, be double stitched like those of men's shirts, which have to withstand frequent launderings. The double-stitched overalls would be less likely to come apart as a result of frequent launderings in a washing machine. These recommendations were adopted, and within a few years substantially changed and expanded the nature of the overall market for young children. The children's parents were more pleased with the overalls because they lasted longer and looked better on the children, and they were far more functional than before.

The special knowledge of the anthropologist has been called into play where there are special subcultural groups to which the marketer wishes to address himself. One beer manufacturer wished to extend his market share among Negroes in a large eastern city in the United States. He was advised about reaching this group by an anthropologist who was familiar with the special subculture of Negroes, and who pointed to the profound effects of Negroes' caste membership on their purchasing behavior. The ambiguity of their role has led many Negroes to be especially aware of articles that have status connotations and of whether a brand symbolizes racial progress. Examination of the manufacturer's marketing program by the anthropologist led to several recommendations for change. The manufacturer began to help in the support of several major social events related to the arts in Negro communities, and to stress that the beer was a national brand with quality-control procedures. He changed the content of his advertising in the direction of enhancing its status and quality connotations. These changes were all directed toward improving the status connotations of the beer to Negroes.

Guidance on related problems with respect to the Puerto Rican and Jewish markets has also been used constructively. Since 35 to 40 percent of the population of the United States consists of minority subcultures, the anthropologist's contributions may be considerable.

Another situation had to do with the selection of specific symbols for various purposes. A major manufacturer of women's products was uncertain about whether to continue using the Fleur de Lis emblem on his package. Anthropological analysis of the symbol suggested that its association with French kings and other cultural connotations of maleness made it more masculine than feminine. The anthropologist's recommendations were confirmed by subsequent field testing.

In a related case, a manufacturer of women's cosmetics conducted an anthropological study of the comparative symbolism in our culture of women's eyes and mouth, which suggested that the eye tends to be experienced as a relatively protecting organ while the mouth tends to be experienced as more nurturing. This knowledge of the differences between the special meanings of eye and mouth could constructively be used in marketing the products, and especially in advertising. The advertising explicitly and implicitly mentioned the role of the eye in protection of the woman. It stressed the role of the mouth as the organ which both symbolically and literally gives love. This replaced the manufacturer's previous advertising, in which both eye and mouth were treated in the same way, as organs which could be made beautiful.

Awareness of Themes

The anthropologist has functioned in situations in which he can use his special understanding of themes of a culture, oftentimes taken for granted.

A major chain of candy shops was suffering a decline in sales. A marketing-research study had established that the brand was usually bought as a gift, either for others or as a gift for the purchaser. The chain was unable to develop any ways of using this finding that were not hackneyed. Anthropological guidance on the symbolism of gift-giving enabled the chain to develop merchandising, packaging, and advertising formats for the gift theme. Anthropological study of the connotations of the major holidays suggested themes for window displays, and advertising of the candy in conjunction with the holidays. The chain's marketing strategy was revised on the basis of the anthropological interpretation and clarification of the marketing-research study. Anthropologists are the only social scientists who have systematically studied gift-giving and gift-receiving.[23]

Another example of anthropological interpretation of a marketing-research study was provided by a shirt manufacturer. The study had established that women buy more than half of men's shirts in a particular price range. The anthropologist was able to interpret this finding in the light of several anthropological studies of the relations between husbands and wives in America. The manufacturer had been thinking of placing advertising for his men's shirts in selected women's magazines. The anthropologist was able to point to a number of studies of husband-wife relations which suggested growing resentment by men over the extent to which women had been borrowing and buying men's clothing, and which suggested that the proposed advertising campaign might not be propitious.

Another anthropologist's special sensitivity to the "rites de passage" helped a shoe manufacturer whose sales were declining because of aggressive foreign and domestic competition. The anthropologist was able to point to the extent to which shoes represent major symbols of our going from one stage of life to another, and to assist the manufacturer in

[23] Marcel Mauss, *The Gift* (London: Cohen & West, Ltd., 1954).

developing methods for using the relationship between shoes and "rites de passage." [24]

A landmark along the road of an infant becoming a child usually is found between the ages of 4 and 6 when he can tie his own shoe laces. The manufacturer developed some pamphlets and other instructional material for parents on how to help children to learn to tie their shoe laces. Distribution by local retailers contributed toward making parents favorably aware of the brand's line for children in this age group.

The teenager signalizes her entrance into a new social world by her first high heels. Window displays and advertising which explicitly stressed the new social activities of the teenager wearing her high heels, and naming specific shoe models after teenage social events ("The Prom") contributed toward associating the manufacturer's name with the excitement of the new world symbolized by the high heels.

Older people see the wearing of special "old people's shoes" as the ultimate reminder that they are becoming old. The manufacturer was able to redesign his line for older people so that it retained its special health features but still looked as stylish as any adult shoe, and had no visible stigma of "old people's shoes."

Sensitivity to Taboos

Marketers may unwittingly violate taboos, whether cultural, religious, or political, especially in selling overseas. Blue, for example, is the color for mourning in Iran and is not likely to be favorably received on a commercial product. Green is the nationalist color of Egypt and Syria and is frowned on for use in packages. Showing pairs of anything on the Gold Coast of Africa is disapproved. White is the color of mourning in Japan and, therefore, not likely to be popular on a product. Brown and gray are disapproved colors in Nicaragua. Purple is generally disapproved in most Latin American markets because of its association with death. Feet are regarded as despicable in Thailand, where any object and package showing feet is likely to be unfavorably received.

The anthropologist can cast light on taboos and on their opposite: favored colors and symbols. The reason for the people in a country or an area liking or not liking a particular color or symbol may be a function of political, nationalist, religious, cultural, or other reasons.

SOME APPLICATIONS IN CANADA

Canada represents a special opportunity for the application of anthropology in marketing situations. Twenty-nine percent of the country's

---

[24] Charles Winick, "Status, Shoes, and the Life Cycle," *Boot and Shoe Recorder*, Vol. 156 (October 15, 1959), pp. 100–202.

entire population is in French-speaking Quebec, and over half of this number know no English. Canada thus offers a changing kind of bilingual and culture contact situation with major cross-cultural differences for anthropological analysis.

Both the farm community and the industrial community of Quebec have been studied by anthropologists.[25] The re-evaluation of the nature of Quebec family and community life sparked by Dean Phillipe Garigue of the University of Montreal and a team at Laval University has led to renewed interest in Quebec on the part of anthropologists. Their studies have produced considerable information on styles of life in Quebec which should be translatable into marketing data on pricing policies, colors, package size, flavor and taste of various food items, texture of fabrics, automobile symbolism, product scents, and related subjects.

Specific Knowledge

Perhaps the most frequent occasion for the anthropologist to demonstrate specific knowledge in Canada has to do with language. One laundry-soap company had point-of-sale material on its soap describing it as extra strong and the best one to use on especially dirty parts of wash ("les parts de sale"). After sales of the soap had declined, an anthropologist who was called in by the company pointed out that the phrase is comparable to the American slang phrase "private parts." This kind of mistake might have been avoided if anthropological guidance had been available before sales declined.

Some products do not sell well in Quebec because the English name may be almost unpronounceable to a French speaker, or the name of the product may be meaningless even when translated idiomatically. Even the English spoken in Montreal differs somewhat from the English spoken in Toronto, creating potential hazards for the marketers who may not know, for example that a "tap" in a "flat" in Toronto is likely to be a "faucet" in a Montreal "apartment."

Awareness of Themes

A study done by an anthropologist for a food manufacturer demonstrated the relationship between the purchases of certain food items and the gradual decline of the wood-burning stove which used to be a staple of Quebec farm kitchens. The wood stove would almost always have a stew pot ("pot au feu") simmering all day. Various ingredients were put into the pot to provide flavor. With the introduction of gas and electric kitchen ranges, it not only became relatively expensive to keep the

---

[25] Horace Miner, St. Denis (Chicago, University of Chicago Press, 1939); Everett C. Hughes, French Canada In Transition (Chicago: University of Chicago Press, 1943).

stew pot going but the simmering could not be sustained because the pot would tend to boil rather than simmer.

This change was accompanied by some radical adjustments in food consumption which were of great relevance to food marketing. The manufacturer was able to begin distribution of canned soups and stews which soon found a very large market and rapidly replaced the "pot au feu."

Taboos

Alertness to taboos was illustrated by an anthropologist's suggestion to a manufacturer of canned fish for changing a series of advertisements which were appearing in Quebec magazines and newspapers. The same advertisement was run repeatedly. The advertisements showed a woman in shorts playing golf with her husband. The caption read that the woman would be able to be on the golf links all day and still prepare a delicious dinner that evening if she used the product. Every element in the advertisement represented a violation of some underlying theme of French Canadian life; the wife would not be likely to be playing golf with her husband, she would not wear shorts, and she would not be serving the particular kind of fish as a main course. In this case, the anthropologist was consulted *after* the series had been running for awhile.

THE MARKETER AS AN ANTHROPOLOGIST

A good case could be made for the thesis that marketing researchers do more anthropological research on modern cultures than do anthropologists. Marketing researchers are studying national character, subcultures, themes, and ways of life. The kind of information which marketing-research studies seek on how people live and what products they use represent first-rate material for the cultural anthropologist.

The questionnaire, panel, audit, sales analysis, and other methods of modern marketing differ in degree but not in kind from the trained observations of the anthropologist, but there is no reason why the two methods cannot complement each other. Greater communication between these two fields can and should lead to mutual enrichment of both.

15. The significance of ethnic groups in marketing new-type packaged foods in Greater New York

MILTON ALEXANDER

To manufacturers and distributors of new-type packaged foods, Greater New York ranks first as a market and as a marketing enigma. On the one hand, it is easily the largest spender for foods among the 168 standard metropolitan areas. On the other, it is most unyielding to product innovations.

Hence, the perennial questions of food marketers: What is it that makes New York so different from other marketing areas? And what, if anything, can and should be done to adjust for the difference? According to a traditional hypothesis, the area's atypical pattern of consumer behavior stems from the heterogeneous nature of its population. New York is said to comprise a melting pot of several fairly distinct ethnic markets in one.

Based on a pilot study, this hypothesis oversimplified local food marketing problems. Furthermore, assumptions of ethnic difference were found to rest on long-established hunch rather than current fact. As such, they were largely unrelated to the present-day ethnic setting and to the new-type products which represent an ever-increasing share of consumer expenditures for food. In short, there was an evident need to modernize the traditional hypothesis and to establish guideposts for marketers in this and other heterogeneous areas. This study represents a beginning attempt to fill both needs. It brings up to date the food habits of four

Reprinted from *Proceedings,* American Marketing Association Conference, 1958 (Stockman, Editor), by permission of the American Marketing Association, pp. 557–561.

major ethnic-groups—Italian, Jewish, Negro, and Puerto Rican. More pointedly, it explores the impact of inter- and intra-group differences on acceptance of six "model" new-type products—frozen food dinner, frozen red meat, frozen fruit pie, instant coffee, cake mixes, and dehydrated soups.

Despite all countervailing socio-economic pressures, ethnic food habits continue to prevail in Greater New York. The ethnic setting, therefore, remains a necessary basis for local food marketing strategy and practice. This is particularly so with regard to new food products. Further, an awareness of ethnic differences and of dynamic internal changes (both socio-economic and dietetic) may lessen the marketer's acceptance of behavioral myths regarding ethnic groups.

From the marketers' point of view, the residual ethnic influence in food consumption is variously affected by demographic trends. In the case of Negroes and Puerto Ricans, by an accelerated rate of in-migration; a clustering in the inner city; and an apartness from the general population. In the case of Jews, by conflicting drives toward cultural assimilation and continued clustering even in the adjacent suburbs. And finally, among Italians, by the increased incidence of inter-marriage with "outsiders."

Meanwhile, ethnic food habits have shown a remarkable resilience even under pressure for conformity. Consumption patterns are still evolving. The following is a sampling of significant ethnic attitudes toward foods new and old.

Beginning with typical second-generation Italian housewives, there appears to be a marked residual antagonism toward processed-packaged foods which, incidentally, fail to appear in 80 percent of the group's lunches, 64 percent of its suppers, and 95 percent of its breakfasts. Also, freshness remains the dominant appeal in Italian usage of coffee, vegetables, and meat. At the same time, more housewives are being swayed toward product innovations by the convenience of new-type packaged foods.

The same is true of second-generation Jewish housewives. Thus, 90 percent of Jewish families were found to prefer fresh to canned or frozen alternatives. And about one of three of their breakfasts and one of five of their suppers featured one or more traditional delicacies.

Many young Negro housewives also tend to adhere to their traditional diets. For example, the use of meat at many breakfasts; the preference for starchy products; and the aversion for "raw foods." On the other hand, many ethnic traditions are weakening. By and large, young Negro housewives are found to rebel against the low-income meat-meal-molasses or rice-beans-plantain diets. And in growing numbers, they adopt processed-packaged foods as symbols of social status.

The Puerto Rican diet represents a unique blend of traditional and new-type food preferences. So strong is the ethnic effect, however, that the low-income tropical diet generally prevails. New-type foods, therefore, are supplements to, rather than substitutes for, traditional favorites. Nevertheless, almost every type of packaged food innovation has breached the group's ethnic loyalties.

Now, specifically, how does this dynamic ethnic setting for some 55 percent of New York's population, affect the acceptance of new-type packaged foods? In partial answer, let us review the major findings for each of the six "model" foods featured in this study.

First, frozen food dinner. Italian acceptance is apparently hampered by deep-seated ethnic preferences for fresh meat and vegetables. Sales prospects are brightened only by two relatively minor offsets in the ethnic diet. First, by the continued simplicity of Italian meals. And second, by the group's traditional liking for processed-packaged fish. In any event, Italians place last in rate of consumption. In the Jewish group, a residual ethnic influence seems to militate against large-scale acceptance. The net upshot: Jews rank last in most indices of acceptance. Product convenience is recognized. But this "like" is outweighed by the "dislike" of product taste and expense. Negroes also tend to resist frozen food dinners —seemingly on traditional grounds. The net result is widespread use but in limited quantities. At the other end of the acceptance scale, Puerto Ricans are found to lead all other groups in rate of consumption, presumably due to the high incidence of working housewives within this group.

Italians rank at least second in ethnic acceptance of the second "model" product—frozen red meat. But consumption by Jews is obviously discouraged by the dietary laws—especially in the case of pork. Regardless of variety, however, Jewish consumers resist the product's taste and price. Frozen red meat is also opposed to the Negroes' traditional preference for fresh and fatty cuts. Their resistance is further hardened by the prevailing inadequacy of refrigeration in Negro homes. In the case of Puerto Rican housewives, ethnic distaste for the product is at least partly offset by the working housewives' need for convenience. Puerto Ricans lead in all indices of acceptance. This showing, however, is almost entirely confined to the more economical luncheon cuts.

Frozen fruit pie, the third "model" product, seems to hold but little interest for Italians. At any rate, they rank last in per-capita consumption —avowedly due to a marked dislike of flavor. Jewish consumers do relish sweet goods, but of a distinctive type—either baked at home or available in the many specialty bakeries throughout the area. Principally for this reason, they rank last in regular usage of the frozen product. Also, as per tradition, Negroes still do not "take to" fruit pies. Hence, their bottom score in rate of consumption. In contrast, the Puerto Ricans' craving for sweets is so intense that it seems to overcome the group's dislike of product taste and expense. Usage of the product is still spotty, however.

A strong residual preference for their special blend sharpens Italian resistance to instant coffee—the fourth "model" food. As a result, Italians trail other ethnic groups (excepting Negroes) in rate of consumption. In contrast, instant meets with a favorable response from Jewish consumers. Due to the group's tea-drinking tradition, the rivalry of regular coffee is minimized. Instant, however, is found to be an addition to the group's cultural inventory rather than a replacement for an established item. While the Negroes' ethnic diet also favors acceptance of instant, countervailing socio-economic forces tip the balance against heavy consumption. Actually, Negroes are found to rank last in terms of actual purchases. As with Italians, the Puerto Ricans's traditional diet also features a distinctive type of coffee. Here, however, opposition to instant is tempered by light coffee-drinking habits. And according to the indices of acceptance, Puerto Ricans rank second in per-capita consumption.

Similar implications may be read into the acceptance ratings of cake mix. Here, for reasons already cited in connection with frozen fruit pie, both Italians and Negroes are found near the bottom of the acceptance index, but just a notch above the Jewish group, which is in last place. Puerto Ricans (for all their difficulty in deciphering package directions) seemingly lead the other ethnic groups.

The sixth "model" food—dehydrated soup—also fares rather badly in the Italian diet, at least in comparison with the sales potential of the generic product. Thus, while Italians rank first in usage (vs. non-usage), users in the group rank only fourth in per-capita consumption. In the Jewish group, non-usage still appears to be the rule. Typically, Negroes seem to use dehydrated soup in limited amounts; and they trail all other groups in the indices of acceptance. In rather familiar contrast, the elastic food habits of the young Puerto Rican group have also yielded to this new-type product in large measure.

Now, one may ask: How can manufacturers and retailers implement these varying manifestations of the ethnic effect? There is no simple answer because there is no pat formula for "segment selling"—one that would cover all products and all groups across the board and regardless of time period. An ethnic marketing approach, therefore, demands a separate and distinct adjustment for each combination of ethnic group and new-type packaged food.

For the manufacturer, this selective approach would find useful application in the formulation of marketing strategy and in estimating sales potentials—even if only as a qualitative guide. It would also help him capitalize on opportunities for sectional listing of new products in the large food chains, in in-store promotion, in couponing, and in the deployment of missionaries. At the very least, a fact-based approach to ethnic groups could reduce losses due to a misdirection of promotional efforts. Similar benefits would accrue to super market operators in developing new store locations and in making optimum adjustments, in their merchandising, for significant ethnic differences.

16. Projective techniques in marketing research

MASON HAIRE

It is a well accepted maxim in merchandizing that, in many areas, we are selling the sizzle rather than the steak. Our market research techniques, however, in many of these same areas, are directed toward the steak. The sizzle is the subjective reaction of the consumer; the steak the objective characteristics of the product. The consumer's behavior will be based on the former rather than the latter set of characteristics. How can we come to know them better?

When we approach a consumer directly with questions about his reaction to a product we often get false and misleading answers to our questions. Very often this is because the question which we heard ourselves ask was not the one (or not the only one) that the respondent heard. For example: A brewery made two kinds of beer. To guide their merchandizing techniques they wanted to know what kind of people drank each kind, and particularly, what differences there were between the two groups of consumers. A survey was conducted which led up to the questions "Do you drink ———— beer?" (If *yes*) "Do you drink the *Light* or *Regular?*" (These were the two trade names under which the company marketed.) After identifying the consumers of each product it was possible to find out about the characteristics of each group so that appropriate appeals could be used, media chosen, etc.

An interesting anomaly appeared in the survey data, however. The interviewing showed (on a reliable sample) that consumers drank *Light* over *Regular* in the ratio of 3 to 1. The company had been producing and selling Regular over Light for some time in a ratio of 9 to 1. Clearly,

Reprinted from the *Journal* of *Marketing*, Volume 14 (April, 1950), pp. 649–656, National Quarterly Publication of the American Marketing Association.

the attempt to identify characteristics of the two kinds was a failure. What made them miss so far?

When we say "Do you drink *Light* or *Regular?*" we are at once asking which brand is used, but also, to some extent, saying "Do you drink the regular run-of-the-mill product or do you drink the one that is more refined and shows more discrimination and taste?" The preponderance of "Light" undoubtedly flows from this kind of distortion.

When we ask questions of this sort about the product we are very often asking also about the respondent. Not only do we say "What is ——— product like?" but, indirectly "What are *you* like?" Our responses are often made up of both elements inextricably interwoven. The answers to the second question will carry clichés and stereotypes, blocks, inhibitions, and distortions, whenever we approach an area that challenges the person's idea of himself.

There are many things that we need to know about a consumer's reaction to a product that he can not tell us because they are to some extent socially unacceptable. For instance, the snob appeal of a product vitally influences its sale, but it is a thing that the consumer will not like to discuss explicitly. In other cases the consumer is influenced by motives of which he is, perhaps, vaguely aware, but which he finds difficult to put into words. The interviewer-respondent relationship puts a good deal of pressure on him to reply and to make sense in his reply. Consequently, he gives us stereotypical responses that use clichés which are commonly acceptable but do not necessarily represent the true motives. Many of our motives do not, in fact, "make sense," and are not logical. The question-answer relation demands sense above all. If the response does not represent the true state of affairs the interviewer will never know it. He will go away. If it does not make sense it may represent the truth, but the respondent will feel like a fool and the interviewer will not go away. Much better produce a cliché and be rid of him.

THE NATURE OF PROJECTIVE TESTS

Still other kinds of motives exist of which the respondent may not be explicitly conscious himself. The product may be seen by him as related to things or people or values in his life, or as having a certain role in the scheme of things, and yet he may be quite unable, in response to a direct question, to describe these aspects of the object. Nevertheless, these characteristics may be of great importance as motives. How can we get at them?

Clinical psychologists have long been faced with a parallel set of problems. It is quite usual for a patient to be unable or unwilling to tell the therapist directly what kinds of things are stirring in his motivational pattern. Information about these drives are of vital importance to the process of cure, so a good deal of research has been directed towards the development of techniques to identify and define them. The development of projective techniques as diagnostic tools has provided one of the most useful means to uncover such motivations, and the market-researcher can well afford to borrow their essentials from the therapist.

Basically, a projective test involves presenting the subject with an ambiguous stimulus—one that does not quite make sense in itself—and asking him to make sense of it. The theory is that in order to make it make sense he will have to add to it—to fill out the picture—and in so doing he projects part of himself into it. Since we know what was in the original stimulus we can quite easily identify the parts that were added, and, in this way, painlessly obtain information about the person.

Examples of these tests come readily to hand. Nearly everyone is familiar with the Rorschach Test, in which a subject is shown a series of ink-blots and asked to tell what they look like. Here the stimulus is incomplete in itself, and the interpretation supplied by the patient provides useful information. This test yields fairly general answers about the personality, however, and often we would like to narrow down the area in which the patient is supplying information.

The Thematic Apperception Test offers a good example of this function. Let us suppose that with a particular patient we have reason to suppose that his relation to figures of authority is crucial to his therapeutic problem. We can give him a series of pictures where people are shown, but where the relationship of authority or the characteristics of the authoritarian figure are not complete. He is asked to tell a story about each picture. If in each story the subordinate finally kills the figure of authority we have certain kinds of knowledge; if, on the other hand, he always builds the story so the subordinate figure achieves a secure and comfortable dependence, we have quite different information. It is often quite impossible to get the subject to tell us these things directly. Either he cannot or will not do so. Indirectly, however, he will tell us how he sees authority. Can we get him, similarly, to tell us how a product looks to him in his private view of the world?

APPLICATION OF PROJECTIVE TEST IN
MARKET RESEARCH

Let us look at an example of this kind of thing in market research. For the purposes of experiment a conventional survey was made of attitudes toward Nescafé, an instant coffee. The questionnaire included the questions "Do you use instant coffee?" (If No) "What do you dislike about it?" The bulk of the unfavorable responses fell into the general area "I don't like the flavor." This is such an easy answer to a complex question that one may suspect it is a stereotype, which at once gives a sensible response to get rid of the interviewer and conceals other motives. How can we get behind this facade?

In this case an indirect approach was used. Two shopping lists were prepared. They were identical in all respects, except that one list specified Nescafé and one Maxwell House Coffee. They were administered to alternate subjects, with no subject knowing of the existence of the other list. The instructions were "Read the shopping list below. Try to project yourself into the situation as far as possible until you can more or less characterize the woman who bought the groceries. Then write a brief description of her personality and character. Wherever possible indicate what factors influenced your judgement."

Shopping List I

Pound and a half of hamburger
2 loaves Wonder bread
bunch of carrots
1 can Rumford's Baking Powder
Nescafé instant coffee
2 cans Del Monte peaches
5 lbs. potatoes

Shopping List II

Pound and a half of hamburger
2 loaves Wonder bread
bunch of carrots
1 can Rumford's Baking Powder
1 lb. Maxwell House Coffee (Drip Ground)
2 cans Del Monte peaches
5 lbs. potatoes

Fifty people responded to each of the two shopping lists given above. The responses to these shopping lists provided some very interesting material. The following main characteristics of their descriptions can be given:

1. 48 percent of the people described the woman who bought Nescafé as lazy; 4 percent described the woman who bought Maxwell House as lazy.
2. 48 percent of the people described the woman who bought Nescafé as failing to plan household purchases and schedules well; 12 percent described the woman who bought Maxwell House this way.
3. 4 percent described the Nescafé woman as thrifty; 16 percent described the Maxwell House woman as thrifty.
   12 percent described the Nescafé woman as spendthrift; 0 percent described the Maxwell House woman this way.
4. 16 percent described the Nescafé woman as not a good wife; 0 percent described the Maxwell House woman this way.

4 percent described the Nescafé woman as a good wife; 16 percent described the Maxwell House woman as a good wife.

A clear picture begins to form here. Instant coffee represents a departure from "home-made" coffee, and the traditions with respect to caring for one's family. Coffee-making is taken seriously, with vigorous proponents for laborious drip and filter-paper methods, firm believers in coffee boiled in a battered sauce pan, and the like. Coffee drinking is a form of intimacy and relaxation that gives it a special character.

On the one hand, coffee making is an art. It is quite common to hear a woman say, "I can't seem to make good coffee," in the same way that one might say, "I can't learn to play the violin." It is acceptable to confess this inadequacy, for making coffee well is a mysterious touch that belongs, in a shadowy tradition, to the plump, aproned figure who is a little lost outside her kitchen but who has a sure sense in it and among its tools.

On the other hand, coffee has a peculiar role in relation to the household and the home-and-family character. We may well have a picture, in the shadowy past, of a big black range that is always hot with baking and cooking, and has a big enamelled pot of coffee warming at the back. When a neighbor drops in during the morning, a cup of coffee is a medium of hospitality that does somewhat the same thing as cocktails in the late afternoon, but does it in a broader sphere.

These are real and important aspects of coffee. They are not physical characteristics of the product, but they are real values in the consumer's life, and they influence his purchasing. We need to know and assess them. The "labor-saving" aspect of instant coffee, far from being an asset, may be a liability in that it violates these traditions. How often have we heard a wife respond to "This cake is delicious!" with a pretty blush and "Thank you—I made it with such and such a prepared cake mix." This response is so invariable as to seem almost compulsive. It is almost unthinkable to anticipate a reply "Thank you, I made it with Pillsbury's flour, Fleischman's yeast, and Borden's milk." Here the specifications are unnecessary. All that is relevant is the implied "I made it"—the art and the credit are carried directly by the verb that covers the process of mixing and processing the ingredients. In ready-mixed foods there seems to be a compulsive drive to refuse credit for the product, because the accomplishment is not the housewife's but the company's.

In this experiment, as a penalty for using "synthetics" the woman who buys Nescafé pays the price of being seen as lazy, spendthrift, a poor wife, and as failing to plan well for her family. The people who rejected instant coffee in the original direct question blamed its flavor. We may well wonder if their dislike of instant coffee was not to a large extent occasioned by a fear of being seen by one's self and others in the role they projected onto the Nescafé woman in the description. When asked directly, however, it is difficult to respond with this. One can not say, "I don't use Nescafé because people will think I am lazy and not a good wife." Yet we know from these data that the feeling regarding laziness and shiftlessness was there. Later studies (reported below) showed that it determined buying habits, and that something could be done about it.

Analysis of Responses

Some examples of the type of response received will show the kind of material obtained and how it may be analyzed. Three examples of each group are given below.

Descriptions of a woman who bought, among other things,
Maxwell House Coffee

I'd say she was a practical, frugal woman. She bought too many potatoes. She must like to cook and bake as she included baking powder. She must not care much about her figure as she does not discriminate about the food she buys.

The woman is quite influenced by advertising as signified by the specific name brands on her shopping list. She probably is quite set in her ways and accepts no substitutes.

I have been able to observe several hundred women shoppers who have made very similar purchases to that listed above, and the only clue that I can detect that may have some bearing on her personality is the Del Monte peaches. This item when purchased singly along with the other more staple foods indicates that she may be anxious to please either herself or members of her family with a 'treat.' She is probably a thrifty, sensible housewife.

Descriptions of a woman who bought among other things,
Nescafé Instant Coffee

This woman appears to be either single or living alone. I would guess that she had an office job. Apparently, she likes to sleep late in the morning, basing my assumption on what she bought such as Instant Coffee which can be made in a hurry. She probably also has can [sic] peaches for breakfast, cans being easy to open. Assuming that she is just average, as opposed to those dazzling natural beauties who do not need much time to make up, she must appear rather sloppy, taking little time to make up in the morning. She is also used to eating supper out, too. Perhaps alone rather than with an escort. An old maid probably.

She seems to be lazy, because of her purchases of canned peaches and instant coffee. She doesn't seem to think, because she bought two loaves of bread, and then baking powder, unless she's thinking of making cake. She probably just got married.

I think the woman is the type who never thinks ahead very far—the type who always sends Junior to the store to buy one item at a time. Also she is fundamentally lazy. All the items, with possible exception of the Rumford's, are easily prepared items. The girl may be an office girl who is just living from one day to the next in a sort of haphazard sort of life.

As we read these complete responses we begin to get a feeling for the picture that is created by Nescafé. It is particularly interesting to notice that the Nescafé woman is protected, to some extent, from the opprobrium of being lazy and haphazard by being seen as a single "office girl"—a role that relieves one from guilt for not being interested in the home and food preparation.

The references to peaches are significant. In one case (Maxwell House) they are singled out as a sign that the woman is thoughtfully preparing a "treat" for her family. On the other hand, when the Nescafé woman buys them it is evidence that she is lazy, since their "canned" character is seen as central.

In terms of the sort of results presented above, it may be useful to demonstrate the way these stories are coded. The following items are extracted from the six stories quoted:

Maxwell House	Nescafé
1. practical frugal likes to cook	1. single office girl sloppy old maid
2. influenced by advertising set in her ways	2. lazy does not plan newlywed
3. interested in family thrifty sensible	3. lazy does not plan office girl

Items such as these are culled from each of the stories. Little by little categories are shaped by the content of the stories themselves. In this way the respondent furnishes the dimensions of analysis as well as the scale values on these dimensions.

Second Test

It is possible to wonder whether it is true that the opprobrium that is heaped on the Nescafé woman comes from her use of a device that represents a short-cut and labor-saver in an area where she is expected to embrace painstaking time-consuming work in a ritualistic way. To test this a variation was introduced into the shopping lists. In a second experiment one hundred and fifty housewives were tested with the form given above, but a sample was added to this group which responded to a slightly different form. If we assume that the rejection in the first experiment came from the presence of a feeling about synthetic shortcuts we might assume also that the addition of one more shortcut to both lists would bring the Maxwell House woman more into line with the Nescafé woman, since the former would now have the same guilt that the Nescafé woman originally had, while the Nescafé woman, already convicted of evading her duties, would be little further injured.

In order to accomplish this a second prepared food was added to both lists. Immediately after the coffee in both lists the fictitious item, "Blueberry Fill Pie Mix" was added. The results are shown in Table 1 below.

It will be seen immediately, in the first two columns, that the group to whom the original form of the list were given showed the same kind of difference as reported above in their estimates of the two women. The group with an additional prepared food, however, brought the Maxwell Coffee woman down until she is virtually undistinguishable from the Nescafé. There seems to be little doubt but that the prepared-food-character, and the stigma of avoiding housewifely duties is responsible for the projected personality characteristics.

Relation to Purchasing

It is still relevant to ask whether the existence of these feelings in a potential consumer is related to purchasing. It is hypothesized that these personality descriptions provide an opportunity for the consumer to project hopes and fears and anxieties that are relevant to the way the product is seen, and that they represent important parts of her motivation in buying or not buying. To test this hypothesis, a small sample of fifty housewives, comparable in every way to the group just referred to, was given the original form of the shopping list (Nescafé only). In addition to obtaining the personality description, the interviewer, on a pretext, obtained permission to look at her pantry shelves and determine personally whether or not she had instant coffee of any brand. The results of this investigation are shown in Table 2.

The trend of these data shows conclusively that if a respondent sees the woman who buys Nescafé as having undesirable traits, she is not likely to buy instant coffee herself. The projected unacceptable characteristics go with failure to buy, and it does not seem unwarranted to assume that the association is causal.

Furthermore, these projected traits are, to some extent, additive. For instance, if a respondent describes the woman as having one bad

Table 1

Personality Characteristics Ascribed to Users of Prepared Foods

If They Use	No Prepared Food (Maxwell House alone)		Nescafé (alone)		Maxwell House (plus Pie Mix)		Nescafé (plus Pie Mix)	
	Number	Percent	Number	Percent	Number	Percent	Number	Percent
They are seen as:								
Not Economical	12	17	24	32	6	30	7	35
Lazy	8	11	46	62	5	25	8	40
Poor Personality and Appearance	28	39	39	53	7	35	8	40
N =	72		74		20		20	

Table 2

The woman who buys Nescafé is seen as:	By Women Who Had Instant Coffee in the House (N = 32)		By Women Who Did Not Have Instant Coffee in the House (N = 18)	
	Number	Percent	Number	Percent
Economical**	22	70	5	28
Not economical	0	0	2	11
Can not cook or does not like to**	5	16	10	55
Plans balanced meals*	9	29	2	11
Good housewife, plans well, cares about family**	9	29	0	0
Poor housewife, does not plan well, does not care about family*	5	16	7	39
Lazy*	6	19	7	39

*A single asterisk indicates that differences this great would be observed only 5 times out of 100 in repeated samplings of a population whose true difference is zero.
**A double asterisk indicates that the chances are 1 in 100. We are justified in rejecting the hypothesis that there is no difference between the groups.

trait only, she is about twice as likely not to have instant coffee. However, if she sees her as having two bad traits, and no good ones (e.g., lazy, can not cook), she is about three times as likely not to have instant coffee as she is to have it. On the other hand, if she sees her as having two good traits (e.g., economical, cares for family), she is about six times as likely to have it as not.

It was pointed out earlier that some women felt it necessary to "excuse" the woman who bought Nescafé by suggesting that she lived alone and hence could not be expected to be interested in cooking, or that she had a job and did not have time to shop better. Women who had instant coffee in the house found excuses almost twice as often as those who did not use instant coffee (12 out of 32, or 42 percent, against 4 out of 18, or 22 percent). These "excuses" are vitally important for merchandising. The need for an excuse shows there is a barrier to buying in the consumer's mind. The presence of excuses shows that there is a way around the barrier. The content of the excuses themselves provides valuable clues for directing appeals toward reducing buying resistance.

CONCLUSIONS

There seems to be no question that in the experimental situation described here:

(1) Motives exist which are below the level of verbalization because they are socially unacceptable, difficult to verbalize cogently, or unrecognized.

(2) These motives are intimately related to the decision to purchase or not to purchase, and

(3) It is possible to identify and assess such motives by approaching them indirectly.

Two important general points come out of the work reported. The first is in the statement of the problem. It is necessary for us to see a product in terms of a set of characteristics and attributes which are part of the consumer's "private world," and as such may have no simple relationship to characteristics of the object in the "real" world. Each of us lives in a world which is composed of more than physical things and people. It is made up of goals, paths to goals, barriers, threats, and the like, and an individual's behavior is oriented with respect to these characteristics as much as to the "objective" ones. In the area of merchandizing, a product's character of being seen as a path to a goal is usually very much more important as a determinant of purchasing than its physical dimensions. We have taken advantage of these qualities in advertising and merchandizing for a long time by an intuitive sort of "playing-by-ear" on the subjective aspects of products. It is time for a systematic attack on the problem of the phenomenological description of objects. What kinds of dimensions are relevant to this world of goals and paths and barriers? What kind of terms will fit the phenomenological characteristics of an object in the same sense that the centimetre-gram-second system fits its physical dimensions? We need to know the answers to such questions, and the psychological definitions of valued objects.

The second general point is the methodological one that it is possible, by using appropriate techniques, to find out from the respondent what the phenomenological characteristics of various objects may be. By and large, a direct approach to this problem in terms of straightforward questions will not yield satisfactory answers. It is possible, however, by the use of indirect techniques, to get the consumer to provide, quite unselfconsciously, a description of the value-character of objects in his environment.

17. Fitting the semantic differential to the marketing problem

WILLIAM A. MINDAK

Advertising and marketing men frequently are faced with the problem of quantifying highly subjective data, representing difficult-to-verbalize reactions of people to the "image" of a brand, product, or company.

Consistent with this attempt to define an "image" is the technique originated by Charles E. Osgood and his associates, called the semantic differential.[1] This technique attempts to measure what meaning a concept might have for people in terms of dimensions which have been empirically defined and factor-analyzed. Since this concept can indeed be something as abstract or nebulous as a company image, the semantic differential has been increasing use in various ways.[2]

Osgood's semantic differential involved repeated judgments of a concept against a series of descriptive polar-adjectival scales on a 7-point equal-interval ordinal scale. These scales were usually selected from 50 pairs of polar adjectives, with heavy factor loadings labeled "evaluative" (on which are based the attitudinal measures), "activity," and "potency."

An example would be:

$$\text{good}-:-:-:-:-:-:-:\text{bad}$$

Reprinted from the *Journal* of *Marketing*, Volume 25 (April, 1961), pp. 28–33, National Quarterly Publication of the American Marketing Association.

[1] Charles E. Osgood, George J. Suci, and Percy H. Tannenbaum, *The Measurement of Meaning* (Urbana, Illinois: University of Illinois Free Press, 1957).

[2] William A. Mindak, "A New Technique for Measuring Advertising Effectiveness," *Journal of Marketing*, Vol. 20 (April, 1956), pp. 367–378. Mogul, Lewin, Williams & Saylor, Inc., "Product Semantic Indices," (private publication) (New York, 1958). John F. Bolger, Jr., "How to Evaluate Your Company Image," *Journal of Marketing*, Vol. 24 (October, 1959), pp. 7–10.

Progressing from left to right on the scale, the positions are described to the subjects participating in the experiment as representing "extremely good," "very good," "slightly good," "being both good and bad," "slightly bad," "very bad," and "extremely bad." Subjects are encouraged to use the scales as quickly and as honestly as possible and not to puzzle over any particular concept.

In scoring the differential, weights can be assigned to each position; and these in turn can be converted to individual or group mean scores and presented in "profile" form. Reliability of the differential is reasonably high, and the measure has a high degree of face validity.

SEMANTIC DIFFERENTIAL IN MEASURING "IMAGES"

The semantic differential has a number of specific advantages for marketing researchers interested in measuring brand, product, or company images:

1. It is a quick, efficient means of getting in readily quantifiable form and for large samples not only the *direction* but *intensity* of opinions and attitudes toward a concept . . . be it brand, product, or company. If desired, these "profiles" can be used as a guide to indicate areas for more intensive research or interviewing.

2. It provides a comprehensive picture of the "image" or meaning of a product or personality. Duncan Hines and Betty Crocker as corporate personalities might both be looked up favorably, but reacted to differently in terms of "activity," "strength," "warmth," "helpfulness," etc.

3. It represents a standardized technique for getting at the multitude of factors which go to make up a brand or product "image." Comparison of one brand with another must take into consideration *specific brand attributes* (size, shape, price, ingredients, etc.) as well as *general product class characteristics* (including competition); the *sources* of the impressions (merchandising, packaging, advertising, media, etc.); the *company* that makes the product; and *types of consumers associated with* the product.

4. It is easily repeatable and quite reliable. Therefore, it can be used as a continuing measure sensitive enough to note changes in consumer reactions from year to year.

5. It avoids stereotyped responses and allows for individual frames of reference. The sheer number of scales and concepts and the speed of administration (both with groups and individuals), encourage quick "top-of-mind" responses. For this reason it has sometimes been called a "semantic projection" test.

6. It eliminates some of the problems of question phrasing, such as ambiguity and overlapping of statements. In addition, it facilitates the interviewing of respondents who may not be too articulate in describing

their reactions to such abstruse factors as a brand, product, or company image.

MODIFICATIONS FOR ADVERTISING RESEARCH

To make the differential even more sensitive in evoking subtle distinctions in the images of physically similar products, researchers have suggested many modifications. The most important of these are:

1. *Descriptive nouns and phrases.* These are in addition to (and sometimes as a substitute for) simple one-word adjectives. The original differential dealt primarily with single-word adjectives such as "good-bad," "weak-strong," "pleasant-unpleasant," etc. The "evaluation," "activity," and "potency" factors are still retained, but with increased shades of meaning provided by these longer, more involved scales.

Here is an example for a beer:

Happy-go-lucky—kind of serious
Something special—just another drink
Little after-taste—lots of after-taste
Really refreshing—not really refreshing
American flavor—foreign flavor

Here is an example for people who drink beer:

Live in average homes—live in expensive homes
Take life easy—always on the go
Drink just to be sociable—really enjoy it
Really know beer—can't tell one from another
Snobs—regular guys
Housewife—career girl

Edmund W. J. Faison, President of Visual Research Inc., in an attempt to match personality types with package designs, labels, colors, etc., has used these phrases as one end of a scale:

Stands out in a crowd
Self-made man
Likes to hunt and fish
Factory worker making $400 a month
Belongs to a higher social class than his parents

2. *Tailor-made scales.* In attempting to set up standardized scales, certain researchers have concentrated on the classic list of 50 word-pairs, factor-analyzed by Osgood. This direction offers comparative possibilities and a hope of generalized attitude scales. In rating TV commercials, Burleigh Gardner of Social Research, Inc., consistently uses 30 word-pairs, with heavy factor loadings on evaluation, activity, strength, etc.

But for many researchers such a standardized list lacks flexibility and appropriateness to the specific problems at hand. They find it necessary to construct tailormade word and phrase lists. Sources for these lists are content analyses of their own and competitive advertising, word association tests with consumers, individual or group interviews, and factor analyses.

In such exploratory or pretests, simple opposites are used, often without the 7-point scale. Once it is agreed that these adjectives and phrases cover the factors best delimiting the image, they are then scaled to permit profile comparisons.

3. *"Connotative" and "non-polar" opposites.* Although in theory every adjective or phrase should have a denotative opposite (true-untrue, good-bad, bright-dull), researchers have found that in practice respondents often refuse to "play the game," as it were. In an advertising context or in rating large well-known companies, subjects often balk at using negative sides of scales or to gradate a concept negatively.

Respondents can, and do, make sharp distinctions as to the level of believability of a company's advertising or of a particular claim. But they either hesitate to rate a concept as unbelievable (feeling that "if it is advertised, it must be true") or they are unable to gradate their feelings of unbelievability.

This failure frequently results in indiscriminate clustering about the middle of the scales, thus making it difficult to differentiate among concept profiles. Some researchers have attempted to circumvent this tendency either by "heightening" the level of the dimensions or by using phrases which, although not necessarily *denotatively* opposite, still seem to fit more logically and naturally into people's frame of reference. Scales such as these are used:

Really modern—sort of old-fashioned
High-quality product—so-so quality product
Heavy beer drinker—a "sometimes" beer drinker
Really peps you up—somehow doesn't pep you up

4. *Built-in control concepts.* As a realistic control, it is helpful to get ratings on such concepts as, "the ideal company," or "my favorite brand," or "brand I would never use." These control profiles can be compared with test concepts or competitive concepts. Although one might expect respondents simply to use the extremes on all scales to represent their "ideal" or their "least-liked," such is not really the case.

5. *Personal interviews and mail questionnaires.* Early experiments with the differential usually were conducted with "captive" audiences, often students in class. In the main, though, the advertising researcher prefers to do field studies and depends on individual personal interviews. The differential has been used in these situations, and respondents show little reluctance in performing the task of checking several concepts on a

variety of scales. The need for tailor-made scales is often quite apparent, however, in that certain age groups and certain socio-economic groups find it relatively difficult to think in terms of various continua and to deal with such abstractions as "concepts."

Other researchers have even experimented with the differential in mail questionnaires, although this means of delivery obviates most of the projective qualities of this test. Respondents have too much time to deliberate over their judgments and have too much control over their ratings. Personal supervision is necessary to assure speed and "top-of-mind" responses.

A BRAND-IMAGE STUDY

The following case study demonstrates the use of the differential, as well as some of the modifications discussed. This particular study's purpose was to determine beer drinkers' reactions to the personalities of three local brands of beer (and specifically Brand Y), compared with three competitive national brands in a large midwest city. Various facets of this image were to be explored, such as specific characteristics of each brand, the attitudes toward advertising, the image of the company, and feelings about various consumers who might be associated or not associated with each brand of beer.

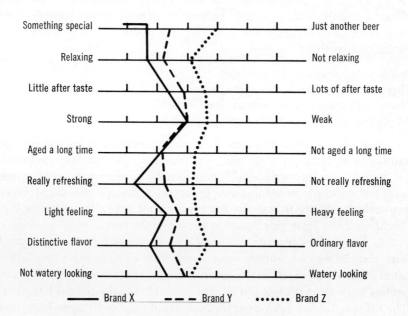

Figure 1. Specific product image

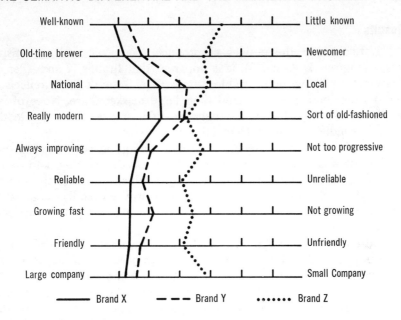

Figure 2. Company image

Respondents were asked to rate these six beers on several dimensions. Scales were selected from content analyses of depth-interview responses, as well as from advertisements for the various brands. The mean ratings were converted into profiles for comparison purposes. Figures 1 through 4 illustrate certain critical scales for three local brands of beer.

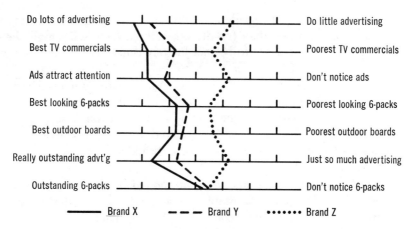

Figure 3. Advertising image

Results

1. Looking at the profiles of products, company, and advertising image (Figures 1, 2, and 3), it is apparent that Brands X and Y enjoy many more positive or favorable ratings than Brand Z. This reflects X and Y's domination of sales and their large market share. None of X's or Y's mean ratings fall on the negative side; and very few are in the neutral or indifferent area (3.5 to 4.5).

Brand X received essentially positive ratings in regard to specific *product* (it was quite refreshing, something special, relaxing, and had a distinctive flavor); *advertising* (it was outstanding, it was attention getting, and there was lots of it); and *company* (it was friendly, large, well-known, and an old-time brewer who still manages to grow fast and always improve).

Although Brand Y's ratings usually were favorable, they were not as extreme as Brand X. The only two exceptions occurred in ratings of the specific products. Beer drinkers rated Y about the same as X on the "weak-strong" scale and the "aged-a-long-time" dimension. *Brand Z,* a relative newcomer to the city, was reacted to quite neutrally—in this case, an indication of little consumer experience with, or knowledge of, the beer. In addition to its "militant indifference," Brand Z was thought to be less well-known than the other two brands, to do less advertising, and to be more of a local beer.

2. In products such as beer, advertising researchers are interested in determining the "types" of consumer most often associated with a particular brand. Social Research, Inc., the Psychological Corporation, the Institute for Motivational Research, Inc., and other organizations increasingly emphasize psychological typologies rather than conventional demographic characteristics.

In this case, Figure 4 shows that the consumer profile ratings, that is, the types of people considered likely to buy each of these beers, tend to cluster much more than for the other three factors. It might be advantageous for a beer *not* to be inordinately connected or identified with a particular type of consumer.

Beer drinkers thought Brands X and Y more "universal" than Z. They were "all things to all beer drinkers." Brand X was thought of as being consumed more at home and by average people who really enjoy and know beer. Brand Y was considered to be drunk more in bars. Brand Z's image tended toward home drinking and use by less discriminating beer drinkers.

The results of this study were interpreted by the management of Y company to be quite favorable, particularly when the advertising budgets of X and Y were compared. Management was pleased with reactions to the company which a few years back had not enjoyed the

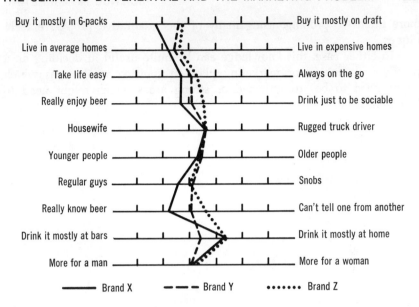

Buy it mostly in 6-packs	Buy it mostly on draft
Live in average homes	Live in expensive homes
Take life easy	Always on the go
Really enjoy beer	Drink just to be sociable
Housewife	Rugged truck driver
Younger people	Older people
Regular guys	Snobs
Really know beer	Can't tell one from another
Drink it mostly at bars	Drink it mostly at home
More for a man	More for a woman

———— Brand X   — — — Brand Y   •••••• Brand Z

Figure 4. Consumer profile

best of reputations. Possible weak areas which might need strengthening were Brand Y's dealer displays (6-packs); the feeling that the company was not as modern as it could be; and the need of upgrading the image of the beer among "higher-class," sophisticated, home beer drinkers.

Implications

A great deal of controversy (some genuine, some "strawman") exists between the "quantifier" and the "qualifier" in attempting to delineate the image of a product, brand, or company. The semantic differential and techniques similar to it help to quantify what too often has been considered abstract, mysterious, and qualitative material regarding consumers' opinions, feeling tones, and emotional reactions. In addition, the modifications suggested by advertising researchers (phrases and nouns in addition to single adjectives, connotative as well as denotative opposites, tailor-made scales) add more scope and direction to what may be superficial quantitative information.

The differential serves as a two-edged tool: (1) It is a simple, large sample, nose-counting device which can be repeated from time to time to detect trends in consumer reactions, and to measure interaction between advertising and consumer attitudes. (2) In addition, the differential "profiles" serve as useful directional indicators for further and more intensive probing, using many of the qualitative projective techniques.

In either case, this knowledge can be quite useful in deciding on a possible advertising or marketing plan, in spotting weak areas which might need to be strengthened or strong areas which might need to be emphasized.

18. The "draw a supermarket" technique

HERBERT E. KRUGMAN

The use of projective techniques of an essentially verbal character
has now become well established in opinion research. For special types
of problem, however, nonverbal methods may also be considered. In
the case described here such a method was developed in response to
a problem in store layout and design.

The general problem was to provide guidance to supermarket
planners about those aspects and areas of present-day store layouts
which create conflict and tension in the shopper. To some extent this
guidance was already available in the form of traffic and conventional
interviewing studies. What still seemed desirable, however, was a technique for enhancing the conventional interview process by recording
the shoppers' stereotyped perception of supermarkets *before* the verbal
questioning or "formal" interviewing began.

The technique selected was a drawing task and used as its materials
a No. 2 lead pencil—without eraser—and a sheet of plain white bond
paper 8½ × 11 inches. However, on each sheet of paper a simple rec-
tangle 5½ × 7 inches was drawn in advance. This was meant to represent
the outlines of the most common (110 × 140 foot) supermarket.

Fifty housewives in New York and adjacent suburban areas were then
asked to "draw a supermarket." Some had to be reassured about "just
making a quick sketch" or "not having to reproduce any particular supermarket"—although concern over drawing skill was the more common
cause for resistance. As each drawing was completed and the parts
labeled, interviewing began. Special emphasis in the interview was
placed on the content of the drawings.

Three aspects of the drawings were of primary interest. These were
(1) store departments omitted, (2) order in which departments were

Reprinted from the *Public Opinion Quarterly*, Volume XXIV, 1960, pp. 148–149.

drawn, and (3) space allotted to each department. The range of these responses may be described as follows:

1. The meat department was omitted in about 1 out of 10 drawings, produce in 1 out of 5, dairy in 1 out of 5, dry groceries in 1 out of 4, etc.

2. The produce department was drawn first in about 2 out of 5 drawings, meats in 1 out of 5, dairy in 1 out of 6, dry groceries in 1 out of 6, etc.

3. The meat department was, on the average, drawn about 50 percent *larger* than the dry groceries department. Actually, it is only about one-third as large as the dry groceries department in a store of the dimensions involved. Produce was drawn 80 percent as large as dry groceries, though it too occupies only about a third of the space actually allotted to dry groceries.

These data suggest that supermarkets do look quite different to different shoppers and, more important, different from actual dimensional layouts. In the present case they have provided a vivid representation for discussion of respondents' feelings and, when used as illustrations of interview findings, have proven useful in communicating the various shades and nuances of those findings to store planning and design personnel.

III. The Consumer

INTRODUCTION

Analysis of the consumer may be done on several different levels. The individual consumer or buyer may be studied to determine his basic desires, attitudes, and responses to varied stimuli. In addition, the influence of groups upon the individual's development has been shown to be of great importance for many of his behavior patterns. These groups may range from family and friends to political and economic associations and to society, each group having its specialized influences on the different individuals within it. These groups can be the focus of study themselves in an effort to understand the group's predominant impact upon heterogeneous individuals.

The marketing man is faced with a maze of knowledge about behavior patterns that influence the consumer. His job is to understand the relative importance of these individual variables upon buyer behavior and how they may combine to produce still new desires or preferences which the market analyst must interpret in terms of products, services, purchasing patterns, and response to promotion. It is the marketing task to match company resources with consumer needs on profitable terms. To achieve this completed task it is necessary to employ every skilled technique available.

19. The significance of social stratification in selling

RICHARD P. COLEMAN

Dating back to the late 1940's, advertisers and marketers have alternately flirted with and cooled on the notion that W. Lloyd Warner's social class concept [1] is an important analytic tool for their profession. The Warnerian idea that six social classes constitute the basic division of American Society has offered many attractions to marketing analysts when they have grown dissatisfied with simple income categories or census-type occupational categories and felt a need for more meaningful classifications, for categorizations of the citizenry which could prove more relevant to advertising and marketing problems. However, in the course of their attempts to apply the class concept, marketers have not always found it immediately and obviously relevant. Sometimes it has seemed to shed light on advertising and merchandising problems and at other times it hasn't—with the result that many analysts have gone away disenchanted, deciding that social classes are not much more useful than income categories and procedurally far more difficult to employ.

It is the thesis of this writer that the role of social class has too often been misunderstood or oversimplified, and that if the concept is applied in a more sophisticated and realistic fashion, it will shed light on a great many problems to which, at first glance, it has not seemed particularly relevant. What we propose to do here, then, is discuss and illustrate a few of these more subtle, more refined and (it must be acknowledged) more complicated ways of applying social class analyses to marketing and advertising problems. In other words, the purpose of this paper is to

Reprinted from *Proceedings*, American Marketing Association Conference, December, 1960 (Bell, Editor), by permission of the American Marketing Association, pp. 171–184.

[1] See W. Lloyd Warner, Marchia Meeker, Kenneth Eells, *Social Class in America* (Chicago: Science Research Associates, 1949).

clarify *when* and *in what ways* social class concepts are significant in selling, and to suggest when they might not be as significant as other concepts, or at least need to be used in concert with other analytic categories.

THE WARNERIAN SOCIAL CLASSES

The six social classes which are referred to in this paper are those which W. Lloyd Warner and his associates have observed in their analyses of such diverse communities as Newburyport, Massachusetts,[2] Natchez, Mississippi,[3] Morris, Illinois,[4] Kansas City, Misouri,[5] and Chicago. These social classes are groups of people who are more or less equal to one another in prestige and community status; they are people who readily and regularly interact among themselves in both formal and informal ways; they form a "class" also to the extent that they share the same goals and ways of looking at life. It is this latter fact about social classes which makes them significant to marketers and advertisers.

Briefly characterized, the six classes are as follows, starting from the highest one and going down: [6]

1. The Upper-Upper or "Social Register" Class is composed of locally prominent families, usually with at least second or third generation wealth. Almost inevitably, this is the smallest of the six classes—with probably no more than one-half of one percent of the population able to claim membership in this class. The basic values of these people might be summarized in these phrases: living graciously, upholding the family reputation, reflecting the excellence of one's breeding, and displaying a sense of community responsibility.

2. The Lower-Upper or "Nouveau Riche" Class is made up of the more recently arrived and never-quite-accepted wealthy families. In cluded in this class are members of each city's "executive elite," as well as founders of large businesses and the newly well-to-do doctors and lawyers. At best only one and one-half percent of Americans rank at this level—so that all told, no more than 2 percent of the population can be counted as belonging to one layer or the other of our Upper Class. The goals of people at this particular level are a blend of the Upper-Upper

---

[2] See W. Lloyd Warner and Paul Lunt, *The Social Life of a Modern Community*, (New Haven: Yale University Press, 1941).

[3] See Allison Davis, Burleigh B. Gardner and Mary R. Gardner, *Deep South* (Chicago: University of Chicago Press, 1941).

[4] See W. Lloyd Warner and Associates, *Democracy in Jonesville*, (New York: Harper & Brothers, 1949).

[5] The writer's observation on the Kansas City social class system will be included in a forthcoming volume on middle age in Kansas City, currently being prepared for publication by the Committee on Human Development of the University of Chicago.

[6] Some of the phrases and ideas in this characterization have been borrowed from Joseph A. Kahl's excellent synthesizing textbook, *The American Class Structure* (New York: Rinehart & Company, Inc., 1957).

pursuit of gracious living and the Upper-Middle Class's drive for success.

3. In the Upper-Middle Class are moderately successful professional men and women, owners of medium-sized businesses and "organization men" at the managerial level; also included are those younger people in their twenties or very early thirties who are expected to arrive at this occupational status level—and possibly higher—by their middle or late thirties (that is, they are today's "junior executives" and "apprentice professionals" who grew up in such families and/or went to the "better" colleges). Ten percent of Americans are part of this social class and the great majority of them are college educated.

The motivating concerns of people in this class are success at career (which is the husband's contribution to the family's status) and tastefully reflecting this success in social participation and home decor (which is the wife's primary responsibility). Cultivating charm and polish, plus a broad range of interests—either civic or cultural, or both—are also goals of the people in this class, just as in the Lower-Upper. For most marketing and advertising purposes, this class and the two above it can be linked together into a single category of "upper status people." The major differences between them—particularly between the Upper-Middle and the Lower-Upper—are in degree of "success" and the extent to which this has been translated into gracious living.

4. At the top of the "Average Man World" is the Lower-Middle Class. Approximately 30 percent or 35 percent of our citizenry can be considered members of this social class. For the most part they are drawn from the ranks of non-managerial office workers, small business owners, and those highly-paid blue-collar families who are concerned with being accepted and respected in white-collar dominated clubs, churches, and neighborhoods. The key word in understanding the motivations and goals of this class is Respectability, and a second important word is Striving. The men of this class are continually striving, within their limitations, to "do a good job" at their work, and both men and women are determined to be judged "respectable" in their personal behavior by their fellow citizens. Being "respectable" means that they live in well-maintained homes, neatly furnished, in neighborhoods which are more-or-less on the "right side of town." It also means that they will clothe themselves in coats, suits, and dresses from "nice stores" and save for a college education for their children.

5. At the lower half of the "Average Man World" is the Upper-Lower Class, sometimes referred to as "The Ordinary Working Class." Nearly 40 percent of all Americans are in this class, making it the biggest. The proto-typical member of this class is a semi-skilled worker on one of the nation's assembly lines. Many of these "Ordinary Working Class" people make very good money, but do not bother with using it to become

"respectable" in a middle-class way. Whether they just "get by" at work, or moonlight to make extra, Upper-Lowers are oriented more toward enjoying life and living well from day to day than saving for the future or caring what the middle class world thinks of them. They try to "keep in step with the times" (indeed, one might say the "times" are more important than the "Joneses" to this class), because they want to be at least Modern, if not Middle Class. That is, they try to take advantage of progress to live more comfortably and they work hard enough to keep themselves safely away from a slum level of existence.

6. The Lower-Lower Class of unskilled workers, unassimilated ethnics, and the sporadically employed comprises about 15 percent of the population, but this class has less than 7 or 8 percent of the purchasing power, and will not concern us further here. Apathy, fatalism, and a point of view which justifies "getting your kicks whenever you can" characterize the approach toward life, and toward spending money, found among the people of this class.

Now, we do not mean to imply by these characterizations that the members of each class are always homogeneous in behavior. To suggest such would be to exaggerate greatly the meaning of social classes. To properly understand them, it must be recognized that there is a considerable variation in the way individual members of a class realize these class goals and express these values.

For example, within the Upper Middle and Lower Upper Class, there is one group—called Upper Bohemians [7] by Russell Lynes—for whom cultural pursuits are more important than belonging to a "good" country club. As a result, the tastes in furniture, housing accommodations, and recreations exhibited by the men and women of this "issues-and-culture set"—leaning toward the avant garde and eclectic, as they do—are apt to be very different from those practiced by the more conventional, bourgeois members of these status levels. Nevertheless, to both the Upper Bohemians and the Upper Conventionals, displaying "good taste" is quite important, with the differences between them not so much a question of good-versus-bad taste as one of whose form of good taste is preferred (though, to be sure, the Upper Bohemians are usually quite certain theirs is better).

Other sub-categories can be found in these higher classes and parallel kinds of sub-categories can be found in the Lower Middle and Upper Lower classes. Within the Upper Lower Class, for instance, there is a large number of people who are quite concerned with their respectability and spend much of their spare time in church trying to do something about it. Their respectability concerns are not quite like those of the Lower Middle Class, however, for they seem to care more about The Almighty's view of them than of their fellow man's. Thus, the Upper-

[7] See Russell Lynes, A Surfeit of Honey (New York: Harper & Brothers, 1957).

Lower Class might, for certain analytic purposes, be sub-divided into Church-Going and Tavern-Hopping segments, although this would by no means exhaust all possibilities of sub-categorization here.

All of this is by way of indicating that the millions of individuals who compose each social class are not necessarily similar or identical in their consumption patterns, even though they are of equal status socially and share a set of goals and points of view which are class-wide. Thus far, the literature on social class in both marketing journals and sociological publications has emphasized the similarities of people within classes and rarely pointed out these variations. This has been necessary, of course, in order to properly introduce the concept and educate social scientists and marketers to its utility, but it has led on occasion to naive misuse of the concept and ultimate disillusion. In my view, it has come time for us to advance into a more sophisticated application of social class to marketing problems, which involves awareness of the differences as well as similarities within each class.

SOCIAL CLASS VERSUS INCOME

Let us proceed now to stating the basic significance of this class concept for people in the selling field. In the first place, it explains why income categories or divisions of Americans are quite often irrelevant in analyzing product markets, consumers' shopping habits and store preferences, and media consumption. For example, if you take three families, all earning around $8,000 a year, but each from a different social class, a radical difference in their ways of spending money will be observed.

An Upper-Middle Class family in this income bracket, which in this case might be a young lawyer and his wife or perhaps a college professor, is apt to be found spending a relatively large share of its resources on housing (in a "prestige" neighborhood), on rather expensive pieces of furniture, on clothing from quality stores, and on cultural amusements or club memberships. Meanwhile, the Lower-Middle Class family—headed, we will say, by an insurance salesman or a fairly successful grocery store owner, perhaps even a Diesel engineer—probably has a better house, but in not so fancy a neighborhood; it is apt to have as full a wardrobe though not so expensive, and probably more furniture though none by name designers. These people almost certainly have a much bigger savings account in the bank.

Finally, the Working Class family—with a cross-country truck driver or a highly-paid welder as its chief wage-earner—is apt to have less house and less neighborhood than the Lower-Middle or Upper-Middle family; but it will have a bigger, later model car, plus more expensive appliances in its kitchen and a bigger TV set in its living room. This family will spend less on clothing and furniture, but more on food if the number of children is greater, as is likely. One further difference: the man of the house probably spends much more on sports, attending baseball games (for example), going hunting and bowling, and perhaps owning a boat of some description.

The wives in these three families will be quite noticeably different in the kind of department stores they patronize, in the magazines they read, and in the advertising to which they pay attention. The clothing and furniture they select for themselves and their families will differ accordingly, and also because they are seeking quite different goals. This has become very clear in studies Social Research, Inc., has done for the *Chicago Tribune* on the clothing tastes of Chicagoland women, for the Kroehler Company on the place of furniture in American homes, and for MacFadden Publications on the purchasing patterns and motivations of their romance magazines' Working Class readers.[8] (These have been contrasted in turn with the motivations of Middle Class women who read service magazines.)

The Upper-Middle Class wife—even of the struggling young lawyer —usually buys all her public-appearance clothes at specialty shops or in the specialty departments of her community's best department stores; she feels constrained to choose her wardrobe according to rather carefully prescribed standards of appropriateness. In furnishing her home, she thoughtfully considers whether a given piece or a combination of pieces will serve as adequate testament to her aesthetic sensitivities, plus doing credit in turn to her husband's taste in wife-choosing. She pays careful attention to the dictates of the best shelter magazines, the "smart" interior decorators in town, the homes of other women in her class, and maybe that of the boss's wife.

The Lower-Middle Class woman is more single-mindedly concerned with furnishing her home so that it will be "pretty" in a way that suits her and hopefully might win praise from her friends and neighbors. She tries to get ideas from the medium-level shelter and service magazines and is perpetually depressed because her home isn't furnished as much like a dream house as she would like it to be. In this she is quite different from the Upper-Lower wife who is apt to care more about having a full array of expensive, gleaming white appliances in her kitchen than a doll's house of a living room. Where the Lower-Middle housewife usually has a definite style in mind which she's striving to follow, the Upper-Lower woman simply follows the lead of newspaper furniture advertising (and what she sees when window shopping) toward furniture which is "modern-looking," by which she means the "latest thing" that has hit the mass market.

[8] This study has been published under the name *Workingman's Wife* (Oceana Press: New York City, 1959) by Lee Rainwater, Richard P. Coleman, and Gerald Handel.

A great many more examples of differences in consumption patterns by class levels could be given, but the principal ones have been well reported already—facetiously by Vance Packard and seriously by Pierre Martineau; [9] for further amplification on this point the latter source is recommended. The significance to merchandisers and advertisers of these findings about motivational differences between classes is fairly obvious, the major idea being that for many products, advertising appeals and merchandising techniques must be differentially geared to the points of view reflected in these three main social classes. Advertising of brands or goods aimed at a specific class must take into account the motivations of that class, and not try to sell everything as if it were an Upper Class or Upper-Middle status symbol.

Up to now, we've been talking about product areas—clothing, furniture, and residential neighborhoods—where the relationship between social class and quality of goods purchased is highest. In these things the so-called "Quality Market" and the Upper Middle (and higher) markets coincide. That is, the purchasers of highest quality clothing and highest quality furniture are more nearly from the Upper-Middle and Upper social classes than from the highest income categories, and so on it goes down the hierarchy. The correlation between price of goods purchased and social class is relatively quite high in these product areas while the correlation between price paid and annual income is lower than one might expect.

There is another group of products which are not linked in such a direct way with social class, but neither are they linked with income categories in any obvious relationship. The current car market provides an instructive example of this situation, for the nature of the market cannot be grasped by using one or the other concept exclusively. What is happening in today's car market can only be understood when income categories are placed into a social class framework.

THE "OVERPRIVILEGED" AS "QUALITY MARKET"

Within each social class group there are families and individuals whose incomes are above average for their class. The Upper-Lower family with an income above $7,000 a year—sometimes a product of both husband and wife working, and sometimes not—is an example of this. So, too, is the Lower-Middle Class business owner or salesman who makes more than $10,000 a year, but has no interest in either the concerts or country clubs of Upper-Middledom and hence is still Lower Middle Class. The Upper Middle Class couple with more than $25,000 a year at its disposal but no desire to play the "society game" of subscription

---

[9] See Pierre Martineau, *Motivation in Advertising* (New York: McGraw-Hill Book Company, 1957) and "Social Classes and Spending Behavior," *The Journal of Marketing*, Vol. 23, No. 2, October 1958, pp. 121–130.

balls or private schools is also in this category. These are what might be called the "overprivileged" segments of each class. They are not "overprivileged" in the absolute sense, of course; they are "overprivileged," however, relative to what is required or needed by families in their class. After they have met the basic expectations and standards of their group in the housing, food, furnishing, and clothing areas, they have quite a bit of money left over which is their equivalent of "discretionary income."

In much the same way, each class has its "underprivileged" members; in the Upper-Middle Class these are the younger couples who haven't made the managerial ranks yet, the college professors, the genteel professionals, and a few downwardly mobile people from high-status backgrounds who are trying to hang on to what fragments of status they have left—for the most part these people are below the $12,000-a-year mark and they can barely meet some of the basic requirements of Upper-Middle life, much less experience any of its little luxuries; in the Lower-Middle Class these are the poorly paid bank tellers, the rows of bookkeepers in railroad offices, the school teachers with considerably more status aspiration than income; and in the Upper-Lower Class it is almost any family earning less than $4,500 or $5,000 a year, at today's rates of pay in metropolitan areas.

In the middle of each class's income range are its "average" members, families who are neither underprivileged nor overprivileged by the standards of their class. You might think of this as the Upper-Middle Class family between $12,000 and $20,000 a year, the Lower-Middle family in the $7,000–$9,000 range, and the Upper-Lower family near $6,000 per annum. However, this word of caution is necessary: a lot of people in the middle income range of their class see themselves as underprivileged because they are aspiring to become one of the "overprivileged" in their class or to move on up the ladder to a higher class.

The relevance of all this to the car market is that when you look at this particular market today, you find it is the "average" members of each class, whether Upper-Middle, Lower-Middle, or Upper-Lower, who constitute the heart of the Low-Priced Three's audience; these are the people who are buying Fords and Chevrolets this year and last, and probably next. No longer is the Ford and Chevrolet market just a lower-middle income market, or (in class terms) a Lower-Middle or a Lower Class market. Rather, it is recruited from the middle income group *within each* social class. Indeed, the $15,000-a-year Upper-Middle "organization man" is apt to choose a Ford or Chevy from the Impala-Galaxie level or else a top-price station wagon once he ventures into this market, whereas the average-income Lower-Middle man will settle for a middle-series Bel Air or Fairlane 500, and the "average-income" Upper Lower guy either splurges for an Impala or "sensibly" contents himself with the spartan Biscayne.

While this has been happening to the Low-Priced Three makes, the heart of the medium-price car market has relocated in the "overprivileged" segments of each class. Today, rich blue-collar workers are joining prosperous Lower-Middle Class salesmen and well-to-do Upper Middle Class business owners in buying Pontiacs, Buicks, Oldsmobiles, Chryslers, and even Cadillacs. In fact, what there is left of big-car lust in our society is found at peak strength among the "overprivileged" Upper-Lowers or else among men who have achieved higher status, but grew up as kids in the Upper-Lower class and have not forgotten their wide-eyed envy of the big car owner.

Finally, as you may have guessed by now, the compact car market's heart is to be found in the "underprivileged" segments of each class (here we are speaking of the market for a compact as a first car). The overwhelming majority of Rambler purchasers, Falcon buyers, and foreign economy car owners come from this socio-economic territory. Thus, it is not the really poor who are buying these cheapest, most economical cars —rather it is those who think of themselves as poor relative to their status aspirations and to their needs for a certain level of clothing, furniture, and housing which they could not afford if they bought a more expensive car.

The market for compacts as second cars is somewhat more complicated in its socio-economic geography, being located in the middle range of the Upper-Middle Class, and the "overprivileged" segment of the Lower-Middle. The "overprivileged" Upper Middle may have one as a third car, but he prefers either a T-Bird, a foreign sports car, a Pontiac convertible, or a beat-up station wagon as his second car, while the "overprivileged" Upper Lower is apt to go for a used standard if he wants a second car.

If marketers and advertisers had assumed that the market for compacts was going to be the lowest-income or lowest-status members of our society, they would have seriously miscalculated in their merchandising and advertising approach. Rambler, for one, did not make this mistake. American Motors advertised its cars as "bringing sense into the auto market" and thus enabled people who bought one to pride themselves on the high-minded rationality they had displayed. Rambler owners, as they drive down the street, are not ashamed that they couldn't afford better— instead, as the company has told them to be, they are proud that they did not yield, like their neighbors, to base emotional desires for a car bloated in size beyond necessity and loaded in gadgetry beyond reason. Compact car owners have their own form of snobbery—what might be called "sensibility snobbery"—with which to content themselves and justify their purchase.

This analysis of the car market is one example of what I mean by the sophisticated application of social class concepts to marketing and advertising problems. There are many products and many brands which, like cars, are more nearly symbols of high status class within class than symbols of higher status per se. A color television set is such a product, or at least it was two years ago when Social Research, Inc., studied its market. At the time color television manufacturers were puzzled because sales were thinly spread throughout the income scale, without any noticeable increase in concentration until an extremely high level was reached. Furthermore, they were unable to see any particular relationship between social class and color set ownership, since about as many Upper-Lower Class people owned them as did Upper-Middles. However, when the two factors of income and class were put together, in the manner described above, it became clear that the color television market was concentrated among high-income or "overprivileged" members of each social class. Other products which bear this complicated relationship to class and income are the more costly brands and larger sizes of home appliances. Fairly expensive recreational equipment like outboard motor boats also tend to be in this category.

In summary, today's market for quality goods and quality brands is not necessarily drawn from what has historically been described as the "Quality Market" of Upper-Middle and Upper Class people, nor even necessarily from the highest income categories. Rather, in many instances, it is drawn from those people within each social level who have the most discretionary income available for enjoying life's little extras above and beyond the requirements of their class. Every merchandiser and advertiser ought to take a good hard look at what he is selling and ask himself if it bears this particular relationship to the class and income picture. If his product does, and if his brand is one of the more expensive, then he should merchandise it not as if it were just for social climbers or for the upper classes, but rather as part of the Better Life, U.S.A. If, on the other hand, his brand is one of the least expensive, then he is not just selling to the poor, but rather to those in all classes who feel it is only sensible on their part to settle for a brand such as his and save the difference for other things which are more important in their statement of social class aspiration and identity.

SOCIAL CLASS ISN'T ALWAYS IMPORTANT

Now, to make the picture complete, it must be pointed out that Social Research, Inc., has found some products in which the income factor is all-important and the social class variable is relevant only to the extent that it is correlated with income. Perhaps the most perfect example of this is the market for air conditioners in Southwestern cities. There, everybody—except the sickly and the extremely old-fashioned— agree that air conditioning one's home is imperative if summer is to be survived with any degree of comfort. Consequently the expensiveness of a family's air conditioning equipment—whether centrally installed, or window units to the number of four, three, two, or one—is directly correlated with family income. It is not merely a function of discretionary income—as in our example about purchase of medium-priced cars; it is instead almost completely a function of total annual income. If more Upper-Middles than Upper-Lowers are fully air-conditioned it is only because more of them can afford to be; it is not because Upper-Middles as a group are placing higher priority on the air-conditioned existence.

Undoubtedly air conditioners are not alone in being classless—so that one more thing the marketer who uses social class in a truly sophisticated way needs to understand is that there can be occasions when it is an irrelevant variable. Realizing this, he will not become disenchanted with social class when he finds a marketing problem where it does not shed light or where it does not seem pertinent. Of course, he will want to make sure that in advertising such a product there is indeed no need to take class into account. After all, some apparently classless products are properly sold to the market in a segmental approach, appealing first on one ground to one class, then on other grounds to another.

There are other products—and probably air conditioning is one of them and children's play clothes may be another—where this is not necessary. For such products some factor, such as physical comfort (in the one case) or simple durability (in the other), is so basic in the consumer's consideration that all other motivations pale into insignificance beside it. There are even products, like beer, where the democratic approach—that is, a tone of "let's-all-be-good-fellows-together" is exactly right and segmental appeals or snob stories are all wrong.

Another aspect to the sophisticated employment of social class refers back to the point made earlier that social class groups are not always homogeneous. It must be recognized that at times at product's market is formed by "highbrows" from the Upper-Upper Class on down to the Lower-Middle, or by "suburbanites" and suburban-minded people of all classes—in which case the social class variable may confuse a market analysis more than clarify it.

Particularly must merchandisers and market analysts beware of equating "Class" with "Brow"; for they are not synonymous. For example, the Upper-Middle Class and those above it are mainly middlebrow in taste (veering toward an all-American lower-middlebrow level of preferences in television shows and advertising messages) even though the majority of highbrows are found at this level. At times advertisers have made the mistake of assuming that the Upper-Middle Class should be appealed to in a highly sophisticated fashion—and though this is just fine if the product itself is likely to appeal primarily to the Manhattanized type of Upper-Middle, it is not correct if it is expected to sell to the kind of doctor in Dubuque who enjoys a visit to New York every now and then but would never want to live there.

In short, not only must the sophisticated marketer abandon social class in favor of income categories on occasion in his analysis and interpretation of a market, he must recognize that at times both income and class are superseded in importance by divisions of the public into brow levels, by divisions into "high mobiles" and "low mobiles," innovators and non-innovators, inner-directed and other-directed, urbanites, suburbanites, exurbanites, ruralites, and Floridians, or what have you. Usually, of course, fullest understanding of a market will require that social class be linked in with whichever sub-categorization proves pertinent from among those in the catalogue just recited, much as income and class were linked together for fullest comprehension of the car market.

As a final point, let it be noted that the way of life and the goals of people in each social class are in perpetual flux. Neither the "who" of each class nor "what motivates them" are constants to be assumed without continual re-evaluation. Right now, particularly, it is very clear that our society is changing. Every year the collar-color line is breaking down further. More blue-collar workers are becoming Middle Class as well as middle income and Modern, and a white-collar position is less and less a guarantee of Lower-Middle status. As a consequence of this, the Lower-Middle Class is perhaps somewhat more "materialistic" in outlook and slightly less "respectability" conscious than it was 25 years ago, or even 8. Meanwhile, for men and women to achieve Upper-Middle status without college backgrounds is becoming more and more difficult, so that this class is turning much more worldly-wise and well-read, much less conventionally bourgeois than it was in the zenith of Babbitt's day.

In short, the form of our society and its division into social classes is not fixed as of Yankee City in 1931, Jonesville in 1944, Kansas City in 1952, or St. Louis in 1960. We won't be able to say exactly the same things about either the classes themselves or their relationships to specific markets by next year at this time. This fact about the American class structure, that it is not static, that it is in the process of change, is in itself important to merchandisers, to advertisers, to anyone in selling. Among other things, it means that undoubtedly they have played a part in past changes and can play a leading role in directing future changes. But of more direct concern here, to the marketing analyst it means that if he allows his stratification concept to become dated, his use of it will cease as of that moment to be sophisticated.

20. Behavioral science concepts for analyzing the consumer

HERTA HERZOG

In earlier years, marketing, strongly influenced by economic theory, emphasized the objective factors in buying behavior although it was never unaware of the importance of "emotional" factors. It struggled with the problem but it had no systematic way of approaching the question as to the kind of psychological factors present in a given situation and as to the why and how of their importance. This was one of the main troubles with the application of the early "lists" of buying motives.

Psychological research, or what commonly goes under the name of "Motivation Research," has received new attention during the last decade when the post-war seller's market changed into a buyer's market. This economic change stimulated widespread recognition of the need to understand the consumer thoroughly. At the same time, the behavioral sciences had developed to a point where it seemed promising to attempt application of some of their concepts and methods to the specific problems of buying and consumption behavior.

The attempts so far have been quite encouraging but they represent only a beginning. Motivation researchers have been busy doing specific studies; we have not yet had enough time to think through what we are doing and what general findings emerge. We have made uneven use of the available behavioral science concepts, and for some of the marketer's problems the behavioral sciences do not yet offer concepts or methods.

Application of existing behavioral science material is further complicated by the fact that we are not yet dealing with a unified theoretical system. Interdisciplinary integration is far from complete and so is con-

Reprinted by permission of D. J. Duncan, editor, *Proceedings, Conference of Marketing Teachers from Far Western States.* 1958, pp. 32–41.

sensus within the various disciplines. Psychology, for instance, offers at least three major approaches to motivation.

There is the approach of the laboratory psychologists who in many instances use animals for their subjects and who have tended to focus on the physiological tensions or "body needs" as motivational forces.

There is the work of the clinical psychologists, and of dynamic psychology in particular, which has focused on the role of psychological factors. They see in the handling of the biological drives within the mores of society a key problem, and also a possibility for influencing behavior. Conflicts between basic drives or motives and social restrictions, they say, put great stresses on the individual. Since he cannot tolerate them, the motives become repressed, unconscious but not eliminated as driving forces. They continue to make themselves felt in a variety of ways.

A third approach to the study of motives is represented by the Gestalt psychologists and, particularly, the work of Kurt Lewin. This sociopsychological approach emphasizes the fact that people are reacting in an environment and that behavior must be understood as a function of the person and the environment in which he lives, with both of these being mutually dependent variables. Behavior, as these psychologists see it, is largely goal-directed and results from a person's motives as well as his perception of the environment at a given time.

In short, at this point the behavioral sciences offer a variety of differing theories and approaches to the understanding of behavior. Thus you will find that the application of behavioral science concepts to marketing varies with the theoretical orientation of the researchers, or that market researchers borrow eclectically depending on which theoretical concepts seem most applicable and fruitful in a particular case.

What are some of the more widely used concepts and the areas of their application?

1. WHAT IS A PRODUCT?

Let me begin with the question "What is a product"—a question of concern to every marketer. From a strictly technical manufacturing standpoint, a product consists of a number of raw materials so put together that the end result, the product, serves a useful purpose of consumption, be it in feeding, clothing, housing, transporting the consumer, etc.

You need only to think about your car, however, to realize that it represents neither the sum total of its parts for you, nor merely an instrument of transportation. This has, of course, been long recognized and one of the concerns of marketing has been to determine just which product "features" are important to the consumer. Thus market research on a food product has tried to measure the relative appeal of such features as taste, color, consistency, quality of ingredients, price, etc. Studying cars, we have tried to assess the interest in engineering features such as power steering, power brakes or automatic transmission as compared with appearance, comfort, up-keep, trade-in value, etc.

These familiar classifications are not fully satisfactory. Obviously, "trade-in value" is a feature of a rather different kind than some of the others I have mentioned. To know that a consumer values "comfort" does not tell us too much. What constitutes comfort to him, we want to know: is it the upholstery, leg room, head room, trunk space, good springs, or what? Is it correct to interpret a car owner's concern with power steering as an expression of interest in engineering features or, rather, does it mean "easy parking," another comfort item to the consumer? Will the consumer tell us what he wants when we ask him to compare looks with, let's say, economy or technical quality?

In short, the traditional methods of classification are somewhere in-between a product definition in terms of the manufacturer and a product definition in terms of the consumer. Thus they tend to fall short of telling the manufacturer how and what the consumer sees in a car so that he can build a car that will deliver these consumer benefits.

The application of behavioral science concepts, particularly the various psychological theories, has been useful in helping us toward a better understanding of the "product."

In pointing out the subjective component in perception, they suggested that we must go the whole way in determining how the consumer sees the product, not what it is technically. The concept of the "psychological environment" includes the notion that what people "see," depends on the stimulus characteristics as well as their personality—the type of person they are, the state they are in, and their ideology. It contains a strong social and cultural component: we "see" things in the way our culture and the particular social group in which we move have induced us to see them. And we see things in context, not as isolated elements or objects but as part of the "total situation," the inner and outer environment. It is useful to add here a key concept borrowed from psychoanalytic theory, namely, that the "inner environment" may contain repressed needs and wants as well as those the individual is aware of.

These theoretical concepts have led to the notion of the *product image and the exploration of the various meanings, rational and symbolic, which the product* may have to the consumer.

For example, getting at the product image of gasoline, we asked motorists, among a number of questions, what other purchases they consider "similar" to buying gasoline, and why they are similar. We found three main types of conceptions: gasoline was likened to other types of fuel such as electricity, water, etc., by a small percentage; gasoline purchases were likened to other purchases having to do with transportation such as bus tickets, railroad fares, by another small proportion. More than half of the respondents likened gasoline to personal consumption items: things which keep the human body fed such as bread or milk, which keep it protected such as hats or shoes, which keep it pepped up, such as beer or cigarettes.

This particular study was done before the first gasoline additive broke on the market, at a time when in conventional questioning the large majority of consumers stressed that gasoline is rather an uninteresting product, all main gasolines are pretty much alike, and that in buying gasoline they look for station convenience and service rather than the particular product sold at the station. The findings on the product image suggested that via the car, viewed as an extension of the body, there was a good deal more potential interest in the product itself which should be catered to in product development and subsequent product promotion.

Or take another example—airplanes and air travel. In another type of so-called projective questioning, people who like plane travel and those who do not care for it were asked to draw their idea of an airplane and tell a story about their drawings. The responses revealed marked differences in product image among the two groups, which were confirmed by other data. The fan sees himself at the controls of a wonderful instrument, while the non-fan tends to see himself as a passenger, looking at a plane mainly as a perhaps time-saving vehicle of transportation.

The famous Mason Haire study is another example of exploration of the product image. As you know, Haire made up two "shopping lists" containing a series of everyday household purchase items such as a pound and a half of hamburger, two cans of Del Monte peaches, etc. One list contained Nescafe while the other, identical with the first, substituted Maxwell House regular for the instant coffee. When he asked a matched group of housewives to describe the type of woman who would purchase each list of products, he found that a considerable proportion mentioned "lazy" housewives, "women who don't plan well," for the list containing instant coffee. Direct questioning had given no indication that this was a connotation associated with the perception of the new product.

Since the meanings associated with a product are often quite varied, it is useful to employ a variety of questioning techniques which will uncover the rational as well as the emotional connotations: direct questions, open-end type questions and projective devices, some of which I mentioned. Also, the questioning must give the respondent a variety of opportunities to say what he or she has in mind about a product. In addition to asking what she likes about the product or how she rates specific features, one might ask about the "ideal" product in a given category. Or one might invite the respondent to describe how she uses the product, or have her report her thoughts as she actually uses it. One might ascertain memories of outstanding enjoyment of the product, ask the consumer how she would feel if she had to do without the product, and why, etc.

From such types of questioning one can document that an apparently simple product such as cigarettes had a variety of "meanings" —even before the days of health concern. Some smokers, for example, saw in a cigarette something to manipulate, a means of assertion; they were particularly interested in specific features such as firm packing. For others, a cigarette was a means of comfort—deep inhaling, the strength of a cigarette, were some of the things they particularly valued. Some saw in a cigarette an outlet of nervous tension; there were no particular features that interested them more than others. Some saw in a cigarette primarily an oral sensation; taste of course was one of the features they were interested in. In each case it could be shown that the product definition was strongly linked to basic tendencies on the part of the smoker and linked also to an interest in particular product attributes.

Studies relating to product image have also taught us that the same word used loosely by the consumer, may have very different meanings. Take "taste," for example. In a study of Kippers we found that a large proportion of respondents who in direct questioning said they didn't use the product because they didn't like its taste, actually had never tasted it. In depth interviewing, it turned out that dislike of "taste" in this case was merely a way of talking about something that was unfamiliar, foreign, unacceptable, unconventional. The average American housewife had a kind of mental image of barefoot dock workers slopping around in these slimy fish in some far away port. In the case of soda crackers, liking for "taste" stands primarily for texture characteristics. In the case of toothpastes, "taste" stands for the total sensation in the mouth, not just a particular flavor. And in the case of hard liquor, "taste" is a means to describe and to anticipate effect characteristics.

Product image studies need to be repeated. Consumer conceptions about a product do not stand still: technical developments, degree of market saturation, availability, are some of the environmental factors which may restructure the consumer image. There was a time when ammoniated toothpastes had a special health connotation attractive mainly to the hypochondriac. With the subsequent advent of chlorophyll and anti-enzyme ingredients, the image of a toothpaste changed; today the anti-decay feature is a part of a modern, up-to-date toothpaste that the majority of consumers would not want to do without.

2. WHAT IS A BRAND?

You will have gathered from the preceding that brands, like product types, are perceived by the consumer in the form of "brand images." This is the sum total of impressions the consumer receives from many sources: from actual experience and hearsay about the brand itself as well as its packaging, its name, the company making it, the types of people the individual has seen using the brand, what was said in its advertising, as well as from the tone, format, type of advertising vehicle in which the product story was told.

All these impressions amount to a sort of brand personality which is similar for the consuming public at large, although different consumer groups may have different attitudes toward it. For instance, users generally interpret the brand image more favorably than non-users although both groups agree on its essential outline. The user may like a brand because it is "tried and true," the "first and best on the market," while the non-user may call the same brand "old-fashioned," with both agreeing that it is an old, well-established brand.

The brand image contains objective product qualities, particularly if there are observable product characteristics such as differences in strength or taste or shape or texture. These qualities themselves have rational as well as symbolic meanings which merge with the meanings created by all the other sources through which the public meets a brand.

In the gasoline study quoted before, it was found that motorists tended to think of Gulf, among other things, as a "friendly" gasoline— a notion that stemmed from associations with the name which reminded of "outdoor sports," the "Gulf of Mexico," etc. These notions were supported by the "sunny" yellow color used in its emblem, the "friendly" approach in its advertising copy (Go Gulf), and the nature of the advertising vehicle, a program called "We the People" which, although no longer on the air at the time of the study, had done its share in contributing to the brand image.

Interviews with smokers done by various motivation researchers, indicate that although they may not be able to tell brands apart in a blindfold test, they nevertheless have quite clear-cut images of various brands. Both Camels and Luckies, for example, are thought of as "strong" cigarettes as compared with Philip Morris which is associated with mildness. But there are further marked differences in the images of Camels and Luckies. This was measured, for example, by a set of questions in which people were asked to "match" each brand with a series of socioeconomic and psychological characteristics, which presumably were "typical of the person likely to smoke the brand."

The concepts consumers have of a brand result from objective facts; at the same time, these concepts serve to shape sales patterns. For we find rather frequently that consumers tend to prefer the brand whose image is congenial to them. This brings me to a third point—the question "What is a consumer?"

3. WHAT IS A CONSUMER?

Marketing has always thought of the consumer in terms of who buys what, for what purpose, at what price, where, etc. This kind of information, derived from observable consumer behavior data, is very important in locating a product or brand in the total market picture. But certain marketing needs, specifically those of the people concerned with the creative aspects in product development and brand promotion, require more qualitative dynamic knowledge about the consumer than his age, income or family status. They require an answer to the question why consumers buy a particular product and how current non-users can be switched to a specific brand.

This statement of the problem of consumer motivation is in itself different from the way in which it used to be stated, and strongly influenced by the application of behavioral science concepts.

From trying to apply a general list of buying motives to the purchase of a particular product or brand, market research proceeded to ask the user why he bought or preferred the brand, to find out from the former user why he switched to it, and from the non-user why he never used it. This was a step ahead because it attempted to trace the purchase decision for a particular brand, and included the user and the non-user.

As you can well imagine, the non-user in particular finds it difficult to explain why he doesn't use the brand. "I just never thought of it," "I don't need it," "I like my current brand," are rather typical answers. Even more specific ones such as "I don't like the color," and "It's too expensive" do not indicate with enough certainty what appeal would be effective in inducing purchase. If one were to take the answers seriously and changed the color or reduced the price, two drastic changes on the part of the manufacturer, would the non-user really become a consumer, one wonders? And what impact would these changes have on the current consumer?

In today's third stage of development we are mindful of the concept that the consumer acts in a total situation and we also consider that behavior results from the interplay of his personal make-up and his perception of the environment. Thus we tend to look upon a particular brand as one possible choice the consumer might make among other brands in the category, and even among other kinds of products. And allowing for external situational influences which might have a bearing on buying behavior, motivation research proper attempts to assess the hold the brand has on its current consumers (some of whom might switch away from it tomorrow), as well as the appeal it might offer to its most likely prospects (not *all* non-users). It does so by relating the perception of the brand to the "needs" of the consumer.

In this analysis of needs one must provide for the fact that consumer behavior serves physiological as well as psychological needs; needs the person is aware of and needs he may not be conscious of although they are "projected" into his buying behavior; needs he is willing to tell and those he doesn't want to admit, falling back on "rationalization." The needs are patterned by the culture and the social class to which he belongs, his stage of development as well as his "personality."

Therefore, a good motivation study must be based on a thorough knowledge of the market in terms of such background characteristics as socio-economic status, age, city size, region; and it employs the total arsenal of methods that the behavioral sciences have at their command so far to get at conscious as well as unconscious needs. This means personality tests and depth interviewing, as well as direct questioning.

One of the general findings that has emerged from this type of research is the concept of *psychological market segmentation* which cuts across and refines the traditional concept of market segmentation based on such characteristics as age or income. Consumers tend to buy the brand whose image most closely corresponds to their own needs; the image selects the type of consumer for whom the brand promises particular satisfaction. This is true in product categories where you would expect it, such as in the cigarette field or the use of hair tonics among men. It also holds for durable goods such as cars, for foods down to peanut butter, for household supplies down to disinfectants.

The main research task in finding out what motivates the consumer toward product use and brand preferences is to find the psychological dimension(s) which characterize the user and differentiate him from the non-user. These might have to do with the "self-image" which the consumer acts out, as it were, in his consumption behavior. The self-image is important, for example, in determining whether or not a man (with enough hair on his head) will use a hair tonic, and what type of hair tonic he will use. The basic compulsivity of a woman and the way she sees her role as a housewife, have a marked bearing on the type of household items she uses. People on comparable income levels handle the conflict between the impulse for self-indulgence (buying) and the demands for self-restraint (postponement of buying) in ways which differentiate the saver from the non-saver. In a study dealing with a service from a "big" company, we found that this key characteristic of the image had a positive attraction for at least two consumer groups. Those who as personalities sought and needed protection, bought the company's products because bigness provided assurance. At the other end of the pole were the assertive, aggressive people who also reacted positively because bigness provided a self-conscious gratifying indentification with success.

However, there were also groups representative of many consumers who reacted negatively for a variety of reasons. In some instances the resistance against a "big" brand was as basic as its appeal to other consumer groups. In other instances, the negative responses expressed merely a feeling that the company was remote, aloof, efficient but not close enough to the consumer.

The data not only indicated that these non-users could be interested but the interviews contained a number of important clues as to just what the brand must do to hold its current customers and come closer to these prospects. The clues included changes in marketing strategy, media policy and selling arguments.

4. WHAT IS AN AD?

I will be very brief on a fourth question. . . . "What is an ad," because you are probably least interested in this area of application.

Let me make one point on layout, the physical appearance of the ad, since the application of behavioral science concepts to advertising copy follows pretty much from what I have already said about findings on consumer motivations.

Thousands of readership checks in the past have served to indicate that on the average photographs or life-like drawings are in most product fields a means of obtaining attention. Borrowing some of the concepts developed particularly by scientists working on theory of instincts, we have come to understand what accounts for the occasional very high readership obtained by ads that do not use the photographic technique.

These scientists, working with animals, have come up with the concept of "perceptual releasers." These are attributes of the stimulus which are sufficient to activate memory traces which then produce the response. For example, studying the courtship behavior of the Stickleback fish, they found that the male will pursue the dummy of a female, held into the aquarium by the experimenter, as long as it has a swollen abdomen (even though it may be only a very crude model), in preference to a lifelike reproduction of a normal female. He will court the dummy particularly if it is lowered into the aquarium in the typical position of the female Stickleback in the courting situation.

The perception of an ad apparently works similarly. For example, one successful campaign featured an insurance salesman, Mr. Friendly, who was drawn in almost cartoon fashion. It was certainly not a life-like portrayal but copy research indicated that this piece of artwork served indeed to catch and release the reader's ambivalence about insurance and insurance salesmen. It was real in the sense of touching a real experience.

In conclusion, I should like to apologize that I know little or nothing about your special area of interest, the teaching of marketing. If the behavioral science approach is not already a part of your curriculum, I should think it worthy of your consideration—even if its application to marketing problems is not yet fully developed.

21. Symbolism and life style

SIDNEY J. LEVY

The symbolic nature of consumer objects has received much attention in recent years. At least it has been fashionable to designate various
outstanding objects as symbolic, thereby giving lip service to this idea.
We comfortably note that language is symbolic, as are visual materials
in modern art, and television commercials. Having noted this, or used the
term to accuse someone of striving for status symbols, the matter is commonly dropped. This usually occurs because it is hard to keep thinking
about the symbolic meanings of objects and behavior. To do so requires
practice in adopting a view of actions that is sufficiently detached to
permit analysis and interpretation, and sufficiently empathetic to produce
insights. It is usually simpler to deal with the objects and behaviors
themselves.[1]

It is easier to take for granted that people do what they do because,
being themselves, they must, with no more need for explanation than we
normally feel we must offer to explain our own actions. It is easier to
explain behavior by categorizing it as the result of the person's being
between the ages of 40 and 45, upper middle class, and in the over
$15,000 income bracket. If we are daring, we may go so far as to hint
that these consumers are sociable or introverted or discriminating in personality. These are all legitimate rubics, and provide convenient and
useful ways of dividing up data in order to compare frequency distribution.

Reprinted from *Proceedings,* American Marketing Association Conference,
December, 1963 (Greyser, editor) by permission of the American Marketing Association, pp. 140–150.

[1] David McK. Rioch has a relevant discussion in distinguishing between two
separate problems in communication which face the physician—"that of commitment
to the patient as a person and that of analyzing the mechanisms involved and their
disorders." See: David McK. Rioch, "Communication in the Laboratory and Communication in the Clinic," *Psychiatry,* (1963) Vol. 26, #3, pp. 209–221.

But we are challenged to try to analyze *meaning*—and thus become engaged with the study of symbolism and the role of symbols in the daily life of average citizens. Here I must emphasize that in speaking of symbols and symbolizing, I am not referring shyly and euphemistically to the study of phallic objects on cars or to dreams of nudity in the streets—although I would not, of course, exclude such curious phenomena from consideration. As Langer points out:

Obvious only in man, is the *need of symbolization*. The symbol-making function is one of man's primary activities, like eating, looking, or moving about. It is the fundamental process of his mind, and goes on all the time. Sometimes we are aware of it, sometimes we merely find its results, and realize that certain experiences have passed through our brains and have been digested there.[2]

If this is so, there are several implications. First, as I have mentioned, it is hard to notice people's symbolizing any more than we notice their breathing or blood circulating, unless something goes wrong with these functions. Similarly, we notice symbolizing with it becomes dramatic, blatant, or so alien to our understanding that we are struck by the discrepancy between someone else's meanings and our own. Moreover, since symbolizing is so implicit, asking people about it may elicit no simple answers since the symbolizer may not be self-conscious about what he is doing.

Nevertheless, the pervasive and inescapable nature of symbolizing means that analyzing it is what we are really doing whenever we study human behavior. This then applies to the ordinary actions that constitute consumer behavior as well as the extraordinary. Now, how can we examine symbolizing as a life style force? I would like to start by offering the view that an individual's life style is a large complex symbol in motion. It is composed of sub-symbols; it utilizes a characteristic pattern of life space; and it acts systematically to process objects and events in accordance with these values.

A LARGE COMPLEX SYMBOL IN MOTION

Everyone's life has a cycle of some kind. As a total entity moving through time, a person builds a characteristic assertion of who he is and how he regards his own being, and he expresses it in the specific manner of his actions. To realize this is merely to note that people have recognizable personalities that remain familiar to us—they do not appear as strangers each time we meet them. But this also means that there is more to them than that they eat when hungry, sleep when tired, and love when stimulated. They develop the wish to do these things in particular ways

[2] Susanne K. Langer, *Philosophy in a New Key*, Harvard University Press, 1951, Cambridge, Mass., p. 41.

regarded as suitable for themselves. And *what is thought suitable rests in who they are, how they grew up, their nationality, the groups they participate in or seek, and ultimately in all of this, the individual person they aim to be.*

In a sense, everyone seeks to prove something, and this—or some central set of recurring motifs—is identifiable as the summary fashion of his wrestling with existence. To observe this takes some largeness of view; perhaps it can never be fully observed until a man is dead, and then the one person who experienced it all and might know most about it is gone. Still, we do observe other people's life styles, even if we capture only fragments and part-motifs.

We can think of people in categorical terms derived from their customary behavior, emotional tone, expressed wishes; by being donors and recipients to their special forms of taking and giving. So the person oriented to display may take attention and admiration from us, the ambitious leader wants us to obey, the careless driver may want to share an accident with us. As they show us themselves, order us about, or collide with us, they bring their life styles to our attention. We discover something about the content of their personalities and the special fashion or form they give to it. So perhaps this driver apologizes profusely—as perhaps he always does when he hurts others; this leader keeps insisting it is all for the good of others; and this exhibitionist does it by putting on striking clothes rather than removing them.

As we sense the meaningful currents in people's behavior and emotional expression, we become aware of what they are trying to do and the means they employ. We decide they are generous, moral, corrupt, subtle, bitter, active, sweet; and when we pronounce such as judgments we are usually referring to the ongoing symbolic quality of the person rather than to a specific action. We mean the deeper attributes that go on despite the times he is not generous, subtle, or active.

Contrasting Styles of Life

In expressing their values, in describing the kinds of roles they play in life and how they think those roles should be fulfilled, people reveal both real and ideal life styles. In one marketing study in Montana, life was described as slow-paced, with the people geared to the rigors and virtues of frontier life where it is cold and demanding; where the skills and rewards of hunting and fishing loom large; where men are rugged, touched with the nobility of the natural man and superior to the wan and tender Eastern city man. A man's life style was generally conceived as one of good fellowship, whether with a gun, a rod, or a drink. This may sound like parody; to show the reality of these views, I quote the comments of some of the men describing the people and life style of Montana.

The men here are real good, you can trust them. Most of them are outdoor men; they have to be or else they wouldn't live here. Most of them are honest.

The men here are true Westerners; big, tough and rugged.

Men are men here, and they are manly. Somewhat more honest and less sharp dealing than in the more civilized parts of the country.

It's wonderful here. It's God's country. I like the frontier atmosphere. Life is casual and leisurely here, no frantic big city pace.

This contrasts with the kinds of life style men in metropolitan environments offer to sum up who they are. Here we find the familiar tunes of urban-suburban people, where men are first husbands and fathers, and run to the ragged rather than the rugged.

The men here are very nice, a well-educated group of men who have many outside interests and are very congenial. They're home-loving and conscientious.

Most of my neighbors are young families and pretty well child-oriented. The men are typical suburbanites, very much concerned with crab grass and PTA. They all work hard and bring home brief cases.

To grasp these life styles and how they are exemplified in individual lives requires an orientation to configurations, to patterns of ideas, feelings, and actions. We need to sense the man at work, to feel with him the peculiar flavor with which he invests his work or draws from it joy, irritation, monotony, impatience, anticipation, anxiety about today or tomorrow, comfort, competence, pride, a restless urge to succeed visibly, or a restless urge to reach five o'clock. We can think about what kind of motivation is useful in distinguishing the achieving executive from the adequate one, the upward striving white collar worker from the man who just wants to make a living. *To explore this large, complex symbol in motion that is a man's grand life style is to seek to define his self-concept,* to describe the central set of beliefs about himself and what he aspires to, that provide consistency (or unpredictability) to what he does. Information about such self-concepts may come from various directions. Two students writing class autobiographies conveyed the contrasting sense of focus each felt about what he sought to achieve in life—one summing up that he wanted to live in accordance with "intelligence, truth, and justice," while the other said his aims boiled down to "thrift, security, and cleanliness." Presumably, the former young man represents a better potential market for books, the latter is possibly more geared to soap.

Such self-definitions can help us perceive the coherence of behavior in housewives who relentlessly pursue antiseptic cleanliness, in children accomplishing characteristically in school, as well as in doting or dismal fathers. This idea of one's self as "naturally" following its bent, accompanied by the feeling "doesn't everyone?" is the core personal symbol. When we understand this about a person, we can start to trace out the intricate pattern of his actions, to see how it affects the handling of money, choice of clothes, food preferences, interest in shopping, cooking, giving gifts, home workshopping. We can see how the persisting needs of one man to bend people to his will can make him a topnotch salesman, or where the urge to resist produces an obdurate purchasing agent.

In anthropological analogue to this thought, Redfield noted the significance of maize as a vital symbol to the Mayan villagers of Chan Kom in the Yucatan.

So I began to form another way of conceiving parts as related to one another in a system of activity and thought. This third system is neither chainlike or maplike. It is radial: maize is a center and other things are grouped around it, connected to it in different ways, some by a series of useful activities, some by connections of symbolic significance. The mind goes out from maize to agriculture, from maize to social life, from maize to religion. Maize is always the center of things.[3]

LIFE STYLE IS MADE OF SUB-SYMBOLS

If we can thus think of the life style of a person or a group as having a general symbolic character, one that refers to and expresses a certain central emphasis in motivation and action, we can describe as sub-symbols the things—objects, activities—that are used to play out this general symbolic meaning and to embody it. The clotheshorse needs clothes, the bookworm needs books, the cliffdweller needs cliffs. For example, *housing has a meaning that varies with who is to live in it.*

Back noted that in Puerto Rico a public housing project could be regarded as a custodial institution or as a technique for upward mobility, making the most progressive and the most dependent families inclined toward the project. Families falling between these extremes tend to prefer to stay in private housing, even though it may be objectively inferior.[4]

Apartment living versus living in a house provides a contrast in the meanings of sub-symbols. Apartment dwellers who are not familially oriented and who use housing that exemplifies the exciting values of urban life, like the freer kind of life it represents

I like living in apartments . . . The thing I like best about it is the convenience of having everything taken care of.

Apartment life is very relaxing—no fires to tend to, sidewalks to shovel, and no painting. More time for enjoyment.

[3] Robert Redfield, *The Little Community*, The University of Chicago Press, 1955, p. 22.

[4] Kurt W. Back, *Slums, Projects, and People*, Duke University Press, 1962.

Those with a greater yearning to belong and to share in a feeling of some social responsibility see apartments as a stopgap that falls short of true participation in life.

The only advantage to apartment living is that it is a stopgap until you can buy a house.

There is very little opportunity for a sense of community life in an apartment.

Multiple Meanings

As these contrasting views of apartment living so aptly illustrate, a complication for understanding marketing problems is caused by the multiple meanings of objects and communications. The same person may see several meanings and different people may see different meanings. A picture of a skier shows a man standing on two sticks: this may signify a pleasant sport, a dangerous sport, an expensive pastime, new ways of leisure in America, superior social status at an elegant resort, the competitiveness of the Olympics, even a cause of perspiration in a deodorant advertisement.

Examples could be multiplied to show how people behave in accordance with their own view of themselves and how they want to do things that fit this view. This extends into interesting realms of action and non-action. A study of why women do not visit physicians for examination as often as they should to detect cancer showed that one reason was a reluctance to change one's underwear habits—for example, to iron a brassiere in order to seem like the kind of women the doctor is presumably accustomed to examining. It was also clear that some women did not want to explore the possibility of having cancer because they believe it is a venereal disease and would reveal their sexual practices. Such anxieties are similarly related to skin problems among young people, where ideas about self-indulgence, sex, and hostility become interwoven with the sense of self, producing feelings of shame and guilt. For example:

"I saw an ad—it was either for pimples or athlete's foot—that was pretty gruesome. It was like some of the awful pictures shown in the windows of the cheap low class drug stores for skin diseases, and everyone knows what they are trying to show without coming right out and saying venereal disease."

The utilization of sub-symbols affects all customers, not merely buyers of consumers' goods looking for "status symbols." A study of institutional food buyers showed the pervasive effects of how the buyers defined themselves, their institutions, and their customers, to give their food purchasing its special flavor and meaning. Dietitians and home economists, pursuing their professional roles, tended to emphasize nutritional values and balanced menus; buyers oriented to cooking or the clientele of an establishment devoted to the arts thought in terms of the palate and visual esthetics; more business-oriented managers made money a foremost consideration in the style of planning they showed. These were occupational life styles, each reflecting the typical symbolic configuration that had developed as suitable. The sub-symbols of place, titles, preferred suppliers, utensils, foods, all played roles in sustaining the larger significance these people sought to convey.

It is easiest to see objects being employed symbolically where the goal is to display, where visibility is high; and it is in these situations where they probably do reach their fullest flowering and elaboration. In dress furniture, when "company is coming," and so on, the importance of audiences intensifies the presentation of life style. Nevertheless, one's life style is always going on, even if privately at a different level. It is hard for us to believe that there is ever a time when no one is looking—there is always God. And even if we relax our standards with Him and scratch our behinds, wear our socks a second day, or read faster than comprehension can keep up, our lapses are also part of ourselves. They support the purchase of sub-symbolic products that make up the covert life styles that let one sneak a secret drink, consume pornography, or watch more television than one likes to admit.

A CHARACTERISTIC PATTERN OF LIFE SPACE

An interesting aspect of symbolism is the significance of life space. As a person expresses his life style, he moves through his environment, perceiving it and using it in his own special ways. Probably we can observe a typical continuum ranging from expansive to constricted use of the environment. Higher status people have a larger world view, they look toward and move toward more distant horizons. They are among that classic 20 percent of the population who do 80 percent of the living, using airplanes and long distance telephones in sharply disproportionate degree. Lower status people are apt to use even their own city in narrower fashion, some never going downtown or leaving the home neighborhood. This is not merely a matter of economics, although money (and its relative availability) is a related parameter.

Individuals vary in their yearnings for space, some loving roomy old houses, others preferring restricted, efficient space. Michael Balint [5] has devoted a book to exploring the psychological consequences of basic interest in things versus basic interest in the spaces between things. He believes that people have fundamental orientations that lead them either to emphasize clinging to objects or to emphasize moving between

[5] Michael Balint, *Thrills and Regressions*. International University Press, 1959.

objects. The latter orientation is characteristic in the thrill-seeking of skiing and rollercoasting, whereas clinging to objects turns ocnophils (as Balint calls them) toward stability and security. A study of mobile home dwellers highlighted this contrast with cases of women who bewept the fact that their less root-minded husbands did not provide homes with entrenched foundations and space to accumulate more objects.

Such concerns can be extended into assessments of how people organize objects in the space available. Are they orderly and precise or do they want things to "look lived in?" We may judge people and companies for their life style by how they use space, ranging from Japanese austerity to Victorian clutter, understanding perhaps that a clear desk means efficiency, high status, or a figurehead who lets others do the work. A desk piled high may be interpreted as sloppy; comfortable; the home of a drudge, a procrastinator, or a hard worker. Modern architectural design struggles with whether to "waste space" by leaving open areas or allot everyone a tight cubicle; should an office building be like a hospital or like an atrium, will the public think better of the corporation if the street level is built like an expensive garden plaza instead of having convenient and profitable shops flush to the sidewalk?

PROCESSING OBJECTS AND EVENTS

What are the practical implications of this view of life style that stresses its symbolic character? It emphasizes the fact that buyers see objects and events in the real world as having certain potentialities. These potentialities are scanned, screened, and processed for their symbolic suitability, not only because the products can provide some specific results, but because they become incorporated into the life style of the person. This does not mean all product choices are razor's edge decisions between the real-me and the not-me, with a nod to the fake-me. But still, what do they all add up to?

From a marketing point of view—one that might startle traditional academicians (other than anthropologists, perhaps)—*a consumer's personality can be seen as the peculiar total of the products he consumes.* Shown a picture of a young man in an advertisement, one female respondent deduced the following:

He's a bachelor, his left hand is showing and it has no ring on it. He lives in one of those modern high-rise apartments and the rooms are brightly colored. He has modern, expensive furniture, but not Danish modern. He buys his clothes at Brooks Brothers. He owns a good Hi-fi. He skis. He has a sailboat. He eats Limburger or any other prestige cheese with his beer. He likes and cooks a lot of steak and he would have filet mignon for company. His liquor cabinet has Jack Daniel's bourbon, Beefeater gin, and a good Scotch.

Through his life style does she know him.

If we think of a housewife who uses Crosse and Blackwell soups, subscribes to *Gourmet* magazine, flies live lobster in from Maine to Chicago to serve guests, drives a Renault, and doesn't shave under her arms, we sense a value system engaged in choosing things from the marketplace that add up to a life style quite different from that of the woman who uses Campbell's, reads *Family Circle* for ideas on how to furnish a playroom, makes meat loaf twice a week (stretching it with oatmeal), rides in her husband's Bel Air, and scrubs the kitchen floor three times a week.

By studying these configurations of life style, by observing how people put together those ways of living they think appropriate for a 40 year old surgeon on the make, a prosperous factory foreman in a working class suburb, a woman who feels she leads a dog's life and likes to "go out and eat," or "a woman who feels she is not a raving beauty, but is attractive to men," we can find out how they use products most meaningfully for themselves. Close analysis of consumption systems of different kinds of people is revealing,[6] as is accumulating life history information which does not focus so closely on products that it loses the larger ongoing symbolic aims I have been discussing.

CONCLUSION

The descriptions I have made here to capture or convey some of these life style issues seem awkward and inadequate. Much work is needed to study consumer life styles, to create a taxonomy of life styles that helps us to think more systematically about different kinds of people, to build a theory that illuminates the dynamic process by which people turn their primitive needs into nuanced and elaborated sets of discriminations among the objects in the market place. We each know that such a process is true of ourselves, but so often when studied, it seems to fall between the meshes of the research net. It laughs at the grossness of personality inventories or the stodginess of questionnaires that fail to take account of the ludicrous, shy, quicksilver, or perverse elements of life style, the felt absurdity of caring about invisible differences in unessential products.

Earlier work has suggested the importance of symbols in the marketing world, particularly in regard to age, sex, and social class. My present purpose is to reaffirm this importance. It is also to point attention to the fact that *marketers do not just sell isolated items that can be interpreted as symbols; rather, they sell pieces of a larger symbol—the consumer's life style.* Marketing is then a process of providing customers with parts of a potential mosaic from which they, as artists of their own life styles,

[6] See Harper W. Boyd, Jr., and Sidney J. Levy, "New Dimension in Consumer Analysis," *Harvard Business Review*, November–December, 1963, pp. 129–140.

can pick and choose to develop the composition that for the time may seem the best. The marketer who thinks about his products in this way will seek to understand their potential settings and relationships to other parts of consumer life styles, thereby to increase the number of ways he fits meaningfully into them.

22. The competitive marketing simulator—a new management tool

PHILIP KOTLER

Business decisions are growing increasingly complex and expensive. This has stimulated the interest of business executives in refined models for decision making. Many executives have welcomed the development of operations research models for capital budgeting decisions, traffic decisions, inventory and production decisions.

Of all the functional areas, marketing seems to be marked by the least analytical progress. Personal intuition continues to play a much more important role in this type of decision making than formal analysis. This is due not so much to intellectual apathy or resistance on the part of marketing executives as to the intrinsically more difficult nature of marketing decisions. Marketing phenomena tend to exhibit fewer tractable quantitative properties than production and finance phenomena.

SIX FACTORS

Suppose a company wants to estimate likely sales at alternative levels of advertising expenditure. There are at least six factors which burden the investigation.

1. *Nonlinearity*. The relationship between sales volume and advertising expenditure is direct but not linear throughout. Sales may increase at an increasing rate as advertising expenditures attain some volume, and later increase at a decreasing rate as the upper limit of potential demand is reached. This particular conception of the sales/advertising curve is shown in Figure 1.

Reprinted from the *California Management Review*, Volume VII, No. 3, Spring, 1965. Copyright 1965 by the Regents of the University of California.

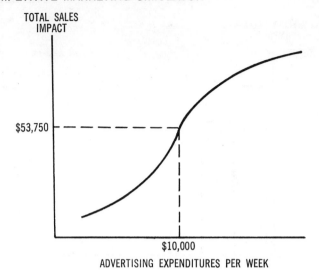

TOTAL SALES
IMPACT

$53,750

$10,000
ADVERTISING EXPENDITURES PER WEEK

Figure 1. One Conception of the Relationship of Total Sales to Advertising

2. *Time lags and decay.* An advertising expenditure produces both immediate and delayed effects. The delayed effects tend to decay in importance with the passage of time at a rate depending on the nature of the advertising. This particular conception of the effects of an advertisement through time is shown in Figure 2.

3. *Other elements in the company's marketing mix.* The sales impact of an advertising expenditure is conditional upon the qualities and levels of the other elements in the company's marketing mix. Thus, an advertisement may produce large sales if the company's price is low and only small sales if the company's price is high. An example is given in the boxed exhibit.

4. *The state of the particular market.* The sales impact must be estimated under assumed conditions concerning the size of the particular market, the needs, motives, and attitudes of people in the market, the available products, and so forth.

5. *Environmental conditions.* The sales impact must be estimated under assumed conditions concerning the level and distribution of income, possible changes in legislation, the likely weather pattern, and so forth.

6. *Competitive maneuvers.* The sales impact must be estimated under assumed responses of competitors and its own counter responses. Competitors are likely to respond in varying ways depending upon which marketing variable was changed and the amount of change. For example, firms in pure oligopolistic competition are likely to meet a price cut but are less likely to react immediately to a new packaging design introduced by a competitor.

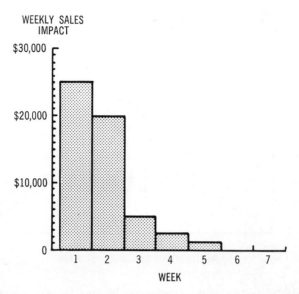

Figure 2. A Hypothetical Distributed Lagged Sales Impact of a $10,000 Advertising Expenditure at the Beginning of Week One (See Figure 1 to compare the temporal pattern of the impact to its aggregate impact)

MARKETING ENVIRONMENTS

These six factors characterize a *complex marketing environment*. We know very little either conceptually or empirically about the likely impact of a new marketing decision in this type of environment. Many of the present mathematical decision models seem to be too simple to portray dynamic marketing processes. Thus programming models tend to require several unrealistic simplifications in solving for the optimal marketing mix; and formal game theory offers very little actual guidance in competitive decision making. At this stage, pure mathematical representations of marketing problems are suggestive rather than adequate.[1]

Yet the mathematicians are the last to give up hope. "When all else fails, simulate!" is their cry in an age of computers. *The aim of a computer simulation is to reproduce in miniature the characteristics of a*

[1] For a guide to the literature, the reader should refer to Robert Buzzell, *A Basic Bibliography on Mathematical Models in Marketing* (Chicago: American Marketing Association, 1962). Some of the listed articles have found their way into the following edited collections: Frank M. Bass, *et al.*, *Mathematical Methods and Models in Marketing* (Homewood, Ill.: Richard D. Irwin, Inc., 1961); Ronald Frank, *et al.*, *Quantitative Techniques in Marketing* (Homewood, Ill.: Richard D. Irwin, Inc., 1962); and Wroe Alderson and Stanley Shapiro, *Marketing and the Computer* (Englewood Cliffs, N.J.: Prentice-Hall, Inc., 1962). See also my article, "The Use of Mathematical Models in Marketing," *Journal of Marketing*, October 1963.

system too complex to be represented and analyzed by ordinary mathematical methods.

ILLUSTRATION OF THE INTERACTION AMONG MARKETING VARIABLES

Suppose the quantity sold (Q) depends upon the price charged (P), the level of personal selling expenditure (S), and the level of advertising expenditure (A). Economists often try to fit a multiple exponential function to explain a demand relationship. Suppose the particular equation is:

$$Q = 100{,}000P^{-2}A^{1/8}S^{1/4}$$

Then if $P = \$16$, $S = \$10{,}000$, and $A = \$10{,}000$, the predicted quantity sold is 12,400. If advertising expenditures are increased to \$50,000, holding P and S constant, then the predicted quantity sold is 15,100. Thus, a \$40,000 increase in advertising expenditure increases predicted sales by 2,700 units (15,100–12,400). But this result depended on the level of the other variables. Had the product been priced at \$24 instead of \$16, while S remained constant, an increase in advertising expenditures from \$10,000 to \$50,000 would have caused sales to go from 5,500 units to 6,700 units, an increase of only 1,200 units. In this example, the elasticity of advertising remained constant (at ⅛), but not its absolute impact on sales. In fact, the impact of a marketing variable not only depends on the levels of the other marketing variables but also on the initial levels of the particular marketing variables whose changes are being contemplated.

A USEFUL REPRODUCTION

I believe that some of the major features of the marketing environments of particular industries can be usefully reproduced in computer model terms. I will propose how a Competitive Marketing Simulator can be constructed and used. The components of the simulator will be firms and customers whose operating characteristics are specified as realistically as possible on the basis of available knowledge and data on the industry. Each behavioral unit would make periodic decisions which are influenced by preceding events and which in turn influence subsequent events.

A Competitive Marketing Simulator should suggest better ways to conceptualize market processes and decision problems in marketing. Furthermore, it should help define what data are needed for decisions as well as how to analyze existing data. Finally, when tailored to reflect the marketing environment of specific companies, it might provide a useful analytical tool. In particular, it might aid the company in its estimating of the sales and profit implications of alternative *marketing strategies* directed at alternative *market segments.*

SOME EXISTING MODELS

A Competitive Marketing Simulator would combine elements which are drawn from various types of existing simulation models. As background, five major types of existing models will be reviewed and contrasted.

Enterprise models. This type of model is used to investigate how the existing information and decision systems *within* an enterprise system affect the flow of material, men, machines, and money. A model of the existing system is constructed and then experimented with in the hope of finding alternative information-decision rules and arrangements which improve various flows according to some specified criteria.

Two somewhat different simulation approaches have attracted major attention in this area. The first is "industrial dynamics" associated with the name Jay W. Forrester at M.I.T.[2] Forrester has been interested chiefly in the phenomena of amplification, that is, the intensification of certain flows caused by various system delays and the lack of decision co-ordination in the firm. His estimates on delays come largely through fitting curves to historical company records. The other approach is associated with studies done at the Graduate School of Industrial Administration at Carnegie Tech.[3] The Carnegie approach contrasts to that of Forrester in being more behavioral. It utilizes actual observations of business practice and behavioral propositions drawn from economics and social science to model the behavior of component units.

OVERSIMPLIFIED FORMULA

From the point of view of marketing analysis, the major deficiency of these enterprise models lies in their generally oversimplified formula for sales determination. Sales typically are treated as an exogenous input characterized by a specified trend, seasonal pattern, cycle, and random disturbances. The original motivation for treating sales as exogenously determined is to discern how a firm's production and cash flows would respond to different uncontrollable patterns of sales. In Forrester's case, he later recognized that the magnitude and timing of sales are affected partly by company marketing decisions. Forrester specifically examined how poor timing of advertising expenditures could cause undesirable amplifications in some of the enterprise flows.

Bonini's enterprise model is the most advanced in a marketing sense

[2] Jay W. Forrester, *Industrial Dynamics* (New York: John Wiley & Sons, Inc., 1961).

[3] See R. M. Cyert and J. G. March, *A Behavioral Theory of the Firm* (Englewood Cliffs, N.J.: Prentice-Hall, Inc., 1963); K. J. Cohen, *Computer Models of the Shoe, Leather, Hide Sequence* (Englewood Cliffs, N.J.: Prentice-Hall, Inc., 1960); C. P. Bonini, *Simulation of Information and Decision Systems in the Firm* (Englewood Cliffs, N.J.: Prentice-Hall, Inc., 1963).

in that he made actual sales a function of the type of salesman, the pressure he worked under in the current period, the sales potential of his district, the market trend, prices, and a random element.[4] But he did not incorporate advertising, product attributes, and some other important mix elements. In general, most enterprise models lack an adequate description of marketing processes from two points of view:

1. They tend to postulate only a few marketing mix variables and treat them in a gross way.

2. They make no specific allowance for competitive interactions. Company sales are made a direct function of company decisions and the economic climate. These deficiencies are remedied in other types of models.

BUSINESS GAMES

Marketing mix models. This type of model is used to investigate the impact of alternative company marketing strategies on sales and profits. The models which come closest to serving this purpose are those incorporated in business games. Although business games are designed primarily for educational purposes, their potential use as a research tool is being increasingly recognized. For example, the researcher could dispense with the live players and program explicit competitive strategies for each decision unit. The implications of alternative programmed strategies can be investigated through simulation.

Virtually all business games provide for some marketing decisions to be made by the players. But the marketing function is highly simplified in the typical game. The players set a price, determine separate budgets for advertising and personal selling, and possibly allocate these budgets over three or four products and/or regions. Such games are of insufficient marketing complexity for our purposes. The Carnegie Tech Management Game, modeled after the household detergent industry, provides a richer marketing set of alternatives. It calls for decisions on advertising, distribution, prices, product development, and the purchase of various types of market information.[5] The M.I.T. Marketing Game, in the writer's opinion, offers the most complex marketing environment of any existing game.[6] Modeled around electric floor polishers for household use, this game requires the players to determine product quality, price, dealer margins, channels of distribution (including number and type of dealers), market

[4] Bonini, *op. cit.*

[5] *A Manual for Players of the Carnegie Tech Management Game* (Graduate School of Industrial Administration, Carnegie Institute of Technology, February 1960).

[6] Peter S. King, William F. Massy, Arnold E. Amstutz, and Gerald B. Tallman, "The M.I.T. Marketing Game," in Martin L. Bell, ed., *Marketing: A Maturing Discipline* (Proceedings of the Winter Conference of the American Marketing Association, 1960), pp. 85–102.

area, advertising expenditures, advertising media and appeals, the number and disposition of salesmen, and promotion within the retail store.

DESIGNING PROBLEMS

The designer of a business game has the task of determining plausible mathematical relationships between company sales on the one hand and company marketing decisions, competitors' marketing decisions, and economic climate factors on the other. Yet in several existing games, some of the functions seem highly artificial, both in their form and in their choice of parameters. The parameters do not appear to have been derived from an intensive statistical analysis of existing industry and company data.

The major shortcoming of these games from the point of view of a genuine marketing simulation lies in their superficial treatment of the market. The market is not conceived of as a diverse collection of individual buyers but rather as a vague aggregate which responds in a nonlinear and lagged way to company marketing decisions and changes in the economic climate. Instead of a separate function representing the brand choice of each type of buyer, there is an aggregate function representing the whole market's distribution of brand choices. Thus, even those games which boast of an environmentally rich marketing function fail to supply an environmentally rich market. For this we must turn to market models.

A SAMPLE UNIVERSE

Market models. A market model is a hypothetical sample universe of customers on which the effects of alternative marketing mixes can be tested. For example, the Simulmatics Corporation created a sample universe of 2,944 hypothetical persons supposedly representing a cross-section of the American population.[7] One hundred and forty different types of persons were defined by stratifying according to sex, age, type of community, employment status, and education. Several representatives of each type were located at ninety-eight sampling points in the continental United States.

This population was created specifically to test alternative media schedules and not buyer brand choice. An individual's media choices were determined probabilistically from his social-economic characteristics. Thus the probability that a particular man would read *Life* on a given week was treated as a multi-variate stochastic function of his age, education, etc. A particular client media schedule would be exposed to all the individuals in this hypothetical population. The computer would calculate which individuals viewed which media and would prepare

[7] *Simulmatics Media-Mix: Technical Description* (New York: The Simulmatics Corporation, October 1962).

various summary audience tabulations. The advertiser would examine these tabulations and decide whether the audience profile and the reach and frequency characteristics of the proposed media schedule were satisfactory.

WISCONSIN MODEL

At Wisconsin, Guy Orcutt and his co-workers have developed a demographic model consisting initially of 10,000 individuals having an age, sex, marital distribution, etc., resembling that found in the United States in 1950.[8] The computer makes a "pass" each period—representing a month—to determine births, marriages, divorces, and deaths. These events are determined probabilistically on the basis of functions whose coefficients have been estimated from actuarial data. Ultimately Orcutt wants to attribute economic behavior to these individuals and has already assigned debt and liquid asset characteristics to each household spending unit. But to date, the model had not been programmed to simulate buyer behavior.

In contrast, an industrial market model is found in the Pitt-Amstan Market Simulator.[9] This was designed at the University of Pittsburgh to represent the marketing problems of wholesale branch sales managers. It emphasizes particularly the problem of allocating salesmen and sales effort to over 300 business accounts. For each account, past purchases, past sales calls, and certain other vital statistics are made available to the players who represent competing wholesalers. The computer is programmed to award each individual customer's business to the several wholesalers according to the customer's characteristics and the wholesalers' relative efforts.

The three market models described above are specialized, one to the media selection problem, the second to the demographic process, and the third to the sales force allocation problem. To my knowledge there is no published account of a household market set up to explore brand choice behavior. Furthermore these market models, with the exception of the third, are not designed primarily for investigating the problem of competitive interaction.

SIMULATED COMPETITION

Competitive response models. These models are designed to explore the likely reactions of competitors to each other's moves. Cyert, Feigen-

[8] Guy H. Orcutt, Martin Greenberger, John Korbel, and Alice M. Rivlin, *Microanalysis of Socioeconomic Systems: A Simulation Study* (New York: Harper & Brothers, 1961).

[9] William B. Kehl, "Techniques in Constructing a Market Simulator," in Martin L. Bell, *op. cit.*

baum, and March developed an elaborate duopoly model in which each duopolist forecast the reactions of its competitor, revised its estimate of the demand curve and its own cost curve accordingly, specified its profit goal, and evaluated its alternative. Further revisions were made if no alternative met its profit goal. The model was simulated with specific parameters and the designers managed to generate competitor profit ratios and market shares which agreed in a rough way with observed values arising from the competition between the American Can Company and the Continental Can Company between 1913 and 1956.[10]

There also exist oligopoly models describing the likely reactions of competitors to price changes initiated by one of the oligopolists. But few models have come to this writer's attention which specified the likely reactions of competitors to other types of marketing challenge initiated by a particular oligopolist, such as an improvement in product quality, a change in packaging, increased advertising activity, the use of premiums, etc. On the other hand, a Competitive Marketing Simulator would be designed specifically to test competitive reaction rules to meet a variety of marketing challenges.

DECISION BEHAVIOR

Distribution models. Some models in this final classification have a tangential bearing on the Complex Marketing Simulator. Kalman Cohen designed a model which imputed specific decision rules regarding pricing and purchasing to five different channel levels in the leather shoe industry.[11] His objective was to see whether the attributed behavior could explain the actual historical behavior of the industry as reflected in past time series.

With a somewhat different objective, Balderston and Hoggatt developed a model based on the West Coast lumber industry in which the behavioral units were suppliers, wholesalers, and customer firms.[12] The wholesalers were brokers who attempted to match suppliers and customers. The brokers' major costs arose from searching, ordering, and confirming orders. A major purpose of the simulation was to examine the effects of changes in the availability and cost of information on the survival and efficiency of participant firms.

Physical distribution aspects of marketing channel arrangements also have been simulated. Gerson and Maffei have described a computer model for evaluating a system of up to 40 warehouses, 4,000 customers,

[10] Cyert, *op. cit.*
[11] Cohen, *op. cit.*
[12] Frederick E. Balderston and Austin C. Hoggatt, *Simulation of Market Processes* (Berkeley: University of California, Institute of Business and Economic Research, 1962).

and 10 factories.[13] The objective is to explore the cost of proposed alterations in the existing number and locations of factories and warehouses.
Simulation is proposed as a more flexible instrument than linear programming although this comes at the price of not having an algorithm leading
to the least cost system under the given assumptions.

COMBINED ELEMENTS

A *Competitive Marketing Simulator*. The previous discussion was
undertaken to indicate that none of the existing computer models have
enough marketing complexity to permit a realistic exploration of issues
related to market segmentation, marketing mixes, and competitive marketing response. The M.I.T. Game provides for many marketing decisions
but does not define a market of individual buyers; market reactions are
treated in terms of aggregate functions. The Simulmatics Corporation
consumer model provides a rich sample of hypothetical people but does
not provide for brand choice behavior or competitive marketing activity.
On the other hand, a Competitive Marketing Simulator would bring together an "environmentally rich" market of individuals and a "decision
rich" marketing function. *The brand behavior of individuals would be
linked intimately with the marketing decisions of firms. And the marketing decisions of a particular firm would be linked intimately with the
marketing decisions of competitors.* Thus a simulation on this model
would combine the elements found in market models, marketing models,
and competitive models.

ALTERNATIVE PATTERNS

In principle, the model could be created to represent a generalized
marketing environment or could be patterned after some specific marketing environment. Although Bonini's enterprise model and many business
games are not designed after any specific industry, a specific industry
model is likely to be more constructive. One of the major purposes is to
determine whether a Competitive Marketing Simulator could be made
sufficiently descriptive to be fairly useful as a company predictive tool.
The direct way to answer this question is to construct a model which
represents plausibly the behavior of buyers, the marketing alternatives
open to firms, and the pattern of competitive behavior of a particular
industry.

The details of the model would depend upon whether the industry
product was a frequently purchased consumer good, a durable consumer
good, an industrial raw material, or some other type of good. For ex-

[13] Martin L. Gerson and Richard B. Maffei, "Technical Characteristics of Distribution Simulators," *Management Science*, October 1963, pp. 62–69.

ample, sales force decisions—such as hiring, training, remuneration, and quota setting—tend to be much more important in the case of industrial products than consumer products.

The principles to be used in constructing a Competitive Marketing Simulator can be illustrated in connection with the writer's preliminary research on the *household market for regular coffee*.[14] This market provides a good subject because of both the characteristics of the product and the availability of data.[15] The Competitive Marketing Simulator would consist initially of two types of micro-units, individual households and coffee firms, although a retail sector may be added later.

A LOCAL MARKET

Individual households. The hypothetical households are designed to represent a local market—Chicago—rather than a national market. As a result, the competing firms do not confront the problem of evaluating the market potential of different regions and deciding on the relative allocation of competitive marketing effort to these regions. On the other hand, the local market serves as a common test market to which the competing firms resort to pre-test proposed changes in marketing strategy.

The individual households—whose buying representative is the housewife—are diversified (Table 1) in terms of:

Socio-economic characteristics such as income, family size, and national origin.

Past brand choices.

The typical amount purchased per week.

[14] This model should be compared to the one in William D. Wells, "Computer Simulation of Consumer Behavior," *Harvard Business Review*, May–June 1963.

[15] The product is one which is purchased frequently and this makes it possible to generate individual household purchase sequences as well as market share behavior over time. The product is in the competitive stage of its life cycle and this allows a focusing on the problem of market share rather than total sales growth. Furthermore, real differences can be found among brands in terms of flavor and strength and this permits competition along brand quality lines. The existence of real differences in brand qualities also gives rise to the phenomena of consumer learning and brand loyalty. Yet the loyalties are not so strong as to prevent brand switching in response to changing market strategies. The marketing strategy decision set itself is rich in possibilities: price and price deals, premiums, packaging, shelf space, advertising, product quality, etc. These and other characteristics of the household coffee market render it a good subject for a marketing model. Furthermore, data on product, buyer, and company characteristics of purchases of this market are available from a number of sources. The weekly coffee purchases of over 500 Chicago households over several years are obtainable from the Chicago *Tribune*'s consumer panel. A description of the social-demographic characteristics of each family is also available as well as information on any price deals which surrounded individual purchases. Periodic surveys of coffee buyers and their consumption habits and attitudes have been conducted by the Corby Research Service under the sponsorship of the Pan-American Coffee Bureau. Motivational aspects of coffee purchasing have been investigated by Social Research, Inc. Additional data are obtainable from the Marketing Research Corporation of America and the A. C. Nielsen Company.

Table 1.

Some Characteristics of Twenty Hypothetical Households

Household	Social-Economic Characteristics		Amount Purchased per Household per Week in Pounds	Brand Choice History Week				
	Mean Annual Income	Number of Household Members over 14 Yrs. of Age		-4	-3	-2	-1	0
1	$8,100	2	.2	A	A	A	A	A
2	9,500	3	.9	A	A	A	A	A
3	7,300	2	.3	A	A	A	A	B
4	7,500	1	.1	A	A	A	A	B
5	6,200	2	.2	A	A	A	A	C
6	5,300	2	.8	A	A	A	B	A
7	7,300	2	.6	A	A	B	A	A
8	5,000	4	1.0	A	B	B	B	C
9	4,000	3	.7	A	B	C	C	C
10	5,400	5	1.6	A	C	A	B	B
11	6,100	2	.5	B	A	B	B	B
12	5,000	2	.3	B	B	B	B	B
13	7,400	2	.2	B	B	C	B	B
14	4,200	1	.2	B	C	C	C	C
15	4,300	3	1.1	B	C	C	C	C
16	7,100	3	.2	B	C	C	B	B
17	5,800	4	.9	C	B	B	C	B
18	6,200	2	.6	C	B	A	C	C
19	4,000	6	1.3	C	C	C	C	C
20	5,300	3	.6	C	C	C	C	C

The actual characteristics are derived from the records of a Chicago consumer panel. Each household will represent a discernible segment of the coffee-drinking market. A household's brand choice in a particular week will be multiplied by a factor reflecting the relative size of this segment. A few hundred households will ultimately be included in this model.

Each household will be assumed to purchase coffee once a week.[16] Since its last purchase, the household has been exposed to certain stimuli. The major stimuli are the number of advertising exposures to various brands and any changes in business activity. In the case of the latter, a shift toward recession causes certain households to switch to less expensive brands. Other interim stimuli, such as peer influences, taste maturation, etc., are not feasible to include in a first model. In addition to the interim stimuli, the household buyer is influenced by her in-store experience in the act of making her coffee purchase. She confronts a set of prices, promotion deals, point-of-purchase displays, variations in shelf space, and, possibly, new packaging for an old brand or even for a new brand. Thus a particular household buyer's choice is a function of her:

Socio-economic characteristics.
Previous brand choices.
Interim experience.
In-store experience.

The first two represent the household's *status variables,* the second two represent the *input variables,* and the household's brand choice is the *output variable.*

Furthermore the output variable is related to the input and status variables in a probabilistic way. Specifically, purchase behavior is represented by a brand *probability vector* showing the respective probabilities of a household i buying the various brands at time t. For example, $(.60, .30, .10)_{it}$ says that for household i at time t, the probability is 60 percent that it will buy Brand A, 30 percent that it will buy Brand B, and 10 percent that it will buy Brand C. The probabilities are made to sum to one on the assumption that each household is addicted to coffee and would not leave this market or change its consumption level. Note that this model, in contrast to Orcutt's, does not provide for new family

---

[16] This in an admitted oversimplification in that the purchase period varies according to the amount purchased on each occasion, the daily amount consumed, holidays, and so forth. Furthermore, in practice more than one brand may be bought at a time. Yet it would have been difficult, though not impossible, to build in different purchasing habits and use a variable rather than discrete time interval between purchases. The choice was made in favor of a discrete time interval, a single brand choice, and a specific amount purchased by each household. It is expected that no substantive price will be paid for this simplification.

formations, deaths, etc. The population is completely stable and ageless. Each "week," the computer will cycle through each household and compute its new probability vector on the basis of interim and in-store experiences created by the marketing efforts of the competitors and changes in business activity. The household's actual brand choice is determined by the drawing of a random number from a distribution with the probabilities shown in the household's current brand vector. Thus, the brand which had the highest probability in the household's vector is the expected choice, but it may not be the actual choice. Consumer choice, especially with respect to convenience goods, is not entirely premeditated.

THREE COMPANIES

Firms. Three specific companies are contemplated to operate in this industry. Before the beginning of the simulation, company A sells a high-quality coffee and charges a high price; company B sells a medium-quality coffee and charges a medium price; and company C sells a low-quality coffee and charges a low price. Although more than three companies could be specified which differed along other dimensions as well, it is felt that existing firms in the industry fall into the types A, B, and C and the real problem is to consider what are the best marketing strategies for a firm in A's position, B's position, and C's position, respectively.

Before the start of the simulation, each firm will enjoy a certain market share in terms of the total pounds sold. Using the twenty hypothetical households in Table I as an example, the market share for the last week —week O—can be found by summing the household purchase amounts for each brand. The market shares turn out to be .23, .31, and .46 for A, B, and C, respectively. In the absence of any new moves by any of the firms, or any changes in economic activity, these shares are preserved approximately, except for chance movements. That is, the probability vector for each household remains as it was in the last period in the absence of new stimuli. Therefore the future *market share vector* remains close to (.23, .31, .46).

STRATEGY ALTERATIONS

However, a major purpose of the computer simulation is to investigate the sales and profit implications of alterations in marketing strategy. Suppose a particular firm wants to increase its market share. The model will provide that this firm—or its competitors—can alter one or any combination of the following marketing decision variables:

1. Permanent list price.
2. Special temporary price deal.
3. Premiums.
4. Packaging.
5. Product quality.
6. Shelf space.
7. Co-operative advertising budget.
8. Point-of-purchase displays.

Now altering the status of a marketing variable is only accomplished at a cost. Otherwise a company could achieve a much larger market share by simply halving its price, doubling its advertising budget, and ignoring profits. The cost of each possible change is assumed to be known in advance. Thus special premiums attract more customers at a specific cost to the firm. Or the company can obtain a larger proportion of shelf space by hiring additional retail salesmen and/or allowing higher dealer margins. Or the company can improve the quality of its product or packaging for specified dollar investments.

The simulation is initiated when a particular firm in the model alters its strategy. The new strategy is one which an actual company may want to test. As a result of the new strategy, the probability vectors of the individual households undergo individual alteration in the following week. They may not undergo full alteration in that week to the extent that distributed lagged reactions are built into the model. In other words, the probability vector of household i may move toward a new equilibrium but may not move all the way in one week. In any event, the random number generator is used to determine actual brand choices in the following week in line with the new probability vectors. New market shares are then computed.

The computer will prepare a weekly profit and loss statement for each company based on its sales and its costs. The production and financial aspects are highly simplified in this model so as not to burden the computer program any further. The price paid for this simplification is that a seemingly good marketing strategy may be sub-optimal when the production, inventory, and financial implications are considered. It would be desirable eventually to build a complex enterprise model which included the complex marketing model as one of its components. This would enable a more systematic study of global criteria for marketing strategy.

In the accounting model, each firm will bear the same total fixed cost per period. The unit variable production cost will depend on the quality of the coffee and the packaging. Total marketing cost for each firm will be the sum of advertising expenditures, sales force salaries, point-of-purchase displays and premiums. Weekly company revenue will be equal to the net price multiplied by the number of units sold. The difference between costs and revenues will represent the company's current profit.

THE FIRM'S REACTION

Firms will not necessarily react immediately to a new competitive challenge. Weeks can pass before a firm is able to, or willing to, revise its own strategy. The elapsed time will depend upon the nature of the challenge. For example, a company can match a competitive price reduction within one week, although it may want to wait longer to see what effect the competitor's move has on market share and profits. Yet the same company may require a few months before it can meet the challenge of a new competitive packaging approach.

The specific reaction of the competitors can be simulated on a judgment basis or on a programmed basis. In the former case, alternative plausible responses by each competitor are simulated and the results observed. In the latter case, *formal reaction decision rules* are specified in advance for each of the three competitors. A rule may take the following form: when the firm's market share falls to a certain level, a specified action is taken depending upon the assumed cause of the decline. The *input variables* in the firm's behavior would be the new market share and the new competitive challenge; the *status variables* would be the company's existing marketing mix characteristics; and the *output variables* would be the firm's new marketing mix. If responses to major types of provocations are specified in advance for all three competitors, it may be possible to initiate the simulation with a specified marketing mix change by one competitor and then let it run week after week on its own momentum. A provision can be made for a firm to pass out of existence when its profits persist below a certain level for a certain length of time. In any event, this model would generate a time series of weekly shares and company profits. Under certain circumstances, the market shares may appear to move toward, or oscillate around, some equilibrium values. Those values would signify the ultimate market share each company could expect under a continuation of the prevailing formal reaction decision rules.

A RESEARCH TOOL

Summary. This is a brief description of a Competitive Marketing Simulator for the household coffee market. It would combine a market simulation, a company marketing simulation, and a competitive simulation. In addition to the marketing variables listed earlier, the model could be modified to aid in the analysis of new product introduction and also to probe the value of a company's buying different types of information about the market and competitors.

In designing a Competitive Marketing Simulator, the major anticipated challenges relate to the development of a representative market of individual buyers, the formulation of an adequate mathematical apparatus for linking the three simulations, and the estimation of the appropriate parameters. Beyond this, the question to resolve is whether the model would have enough merit as a research and management tool to justify its painstaking construction. Finally, there is the philosophical question of what would be the nature of marketing strategy if every competitor in an industry had its own Competitive Marketing Simulator.

ANALYZING COMPLEXITIES

Marketing executives have the task of analyzing the firm's market opportunities, planning the marketing mix strategy, and controlling the marketing effort. Their task is complicated by the existence of complex properties in the marketing environment. The impact of a marketing decision is neither immediate, nor linear, nor independent of other marketing variables, nor necessarily stable through time. Furthermore, the final impact depends upon competitive response and the level of economic activity. Existing company decision procedures often do not recognize or adequately deal with these properties. On the other hand, a Competitive Marketing Simulator may provide a chance to generate predictions for such an environment and therefore could become a useful management tool.

23. The role of the consumer in image building

WILLIAM H. REYNOLDS

Product and brand images are created by consumers. Herta Herzog
has defined an image as "the sum total of impressions the consumer
receives from many sources. . . ." [1] This definition (which may have been
an intentional oversimplification) tends to emphasize what might be
called the "message milieu" and to look upon the consumer himself as a
passive recipient of impressions. An image is actually the result of a more
complex process. It is the mental construct developed by the consumer
on the basis of a few selected impressions among the flood of total impressions; it comes into being through a creative process in which these
selected impressions are elaborated, embellished, and ordered.

The exotic word "infundibular," or funnel-shaped, describes the
image-building process. A great deal of work has been done in marketing
on the elements in a marketer's total communications mix which actually
get through to the consumer. This is the first half of the process dia-
grammed. [2] Less has been done on what the consumer does with the bits
of information that reach him. Yet research in this area is vital if marketers are to control their image.

To cite one example, suppose that a manufacturer of cooking oils
finds that his product has an image of heaviness and viscosity and he
takes steps to correct the problem. Actual reductions in viscosity—as

Reprinted from the *California Management Review*, Volume VII, No. 3, Spring,
1965. Copyright 1965 by The Regents of the University of California.

[1] Herta Herzog, "Behavioral Science Concepts for Analyzing the Consumer," in
Perry Bliss, ed., *Marketing and the Behavioral Sciences* (Boston: Allyn and Bacon, Inc.,
1963), p. 82.

[2] John A. Howard, *Marketing: Executive and Buyer Behavior* (New York:
Columbia University Press, 1963), pp. 28–29; 136, and John C. Maloney, "Is Advertising Believability Really Important?" *Journal of Marketing*, XXVII (Oct. 1963), 3; 5.

MESSAGE   SELECTED   ELABORATED
MILIEU   IMPRESSIONS   IMAGE

measured by laboratory techniques—are unlikely to be effective. House-wives apparently judge viscosity in cooking oils on the basis of color. Light-colored oils are seen as less viscous. The manufacturer could change the image of his oil more successfully by changing its color than by changing its viscosity.

IMAGE AS REPUTATION

Belief versus *fact*. Often, of course, the word "image" is used as equivalent to reputation. Daniel Boorstin's *The Image* in effect deplores in an old-fashioned way the apparent current emphasis on reputation, what people believe about a person or an institution, *versus* character, what the person or institution actually is.[3] This usage of "image" to mean reputation tends to focus attention upon the problem of the congruity of semblance and reality. George H. Brown took this point of view in an illustration in his "Brand Images Among Low Priced Cars":

A particularly interesting case, from the point of view of marketing strategy, would arise in our scouring powder example if a particular brand should have an image of being hard on the hands, possibly due to an early version of the product, but which is in fact not at all irritating to the skin. Here, the manufacturer has the option of attempting to change the brand image through promotional efforts or of bringing out the current product under a new brand, or doing both.[4]

The question of belief *versus* fact can obscure the actual nature of an image. Images are not isolated empirical beliefs about a product or brand but are *systems of inferences* which may have only a tenuous and indirect relationship to fact. The scouring powder mentioned in the illustration above might be seen—because of its roughness—as an especially effective cleanser. (Some of us have a tendency to put more confidence in medicine which has a bad taste.) The powder might be associated with a good housekeeper who cares more for her home than for frivolous white hands. The roughness might carry connotations of health and sanitation ex-

[3] Daniel J. Boorstin, *The Image: Or, What Happened to the American Dream* (New York: Atheneum, 1962).

[4] George H. Brown, "Brand Images Among Low Priced Cars," in Richard M. Hill, ed., *Marketing Concepts in Changing Times* (Proceedings of the 42nd National Conference of the American Marketing Association, Dec. 1959), p. 62.

tremely important as purchase motives to the principal customers of the powder.

In other words, a particular belief about a product or brand (whether true or false) can lead to dozens of other interdependent beliefs. Given a starting point, possibly only a single fact, a consumer can create (in the same way that a paleontologist can reputedly reconstruct a dinosaur from a single bone) an amazingly detailed image of a product, the people likely to use it, and the homes in which it might been seen, complete with evaluative attitudes and emotional overtones. The proper question to ask about a belief concerning a product is not whether it is true or false but how it is interrelated functionally with other beliefs.

"OBJECTIVE CORRELATIVE"

The literary analogy. In a way, the image-building process is analogous to literary composition. The information on the basis of which people construct images is roughly equivalent to T. S. Eliot's famous concept of the "objective correlative":

The only way of expressing emotion in the form of art is by finding an "objective correlative"; in other words, a set of objects, a situation, a chain of events which shall be the formula of that particular emotion; such that, when the external facts, which must terminate in sensory experience, are given, the emotion is immediately evoked.[5]

A writer, in attempting to communicate a particular emotion or experience, does so by presenting in his writing an objective correlative (or significant datum) which he hopes will evoke in his readers the emotion or experience. The following quote from *Death in the Afternoon* describes Hemingway's search for the significant datum in a goring he had witnessed in the bull ring:

For myself, not being a bullfighter . . . the problem was one of depiction and waking in the night I tried to remember what it was that seemed just out of my remembering and that was the thing I had really seen, and finally, remembering all around it, I got it. When he stood up, his face white and dirty and the silk of his breeches opened from waist to knee, it was the dirtiness of the rented breeches, the dirtiness of his slit underwear and the clean, clean, unbearably clean whiteness of the thigh bone that I had seen, and it was that which was important.[6]

Some products and brands—or certain aspects of them—have what might be called "plot value." [7] They provide a starting point for imagery

---

[5] T. S. Eliot, "Hamlet and His Problems," in *Selected Essays* (New York: Harcourt, Brace and Co., 1950), pp. 124–125.

[6] Ernest Hemingway, *Death in the Afternoon* (New York: Charles Scribner's Sons, 1932), p. 20.

[7] The Marlboro tattoo is an instance of deliberately building plot value into a product; it functions as a significant datum to establish that the sophisticated and

going beyond the original stimulus. Mason Haire's famous shopping list study of instant coffee is still the best example of this. Haire's data indicate that a writer could communicate that one of his female characters is a shiftless housewife by showing her husband forlornly mixing himself a cup of instant coffee.[8]

Writers are more aware than most of us of expressive values and a screening of the way branded products are presented in popular fiction, possibly using a sample of paperback books, might be revealing. For example, a recent novel, *The Fly Girls*, described two girls driving a Corvette in downtown Miami:

. . . it was all I could do to remain impassive when kids wolf-whistled at us. Not only kids, either. We even wowed the cops on traffic duty. . . . Frankly, I don't dig it. What's so sexy about a couple of airline hostesses driving a Corvette? I mean, where's the actual sex? [9]

Where *is* the actual sex? Obviously, it is part of the author's conception of the image of the Corvette. He thinks, probably correctly, that other people will see the situation as he does, that "girls in a Corvette" will evoke in his readers the image—including sex—which he was trying to communicate. (The villain in this story, incidentally, is a professional gambler who drives a metallic gray Lincoln Continental.)

Thus, a writer can often guess accurately at the images which will be evoked by the significant details he deploys. Sometimes, of course, he may fail. A marketer faces a similar problem in trying to predict or control the product image that consumers will form on the basis of the messages he directs to the market. He is helped in this task—as is the writer—by the fact that images tend to be consistent from person to person, partly because of common consumer experiences and expectations. Also, several well-known psychological phenomena operate in the image-building process to force images into certain directions.

THE SIMPLEST PROCESS

The halo effect. The halo effect is the simplest process contributing to the development of an image from a relatively small amount of data. Someone liking a product because of a particular attribute with which he happens to be familiar can—and does—form opinions on other attributes of the product regardless of whether he knows anything about them or not. A food product which is liked (for whatever reason) may

---

successful Marlboro Man must have had an interesting and adventurous past. See Edward L. Brink and William T. Kelley, *The Management of Promotion* (Englewood Cliffs, N.J.: Prentice-Hall, Inc., 1963), p. 164.

[8] Mason Haire, "Projective Techniques in Marketing Research," *Journal of Marketing*, April 1950, pp. 651–652.

[9] Bernard Glemser, *The Fly Girls* (New York: Random House, 1960), p. 268.

—because of halo—be rated high on all of its characteristics, such as quality, nutrition, and flavor. An image produced by halo looks like a real image and may function like one.

For example, college students are attracted to General Electric and consider it a good place to work. Historically, there is some probability that this attitude stems from GE's past (and present) reputation, which has filtered through faculty to students, for an atmosphere conducive to research. Currently, however, the favorable attitude toward GE seems to "float," unconnected with any specific reputational factor. The underlying reasons for the generalized attitude are almost irrelevant. GE is considered a good place to work by accountants, marketers, management types, and researchers alike. The halo consequently may cause an accounting major to sign with GE. An image strong enough to influence career decisions must in some sense be taken as real.

If a product has an unfavorable reputation with respect to one of its attributes, a manufacturer should not leap to the conclusion that this attitude is unique and singular and unrelated to other attitudes. It may stem from halo. Strategically, it may be easier for him to change other attitudes than the one in question. A garment manufacturer whose dresses are considered unfashionable and ill-made might find it hard to convince buyers that his workmanship is good. This quality would not be visible to potential customers nor would it be something they could assess for themselves. By changing styles and aggressively promoting the fact, he might, however, be able to overcome his reputation for poor fashion. If so, halo—as people came to like his clothes—could cause his reputation for workmanship to improve concurrently.

PLOT VALUE

Simple inference. People feel that certain attributes "go together." A beehive hairdo "goes" with eye make-up. A suit made of good materials is usually well-cut. White Levis are youthful. Expensive stores have salesladies who may snub you. Instant coffee is used by lazy women. These inferences may be right or wrong, but all of them have some prima facie validity.

Inferences can sometimes seize on one aspect of a product to the neglect of others. A product may have attributes A, B, C, and D; if A possesses more plot value than the other attributes, or—for whatever reason—attracts the attention of more consumers, it may play a disproportionately large role in the image of the product.

The respondents in a recent study were given the opportunity to examine in detail two quite different automobiles and were then asked to rate them on a list of image-type characteristics. Questions were asked about the perceived attributes of the cars themselves—sporty, elegant,

fast—the people who might drive them—banker, suburban couple, teenager—and where and under what circumstances the cars might be seen
—shopping center, opera, beach.

The same questionnaire was then administered to another group of
respondents who were not shown the cars but who were told only that
one of the cars was big and black and that the other was small and white.
The results were substantially similar to those obtained when people
were looking at the actual cars, knew their brands, and had been given a
chance to become thoroughly familiar with them. The big black car, for
example, was seen in both phases of the research as elegant, suitable for
a banker, and likely to be seen at the opera. The images based on color
and size alone were as elaborated and as detailed as those based upon
the vastly greater amount of information given the first group of respondents.

Similarly, Pierre Martineau compared the images held by women
familiar with two department stores with the images of the same two
stores developed by another group of women, unfamiliar with the stores,
but who had been shown advertisements. Again, the images based upon
the limited amount of information in the advertisements were in close
correspondence with the images based upon detailed information and
long familiarity.[10]

Building an image with inferences from observed details is analogous
to the process of concept formation described by Bruner, Goodnow, and
Austin:

We have found it more meaningful to regard a concept as a network of sign-
significate inferences by which one goes beyond a set of *observed* criterial properties exhibited by an object or event to the class identity of the object or event
in question, and thence to additional inferences about other *unobserved* properties of the object or event. We see an object that is red, shiny, and roundish
and infer that it is an apple; we are then enabled to infer further that "if it is
an apple, it is also edible, juicy, will rot if left unrefrigerated, etc." [11]

A marketer may be able to build an image by doing no more than establishing that his product is of a certain class; the consumer can then go on
to make further inferences and, in effect, create the image himself.

PERSONAL ASSOCIATIONS

Associational structures. Associations may be idiosyncratic. For example, Caroline Spurgeon in *Shakespeare's Imagery* has shown how
Shakespeare associated the words "dog," "candy," and "melting," and

---

[10] Pierre Martineau, *Motivation in Advertising* (New York: McGraw-Hill Book
Co., 1957), p. 164.

[11] Jerome S. Bruner, Jacqueline J. Goodnow, and George A. Austin, *A Study of
Thinking* (New York: John Wiley and Sons, Inc., 1960), p. 244. This paper is indebted
throughout to Bruner's work.

used them in situations in his plays involving fawning and cringing.[12] Lowe's *Road to Xanadu* details the highly personal associations underlying much of Coleridge's language in *The Ancient Mariner*.[13] All of us similarly have personal associations peculiar to ourselves. Idiosyncratic associations are frequent enough, as a matter of fact, that word association tests can be used as diagnostic tools by psychologists concerned with individual personalities.

There are nevertheless sufficient uniformities from person to person in associational structures that association can be important in image building. This is generally recognized in the research conducted on names proposed for new products. It is standard practice in this research to inquire into the words suggested by a name. Consistencies are ordinarily found.

Name research is not the only area in which word association tests can be used. The word "expensive," for example, means "high-priced" or "dear" to a few people and "ostentatious" to a few others. Overwhelmingly, however, the word is associated with "quality," "fine," "elegant," "the best." An expensive product, to most people, is a good product. (The respondents in this research were asked to give the "first word to come to mind.")

Osgood's work with the semantic differential has shown that in one way associational structures are relatively simple and in another way discouragingly complex. Responses obtained when a concept is rated against a large number of adjective scales seem to be governed by three main factors, good-bad, strong-weak, and active-passive. These three factors account for almost 50 percent of the variance when the "meaning" of particular concepts is measured, using factor analysis techniques, almost regardless of the concept, the adjectives against which it is judged, or the people doing the judging. It is in this sense that associational structures can be said to be simple; they are complex in that many opaque factors with light loadings account for the remaining unexplained 50 percent of the variance.[14]

Associations are usually meaningful configurations. Other things being equal, a more expensive product is likely to be a better product. It is hard to establish an association between two items by repetitive juxtaposition unless the items are structurally related to each other in some way. "Progress" can be associated with General Electric but not with a buggy-whip manufacturer.

[12] Caroline Spurgeon, *Shakespeare's Imagery* (Boston: Beacon Press, 1958), pp. 195–199. (Originally published by Cambridge University Press, 1935.)

[13] John Livingston Lowe, *Road to Xanadu* (New York: Vintage Books, 1959). (Originally published by Houghton Mifflin Co., 1927.)

[14] Charles E. Osgood, George J. Suci, and Percy H. Tannenbaum, *The Measurement of Meaning* (Urbana: University of Illinois Press, 1957), pp. 36–39, *passim*.

DISSONANT ELEMENTS

Cognitive dissonance. An effort to associate "progress" with a buggy-whip manufacturer would be an instance of Feistinger's "cognitive dissonance." [15] Dissonance creates tension and people have evolved strategies for handling it. One strategy is to deny or to refuse to admit the existence of one of the dissonant elements—to insist, for example, that the buggy-whip manufacturer is not progressive, or that he is progressive but no longer manufactures buggy-whips.

Another strategy is to search for additional information or to develop broader concepts which will resolve the dissonance. A watch for ladies might be seen as both delicate and sturdy, a dissonant combination of attributes. The manufacturer could resolve this dissonance by advertising that his watch represents a breakthrough in watch design: "Incredibly light, incredibly sturdy, through space-age miniaturization!"

A dissonance offers a real opportunity for the exercise of creativity; a confused image, if handled adroitly by a marketer, can be turned into an asset. A bank, for example, might offer higher interest rates than competitors but be considered "unfriendly." The obvious and usual way to counter this would be to deny the "unfriendly" element in the dissonant image and to try to create a folksy, friendly image through advertising and promotion. Another way, possibly more effective, would be to try to bring the two dissonant elements into consonance: "We offer higher interest rates because we're strictly business. Don't come to us if you want colored checks." The current Avis campaign—"We're second in rent-a-car and so we try harder"—is an attempt to bring "second" and "best" into consonance.

USE OF CODES

Information theory. Information theory, as developed from the original work of C. E. Shannon and Bell Laboratories, offers perhaps the most general explanation of the nature of the image-building process.[16] The transmission of information can be extraordinarily efficient if codes are used which make reference to information already available to the recipient. Western Union's numbered birthday messages are an example. Transmission of one or two digits will tell the operator at the other end of the line which birthday message to pull from his file to deliver to the addressee. Similarly, computer codes such as Fortran simply tell computers conceptually which of several stored programs to use.

The consumer also has stored programs which can be activated by

[15] Leon Feistinger, *A Theory of Cognitive Dissonance* (Stanford: Stanford University Press, 1957).

[16] C. E. Shannon, *The Mathematical Theory of Communication* (Urbana: University of Illinois Press, 1949).

appropriate codes. The word "sweet" or the quality "sweetness" will prompt an array of stored associations and inferences which will differ from those which would be prompted by other code words or qualities. The word "sweet," in effect, is a constraint, which tends to reduce the uncertainty of response by making some responses more likely than others.

Sequential constraint, as the concept is used in the highly mathematical literature on information theory, refers to the reduction of uncertainty. An example is that the next item in a sequence of letters, words, or musical sounds is often predictable. If the item is completely predictable, it adds no new information and is consequently redundant. Garner points out that this can be affected by prior familiarity; a guess at the next letter in the sequence, "Now is the time for all go—" is almost certain to be an "o" to complete the sentence "—od men to come to the aid of their party." [17]

PROBABILITIES

It should be emphasized that the process is a matter of probabilities. Constraint is rarely absolute. Osgood comments:

To use another example, "The old man ——— down the road"; it is clear that the structure of English requires some verb (flew, limps, crawls, traveled, etc.), though the tense is not specified by the context; on the other hand, the presence of "old man" and "road" clearly exerts semantic selectivity on the alternatives—*limped* or *hobbled* are certainly more probable semantically than *slept, swam,* or even *ran.*[18]

A knowledgeable consumer with some background who is given a few items of information about a product or brand is often put under a similar constraint. Certain associations, attitudes, and inferences become more likely than others. The consumer will know, for example, that a car described as "big and black" would probably be heavy, expensive, conservative, comfortable, and prestigious.

Image building in fact is not usually this predictable.

People differ in the prior information at their disposal and in their creative ability to elaborate an image.

A product or brand is a combination of attributes, and one person might construct his image on the basis of one feature and another person on another. (The story of the blind men and the elephant comes to mind.)

[17] R. Garner, *Uncertainty and Structure as Psychological Concepts* (New York: John Wiley and Sons, Inc., 1962), p. 213.

[18] E. Osgood, "The Representational Model and Relevant Research Methods," in Ithiel de la Sola Pool, *Trends in Content Analysis* (Urbana: University of Illinois Press, 1959), p. 79.

Uncertainty is hardly ever reduced to zero; almost always, alternative inferences from the same facts or the same sequence of items are conceivable. For
these reasons, images are statistical in nature. Different people will have different images of the same product; the number of people with a particular image
is always a percentage and not the total population.

CONCLUSIONS

Images are ordered wholes built by consumers from scraps of significant detail in much the same way that writers and artists use significant
detail to illumine complex totalities. *Marketers who fail to recognize the
internal structure of their images and who try to correct an image problem by a frontal head-on attack are choosing, whether they know it or
not, the path of most resistance.* Millions of dollars have been spent trying
to convince consumers of something about a product which they know
cannot be true because it is inconsistent with the total complex of attitudes, expectations, and beliefs associated with the product. Instead, the
marketer should ask himself:

1. Are there key elements in my image—not necessarily the most conspicuous—
   which, if changed, might lead to dissonance and to changes in the total
   configuration?

2. What elements in my image are structurally interrelated and give mutual
   support to each other? Do some of my "bad" points make my "good" points
   more believable?

3. How can plot value be exploited in my product design and advertising? Can
   I make some elements in my image more salient than others?

4. What constraints can I build into my message mix to reduce uncertainty and
   make consumer response more predictable?

   Product and brand images arise out of a complex interaction between marketer messages and consumer creativity. It is only by recognizing the contribution of the consumer that a marketer can obtain a measure
of control over the image-building process.

IV. Marketing Management

INTRODUCTION

The elements of a marketing mix are listed under many titles and classification schemes. It is difficult to defend a universally applicable marketing mix since some firms emphasize one mix successfully while others argue that another mix is their key to sales and earnings. With such diverse claims in mind, the student should approach this section ready to review critically the claims that every innovation and development is the most important factor in marketing success. These and similar writings should not be dismissed as extravagant propaganda but should be considered as a reflection of the interdependence of marketing variables.

The task of every marketing manager is to formulate the best possible marketing mix necessary to achieve the firm's marketing objective. Knowledge of many disciplines can be applied to this task and, as illustrated by the selections in this section, many have been.

A. Product Policy

24. A probability model for early prediction of new product market success

WILLIAM D. BARCLAY

Early evaluation of the success of new products in the market is one of the difficult problems facing manufacturers of packaged goods. For example, store audit methods can be quite misleading over the short term because the global data they generate may mask the underlying consumer dynamics. Data from consumer purchase panels, although getting closer to the basic components of net sales figures, often present the analyst with an intractable mass of detail that defies simple summary. The mixture of regularity and randomness found in individual family records is particularly confusing and of little value for the early evaluation of product success.

In response to this situation, a number of formal attempts have been made to devise new product prediction schemes based on standard information sources. Best known, perhaps, is MRCA's prediction model, based on repeat buying patterns developed by the National Consumer Panel.[1]

The present article presents a different application of consumer panel data to the problem. The same probability approach is used as employed by T. W. Anderson in examining changes in political attitudes over time, and by Benjamin Lipstein in analyzing the dynamics of brand loyalty and brand switching.[2] We begin with a statement of the mathe-

Reprinted from the *Journal of Marketing*, Volume 27 (January, 1963), pp. 63–68, National Quarterly Publication of the American Marketing Association.

[1] Louis A. Fourt and Joseph W. Woodlock, "Early Prediction of Market Success for New Grocery Products," *Journal of Marketing*, Vol. 25 (October, 1960), pp. 31–38.

[2] T. W. Anderson, "Probability Models for Analyzing Time Changes in Atti-

matical model, demonstrate its use with actual data, examine the adequacy of the resulting prediction, and conclude with some extensions of the approach.

THE MATHEMATICAL MODEL

The basic assumption of the approach to be used is this: *The probability that a consumer buys a particular brand during a unit time period depends only on whether she bought that brand during the immediately preceding period.*

This assumption can best be appreciated by a symbolic formulation. Suppose that if a woman buys Brand X in an initial unit time period, there is a probability P_1 that she will buy it again the following period. If she did not buy X during the first period, there is a probability P_2 that she will buy it the next period. These hypothetical probabilities, together with the corresponding chances of not buying, may be arranged as follows:

		Probability of
Purchase of brand X in first period	Buying brand X during second period	Not buying brand X during second period
Bought	P_1	$1-P_1$
Did not buy	P_2	$1-P_2$

This array is called a *matrix of transition probabilities*. A matrix of transition probabilities, together with the probability that the process begins in each of its possible initial states, defines a so-called *Markov chain process*. This branch of probability theory is named for its inventor, the Russian mathematician, A. A. Markov. The present article is based on this theory.[3]

The individual entries are known as transition probabilities, since they denote the chances of passing from a specified purchase "state" (bought or did not) during one period to a specified purchase state during the next.

---

tudes," in *Mathematical Thinking in the Social Sciences,* by Paul F. Lazarsfeld, Editor (Glencoe, Illinois: The Free Press, 1954), Chapter 1, pp. 17–66; Benjamin Lipstein, "The Dynamics of Brand Loyalty and Brand Switching," in *Proceedings: Fifth Annual Conference, Advertising Research Foundation* (New York: Advertising Research Foundation, Inc., 1959), pp. 101–108.

[3] A readable introduction to the subject may be found in J. Kemeny, J. Snell, and G. Thompson, *Introduction to Finite Mathematics* (Englewood Cliffs, New Jersey: Prentice-Hall, Inc., 1957).

Note in the matrix that P_1 is an index of repeat buying, specifically the probability that a woman buying Brand X in Period #1 will rebuy in Period #2. The probability P_2 is the chance that a first period nonbuyer will buy X during the second period. Observe also that the probabilities in each row add up to 1. This must be the case, since a woman either buys Brand X or not during the second period.

The potential utility of this model in the context of early new product evaluation appears to lie mainly in two facts. (1) The model represents the simplest mathematical characterization of the notion that buying behavior in a particular period depends, in a probabilistic sense, on recent previous buying behavior. (2) Latent in this model is a *prediction* of the long-run probability that Brand X will be purchased in a unit time interval.

It is the model's capacity for prediction which is of interest. It can be proved mathematically that if P_1 and P_2 remain constant, then ultimately the proportion of consumers who will buy Brand X during a unit time period will approach:

$$P = \frac{P_2}{1 + P_2 - P_1}.$$

A mathematically sufficient condition is that all entries in the matrix be positive.[4]

The direct significance of this mathematical fact for early new product evaluation is this. If (1) early in the life of a new product, it is possible to estimate P_1 and P_2 with satisfactory precision, and if (2) the conditions which generate P_1 and P_2 are sufficiently "constant," then it is possible to predict the "long-run" probability of purchase for the product during a unit period. That is, this critical dimension of new product success may be predicted, provided the appropriate conditions are met in adequate approximation.

So much for the potential value of this simple model; what of its practical applicability? At the outset, it is evident that no simple model can predict complex marketing consequences with perfect fidelity. There are several reasons why the predicted proportion, P, can be at best a satisfactory approximation.

1. It is implicitly assumed that all Brand X buyers for a given period have the same probability (P_1) of buying the following period. There is a similar assumption for nonbuyers: a common purchase probability of P_2. Neither of these is strictly true.

2. The values of P_1 and P_2 must be estimated from sample data.

3. The constancy of P_1 and P_2 implied in the prediction of P is

---

[4] For a derivation, see reference to J. Kemeny, J. Snell, and G. Thompson in footnote 3, pp. 221–222.

illusory. Such factors as variations in the promotional pressure exerted on behalf of the new product, and retaliatory efforts by its competitors, will affect P_1 and P_2. Hopefully, these parameters will tend to stabilize sufficiently early in the product's history to permit useful prediction.

4. The prediction formula for P is a mathematical idealization, reflecting the proportion buying per unit period after an infinite time lapse. This is what is meant by "in the long run." This limitation is less severe than it appears, since the asymptotic result may often be nearly realized within a relatively short time. The chief virtue of P is that it represents the long-range value toward which the proportion buying in a unit period is tending. In this sense, it is a measure of the staying power of a new brand.

Despite objections to the model such as those above, the real issue is pragmatic: How well does it work in practice?

APPLICATION OF THE MODEL

In late March, 1956, Brand Y, a then new consumer packaged product, was introduced in Chicago with heavy promotional support. Brand Y secured a good sampling in April, and then showed a declining percent of families buying through July–August. In September, it was stimulated with a cents-off coupon, causing another boost in consumer trial. There were apparently no other consumer deals in the brand's first year. See Table 1.

Table 1
Consumer Purchasing of Brand Y, 1965[a]

Period	% of families buying brand Y
January–February	00.0
March–April	20.0
May–June	16.1
July–August	10.1
September–October	22.4
November–December	14.9

[a]Source: Chicago Tribune Consumer Panel.

By any standards, Brand Y proved to be a very successful product in Chicago. Could this have been predicted at a fairly early stage by our simple probability model? To test the model with this case, purchase records were secured from the *Chicago Tribune* of all its panel families who had bought Brand Y at some time during March–September, 1956. This information, along with total panel size, enabled us to estimate P_1

and P_2 month by month through September, and hence to estimate P for each.

To exemplify the calculations, consider the April–May data. Among the total panel, 120 families bought Brand Y during April. Of these, 62 or a proportion $P_1 = .517$ repeated in May. From here on, the notation ought to show that we are dealing with *estimated values* of P_1, P_2, and P *rather than true, population values*. But we have deliberately avoided new notation, since it would complicate this presentation.

Of April nonbuyers, $P_2 = .054$ bought in May. The transition probability matrix for April–May is estimated to be:

	May probability	
April purchase	Of buying brand Y	Of not buying brand Y
Bought brand Y	.517	.483
Did not buy brand Y	.054	.946

Based on this estimated matrix, and assuming these conditions persist, the long-run proportion of families buying Brand Y per month would approach

$$P = \frac{.054}{1 + .054 - .517} = .101$$

The analogous results for the remaining months are exhibited in Table 2. To simplify presentation, only the matrixes and the estimated values of P are presented.

As to the meaning of the results, it is desirable to imagine oneself back in 1956 and trying to interpret these data as they became successively available. This simulates how one would have to operate if he were making an actual prediction.

One's reasoning at that time might have proceeded along the following lines.

1. Based on April–May alone, Brand Y would have been correctly predicted as a success—very few brands in this field do as well. By almost any definition of "success" that might have been used, the prediction based on the April–May data alone would have signaled that the product would be a winner. (There are many profitable brands in this field bought by less than 5 percent of the families in a month.)

Ideally, *before* a study of this kind is made, the analyst should have a firm, quantitative definition as to what kinds of results are to be interpreted as indicative of new product "success." In effect, he should partition the set of all possible predictions into two groups of results: those

Table 2
Estimated Transition Matrixes and Resulting Predictions

	May		
April	.517	.483	Estimated P = .101
	.054	.946	

	June·		
May	.370	.630	Estimated P = .032
	.021	.979	

	July		
June	.674	.326	Estimated P = .050
	.017	.983	

	August		
July	.667	.333	Estimated P = .107
	.040	.960	

	September		
August	.774	.226	Estimated P = .266
	.082	.918	

consistent with a particular *a priori* definition of "success," and those that are not. Then, when the data become available, the analyst can refer the obtained prediction to one or the other of these groups. Obviously, since this article reports a retrospective study, it was not possible to carry out this ideal procedure.

It should also be observed that probably no one would want to make a prediction based on only two months of data. Nevertheless, had such a qualitative evaluation been required, the model would have performed satisfactorily.

2. Examination of the May–June returns would have reduced confidence in the earlier prediction. Because both P_1 and P_2 in this matrix were below April–May, the prediction is less optimistic. About all that might reasonably have been inferred at this point is that the basic dynamics of the process had changed.

3. June–July continued to show instability, although repeat buying was considerably stronger.

4. The July–August matrix, being fairly similar to June–July, would suggest that approximately the same underlying process was at work.[5] At this point, the analyst would likely have felt that *the process was sufficiently stable to permit a firm numerical prediction* of P, assuming no basic changes in market activity. He would probably have pooled the

[5] See Anderson, same reference as footnote 2, pp. 49–51, for a statistical test of the hypothesis that both matrixes reflect the same underlying process.

data to obtain a more reliable estimate of the process. (There are different ways of pooling the sample data, ranging from a simple averaging of corresponding elements in the sample matrixes to more complex weighting schemes.[6]) The result is:

$$\left\| \begin{array}{cc} .670 & .330 \\ .029 & .971 \end{array} \right\|$$

which gives a predicted, long-range proportion of families buying Brand Y in a month of P = .081.

5. The August–September matrix would add little information. The data there reflect consumer dealing—the cents-off coupon in September increased both P_1 and P_2. Hence, the analyst seeing these data at the time they were first available would have been very skeptical of their value for projection under normal circumstances. (The predicted P reflects a hypothetical market situation in which the coupon offer would be repeated monthly.)

At this point, the analyst would probably have concluded that P = .081 is the best available prediction of the proportion buying Brand Y in a month, as a long-run projection.

ADEQUACY OF THE PREDICTION

In the highly-competitive markets typical of packaged goods, it is difficult to judge the adequacy of any prediction. Because all prognostication involves assumptions about the future environment, any deviation from assumption will necessarily influence the apparent adequacy of a projection. Moreover, the prediction in this case was based on fewer data than would be desirable ordinarily; in practice, the estimation procedure would have been continued at least through 1956 and perhaps longer. Nevertheless, confrontation of a prediction with actual data is necessary, if insights into the effectiveness of the model are to be obtained.

We have estimated that the proportion of families buying Brand Y per month would approach 8.1 percent. However, because the only regular *Chicago Tribune* panel estimates of proportion buying are for *bimonthly* periods, it is necessary to convert this result into a bimonthly projection. If 8.1 percent buy in the first month of a bimonthly period, and 2.9 percent of those not buying the first month do buy the second month (see the transition matrix above), then the percent buying during a bimonthly period is predicted to be:

$$8.1\% + (.029)(91.9\%) = 10.8\%$$

[6] The procedure used here was that discussed by Anderson, same reference as footnote 2, pp. 45–53.

The adequacy of the model may be judged by comparing this prediction with Brand Y's bimonthly percent of families buying during the time since introduction, as shown in Table 3.

Table 3
Consumer Purchasing of Brand Y, 1957-1961a

	% of families buying brand Y				
Period	1957	1958	1959	1960	1961
January-February	13.0	16.7	15.8	17.0	17.2
March-April	12.2	14.2	20.0	22.7	17.0
May-June	22.6	13.2	16.8	19.6	17.4
July-August	16.5	11.5	13.0	14.6	
September-October	22.2	19.6	18.2	22.6	
November-December	17.5	18.9	19.3	20.1	

aSource: Chicago Tribune Consumer Panel.

The predicted proportion is always less than the observed values. This consistent underestimation traces in part to three facts.

1. The prediction is based on buying activity during the summer months, a seasonal low for this market. While there does not appear to be any simple way to accommodate such seasonal variations directly in the model, a practically satisfactory adjustment might be made along the following lines. Suppose that, during the period used to obtain the prediction, the proportion of families buying any brand in the category of interest is seasonally C percent below the corresponding annual average. Then the prediction could be multiplied by a factor of $\left(\dfrac{100}{100-C}\right)$ percent to compensate approximately for this. The result would be a "seasonally adjusted" prediction. An analogous adjustment could be made if the prediction were based on a seasonally-high period.

2. The prediction also tends to be generally lower than reported buying, because we have chosen to regard the June–July and July–August matrixes as "stable" for practical purposes and hence have pooled the data for these. This was done because a conservative analyst probably would have acted this way at the time the data were first available. A prediction based on July–August alone (10.7 percent buying per month, 14.3 percent for a bimonthly period) would have accorded more closely with the observed proportions buying.

3. Brand Y was offered to consumers at a substantially reduced price at least once, and usually twice, a year. This had the effect of increasing the proportions buying above the prediction during the deal periods. It seems likely also that these repeated consumer inducements may have had the longer-range effects of increasing P_1 and P_2 above the levels

estimated very early in the brand's development. Had the estimation procedure been continued over a longer time interval, better measures of these might have been obtained.

At the same time, we know that Brand Y's competitors did not "sit by idly" as it gained acceptance. Their attempts to fight back would tend to reduce the reported proportions buying below the prediction.

Unfortunately, there is no way of balancing off these opposing tendencies to evaluate the projection more accurately. Nor is there any way to account for the possible sampling errors and biases inherent in both the original prediction and the reported proportions buying we have used as an "infallible" criterion for comparison.

Finally, note that regardless of one's judgment concerning the significance of the gap between prediction and observed values, two things are significant.

1. The simple probability model would have predicted success for Brand Y, based on only two months' data after introduction.

2. At a time when the gross panel data were showing continuing declines in proportion buying after introduction (see Table 4), simple probability analysis of the data suggested that the underlying process was sufficiently stable (at least temporarily) to permit a quantitative prediction of ultimate product success.

Table 4
Consumer Purchasing of Brand Y, March-August, 1956

Period	% of families buying brand Y
March–April	20.0
May–June	16.1
July–August	10.1

EXTENSIONS OF THE METHOD

The simple probability model used in this article as an approach to early prediction of market success for a new product can be extended in terms of: kinds of problems for which it may be helpful, number of "purchase states" considered, opportunity for subpopulation analyses, and mathematical complexity. Here is an overview of these possible extensions.

1. *Kinds of Problems.* The method can be used to summarize buying behavior with regard to *established products, as well as new products.* In addition to the descriptive role that the transition probability matrix can play, it is also possible to predict long-range staying power. At least conceptually, one may compare the relative effectiveness of alternative

advertising programs, levels of pricing, etc. Whether these possibilities lend themselves to practical experimentation is another matter.

2. *Number of "Purchase States."* This article has dealt with a two-state case—either bought or did not. The model may be extended directly to K mutually exclusive and exhaustive states, with transition probability matrix, as in Table 5.

Table 5
Transition Probability Matrix for K Brands

Brand bought during second period

		A	B	K
Brand bought in first period	A	P_{AA}	P_{AB}	P_{AK}
	B	P_{BA}	P_{BB}	P_{BK}
	K	P_{KA}	P_{KB}	P_{KK}

The leading diagonal in this matrix (P_{AA}, P_{BB}, .., P_{KK}) measures the brand loyalties of the respective brands: A, B, .., K. That is, of first period Brand A buyers, a fraction P_{AA} repurchased during the second period, etc. Further, of first period A buyers, a fraction P_{AB} moved to Brand B during the second period, P_{AC} moved to C, etc. The value of this matrix, as a simple summary of brand loyalty and switching, is evident.

As in the two-state case, it is possible under rather general conditions to make long-range predictions concerning the ultimate distribution of buyers among the various states. We also note that the flow of quantities purchased (not merely buyers) from brand to brand can also be accommodated within this analytical structure. Thus, the model may be useful in predicting long-range brand shares, as well as proportions buying.

3. *Opportunity for Subpopulation Analyses.* In our illustrative example, we have assumed that common probabilities P_1 and P_2 applied to all the members of the panel. It may be worthwhile to examine the transition matrixes separately for demographic and other subgroups.

4. *Mathematical Complexity.* The simple model used here assumed that the probabilities of purchase depended at most on behavior during the directly preceding time period. A more complex model involving behavior during both the preceding period, and the period before that, may be a better representation of reality. The model may be extended backward an arbitrary number of periods, although analysis becomes increasingly more complicated.

Regardless of the ultimate value that the approach used may have for the prediction of new product success, the basic ideas have applicability beyond this specific problem area. In particular, there would appear to be important potential applications in the study of brand loyalty. At the very least, the fundamental idea of a transition probability matrix should be exploitable as a device for providing a simple, compact, and easily understood description of the consumer dynamics of brand purchasing.

25. Phasing out weak products

PHILIP KOTLER

Most companies today are multiproduct organizations. Whether large or small, whether in manufacturing, wholesaling, or retailing, a company will generally handle a multitude of products and product varieties. At the present time, the typical supermarket handles 6,800 items, American Optical manufactures 30,000 different items, and General Electric's products and parts number in the hundreds of thousands.

PRODUCT OVERPOPULATION

Historically, product lines tend to mushroom over a period of time unless a systematic and regular management effort is made at pruning. Yet management tends to find it easier to add products than to remove them.

The fact is that *as products and product lines increase numerically, the range of management problems seems to grow geometrically.*

Major Headaches

Thus management is stalked by the Malthusian specter of product overpopulation—of too many product mouths to feed. Its limited productive financial and marketing resources must be spread thinner over a larger number of products. This, in turn, leads to two major headaches:

Management's efforts at sales forecasting and pricing must contend with increasing mutual-*demand* relationships among its products.

Reprinted from the *Harvard Business Review* (March/April, 1965), pp. 107–118.
AUTHOR'S NOTE: I wish to acknowledge the helpful comments of Professor Richard M. Clewett of Northwestern University and the assistance of Hugh Hopkins, a Northwestern University Graduate School of Business Administration student.

Its efforts at production scheduling, costing, and equipment purchasing must contend with increasing mutual-*supply* relationships among its products.

Product overpopulation also poses baffling problems for management in resource allocation and coordination. The antidote lies in top management giving more attention to product simplification than it has in the past. As the pace of competition quickens and as consumer tastes become surfeited, the need for pruning company product lines of casualties becomes as great as that for finding replacements.

Gradual Recognition

This need is gradually being recognized in many companies. Well-known instances of product pruning in recent years include:

American Motors Kelvinator Division's drastic reduction of the number of models in its refrigerator, air-conditioning, and kitchen-range lines.

Seiberling Rubber's cutdown on the number of its passenger-car tire offerings by over one third.

Champion Papers' elimination of certain lines when a full-scale study showed that 20 percent of its products were producing 80 percent of its sales.[1]

These are but a few reflections of the growing concern of corporate management about obsolete lines and slow-moving products and models.

Yet, though these efforts point in the right direction, by their very abruptness and scale they indicate the lack of regular and systematic product-pruning programs. Most executives will see a physician at least once a year to check on their health but will let their product mix go unchecked until a crisis develops. During this time, many products lie infirm in the mix until they fade away or are suddenly massively ejected in a crisis-inspired housecleaning.

Developing Perspectives

The purpose of this article is to describe a new control system currently under development for conducting efficient and rapid annual product checkups. I shall try to discuss this new approach in enough detail so that it can be implemented by any company concerned with limiting its product population to the more vigorous contenders. Although this system will be described as designed for a manufacturing company, it can easily be adapted by large retail and wholesale organizations, where the problem of dropping weak products is as, if not more, serious.

[1] See "More Companies Drop Slower-Moving Goods to Improve Earnings," *The Wall Street Journal*, August 9, 1962.

Before turning our attention to the elements of the system, however, it is desirable to develop certain perspectives suggested by the following questions:

What is the basis of product obsolescence?
How much does carrying weak products cost a company?
Why does management shy away from dropping these products?
What are current practices on product-line pruning?

PRODUCT LIFE CYCLE

No branded product can be expected to hold a permanent franchise in the marketplace. The lifetime sales of many products reveal a typical pattern of development. This pattern, known as the *product life cycle*, consists of four distinguishable stages:

1. *Introduction*—The product is put on the market; awareness and acceptance are minimal.
2. *Growth*—The product begins to make rapid sales gains because of the cumulative effects of introductory promotion, distribution, and word-of-mouth influence.
3. *Maturity*—The rate of sales growth begins to taper off because of the diminishing number of potential customers who either are unaware of the product or are aware but have taken no action.
4. *Decline*—The sales begin to diminish as the product is gradually edged out by newer or better products or substitutes.

Variable Histories

The product life cycle concept represents a useful idealization rather than a rigid description of all product life histories.[2]

In the first place, there is nothing fixed about the length of the cycle, or the length of its various stages. According to Joel Dean, the rate of product degeneration is governed by the rate of technical change, the rate of market acceptance, and the ease of competitive entry.[3] Thus each year some new dress styles are introduced in the knowledge that their whole life cycle may span only a year or a season. On the other hand, new commercial aircraft are introduced in the expectation that they will enjoy good sales for at least a decade.

In the second place, products have been known to begin a new cycle

[2] See Arch Patton, "Top Management's Stake in the Product Life Cycle," *The Management Review*, June 1959, pp. 9–14, 67–71, 76–79.
[3] See "Pricing Policies for New Products," HBR November–December 1950, p. 28.

or to revert to some earlier stage as a result of the discovery of new uses, the appearance of new users, or the invention of new features. Thus television sales have exhibited a history of spurts as new sizes of screens were introduced, and color television may well put television sales back into a rapid growth stage.

Important Considerations

Yet, despite these and other difficulties concerning the concept of the product life cycle, the concept remains very useful in that it reminds us of three important phenomena:

1. *Products have a limited life*—They are born at some point, may (or may not) pass through a strong growth phase, and eventually degenerate or disappear.
2. *Product profits tend to follow a predictable course through the life cycle*—Profits are absent in the introductory stage, tend to increase substantially in the growth stage, stabilize and then decline in the maturity stage, and all but disappear in the declining stage.
3. *Products require a different marketing (as well as production and financial) program in each stage*—Management must be prepared to shift the relative levels and emphasis given to price, advertising, product improvement, and so forth during different stages in the product life cycle.

To these must be added a fourth consideration. Under modern conditions of competition, a new product's life span is apt to be shorter than it has ever been in the past.[4] There are too many competitors with fast-moving research laboratories, ingenious marketing techniques, and large budgets who stand ready to woo away the customer. The customer himself is generally unloyal, fickle in his tastes, and a prey to gimmicks.

Dual Problem

Executive conversation is rich with talk of "sick" products, "slow movers," "superannuated" products, "senior citizens," "parasites," "former heavyweights," "obsolete lines," and "fizzled-out" products. All kinds of products are involved, including those which never quite got off the ground, those whose profit returns were fair for a while and are now vanishing, and those which were huge successes but are now riding a sea of troubles.

The problem is not only one of the health of whole product classes but also one of individual styles, models, and choices within the classes which add so much to cost. We are talking about any product or product variation of dubious value in the scheme of corporate objectives.

---

[4] For some interesting examples, see "The Short Happy Life," *Time*, March 29, 1963, p. 83.

WEAK-PRODUCT BURDEN

Every weak-selling product which lingers in a company's line constitutes a costly burden. Businessmen often do not realize the magnitude
of this burden because of a fixation with the more direct costs. They are
complacent as long as the revenues of the weak product cover at least
the direct costs of producing it, relieved if the revenues cover most of
the overhead. Their attitude toward the weak product is like that of
Damon Runyon's character, Harry the Horse, who said, "I am going to
bet on the races today. I hope I break even. I need the money."

Hidden Costs

The cost of sustaining a weak product in the mix is not just the
amount of uncovered overhead and profit. No financial accounting can
adequately convey all the hidden costs. Thus:

The weak product tends to consume a disproportionate amount of management's time.

It often requires frequent price and inventory adjustments.

It generally involves short production runs in spite of expensive setup times.

It requires both advertising and sales-force attention which might better be
diverted to making the "healthy" products more profitable.

Its very unfitness can cause customer misgivings and cast a shadow on the
company's image.

Furthermore, as if these hidden costs were not burden enough, the
biggest cost imposed by carrying weak products may well be in the
future. By not being eliminated at the proper time, these products delay
the aggressive search for replacement products; they create a lopsided
product mix—long on "yesterday's breadwinners" and short on "tomorrow's breadwinners"; [5] they depress present profitability and weaken the
company's foothold on the future.

Potential Savings

The tremendous savings which can be effected by product-pruning
programs are dramatized in the following two cases:

Hunt, a medium-sized canner, began to cut its thirty-some-odd lines in 1947.
By 1958 it had only three products: fruit cocktail, tomato products, and

---

[5] See Peter F. Drucker, "Managing for Business Effectiveness," HBR May–June
1963, p. 53.

peaches. Within these lines, Hunt reduced the variety offered. For example, in peaches Hunt packed only one grade (choice) in one type of syrup (thick). This simplification was apparently very successful for Hunt. Its sales increased from $15 million in 1947 to $120 million in 1958. By that time it had the top brand in tomato sauce and tomato paste and was second in peaches and catsup. In addition to cutting down on the number of lines, Hunt also began a diversification program by buying out nonrelated companies, such as a manufacturer of matches.[6]

After a survey one company with annual sales of $40,000,000 eliminated sixteen different products with a total volume of $3,300,000. It also made a number of improvements in methods of handling the products retained.

Over the next three years the company's total sales increased by one-half and its profits by some twenty times. Among the many factors contributing to these spectacular increases, top executives have stated that dropping unsatisfactory products was one of the most important.[7]

ABANDONMENT AVERSION

In view of the costs of carrying weak products, why does management typically shy away from product-pruning programs? Certainly sentimentality, as R. S. Alexander suggests, is a part of the aversion to product abandonment:

But putting products to death—or letting them die—is a drab business, and often engenders much of the sadness of a final parting with old and tried friends. The portable, six-sided pretzel polisher was the first product The Company ever made. Our line will no longer be our line without it.[8]

Retention Rationale

There are, in fact, many reasons for this aversion, logical as well as sentimental.

Sometimes it is expected—or hoped—that product sales will pick up in the course of time when economic or market factors become more propitious. Here management thinks that the poor performance is due to outside factors which will improve.

Sometimes the fault is thought to lie in the marketing program, which the company plans to revitalize. It may be felt that the solution lies in reviving dealer enthusiasm, increasing the advertising budget,

[6] Ralph Westfall and Harper W. Boyd, Jr., *Cases in Marketing Management* (Homewood, Illinois: Richard D. Irwin, Inc., 1961), p. 181.

[7] Charles H. Kline, "The Strategy of Product Policy," HBR July–August 1955, p. 100.

[8] "The Death and Burial of 'Sick' Products," *Journal of Marketing*, April 1964, p. 1.

changing the advertising theme, or modifying some other marketing factor.

Even when the marketing program is thought to be competent, management may feel that the solution lies in product modification. Specifically, the thinking might be that sales could be stimulated through an upgrading of quality, styling, or features.

When none of these explanations exist, a weak product may nevertheless be retained in the mix because of the alleged contribution it makes to the sales of the company's other products. The weak product may provide the salesman with an entrée to important accounts. It may be used as bait to attract prospect interest in looking at the rest of the line. It may be the sacrificial lamb in full-time merchandising to court those buyers who like to obtain their "nuts and bolts" from the same supplier.

If none of these functions are performed by the weak product, then the retention rationale may be that its sales volume covers more than just actual costs, and the company temporarily has no better way of keeping its fixed resources employed. Any sales receipts above out-of-pocket costs make some contribution to overhead charges. Unless another product is available which could make an even larger contribution to overhead, the weak product ought to be retained in the short run until a decision has to be made on renewing a major fixed resource.

Die-Hard Interests

The foregoing are all logical arguments for retaining weak products in the mix. But there are also situations where the persistence of weak products can only be explained by the presence of vested interests, management or consumer sentiment, or just plain corporate inertia. A lot of people inside and outside an organization grow to depend on a particular product. Among them are the product manager, the employees, and certain customers. Eliminating a product from the mix is organizationally disruptive. Personnel may have to be shifted or, in some extreme instances, released. In such cases sentiment becomes a powerful factor in the decision-making process and often explains the slow decay of many weak products.

Those in the organization whose interests may be adversely affected by a product's elimination may engage in practices designed to conceal its weakness. Through hard selling, the product may be pushed into the dealers' stocks although the consumer "pull" is known to be feeble. The product manager may use some of his budget to stimulate sales in artificial ways to postpone the day of judgment. While these and other ruses may conceal the true facts from top management for a period of time, fortunately they cannot work indefinitely.

ABANDONMENT PRACTICES

The vast majority of companies, including some of the most progressive ones in industry, have not established orderly procedures for pruning their products. Such action is usually undertaken either (1) on a *piecemeal* basis, as in instances where the products' money-losing status is incontrovertible, conspicuous, and embarrassing, or (2) on a *crisis* basis, wherein the precipitating event may be a financial setback, a persistent decline in total sales, piling inventories, or rising costs.

But neither piecemeal pruning nor crisis pruning is really a satisfactory practice. Each leaves too many dated products lingering in the lineup for too long. Each leads to hasty "hatchet" jobs under improvised standards. Each is abrupt and possibly traumatic to the morale of certain parties inside and outside the company.

Partial Stride

A somewhat more systematic approach has been described as follows:

A major manufacturer of consumer durables . . . makes a review every six months of all products whose profitability is less than the corporate average; for each such product, the manager responsible is requested to recommend action for improving earnings or elimination of the product.[9]

Although faults can be found with this approach, it represents a step in the right direction. It provides a standard for appraisal; it communicates a performance objective; it inspires the preparation of plans; and it sets a day of judgment. These features constitute the beginning of a control system for the problem of weak products. However, the system can be improved by developing more comprehensive criteria than profits alone and by involving a management team and the marvelous capacities of a computer. In the balance of this article this more advanced approach will be described.

PRODUCT CONTROL SYSTEM

A company which wishes to maintain a strong product mix must commit itself to the idea of a periodic product review. Such a review can be expected to accomplish two objectives:

1. The *formal* objective of increasing over-all company profits through identification of those products which require modification or merit elimination from the mix in the light of changing conditions.

[9] See D'Orsay Hurst, "Criteria for Evaluating Existing Products and Product Lines," in *Analyzing and Improving Marketing Performance* (American Management Association, Management Report No. 32, 1959), p. 91.

2. The *organizational objective* of providing a periodic incentive for better performance on the part of those executives who share product responsibility.

Awareness of Need

We shall assume, for illustrative purposes, that we are dealing with an established company which produces hundreds of products and models, and whose energies until now have been directed toward further product development. Although several company products produce an exceptionally good return, the over-all rate of return on company investment is below that of the industry. The sales of some of the company's mainstay products are slipping, and many models are gathering dust in inventory. The president is concerned with this problem—one that occurs repeatedly in industry—and yet line executives reassure him that the slower moving products are suffering only temporary setbacks.

It is the kind of situation where a reputable management consultant could profitably be brought in. In nine out of ten cases, the consultant would document the case that the high profits on a few good products are being dissipated to support too many has-been products. Such a report would provide an opportunity for the president to accomplish two useful things in one stroke: purge his existing mix of superannuated products and institute a new control system so that the product mix will not become overpopulated again.

An over-all view of a practical control system is charted in Exhibit 1. The first two parts are the *creation* stages and take place only when it has been decided that a control system should be installed. The *operational* steps, 1 through 6, represent the system as it is re-activated annually thereafter for product-pruning purposes.

Creation Stages

Product pruning is not a task which can be entrusted to any one man or department in the organization. There are too many parties involved and too many honest differences of opinion on appropriate criteria.

Representative Corporate Team. Therefore, the first creation stage is the appointment of a management team to assume responsibility for this problem. Because important policy questions are involved, as well as potentially large savings, the product review committee should consist of high-level executives. A representative corporate team, for example, could include executives from the following departments:

Marketing—to provide views on marketing strategy, customer relations, competitive developments, and future sales outlook.

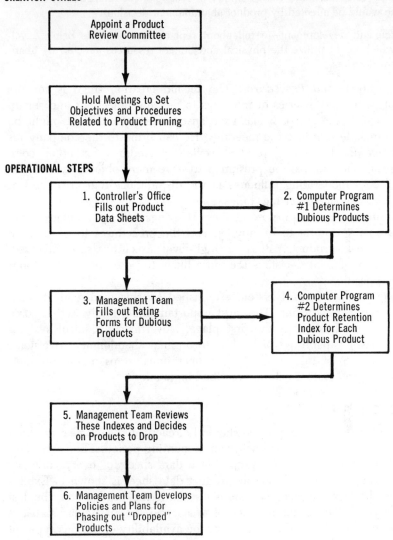

CREATION STAGES

> Appoint a Product
> Review Committee

> Hold Meetings to Set
> Objectives and Procedures
> Related to Product Pruning

OPERATIONAL STEPS

> 1. Controller's Office
> Fills out Product
> Data Sheets

> 2. Computer Program
> #1 Determines
> Dubious Products

> 3. Management Team
> Fills out Rating
> Forms for Dubious
> Products

> 4. Computer Program
> #2 Determines
> Product Retention
> Index for Each
> Dubious Product

> 5. Management Team Reviews
> These Indexes and Decides
> on Products to Drop

> 6. Management Team Develops
> Policies and Plans for
> Phasing out "Dropped"
> Products

Exhibit 1. Creation and Operation of Annual Product Review System

Manufacturing—to describe any scheduling, manufacturing, or inventory problems connected with the products.

Purchasing—to discuss estimates of future costs of materials.

Control (accounting and finance)—to offer data on past sales, costs, and profits and also to develop the implications of product abandonment for cash flow and over-all corporate rate of return.

Personnel—to speak about the feasibility of reassignment for company personnel who would be affected by product abandonment decisions.

Research and development—to tell about replacement products being developed which might utilize the physical and human resources affected by abandonment decisions.

Objectives and Procedures. The second creation stage is for the committee to hold a series of meetings to develop objectives and set up procedures. If the company has used an outside consultant, it might be well to include him in these meetings. He can bring to the company his experience in developing product review procedures for other companies, and he can also be presumed to have more objectivity. At best he will be a moderating influence in the disputations that arise, and at worst a scapegoat for getting things done.

In any event, the purpose of these meetings will be to achieve concensus on the criteria to be applied and the procedures to be used in judging weak products. Because high-level executives are involved, future abandonment decisions are more likely to be carried out without active opposition.

The product control system established by this management team can take numerous forms. The most important thing really is that some system be established in the first place. Nevertheless, control systems differ in their capabilities of leading to optimal abandonment decisions. In the balance of this article the six operational steps of the product-pruning control system will be described in detail.

Step 1: Data Sheet

The product review process should be reactivated each year at about the same time, generally following an accounting period. The controller's office takes the first step by preparing a data sheet for every company product and/or model. A sample product data sheet is shown in Exhibit 2. This sheet summarizes key statistics about the product for the last several years. The exact number of years and the particular statistics depend on the nature of the business, the availability of various types of information, and the judgment of the management team as to what data might indicate that the product is of questionable worth.

The purpose of the data sheet is to provide the informational basis for judging whether the product is in a good state of health or merits further study for an abandonment decision. It is not assumed to contain sufficient information for making the abandonment decision.

Two-Stage Decision. What is the advantage of this two-stage separation of the abandonment decision—first judging which set of products out of the entire set are dubious, and later judging which of these dubious products should actually be eliminated? *The fact is that it takes much*

PRODUCT NO. _____

MODEL NO. _____

DATE _____

		Past Years			
		3	2	1	Current
Industry sales	$				
Company sales	$				
Physical volume					
Unit total cost	$				
Unit variable cost	$				
Price	$				
Cyclical adjustment factor					
Overhead burden					

COMMENTS: _____

Exhibit 2. Sample Product Data Sheet

less information to detect whether a product is weak than to make a judgment on whether it should be dropped.

The product data sheet can be easily prepared, and it serves as a quick means for separating the company's products into the weak and the strong. Since the strong are no longer considered in the context of abandonment decisions, the weak can then receive the focused attention of the management group.

Spotting Dubious Products. How does the information on the product data sheet clew the management team that a product should be considered for possible deletion? Signs of product weakness are declining gross margin, declining sales in relation to total company sales, low coverage of its overhead, and so forth. Undoubtedly, experienced executives who studied the product data sheets would be able to spot a weak or faltering product. But herein lies a difficulty: high-level executives on the review committee can ill afford the time to scan the thousands of product sheets for signs of trouble. One recourse is to turn the task over to middle- or lower-management executives. A more efficient, speedy, and inexpensive recourse is to utilize the versatile capacities of a computer to do the job.

Step 2: Determining Candidates

That is the suggested route shown in the second step of the product review program. The challenge is to develop a computer program which

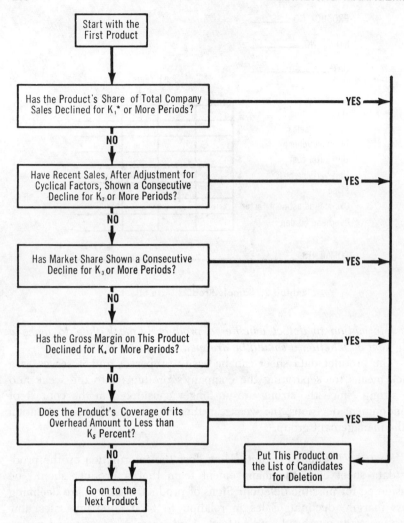

Exhibit 3. Flow Chart of Computer Program #1 Decision Rules (Note: The K's are chosen by the management team. For example, if the team sets $K_1 = 3$, then management thinks that 3 or more periods of sales decline should put a product on the dubious list.)

can "intelligently" scan the product data sheets (in the form of key-punched cards) for signs of weakness in much the same way the management team would. The best approach is to ask the executives what they look for and to embody these principles in computer decision rules.[10]

A very simple program of decision rules is shown in Exhibit 3,

[10] See R. M. Cyert and J. G. March, *A Behavioral Theory of the Firm* (Englewood Cliffs, New Jersey: Prentice-Hall, Inc., 1963), Chapters 7 and 8.

which raises five critical questions—more could be listed—about recent trends in sales, market share, gross margin, and overhead coverage. These trends can be calculated from the product data sheets obtained in Step 2. The questions are hooked in series so that a product must earn a negative answer to all questions to avoid an investigation of its status. Each company sets the retention values it regards as critical for placing a product on the dubious list.

Step 3: Rating Form

After the computer has produced a list of the dubious products, the management team meets to review the list. It might seem that now they should decide which products on the list should actually be dropped. But a judgment at this stage would be premature. In the first place, the executives would find themselves lacking vital information bearing on each product. In the second place, they would lack the guidance of formal criteria.

The major purposes of the meeting are for the team members to sense the over-all pattern and magnitude of the company's weak-product problem, to remove from the list products which their good sense—as opposed to the computer's intelligence—tells them do not belong there, and to implement a formal product rating device. A formal rating device is quite essential if abandonment decisions are to be guided by consistent and explicit standards.

Developing Comprehensive Criteria. Without such a device, the committee executives are likely to raise expedient criteria for each product and to vary the importance they attach to different criteria from case to case. But what criteria should the product rating form embody? In this connection there are likely to be sharp differences of opinion, depending on the orientation of the team's members.[11]

Some executives take the view that products which do not cover their full costs (including historical and arbitrarily allocated costs) should be eliminated. Others are less concerned with historical costs and more concerned with present opportunities. Therefore, if a dubious product is covering its direct costs and contributing more to overhead than an alternative use of resources would contribute, they would recommend retention. Still others traditionally prefer to make a judgment on a more intuitive basis. Their prime concern is dollar volume and the full exploitation of sales resources. The only products they care to see abandoned are those which cause a lot of trouble in relation to their volume or to their contribution to the sales of other products.

Each executive's view would lead to quite different sets of criteria

[11] See Conrad Berenson, "Pruning the Product Line," *Business Horizons,* Summer 1963, p. 63.

for product elimination and therefore would have different long-run sales and profit implications. It is hoped that the meetings held in the creation stage discussed earlier would lead to the development of comprehensive criteria which would blend the more valid aspect of each point of view. A product rating form incorporating a number of important considerations is shown in Exhibit 4.[12]

Rating and Weight Values. This form calls for a *rating value* for each dubious product against seven different scales. Most of the scales are invariably subjective in this area. Each scale ranges from zero to one, with zero representing strong grounds for eliminating the product and one representing strong grounds for retaining the product.

The first scale, for instance, calls for evaluating the future market potential of the product. A product which is becoming hopelessly obsolescent, such as a detergent which is not able to clean modern synthetic fabrics as well as it cleans cotton and linen, would be rated close to zero on this scale.

Since all scales may not be considered by management to be equally important, each scale is also assigned a *weight value*. These weight values are presumably agreed on earlier in the creation stage and remain constant for all product judgments.

The product rating form serves as a discussion guide for each product case and helps to highlight the informational needs. Ultimately the committee must agree on a rating value for each question for each dubious product. Sometimes additional meetings may have to be held before the necessary information is available or sufficient concensus develops.

Step 4: Retention Index

When this work is completed, the product rating form can then be processed to yield a single number, the "product retention index," indicating the degree of product desirability. (The fate of some products may already have been decided in the process of the management team's discussion of the ratings in Step 3.) This single number will be the sum of the weighted ratings on the product rating form.

The sum can range from a maximum value of 7, if the product shows superior grounds for being retained on all counts, to a minimum value of 0, if the product shows minimal grounds for retention on all counts. Although the single number can be obtained by using a desk calculator, when many dubious products are involved, it is best to enter the rating values on a mark-sensing card and to use the computer to calculate the index numbers. Thus Computer Program #2 normally consists of a straightforward calculation of products and sums.

[12] See, for example, Barry Richman, "A Rating Scale for Product Innovation," *Business Horizons*, Summer 1962, p. 37; and John T. O'Meara, Jr., "Selecting Profitable Products," *HBR* January–February 1961, p. 83.

PRODUCT NO._____

MODEL NO._____

DATE_____

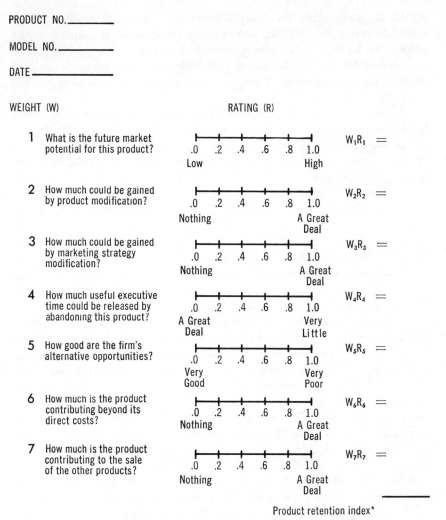

WEIGHT (W)   RATING (R)

1 What is the future market |—+—+—+—+—| W_1R_1 =
  potential for this product?   .0 .2 .4 .6 .8 1.0
                                  Low   High

2 How much could be gained |—+—+—+—+—| W_2R_2 =
  by product modification?   .0 .2 .4 .6 .8 1.0
                                  Nothing   A Great
                                                  Deal

3 How much could be gained |—+—+—+—+—| W_3R_3 =
  by marketing strategy   .0 .2 .4 .6 .8 1.0
  modification?   Nothing   A Great
                                                  Deal

4 How much useful executive |—+—+—+—+—| W_4R_4 =
  time could be released by   .0 .2 .4 .6 .8 1.0
  abandoning this product?   A Great   Very
                                  Deal   Little

5 How good are the firm's |—+—+—+—+—| W_5R_5 =
  alternative opportunities?   .0 .2 .4 .6 .8 1.0
                                  Very   Very
                                  Good   Poor

6 How much is the product |—+—+—+—+—| W_6R_6 =
  contributing beyond its   .0 .2 .4 .6 .8 1.0
  direct costs?   Nothing   A Great
                                                  Deal

7 How much is the product |—+—+—+—+—| W_7R_7 =
  contributing to the sale   .0 .2 .4 .6 .8 1.0
  of the other products?   Nothing   A Great
                                                  Deal
                                                  _____

                                  Product retention index*

Exhibit 4. Seven-scale Product Rating Form
*Each rating (R) is multiplied by the question's importance or weight (W), result-
ing in a weighted rating (WR) for that question. All of the seven weighted ratings
are summed and the sum is the Product Retention Index. The higher this index,
the greater the arguments in favor of retaining the product.

Step 5: Abandonment Decisions

When the indexes are ready, the product review committee again
convenes to make a final judgment on which products to drop. The committee may have already established a retention index number between 0
and 7 so that any dubious product receiving an index number below it

would unquestionably be dropped from the line. Any product which scores, for example, less than one out of a possible seven points must be judged as having very little potential, imposing a large burden on executive time, and contributing very little to profits or to the sale of other company products. There is little reason for retaining such a product.

Products whose indexes exceed the established retention value number have more than minimum justification on one or more criteria, but the management team must examine these individual cases carefully. Product retention indexes supply a formal, albeit subjective, basis for ranking the dubious products in order of the strength of the arguments for retention.

Generally speaking, products that have lower indexes will be the weaker ones, and management will want to concentrate on those. At the same time, it is entirely possible that the committee members may decide to drop a product with a higher index value than another which they decide to retain. The indexes serve as a guide rather than as a final verdict. They are designed to aid in the systematic consideration of product intangibles and not to replace judgment.

Product Interactions. Another reason exists for not using this retention index or any other formal device too mechanically. Various products in the line will have joint demands and/or joint cost and manufacturing relationships. If they are judged only in terms of their individual retention indexes, it may seem desirable to drop a set of them. But management must consider the total effect on its business operations of dropping any set of products. The total effect may be more than the sum of the separate effects because of product interactions. The particular set may spell too great a weakening of the company's position in a certain market, may place too great a strain on certain company personnel, or may lead to costly idling of particular facilities. Because of these factors, the savings which the company expects to realize from eliminating a given set of products may be quite different from the sum of the savings calculated individually.

Simulation Hopes. Is there any tool which can help the management team determine the more global implications of dropping any set of products? Although little work has been done on this problem, computer simulation offers the greatest hope of some breakthrough. Management is interested in what will happen to profits, sales stability, and sales growth as the product mix is changed. A logical approach would be to investigate possible sequences and timings of planned product deletions and additions over some future time period. This approach would require assumptions about the future behavior of sales, costs, and profits for individual products and groups of products.

The computer's contribution would consist of making rapid calculations of profit, stability, and growth characteristics of the many different possible transformations of the product mix through time. By simulating sales and profit patterns of alternative product-mix changes, it would provide management with informative estimates of the expected payoffs and risks of different product-line policies.

Step 6: Phasing Out

There is still one remaining step after management has decided which products to drop, and this is the formulation of the phasing-out policies and plans for the individual products being dropped. (A distinction may be drawn between "dropping" and "milking" a product. In the latter case the company carries the product at a greatly reduced level of promotion and cost, hoping to salvage what it can. Milking amounts to phasing it out very slowly.) For each product, management must determine its obligations to the various parties affected by the decision. Management may want to provide for a stock of replacement parts and service to stretch over the expected life of the most recently sold units. It may want to find a manufacturer willing to take over the discontinued product. Some of the products can be dropped quite easily with little repercussion, while other product eliminations will require an elaborate phasing-out plan.

Influencing Factors. The criteria for this step are quite general. After a decision has been made to eliminate a product, the actual phasing-out plan has to be custom-tailored to the unique product circumstances. Some of the factors which will influence phasing-out tactics and timing are:

How much finished and semifinished stock remains in our inventory; how much finished goods are in distributors' inventories?

What kinds of guarantees and compensations should be offered to distributors and customers?

How soon could the affected executives and employees be shifted to other useful assignments?

How much salvage value could the company get for its machinery and unfinished stock? Could it gain by waiting?

How much will the discontinuation affect the relations with distributors and customers? Could the company gain by waiting?

Critical Timetables. With the answers to these and other questions, management can prepare timetables for the phasing out of its weak products. Where the product involved is one which has enjoyed major distribution, management should consider preparing a critical path program (such as PERT) to ensure efficiency in its phasing out. The program should show when various parties are to be notified about the decision and when various asset-disposal efforts should be made. The objective is to let the news disseminate in a pattern which does not handicap the company's efforts to dispose of certain products and yet does not lead some parties to feel they were unfairly treated.

CONCLUSION

In an age of dynamic product competition, product-line pruning must be considered as a problem on a par with product improvement and new-product development. Yet most managements have no systematic procedure for pruning weaker products; these products often linger in the mix until they just fade away. In the meantime, they depress the company's over-all level of profitability; they complicate the task of allocating scarce company resources; and they hold the company back from aggressively developing new opportunities.

These things are obvious, and yet corporate managements only rarely rise to the occasion. Their attention is riveted on tomorrow's rather than yesterday's products. There is often sentiment about the former heavyweight products which have passed their prime. There is a valid concern about the effect of dropping products on internal organization morale and external customer and supplier relations. There is uncertainty about whether the product is chronically weak or only pausing before the next sales spurt. There is confusion about the right standards to apply in choosing products for deletion. There is a lack of practicable models and precedents for conducting periodic product reviews.

This article has attempted to define the seriousness of this problem and to describe a practical control system for keeping the product mix relatively free of unprofitable products. The system consists of the appointment of a high-level and broadly representative management team which holds meetings at about the same time each year for the purpose of spotting dubious products, evaluating them, choosing those which must be dropped, and developing the phasing-out program for them. In each of these steps, the executives are guided by explicit standards and information, much of which is processed on the computer to expedite the decision making.

The proposed control system for product pruning is expensive in executive time, but this cost must be compared to the greater overt and hidden costs of allowing superannuated products to continue in the product mix. Furthermore, in provoking corporate executives to define standards, gather information, and make decisions, the system brings the company much closer to instituting formal long-range product and market planning procedures which would provide the ultimate answer to achieving an optimal product mix.

26. Behavioral science offers fresh insights on new product acceptance

STEVEN J. SHAW

Few areas of marketing management reveive more attention than new product development. It is estimated that business spends over $10 billion yearly on new product planning, research, and marketing.[1] Yet a recent report of the United States Department of Commerce estimated that 90 percent of all new products fail within four years of their introduction.

Why is this rate of failure so high? Are customers really fickle and unpredictable? Or is failure due to our inadequate knowledge of the *process* by which an innovation is accepted or rejected by consumers?

In the opinion of this writer, the failure of new products can be attributed to the lack of understanding by marketing management of this innovation process. There is a need for management executives to expand their knowledge in this key area of consumer behavior.

Sociology, psychology, anthropology, mathematical biology, and other disciplines that make up behavioral science are providing valuable insights into the highly complex process of the adoption and diffusion of an innovation.

This article, then, focuses on behavioral science concepts that answer, at least partially, the following questions of interest to marketing management: (1) Who are the small group leaders influencing the spread and adoption of innovations? (2) What is the nature of the innovation process? (3) Which attributes of the innovation itself influence its rate of adoption?

Reprinted from *Journal of Marketing*, Volume 29 (January, 1965), pp. 9–13, National Quarterly Publication of the American Marketing Association.
[1] Taylor W. Meloan, "New Products—Keys to Corporate Growth," in Martin L. Bell (editor), *Marketing: A Maturing Discipline*, Proceedings of the 1960 December conference of the American Marketing Association (Chicago: American Marketing Association, 1961), pp. 28–39, at p. 29.

INFLUENCE OF SMALL GROUP LEADERS

The influence of leaders of small groups is now generally acknowledged, because of the pioneer studies of Katz and Lazarsfeld.[2] While their earlier studies indicated that information seemed to flow only down the social pyramid from upper, through the middle, to the lower classes (the "trickle-down theory") their more recent studies have revealed that in many cases the flow of communication is a "two-way street." Thus, a new product or service might be adopted initially by the "tastemakers" (or "innovators," a somewhat comparable term) of a lower-status group and become widely diffused among its members before rising to a higher stratum.

This conclusion is supported by the studies of other anthropologists and sociologists. For example, one study of the rate of adoption of television, canasta, and health insurance, indicated that upper-class respondents were more conservative or slower than lower-class respondents in adopting television, but that the upper-class was much faster to accept canasta. On the other hand, both classes of respondents revealed about the same rate of adoption of health insurance.[3]

In the innovation of household goods, many of the tastemakers may be found among the young and well-educated middle income groups according to the studies of Mueller.[4]

Whyte also made an interesting study of the adoption and diffusion of air-conditioning unit ownership in a typical middle-class community of younger, white-collar workers. Ownership was not uniform throughout the neighborhood, but clustered around certain blocks and was directly related to the social traffic of children and backyard group leaders among the children's parents.[5]

Identification of Tastemakers

The presence of tastemakers in the numerous small and informal groups in American communities is an important factor for the product development department of a firm. The crucial questions are: who are these influential individuals and how does marketing research locate them?

[2] Elihu Katz and Paul F. Lazarsfeld, *Personal Influence* (Glencoe, Illinois: The Free Press, 1955). Elihu Katz, "The Two-Step Flow of Communication: An Up-to-Date Report on an Hypothesis," *Public Opinion Quarterly*, Vol. 21 (Spring, 1957), pp. 61–78.

[3] L. Saxon Graham, "Class and Conservatism in the Adoption of Innovations," *Human Relations*, Vol. 9 (February, 1956), pp. 91–100, at pp. 93 and 94.

[4] Eva Mueller, "The Desire for Innovation in Household Goods," Lincoln H. Clark (editor), *Consumer Behavior Research on Consumer Reactions* (New York: Harper & Brothers, 1958), p. 37.

[5] William H. Whyte, Jr., "The Web of Word of Mouth," *Fortune*, Vol. 50 (November, 1954), pp. 140–143. Edward L. Brink and William T. Kelley, *The Management of Promotion* (Englewood Cliffs, N.J.: Prentice-Hall, Inc., 1963), pp. 61–63.

The Opinion Research Corporation has developed a promising method of identifying tastemakers.[6] To test the hypothesis that they are highly mobile individuals, ORC used a sample of 105 households in Ridgewood, New Jersey, a well-to-do suburban community. The individuals were classified on a scale of mobility: high, medium, and low.

The dimension of mobility were: level of education, travel, job promotion, social contacts, advance in income, intellectual development, kinship mobility, and movement to suburbs and other areas. Thus, the high-mobility classification was designed to consist of families exhibiting the greatest mobility in their overall patterns.

The sample households were given a list of 160 products and services, and were asked to give the first year of usage and their current usage. From this survey it was determined that the "high mobiles" led in the buying of products that relatively were newcomers to a large market. Examples of these were travelers checks, auto rentals, and foreign cookbooks. On the other hand, in the case of new products that had been on the market for some time—station wagons, foreign cars, and electric blankets—the high mobiles accounted for a dwindling share of that market.

The typical high mobiles on ORC's scale were found to be families who traveled extensively, read for intellectual experience, had advanced in their jobs, rose to higher income levels, moved around and met many different types of people, stressed independence in family relations, stressed education for their children, and tried to improve their own.

Of all the mobility factors used, extent of travel showed up as a particularly critical selector. It was found that those who traveled most were far more likely to be early product adopters than the stay-at-homes, even with income held constant. Also, high mobiles were found to read more than the other groups.

However, it was emphasized in these studies that some high mobile families may stand out as leaders in the adoption of new food products, but not of new automobiles; some as leaders in the purchase of household appliances, but not sports equipment. Also, since the initial adoption of a product could start at the top, middle, or lower rungs of the social stratum, class mobility was measured by how many friends the individual had in different walks of life, and not so much by movement to a higher rung on the social class ladder.

Finally, some high mobiles were found quite clearly not to be consumption leaders since their energies were directed to religion or other areas of life that are not closely tied to consumption of goods and services.

[6] America's Tastemakers, Vols. 1 and 2 (Princeton, N.J.: Opinion Research Corporation, April and June, 1959). "Predicting Consumers' Needs: Can Tastemakers Point the Way?" in Thomas L. Berg and Abe Shuckman (editors), Product Strategy and Management (New York: Holt, Rinehart and Winston, Inc., 1963), pp. 223–229, at p. 227.

The Ridgewood experiments have developed a promising hypothesis which needs refinement through sampling on a national scale.

STAGES IN THE ADOPTION PROCESS

In the study of innovations, it is helpful to visualize the adoption process as consisting of a series of distinct but related stages. Behavioral scientists in their study of the diffusion of new products typically conceptualize the adoption process as consisting of the following five stages: *awareness, interest, evaluation, trial,* and *adoption* or *rejection.*[7]

At the *awareness* stage, the individual first becomes exposed to the innovation either through impersonal or personal communication, but lacks complete information. He then may become *interested* in the innovation and seek further information about it. In the succeeding *evaluation* stage, the potential adopter appraises the innovation in the light of his present and anticipated future and then decides whether to *try* it on a small scale. After satisfactory *trial,* the tastemaker may finally decide to continue the full use of the innovation. However, the innovation may be rejected or discontinued at any state in the adoption process.

Using this classification of the adoption process, Rogers [8] has developed some generalizations that could prove of considerable value to sales managers. For instance, as the result of his study of several case histories, he has hypothesized that impersonal mass communication such as radio and television advertising may be more important than personal communication—salesmanship—in stimulating small group leaders initially to become aware of the new product and to seek more information about it. But in the critical evaluation and trial phases of the adoption process, the personal persuasion of informed salesmen probably has greater effectiveness since it permits a two-way exchange of ideas about the product and the prospect's needs.

INNOVATION'S CHARACTERISTICS THAT INFLUENCE RATE OF ADOPTION

Of great importance to marketing management is the identification of innovation characteristics that might reveal a new product's relative speed of adoption and diffusion. Some innovations diffuse from first introduction to widespread use in a few years, while others may require 10 to 50 years.

What attributes of a new product affect the rate at which it diffuses

---

[7] See, for instance, Herbert F. Lionberger, *Adoption of New Ideas and Practices* (Ames, Iowa: The Iowa State University Press, 1960), pp. 3 and 4.

[8] Everett M. Rogers, *Diffusion of Innovations* (New York: The Free Press of Glencoe, 1962), pp. 311–314.

and becomes widely used? As a result of his extensive studies, Rogers [9] concluded that certain basic consumer-perceived product characteristics could be used to predict the rate of adoption. He suggests that *relative economic* or *social advantage, compatibility, complexity, divisibility* and *communicability* are probably the most important attributes. Moreover, he emphasizes that it is the potential adopter's cognizance of these new product or service characteristics that counts.

Relative Economic or Social Advantage

Relative advantage is the yardstick that is traditionally used to evaluate the market possibilities of new products. It is the degree to which an innovation is superior to the product it is trying to replace. One of the keys to a new product's speed of diffusion is the ease or difficulty the adopters have in becoming aware of its particular merits.

It is not the value of an innovation as seen by experts that counts, but what is perceived by the potential adopters and imitators that really matters. This point was stressed by Wasson,[10] who used several case examples to show that "the ease or difficulty of introduction depends basically on the nature of the new in the new product—the new as the customer views the bundle of services he perceives in the newborn." Wasson describes the new in a new product as the "package of consumer-perceived services embodied in it." His list of 13 different ways in which products may be new were grouped into three classes on the basis of whether they eased the job of market introduction, slowed it up, or where ambivalent in their effect. However, Wasson's analysis of the 13 product attributes was largely in terms of economic and social utility—*relative advantage.* He did not identify any of the other important consumer-perceived product attributes such as *compatibility, complexity, divisibility,* and *communicability.*

Compatibility with Existing Values

A significant contribution to an understanding of the innovation process by behavioral scientists may be the concept of compatibility. Compatibility is the degree to which an innovation is consistent with existing values and past experiences of the adopters. An idea that is not compatible with the cultural beliefs and values of a group will not be adopted so rapidly as an idea that is compatible. One easily recognized example of the compatibility idea is the resistance to the use of birth control techniques among certain religious groups in the United States and foreign countries. Then, again, in India the lack of compatibility of beef

[9] Same reference as footnote 8, at pp. 124–133.
[10] Chester R. Wasson, "What is New about a New Product?" *Journal of Marketing,* Vol. 25 (July, 1960), pp. 52–56, at pp. 52 and 54.

production with the country's cultural values prevents the adoption and development of this industry.

Recent market experience supports the compatibility idea. For instance, quite recently Analoze, a cherry-flavored pill that combined analgesic-antiacid qualities and could be used without water, was judged by panel of consumers as clearly superior to competing products in terms of benefits. Yet, despite careful product planning, market testing, and wide advertising support, Analoze did not take in five trial cities and had to be abandoned.

In the postmortem probing, it was concluded that the fatal flaw was the "works without water" feature. Headache sufferers consciously or unconsciously associated water with a cure, and consequently had no confidence in a tablet that dissolved without water. Consumers did not perceive the new product as being compatible with their existing values on the importance of water as part of a headache cure.[11]

As an illustration of the compatibility concept, Rogers points to the failure of an intensive campaign to secure the boiling of drinking water in a small Peruvian village. Despite a physician's frequent public pleas and personal visits to homes by a local hygiene worker most families still refused to accept this innovation. The idea of water boiling conflicted with their belief that only sick people should use hot water. Healthy people drank only cold water. The use of hot water by healthy people was incompatible with traditional beliefs.[12]

Food and dietary habits are imbedded deeply in a society's tradition and are closely related to its cultural values. Innovations which clash with these values are resisted stubbornly. A typical example of such resistance and rejection is the attempted introduction into a Spanish-American community in New Mexico of an improved hybrid seed corn by a county extension agent. A test planting demonstrated convincingly to planters in the area that the hybrid seed yielded three times the normal harvest. Thus, economic advantage was clearly illustrated, and the following year one-half of the growers adopted the hybrid seed. However, two years later nearly all had returned to planting their original varieties, because the ground corn was found to have a strange flavor when made into tortillas. As seen by these consumers, the new corn was incompatible with traditional taste.

Complexity, or Understanding of Idea

Complexity of the innovation is another factor that may affect its rate of adoption. Complexity is the degree to which an innovation is relatively difficult to understand and use. Any new idea may be classified in a

---

[11] Burt Schoor, "The Mistakes: Many New Products Fail Despite Careful Planning, Publicity," *The Wall Street Journal*, Vol. 159 (April 5, 1961), pp. 1, 22.

[12] Same reference as footnote 8, at pp. 7 and 8.

complexity-simplicity continuum. Some innovations are clear in their meaning to members of a social system; others are not.

Although the research evidence is far from conclusive, the generalization is suggested by anthropologists and sociologists that the complexity of an innovation, as perceived by members of a group, affects its rate of adoption. For instance, Graham sought to determine why canasta and television diffused at different adoption rates in the upper and lower classes. He concluded that one of the reasons for this difference was degree of complexity. Canasta had to be learned through detailed personal explanation from other card players. Its procedures were complex and difficult to master. Television, however, appeared to be a relatively simple idea that required only the ability to turn a knob.[13]

Divisibility

Divisibility is the degree to which an innovation may be tried on a limited basis. Some ideas that cannot be divided for small-scale trial may be subjected to a brief trial over time as, for example, a new feed on an entire dairy herd for one week. But some innovations are more difficult than others to divide for trial. Examples of take-it or leave-it innovations are computer systems, bulk-milk tanks, home air-conditioners, and driver-training education in a school system.

There is evidence from several investigations that relatively earlier adopters may perceive divisibility as more important than later adopters. The more innovative individual has no precedent to follow while the latter adopters are surrounded by peers who have already adopted the innovation.[14]

Communicability of New Idea

Communicability is the degree to which the results of an innovation may be diffused to other members of the group. The results of some ideas are easily observed and communicated to others, while some innovations are difficult to describe to others. One illustration is the case of pre-emergent weed killers that are sprayed on before the weeds emerge from the soil. The rate of adoption of this idea has been slow in spite of its relative advantage because there are no dead weeds which the user can show his neighbors.

One of the most comprehensive studies of the effect of the above-described innovation characteristics on the rate of adoption was made by

[13] Same reference as footnote 3, at p. 131.
[14] Elihu Katz, "The Social Itinerary of Technical Change: Two Studies on the Diffusion of Innovation," *Human Organization*, Vol. 20 (Summer, 1961), pp. 70–82, at p. 81.

Kivlin.[15] He found highest correlation between the rate of adoption and (1) relative advantage, (2) complexity (in a negative direction), and (3) compatibility, in this order. In his study no significant relationship was found between rate of adoption and divisibility.

SUMMING UP

Recent studies of consumer innovation behavior by behavioral scientists have strengthened the hypothesis that it is possible to identify community tastemakers—early product adopters—through a mobility scale composed of such criteria as travel, level of education, job promotion, social contacts, advance in income, kinship mobility, and movement to suburbs.

In the study of the diffusion of innovations it might be helpful to think of the adoption process as consisting of five distinct but related stages. Behavioral scientists conceptualize this process as being composed of the awareness, interest, evaluation, trial and adoption or rejection stages.

Behavioral science research also suggests that the speed of acceptance or failure of an innovation is closely related to the ability of the consumer to perceive and evaluate its superiorities. Not only economic advantage, but such product attributes as compatibility, complexity, divisibility, and communicability are important to the early adopters.

Thorough evaluation of an innovation from the viewpoint of the consumer requires that product research and development weigh carefully the answers to basic questions such as the following: Is the innovation compatible with the existing beliefs and values of consumers? Is it easy to understand and use? Is the new product divisible for trial on a limited basis? And, finally, can its superiorities be easily observed and communicated to others?

[15] Joseph E. Kivlin, *Characteristics of Farm Practices Associated with Rate of Adoption*. Unpublished Ph.D. Dissertation, Pennsylvania State University, 1960.

27. New criteria for market segmentation

DANIEL YANKELOVICH

The director of marketing in a large company is confronted by some of the most difficult problems in the history of U.S. industry. To assist him, the information revolution of the past decade puts at his disposal a vast array of techniques, facts, and figures. But without a way to master this information, he can easily be overwhelmed by the reports that flow in to him incessantly from marketing research, economic forecasts, cost analyses, and sales breakdowns. He must have more than mere access to mountains of data. He must himself bring to bear a method of analysis that cuts through the detail to focus sharply on new opportunities.

In this article, I shall propose such a method. It is called *segmentation analysis*. It is based on the proposition that once you discover the most useful ways of segmenting a market, you have produced the beginnings of a sound marketing strategy.

UNIQUE ADVANTAGES

Segmentation analysis has developed out of several key premises:

In today's economy, each brand appears to sell effectively to only certain segments of any market and not to the whole market.

Sound marketing objectives depend on knowledge of how segments which produce the most customers for a company's brands differ in requirements and susceptibilities from the segments which produce the largest number of customers for competitive brands.

Traditional demographic methods of market segmentation do not usually provide this knowledge. Analyses of market segments by age, sex, geography,

Reprinted from the *Harvard Business Review* (March/April, 1964), pp. 83–90.

and income level are not likely to provide as much direction for marketing strategy as management requires.

Once the marketing director does discover the most pragmatically useful way of segmenting his market, it becomes a new standard for almost all his evaluations. He will use it to appraise competitive strengths and vulnerabilities, to plan his product line, to determine his advertising and selling strategy, and to set precise marketing objectives against which performance can later be measured. Specifically, segmentation analysis helps him to—

. . . direct the appropriate amounts of promotional attention and money to the most potentially profitable segments of his market;

. . . design a product line that truly parallels the demands of the market instead of one that bulks in some areas and ignores or scants other potentially quite profitable segments;

. . . catch the first sign of a major trend in a swiftly changing market and thus give him time to prepare to take advantage of it;

. . . determine the appeals that will be most effective in his company's advertising; and, where several different appeals are significantly effective, quantify the segments of the market responsive to each;

. . . choose advertising media more wisely and determine the proportion of budget that should be allocated to each medium in the light of anticipated impact;

. . . correct the timing of advertising and promotional efforts so that they are massed in the weeks, months, and seasons when selling resistance is least and responsiveness is likely to be at its maximum;

. . . understand otherwise seemingly meaningless demographic market information and apply it in scores of new and effective ways.

These advantages hold in the case of both packaged goods and hard goods, and for commercial and industrial products as well as consumer products.

Guides to Strategy

Segmentation analysis cuts through the data facing a marketing director when he tries to set targets based on markets as a whole, or when he relies primarily on demographic breakdowns. It is a systematic approach that permits the marketing planner to pick the strategically most important segmentations and then to design brands, products, packages, communications, and marketing strategies around them. It infinitely simplifies the setting of objectives.

In the following sections we shall consider nondemographic ways of segmenting markets. These ways dramatize the point that finding marketing opportunities by depending solely on demographic breakdowns is like trying to win a national election by relying only on the information in a census. A modern census contains useful data, but it identifies neither the crucial issues of an election, nor those groups whose voting habits are still fluid, nor the needs, values, and attitudes that influence how those groups will vote. This kind of information, rather than census-type data, is the kind that wins elections—and markets.

Consider, for example, companies like Procter & Gamble, General Motors, or American Tobacco, whose multiple brands sell against one another and must, every day, win new elections in the marketplace:

These companies sell to the whole market, not by offering one brand that appeals to all people, but by covering the different segments with multiple brands. How can they prevent these brands from cannibalizing each other? How can they avoid surrendering opportunities to competitors by failing to provide brands that appeal to all important segments? In neither automobiles, soaps, nor cigarettes do demographic analyses reveal to the manufacturer what products to make or what products to sell to what segments of the market. Obviously, some modes of segmentation other than demographic are needed to explain why brands which differ so little nevertheless find their own niches in the market, each one appealing to a different segment.

The point at issue is not that demographic segmentation should be disregarded, but rather that it should be regarded as only one among many possible ways of analyzing markets. In fact, the key requirement of segmentation analysis is that the marketing director should never assume in advance that any one method of segmentation is the best. His first job should be to muster all probable segmentation and *then* choose the most meaningful ones to work with. This approach is analogous to that used in research in the physical sciences, where the hypothesis that best seems to explain the phenomena under investigation is the one chosen for working purposes.

TEN MARKETS

In the following discussion we shall take ten markets for consumer and industrial products and see how they are affected by seven different modes of nondemographic segmentation. The products and modes are shown schematically in Exhibit 1. Of course, these segments are not the only ones important in business. The seven I have picked are only *examples* of how segmentation analysis can enlarge the scope and depth of a marketer's thinking.

MARKET	MODE OF SEGMENTATION						
	Value	Susceptibility to Change	Purpose	Aesthetic Concepts	Attitudes	Individualized Needs	Self-Confidence
Watches	*						
Automobiles	*	*		*			
Perfumes			*				
Bathing Soaps			*				
Hair Care						*	
Other Packaged Goods	*		*	*			
Retail Soft Goods	*						
Adding Machines	*		*				
Computers		*			*		*
Light Trucks		*					*

Exhibit 1. Example of Segmentation in Different Industries

I. Watches

In this first case we deal with a relatively simple mode of segmentation analysis. The most productive way of analyzing the market for watches turns out to be segmentation by *value*. This approach discloses three distinct segments, each representing a different value attributed to watches by each of three different groups of consumers:

1. *People who want to pay the lowest possible price for any watch that works reasonably well.* If the watch fails after six months or a year, they will throw it out and replace it.

2. *People who value watches for their long life, good workmanship, good material, and good styling.* They are willing to pay for these product qualities.

3. *People who look not only for useful product features but also for meaningful emotional qualities.* The most important consideration in this segment is that the watch should suitably symbolize an important occasion. Consequently, fine styling, a well-known brand name, the recommendation of the jeweler, and a gold or diamond case are highly valued.

In 1962, my research shows, the watch market divided quantitatively as follows:

Approximately 23 percent of the buyers bought for lowest price (value segment #1).

Another 46 percent bought for durability and general product quality (value segment #2).

And 31 percent bought watches as symbols of some important occasion (value segment #3).

Defining and quantifying such segments is helpful in marketing planning—especially if a watch company's product happens to appeal mostly to one segment or if the line straddles the three segments, failing to appeal effectively to any. Without such an understanding, the demographic characteristics of the market are most confusing. It turns out, for example, that the most expensive watches are being bought by people with both the highest and the lowest incomes. On the other hand, some upper income consumers are no longer buying costly watches, but are buying cheap, well-styled watches to throw away when they require servicing. Other upper income consumers, however, continue to buy fine, expensive watches for suitable occasions.

Timex's Timely Tactics. The planning implications in value segmentation are very broad for the industry. For one thing, many of the better watch companies in the years between 1957 and 1962 were inadvertently focusing exclusively on the third segment described—the 31 percent of the market that bought a watch only as a gift on important occasions—thus leaving the bulk of the market open to attack and exploitation.

The U.S. Time Company took advantage of this opening and established a very strong position among the more than two-thirds of America's watch buyers in the first two segments. Its new low-price watch, the Timex, had obvious appeal for the first segment, and it catered to the second segment as well. At that time, higher-price watches were making the disastrous mistake in their advertising of equating product quality with water-proof and shock-resistant features. The Timex also offered these low-cost features, at lower prices, thus striking at a vulnerable area which the competition itself created. When Timex pressed its attack, it was able within a few years to claim that "Timex sells more watches than any other watch company in the world."

Even the *timing* of Timex's watch advertising was involved. Much of the third segment was buying watches only during the Christmas season, and so most of Timex's competitors concentrated their advertising in November and December. But since buying by the other two segments went on all the time, Timex advertised all year-round, getting exclusive attention ten months of the year.

Thus, nondemographic segmentation in the watch industry has directly affected almost every phase of marketing, including the composition of the product line. Major watch companies know that they must plan product line, pricing, advertising, and distribution within the framework of the three basic value segments of this market.

II. Automobiles

The nondemographic segmentation of the automobile market is more complex than that of the watch market. The segments crisscross, forming intricate patterns. Their dynamics must be seen clearly before automobile sales can be understood.

Segmentation analysis leads to at least three different ways of classifying the automobile market along nondemographic lines, all of which are important to marketing planning.

Value Segmentation. The first mode of segmentation can be compared to that in the watch market—a threefold division along lines which represent how different people look at the meaning of *value* in an automobile:

1. *People who buy cars primarily for economy.* Many of these become owners of the Falcon, Ford, Rambler American, and Chevrolet. They are less loyal to any make than the other segments, but go where the biggest savings are to be found.
2. *People who want to buy the best product they can find for their money.* These prospects emphasize values such as body quality, reliability, durability, economy of operation, and ease of upkeep. Rambler and Volkswagen have been successful because so many people in this segment were dissatisfied.
3. *People interested in "personal enhancement"* (*a more accurate description than "prestige"*). A handsomely styled Pontiac or Thunderbird does a great deal for the owner's ego, even though the car may not serve as a status symbol. Although the value of an automobile as a status symbol has declined, the personal satisfaction in owning a fine car has not lessened for this segment of the market. It is interesting that while both watches and cars have declined in status value, they have retained *self-enhancement* value for large portions of the market.

Markets can change so swiftly, and the size of key segments can shift so rapidly, that great sensitivity is required to catch a trend in time to capitalize on it. In the automobile market, the biggest change in recent years has been the growth in segment two—the number of people oriented to strict product value. Only a few years ago, the bulk of the market was made up of the other segments, but now the product-value segment is probably the largest. Some automobile companies did not respond to this shift in the size of these market segments in time to maintain their share of the market.

Aesthetic Concepts. A second way of segmenting the automobile market is by differences in *style* preferences. For example, most automobile buyers tell you that they like "expensive looking" cars. To some people, however, "expensive looking" means a great deal of chrome and ornamentation, while to others it means the very opposite—clean, conservative lines, lacking much chrome or ornamentation.

Unfortunately, the same *words* are used by consumers to describe diametrically opposed style concepts. Data that quantify buyers according to their aesthetic *responses*—their differing conceptions of what constitutes a good-looking car—are among the most useful an automobile company can possess.

The importance of aesthetic segmentation can be pointed up by this example:

When Ford changed from its 1959 styling to its 1960 styling, the change did not seem to be a radical one from the viewpoint of formal design. But, because it ran contrary to the special style expectations of a large group of loyal Ford buyers, it constituted a dramatic and unwelcome change to them. This essential segment was not prepared for the change, and the results were apparent in sales.

Susceptibility to Change. A third and indispensable method of segmenting the automobile market cuts across the lines drawn by the other two modes of segmentation analysis. This involves measuring the relative susceptibility of potential car buyers to changing their choice of make. Consider the buyers of Chevrolet during any one year from the point of view of a competitor:

At one extreme are people whose brand loyalty is so solidly entrenched that no competitor can get home to them. They always buy Chevrolets. They are closed off to change.

At the other extreme are the open-minded and the unprejudiced buyers. They happened to buy a Chevrolet because they preferred its styling that year, or because they got a good buy, or because someone talked up the Fisher body to them. They could just as easily have purchased another make.

In the middle of this susceptibility continuum are people who are predisposed to Chevrolet to a greater or lesser degree. They can be persuaded to buy another make, but the persuasion has to be strong enough to break through the Chevrolet predisposition.

The implications of this kind of a susceptibility segmentation are far-reaching. Advertising effectiveness, for example, must be measured against each susceptibility segment, not against the market as a whole. Competitors' advertising should appear in media most likely to break through the Chevrolet predisposition of the middle group. In addition, the wants of those who are not susceptible must be factored out, or they will muddy the picture. Marketing programs persuasive enough to influence the uncommitted may make no difference at all to the single largest group—those who are predisposed to Chevrolet but still open enough to respond to the right stimulus.

If the marketing director of an automobile company does not break down his potential market into segments representing key differences in susceptibility, or does not clearly understand the requirements of each key segment, his company can presevere for years with little or no results because its promotion programs are inadvertently being aimed at the wrong people.

III. Perfume

A segmentation analysis of the perfume market shows that a useful way to analyze it is by the different *purposes* women have in mind when they buy perfume.

One segment of the market thinks of a perfume as something to be added to what nature has supplied. Another segment believes that the purpose of fragrance products is to help a woman feel cleaner, fresher, and better groomed—to correct or negate what nature has supplied. In the latter instance, the fragrance product is used to *cancel out* natural body odors; in the former, to *add* a new scent. To illustrate this difference in point of view:

One woman told an interviewer,

I like a woodsy scent like Fabergé. It seems more intense and lingers longer, and doesn't fade away like the sweeter scents.

But another woman said,

I literally loathe Fabergé. It makes me think of a streetcar full of women coming home from work who haven't bathed.

These differences in reaction do not indicate objective differences in the scent of Fabergé. They are subjective differences in women's attitudes; they grow out of each woman's purpose in using a perfume.

Purposive segmentation, as this third mode of analysis might be called, has been of great value to alert marketers. For instance:

A company making a famous line of fragrance products realized that it was selling almost exclusively to a single segment, although it had believed it was competing in the whole market. Management had been misled by its marketing research, which had consistently shown no differences in the demographic characteristics of women buying the company's products and women buying competitors' products.

In the light of this insight, the company decided to allocate certain lines to the underdeveloped segments of the market. This required appropriate changes in the scent of the product and in its package design. A special advertising strategy was also developed, involving a different copy approach for each product line aimed at each segment.

In addition, it was learned that visualizations of the product in use helped to create viewer identification in the segment that used perfume for adding to nature's handiwork, but that more subtle methods of communication produced better results among the more reserved, more modest women in the second segment who want the "canceling out" benefits of perfume. The media susceptibilities of women in the two segments were also found to be different.

Thus, from a single act of resegmentation, the advertising department extracted data critical to its copy platform, communication strategy, and media decisions.

IV. Bathing Soap

A comparable purposive segmentation was found in the closely related bathing soap field. The key split was between women whose chief requirement of soap was that it should clean them adequately and those for whom bathing was a sensuous and enjoyable experience. The company (a new contender in this highly competitive field) focused its sights on the first segment, which had been much neglected in recent years. A new soap was shaped, designed, and packaged to appeal to this segment, a new advertising approach was evolved, and results were very successful.

V. Hair-Care Market

The Breck-Halo competition in the shampoo market affords an excellent example of another kind of segmentation. For many years, Breck's recognition of the market's individualized segmentation gave the company a very strong position. Its lines of individualized shampoos included one for dry hair, another for oily hair, and one for normal hair. This line accurately paralleled the marketing reality that women think of their hair as being dry, oily, or normal, and they do not believe that any one shampoo (such as an all-purpose Halo) can meet their individual requirements. Colgate has finally been obliged, in the past several years, to revise its long-held marketing approach to Halo, and to come out with products for dry hair and for oily hair, as well as for normal hair.

Other companies in the hair-care industry are beginning to recognize other segmentations in this field. For example, some women think of their hair as fine, others as coarse. Each newly discovered key segmentation contains the seeds of a new product, a new marketing approach, and a new opportunity.

VI. Other Packaged Goods

Examples of segmentation analysis in other packaged goods can be selected almost at random. Let us mention a few briefly, to show the breadth of applicability of this method of marketing analysis:

In *convenience foods,* for example, we find that the most pragmatic classification is, once again, purposive segmentation. Analysis indicates that "convenience" in foods has many different meanings for women, supporting several
different market segments. Women for whom convenience means "easy to use"
are reached by products and appeals different from those used to reach women
for whom convenience means shortcuts to creativity in cooking.

In the market for *cleaning agents,* some women clean preventively, while others
clean therapeutically, i.e., only after a mess has been made. The appeals, the
product characteristics, and the marketing approach must take into account
these different reasons for buying—another example of purposive segmentation.

In still another market, some people use *air fresheners* to remove disagreeable
odors and others to add an odor. A product like Glade, which is keyed to the
second segment, differs from one like Airwick in product concept, packaging,
and type of scent.

The *beer market* requires segmentation along at least four different axes—
reasons for drinking beer (purposive); taste preferences (aesthetic); price/quality
(value); and consumption level.

VII. Retail Soft Goods

Although soft-goods manufacturers and retailers are aware that their
customers are value conscious, not all of them realize that their markets
break down into at least four different segments corresponding to four
different conceptions of value held by women.

For some women value means a willingness to pay a little more for
quality. For others, value means merchandise on sale. Still other women
look for value in terms of the lowest possible price, while others buy
seconds or discounted merchandise as representing the best value.

Retailing operations like Sears, Roebuck are highly successful because they project *all* these value concepts, and do so in proportions
which closely parallel their distribution in the total population.

VIII. Adding Machines

In marketing planning for a major adding machine manufacturer,
analysis showed that his product line had little relationship to the segmented needs of the market. Like most manufacturers of this kind of
product, he had designed his line by adding features to one or several
stripped-down basic models—each addition raising the model price. The
lowest priced model could only add; it could not subtract, multiply,
divide, or print, and it was operated by hand.

Since there are a great many features in adding machines, the manufacturer had an extremely long product line. When the needs of the mar-

ket were analyzed, however, it became clear that, despite its length, the line barely met the needs of two out of the three major segments of the market. It had been conceived and planned from a logical point of view rather than from a market-need point of view.

The adding machine market is segmented along lines reflecting sharp differences in value and purpose:

One buyer group values accuracy, reliability, and long life above all else. It tends to buy medium-price, full-keyboard, electric machines. There are many banks and other institutions in this group where full-keyboard operations are believed to ensure accuracy.

Manufacturing establishments, on the other hand, prefer the ten-key machine. Value, to these people, means the maximum number of laborsaving and timesaving features. They are willing to pay the highest prices for such models.

Both these segments contrast sharply with the third group, the small retailer whose major purpose is to find a model at a low purchase price. The small retailer does not think in terms of amortizing his investment over a period of years, and neither laborsaving features nor full-keyboard reliability count for as much as an immediate savings in dollars.

Despite the many models in the company's line, it lacked those demanded by both the manufacturer and small retailer segments of the market. But, because it had always been most sensitive to the needs of financial institutions, it had developed more models for this segment than happened to be needed. Product, sales and distribution changes were required to enable the company to compete in the whole market.

IX. Computers

One pragmatic way of segmenting the computer market is to divide potential customers between those who believe they know how to evaluate a computer and those who believe they do not. A few years ago only about 20 percent of the market was really open to IBM's competitors—the 20 percent who believed it knew how to evaluate a computer. By default, this left 80 percent of the market a virtual captive of IBM—the majority who did not have confidence in its own ability to evaluate computers and who leaned on IBM's reputation as a substitute for personal appraisal.

Another segmentation in this market involves differences in prospects' attitudes toward the inevitability of progress. Although this factor has been widely ignored, it is a significant method for qualifying prospects. People who believe that progress is inevitable (i.e., that change is good and that new business methods are constantly evolving) make far better prospects for computers than those who have a less optimistic attitude toward progress in the world of business.

X. Light Trucks

The market for light trucks affords us another example of segmentation in products bought by industry. As in the computer example, there are both buyers who lack confidence in their ability to choose among competing makes and purchasers who feel they are sophisticated about trucks and can choose knowledgeably. This mode of segmentation unexpectedly turns out to be a key to explaining some important dynamics of the light truck market:

Those who do not trust their own judgment in trucks tend to rely very heavily on both the dealer's and the manufacturer's reputation. Once they find a make that gives them reliability and trouble-free operation, they cease to shop other makes and are no longer susceptible to competitive promotion. Nor are they as price-sensitive as the buyer who thinks he is sophisticated about trucks. This buyer tends to look for the best price, to shop extensively, and to be susceptible to the right kind of competitive appeals, because he puts performance before reputation.

These ways of looking at the truck market have far-reaching implications for pricing policy, for product features, and for dealers' sales efforts.

CONCLUSION

To sum up the implications of the preceding analysis, let me stress three points:

1. *We should discard the old, unquestioned assumption that demography is always the best way of looking at markets.*

The demographic premise implies that differences in reasons for buying, in brand choice influences, in frequency of use, or in susceptibility will be reflected in differences in age, sex, income, and geographical location. But this is usually not true. Markets should be scrutinized for important differences in buyer attitudes, motivations, values, usage patterns, aesthetic preferences, or degree of susceptibility. These may have no demographic correlatives. Above all, we must never assume in advance that we know the best way of looking at a market. This is the cardinal rule of segmentation analysis. All ways of segmenting markets must be considered, and *then* we must select out of the various methods available the ones that have the most important implications for action. This process of choosing the strategically most useful mode of segmentation is the essence of the marketing approach espoused in this article.

In considering cases like those described, we must understand that we are not dealing with different types of people, but with differences in peoples' *values*. A woman who buys a refrigerator because it is the cheapest available may want to buy the most expensive towels. A man who pays extra for his beer may own a cheap watch. A Ford-owning Kellogg's Corn Flakes-eater may be closed off to Chevrolet but susceptible to Post Toasties; he is the same man, but he has had different experiences and holds different values toward each product he purchases. By segmenting markets on the basis of the values, purposes, needs, and attitudes relevant to the product being studied, as in Exhibit 1, we avoid misleading information derived from attempts to divide people into types.

2. *The strategic-choice concept of segmentation broadens the scope of marketing planning to include the positioning of new products as well as of established products.*

It also has implications for brand planning, not just for individual products but for the composition of a line of competing brands where any meaningful segment in the market can possibly support a brand. One explanation of the successful competing brand strategy of companies like Procter & Gamble is that they are based on sensitivity to the many different modes of market segmentation. The brands offered by P & G often appear very similar to the outsider, but small, marginal differences between them appeal to different market segments. It is this rather than intramural competition that supports P & G successes.

3. *Marketing must develop its own interpretive theory, and not borrow a ready-made one from the social sciences.*

Marketing research, as an applied science, is tempted to borrow its theoretical structures from the disciplines from which it derives. The social sciences offer an abundance of such structures, but they are not applicable to marketing in their pure academic form. While the temptation to apply them in that form is great, it should be resisted. From sociology, for example, marketing has frequently borrowed the concept of status. This is a far-reaching concept, but it is not necessarily the most important one in a marketing problem, nor even one of the important ones. Again, early psychoanalytic theory has contributed an understanding of the sexual factor. While this can sometimes be helpful in an analysis of buying behavior in a given situation, some motivation researchers have become oversensitive to the role of sex and, as a result, have made many mistakes. Much the same might be said of the concept of social character, that is, seeing the world as being "inner-directed," "other-directed," "tradition-directed," "autonomous," and so forth.

One of the values of segmentation analysis is that, while it has drawn on the insights of social scientists, it has developed an interpretive theory *within* marketing. It has been home-grown in business. This may explain its ability to impose patterns of meaning on the immense diversity of the market, and to provide the modern marketing director with a systematic method for evolving true marketing objectives.

28. The process of mass acceptance

When a large investment is required to launch a radically new idea in packaging, two big questions always confront the decision makers:

How can consumers be persuaded to accept the new idea?
How long will it take to put it over?

For years marketers have been searching for a foolproof formula to predict acceptance, whether the question at hand is a new design for an automobile or a pushbutton container for packaging whipped cream.

Whether a universal formula ever will be found is open to question. But in a summary of 35 research studies on how people accept new ideas, conducted in nine states over the past 20 years, there is the promise of more light on this subject than has ever been found before.

The compilation of these research studies has been made and fitted into a framework by Drs. George M. Beal and Joe M. Bohlen, sociologists at Iowa State College, Ames, Ia.[1] Recently, the professors presented some of their findings at the eighth annual United Fruit Forum in New York. Their deduction, based on work done so far, is that the process through which people accept new practices is much the same whether it's frozen foods, synthetic fabrics, mechanical equipment or wonder drugs; whether the people are urban or rural; whether they live in Midtown Manhattan, a small town in Iowa or Arizona.

If this is the case, then an examination of the basic pattern of their thesis should be helpful to all packagers—faced, as they so often are, with a decision on an entirely new packaging concept which may require breaking the barriers of entrenched consumer habits.

Analysis of the behavior pattern indicated by these studies also may provide a key as to where and how to concentrate the promotional pro-

Reprinted from *Modern Packaging*. Copyright 1959, Modern Packaging Corporation, New York.
[1] George M. Beal and Joe M. Bohlen, "The Diffusion Process," Special Report No. 18, Agricultural Extension Service, Iowa State College, Ames, Ia., 1957.

gram—to what age groups, to individuals of what economic levels, with what educational background and with what value orientation.

The data are presented in the framework of two over-all generalizations.

The first is that the process by which people accept new ideas is not a single-unit act, but a series of complex ones—a mental process that can be divided for analysis and action into five stages.

The second is that all people do not adopt new ideas at the same time. Some people are quick to adopt them; others wait a long time, while some never adopt them. And the time span in accepting a new idea can vary from six months to 15 years or more, according to these studies.

In this article we relate to packaging the five stages into which Drs. Beal and Bohlen divide the mental process by which the individual accepts a new idea, accompanied by our own interpretation of its significance in package planning. The five stages, as they have been outlined, are as follows:

1. *The awareness stage.* An individual becomes cognizant of a new idea, such as a cook-in-the-bag food. But the prospective consumer lacks details about it. She may not know a brand name, whether it tastes good or how to prepare it.
2. *The interest stage.* Awareness of the product piques her interest to find out more about it. She wants to know who makes it, how long it takes to prepare, whether the package contains one or more servings, whether it is really a convenience that saves work in the kitchen.
3. *The evaluation stage.* She applies the information obtained in the first two stages to her own situation, gives the cook-in-the-bag package a mental trial —perhaps asking herself: Will my family like this labor-saving food? How much will it cost? Do I have to keep it frozen in the refrigerator before use?
4. *The trial stage.* If the evaluation indicates that the packaged product has possibilities for her, she will buy it and give it a trial. She finds out for herself how easy it is to prepare, whether her family likes it, whether it can be served economically within her budget.
5. *The adoption stage.* The final stage is the adoption stage, characterized by continued use of the product and, most of all, by satisfaction with the idea. It is pointed out that this does not mean a consumer who has accepted an idea must use it constantly, but that she has accepted it as good and intends to include it in her on-going program. She no longer goes through the process of "Should I or should I not buy it?"

The research indicates that mass media—newspapers, magazines, TV and radio—play the dominant role as the source of information in providing awareness and interest. And in the case of rural population, the Government agencies, such as the Agricultural Extension Service, exert a strong influence in the diffusion of new ideas. Families are frequently influenced, also, by new ideas brought from school by the children.

Table 1

Behavior Pattern for the Adoption of a New Idea

Innovators 3-5%	Early Adopters 10-15%	Early Majority 15-20%	Majority 40-60%	Non-adopters 5-10%
High income	Younger	Slightly above average age	Older	Older
High social status	Well educated	Medium-high social and economic status	Less education	Less education
Active in community	More formal participation in formal community activities—hold offices in church organizations, PTA, farm groups	Above-average education	Less social participation	Less social participation
Contacts outside community (travel more)	Receive more news-papers, magazines, specialized publications	Receive more news-papers, magazines, bulletins	Receive fewer news-papers, magazines and other publications	Apt to be satisfied with the status quo
Have direct sources of information beyond that available in mass media		Earlier to adopt than majority		Receive fewer publications

People react to new ideas in much the same way, no matter what product or practice is involved. Drs. Beal and Bohlen conclude after researching more than 40 products from hybrid seed corn to canned frozen fruit juices. First to accept is a small group of innovators, followed in time sequence by other groups as categorized from left to right in the table above. Time span in accepting a new idea can vary from six months to more than 15 years.

290

When it comes to the evaluation stage, neighbors and friends appear to be the most influential. And there is evidence that the further away from the time at which an idea was created, the more people depend upon neighbors and friends as the source of information.

At the trial and adoption stages, the dealer or retailer and salesmen are called on for the detailed information about how to use a new product.

People apparently go through these stages of acceptance at different rates, depending upon their individual characteristics, the social situation in which they live and the type of product involved.

And it is not believed that they go through this process every time they pick up a bar of soap or a tube of toothpaste—an impulse purchase —in the same way they would in the adoption of synthetic textiles as against materials made from natural fibres—a choice that requires longer evaluation before trial and final acceptance. However, the research does show that they go through the process in the adoption of frozen foods as opposed to canned foods, or in the acceptance of new wonder drugs as against old standbys, in much the same way as they did some 40 other products researched in the studies, indicating the validity of the thesis without over-generalizing, say the authors.

The community in which people live affects their values, influencing how rapidly they adopt ideas and the kinds of ideas they adopt, Drs. Beal and Bohlen point out. In some communities there is an attitude toward acceptance of change. When a new idea comes out in that community, it will be accepted rapidly. In other communities, there is an attitude toward the status-quo and it takes hard sell to get people to accept. The communities might be right next to each other within a county, a suburb or a metropolitan area, they say. Also of importance are the groups to which they belong and the values they hold toward the product, the seller and toward change itself.

This being the case, it follows that a knowledge of such characteristics is an important consideration in selecting test markets for a new package.

The findings also indicate, as might be expected, that those practices which cost little seem to be adopted more rapidly than those which are more expensive. The marketer of a popular-priced packaged item whose future success depends on frequency of purchase has a better chance of winning rapid favor than one whose product carries an initial high price. The choice of electrical appliances or farm equipment, for example, re-quires a great deal of time at the evaluation stage and offers little op-portunity of trial before actual adoption. Generally, packaged products are in a favorable position here. A consumer can afford to buy a flip-top box of cigarettes just to try it out, whereas his adoption of an electric refrigerator must depend almost entirely on his evaluation of the various makes and their prices before purchase.

The studies divide people exposed to new ideas into five time-of-adoption categories, with regard to acceptance:

1. *The innovators*, estimated at 3 to 5 percent of any group or community. They are the well-established high-income people, financially able to take risks in being first to try something new. They are not influenced greatly by other local community members. They are active beyond the community; they travel more, secure more technical information and have information sources beyond the local community and therefore are looked up to by the rest of the community. They are change oriented.

2. *The early adopters*, about 10 to 15 percent. These people make up a relatively younger group in the community than those to follow, usually with more education than those who adopt more slowly. They participate actively in community organizations such as churches, parent-teacher and civic associations, often holding elected offices. They receive significantly more newspapers and magazines than the average. There is evidence that this group furnishes a disproportionate amount of formal leadership in a community. Thus, what they do is almost sure to be emulated by other formal and informal group members.

3. *The early majority*, about 15 to 20 percent. These individuals are the informal opinion leaders of the community, usually slightly older than the early adopters. Their contacts are mostly in their own community and the opinions which their neighbors and friends hold of them is their main source of prestige and social status. They are less active in local organizations than those who adopt earlier. Their position of leadership is informal; they are not elected to it. They have a following only insofar as people respect their opinions. If their informal leadership fails a few times, their following looks elsewhere for leadership. But their judgment is usually sound, because they have more limited resources than early adopters and cannot afford to make poor decisions. They seem to be most influential in getting the majority to adopt new practices.

4. *The majority*, about 40 to 60 percent. This group is usually older, with a little less education, and less prone to change. It is composed of individuals who probably form the major part of formal organization membership, but who are less active in leadership. They probably read less, but make up the large percentage group on which the ultimate success of a product or package depends. They seem to be most influenced by what their neighbors and friends do—strive more to conform to group expectation.

5. *The non-adopters*, the remaining 5 to 10 percent are the oldest, with the least education. They participate least in community organizations, come in contact with less direct information, are apt to be resistant to change and, in many cases, probably have fewer consumer needs than the younger groups.

Some families or certain members of it place a high value, apparently, on being first to adopt and thus accept new products more rapidly. The professors think that probably the most influential patterns of association affecting attitudes toward change in the community are the informal groups, the people who play cards together, visit together, ride to work together, engage in sports or other recreational patterns.

In the case of new packages, these findings strongly indicate the need for a carefully planned advertising and promotional program, properly timed with the distribution of the new package. The best package in the world can be a failure if there is a time lag between the promotion and the distribution of the packaged merchandise. Consumers —especially the innovators—must be able to buy it when they become aware of it. The stages in acceptance often suggest the effectiveness of an extensive sampling program to lists of community leaders, followed by store demonstrations, to attract the innovators and early adopters. Also pointed out is the weakness of depending on a one-shot saturation program because not all the potential adopters are reached or even made aware of the product by the one shot.

And in this day of self service, when there is so little clerk service, the process of adoption calls for packages and display materials that give complete information about the product, how to use and how to care for it. More and more today, informative packaging must take over the job of the dealer and salesman in acquainting the prospective consumer with its advantages of convenience, performance and economy.

The research report, of course, does not answer what makes a good idea in the first place. Seemingly, it presupposes that the idea—translated into a commercial product or package—has possibilities for mass acceptance, as previously determined by established market-test procedures. Nor does it cover the question of whether the timing of a new idea is right. For example, one important supplier of cartons reported recently that he went to leading tobacco companies with the idea for a reclosable cigarette carton back in the '30s, but got nowhere. It was not until 20 years later, when the Philip Morris Co. was willing to put money behind its flip-top box in an extensive promotional campaign to put over Marlboros, that the cigarette industry gave serious consideration to a revolutionary change in cigarette packaging. Nor was serious consideration given to the packaging of soft goods in transparent film packages until self-service merchandising forced it.

Perhaps packagers need further study to show (a) how to sell a bright idea to top management and (b) how to put it across to distributors and retailers.

The studies discussed here, however, should be especially useful, it is believed, to point up the importance of delineating the various segments of a potential market and planning the educational and promotional campaign for a new package in relation to adoption process and time of adoption groups.

29. A space age technique to launch new products

JOHN F. STOLLE and JACK C. PAGE

Tension crackled through the slowly circulating air inside the sub-marine—almost in spite of the effort to keep things "routine"—as men followed the step-by-step procedures they'd gone over countless times in rehearsal.

But this was no rehearsal. This was a few moments after 12:30 P.M., July 20, 1960, and the USS George Washington was moving silently downward through the Gulf Stream waters off Cape Canaveral. A 4-year development effort on the Navy's Polaris missile was culminating in the first test firing from a submerged submarine.

Over the murmur of various voices, the loudspeakers snapped to life. A crisp command—"Man battle stations missile"—was followed by the re-peated staccato "beep-beep-beep-beep-beep" of the alarm. Eyes focused on dials and gauges, ears strained to catch the faint sounds whispering into earphones.

Another voice stated flatly, "T minus one and counting." The words flared through the speakers. A momentary pause. "Commence firing." The tension, static-like, drifted away in a flurry of voices. "Stand by . . . stand by . . . stand by. . . . Minus ten seconds. . . . Good. . . ." The familiar countdown numbers rolled through the speakers: "Ten . . . nine . . . eight. . . ." Quickly, "Torpedo room, stand by . . . stand by."

"Fire."

There was a rush of silence that hung within the steel walls . . . and hung . . . and hung.

Suddenly a jubilant voice shouted, "She lit off!" And a moment later a distant and thundering roar rolled down through the waters, not quite drowning out the cheers below.

Reprinted from *Sales Management*, July 3, 1964, pp. 23–27ff.

When the Polaris program was first announced in early 1957, both the Navy and Lockheed Missiles and Space Co., the prime contractor, realized that a precise system of management would be needed to meet a 1960 target date for operational availability. Out of this realization came PERT (Program Evaluation and Review Technique), a space-age system created by a team composed of the Navy's Special Projects Office, Lockheed, and Booz, Allen & Hamilton. Generally credited with a major assist in making Polaris operational ahead of schedule, PERT has since been embraced by industry for a variety of work.

One of the most important applications has been in the development and marketing of new products.

Timely introduction of new products is a key factor for successful marketing in today's competitive climate. Highly essential to corporate growth and marketing effectiveness, new product activity has changed from an occasional project to a continuing effort that requires constant action and demanding management controls. Yet many companies are missing introductory target dates—sometimes by wide margins.

Moving a new product from the idea stage to commercial sales outlets is one of the more difficult and complex coordination efforts a company undertakes. Almost every major department becomes involved at some stage. When coordination fails, product development runs too long, market tests are late, production schedules slip, distribution and warehousing is delayed, and advertising and selling programs go awry. As a result, seasonal sales are lost, the jump on competition is dissipated, and the profitability of the new product is likely to be seriously affected.

To improve this situation, many marketing and new product managers are turning to PERT for planning and controlling new product introductions. Results achieved to date have been gratifying, both in securing lead time on competition and in countering competitors' new items with rapid introductions of their own products.

PERT, as currently developed, is a proven advanced approach to planning and control, which can be applied in marketing as well as other fields. It is particularly effective for complex projects involving many interrelated and interdependent tasks and where completion time is critical. PERT provides *a graphic picture of the entire project* so that management can plan effectively. Using PERT, management can realistically compute project completion time, identify critical activities, and determine the effect that delays in each activity will have on the project as a whole. As work progresses, PERT provides for evaluation of progress, re-estimation of completion dates, pinpointing of anticipated trouble spots, and the pretesting of alternative ways to get the project back on schedule.

With these advantages, it is not surprising to find progressive marketing managers applying PERT to new product introductions. In a study recently completed by Booz, Allen & Hamilton Inc., 13 percent of the companies in the survey had used PERT to schedule and control new product programs. This is the greatest single new use of the technique, surpassed only by the two older PERT uses on construction and R and D projects.

Both consumer and industrial goods producers are using PERT in their new product programs. These include companies in such diverse areas as chemicals food products, electronics, farm equipment, beverages, and others. Among the many firms that have adapted PERT for one or more of their own new product programs are Upjohn Co., Oscar Mayer, Dow Chemical Co., Cummins Engine Co., Inc., Michigan-Carton Co., and Texas Instruments Inc.

PERT IN ACTION

The example of a PERT network described in detail is a simplified section taken from an entire network for the development and introduction of a new consumer product. It was developed for a company that previously had established detailed procedures to guide new product development and introduction. These had substantially helped to maintain a high rate of new product success. However, delays were still encountered in commercializing new products, particularly when the timing was critical as it is in meeting seasonal introduction dates.

The company had expanded its product line into a new consumer market with good results. In order to remain competitive, a particular new product was required to complete the line. It was imperative to introduce the new product by the beginning of the next sales season, less than a year away. Initially this was regarded as an unrealistic target date. In an effort to keep tight control of the project and to reduce all possible time, management decided to use PERT on the project.

First, a network was constructed showing all steps and procedures in new product development and introduction. Here, the basic steps were broken down to the *level of detail needed for control and to show all important interrelationships* throughout the project. For example, consumer testing of the product was required. This activity was divided into such steps as "distribute samples," "samples in use," and "collect samples," in order to assure tight control over progress.

Interrelationships between activities were also depicted. For instance, the sales managers' meeting could not begin until displays were in the warehouses, advertising proofs were approved, and the labels had been approved. In all, there were over *300 activities* in the network representing the development, production, and marketing effort required for this new product.

Since new product programs involve almost every department in the company, *planning could not be confined solely to the marketing department*. Marketing did provide basic strategy, market testing, sales planning, advertising, and other aspects of the marketing program. Other information was needed, however. From manufacturing came data on production, purchasing and plant engineering; R and D provided design and test requirements; the legal department worked on the brand name search; and accounting gave data for profit analysis. In all, 19 departments had responsibility for one or more activities in the new product program.

Time estimates were obtained for each activity in the network from the departments responsible for the activity. Securing these time estimates on a nonsequential basis precluded the possibility of an individual's tailoring his estimates to meet the overall target date. At the same time, the estimate became a time commitment in which to perform the work required for each activity. During this process, *the individual responsible* for each activity in the total program was clearly pinpointed. There is no chance to avoid responsibility in a PERT-controlled project.

After obtaining all the time estimates, the data from the network was processed on a computer to determine which activities were on the *"critical path"* and which activities had *slack time* available. Such data processing presented no problem since virtually all large- and medium-size computers now in service have PERT library programs available. Data processing service bureaus also have computers with PERT library programs.

First results of this data processing revealed that it was *impossible to complete the project on schedule* with existing plans. The critical path ran 40 weeks past the target date. Out of a total project time calculated at 19 months, nine months would have to be saved by replanning in order to meet the target date.

HOW PERT WORKS

The basic concept of PERT is the use of a network to depict a project plan graphically. This example shows the steps required in preparing a new sales promotion display and sales brochure. It is recognized that a project of this simplicity would not normally require a formal PERT network; this is for illustrative purposes only.

The network has two principal components—*events and activities*. *Events*, represented by "bubbles" in the network, are specifically defined and recognizable *benchmarks of accomplishment* in the project. For example, Event #2 occurs when the rough layout of the brochure is completed; Event #6 occurs when the display artwork is approved. The end event in the network represents completion of the total project (Event #12), at which point the total display is complete and available for use.

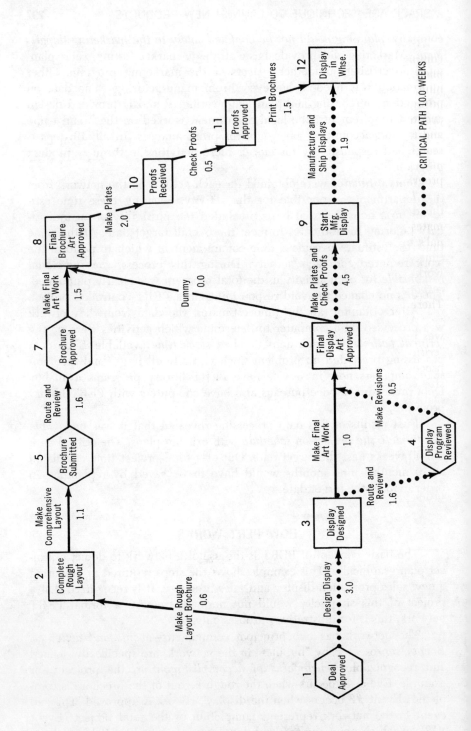

CRITICAL PATH 10.0 WEEKS

Activities represent the *work that must be done* to achieve the events. Activities are shown as arrows connecting events in their proper sequence to form the total network picture of the project. As shown, activities can be *mental or creative work*—"design display" leading to Event #3—or *physical work*—"manufacture and ship displays" leading to Event #12—or a combination of mental and physical work. For each activity a time estimate is made, usually expressed in weeks (or decimal weeks). For example, the activity from Event #9 to Event #12 is expected to take 1.9 weeks.

The principal value of the PERT network over other planning techniques is that it shows *all the principal interrelationships and interdependencies* in the project, as opposed to considering the project as independent items of work to be accomplished. In preparing such a network, the managers and project personnel must carefully think through the project, thus giving assurance that a thorough job of planning is done.

Another point concerning the network is that behind each activity is a *planned assignment of the required manpower, materials, and other resources needed* to get the work done. For example, to arrive at the 1.9 weeks' time estimate for the activity leading from Event #9 to Event #12 (manufacture and ship display), the individual responsible for getting this work done may have figured the work would be done by an outside contractor on an overtime basis. Similarly, all other activities have resources figured into the time estimates (such as one layout artist, two copywriters, one district sales force, and so forth).

Another basic concept of PERT is that of *network paths*. It is important to note that Event #12, project completion, does not occur until both activities (print brochure *and* manufacture display) leading to Event #12 are completed. Similarly, both activities leading to Event #6 must be completed before the event (display approval) occurs and work can begin on activity 6.9, "make plates for display."

Therefore, the network can be viewed as several sequences of activities and events leading from the start event to the end event. In PERT terminology, these are network paths. In the simple example network there are five such paths, which can be followed along these key points:

       Path
       A   1-2-5-7-8-10-11-12
       B   1-3-6-9-12
       C   1-3-6-8-10-11-12
       D   1-3-4-6-9-12
       E   1-3-4-6-8-10-11-12

The reason for defining network paths is that some are more critical than others in affecting the completion date of the project. Once identified, management can focus attention on these.

The final and perhaps the key concept of PERT is the *critical path.* If the time values along each of the five paths are added, the following results:

Path	Time
A	8.8 weeks
B	10.4 weeks
C	8.0 weeks
D	11.5 weeks
E	9.1 weeks

Path D, the longest path at 11.5 weeks, determines the time required to complete the entire project. In PERT terminology this is the critical path. If an activity on this path slips by three days, the total project will slip by the same amount. Conversely, if the project is to be expedited, the activities along Path D must be shortened, since all other paths can be completed in less time. Thus, if timing on the project is critical, management focuses attention on the critical path.

New product introductions are more complex and involve a much larger number of activities than the example above. In practice, PERT can make a major contribution to planning and controlling such complicated new product programs. The *critical path* concept, as a means of directing and redirecting management attention, is an excellent example of the principle of management by exception.

The analysis did not surprise management. "We've been running about that much total time for most of our new product introductions," commented one marketer in the company.

A major advantage of PERT is that a company can identify trouble spots *ahead of time* and pinpoint the major opportunities for saving time. A new products manager, sales manager, or top marketing executive no longer needs to accept *past performance* as the standard for future market timing. In the case cited, the PERT network showed that the project would be delayed at several points in the marketing and manufacturing activities in the project. Market tests would held up the project six or seven weeks. Production would be delayed several weeks, awaiting the carton loader. Critical machinery and tools would be held up, awaiting capital authorization from top management. Design and manufacture of unit tools would greatly delay the project.

On the basis of this information, the project was replanned and the critical path reduced by 44 weeks. Capital appropriations for critical machinery and equipment (which actually involved relatively small dollar amounts) were approved in advance. Non-critical items were approved on the original schedule. Consumer tests were expedited, while other work went ahead in parallel; test results were used as a final check before production began. Because PERT provided close project control, the sales meeting which had been planned after the start of production was advanced to remove it from the critical path.

While a portion of the 40 weeks would have been saved by replanning and by short cuts that would have been taken *during* the project, PERT reduced project time *in the planning stage* when maximum flexibility existed. Top management had a dollars-and-cents blueprint of why it should approve some expenditures at the beginning. Everyone involved had his responsibilities clearly stated. Each saw how his work related to the activities of others, and what time requirements were necessary to meet deadlines.

The actual result was dramatic. The new product went on the market *two weeks ahead of the original target date.* The time saved meant that the company earned several hundred thousand dollars more profit than if it had missed the introduction date. In addition, a market position was protected, and the company gained added capability to react swiftly to competitive moves.

The foregoing example and the experience of many other companies indicate that PERT has a number of specific benefits when used to control new product programs. While some of those are difficult to measure in dollars and cents, they significantly contribute to completing projects on time and within budgets. Among these are:

Planning assured: Building a PERT network imposes a discipline of thoroughly thinking through and planning a project. The technique assures management that planning has taken place, and that project effort will be expended in an orderly and coordinated manner.

Decision points pinpointed: Areas of major expenditure—hence, points of project review and decision—are highlighted in PERT networks. Product managers can clearly show top management the effect a delay in these decisions will have on the total project, and pinpoint the latest allowable date for key decisions if the original target date is going to be reached on schedule.

Responsibility clarified: PERT clearly defines what is expected from the individual responsible for each activity, and with whom he must coordinate his work. This removes the fuzziness that often exists on complex projects as to who is responsible for what.

Decisions pre-tested: One of the most outstanding advantages of PERT is its ability to pre-test decisions. Several alternative timesaving solutions can be tested and their effects evaluated before a decision is made and instructions are issued to operating personnel. Management is thus assured its decision is the best under the circumstances.

Delays evaluated: Many activities in a project are subject to delay without its affecting the project completion date. In the past, management has applied crash efforts at high cost to almost all activities in order to expedite the 15 percent that PERT shows are really critical. Now extra effort need be expended only on those activities that control the project time. Delays in other activities can be put in proper perspective and often ignored, thus reducing costs while improving performance.

While different users find these individual benefits of varying importance to their particular operations, they represent major advantages being realized by most PERT users.

Other Marketing Uses

In addition to new product introduction, marketing management can use PERT effectively for a number of other project-type marketing activities. Among these, in which coordination and timing are critical, are *special promotions.* While fewer activities are involved here than in new product programs, critical introduction time and quick reaction to change are essential. Even though most companies have standard planning and control procedures covering production, distribution, and marketing of special promotions, a competitor's action often precipitates a rapid change of plans. Standard programs are then usually abandoned and "crash" efforts employed. Frequently this results in high cost with only slight improvement in timing. PERT can often save time and money in such cases.

PERT can also be used effectively in realignment of sales territories scheduling and preparing for sales meetings, planning advertising programs, and planning shows and conventions. In many of these instances the PERT network will involve few activities and will not require use of a computer. The principal value of PERT in these areas is that the project will be thoroughly planned.

In the few years since its development, PERT has found wide acceptance. Having relied heavily on barcharting techniques developed in the early 1920's, industry was ready for a more effective tool. Early applications of PERT were in research and development because of the Polaris origin. However, PERT was rapidly extended to building construction, maintenance, production planning, computer installation, and a variety of other functions of business. The latest and most promising application of PERT is to the total new product program and marketing work. We can expect increased usage in these areas as management becomes more familiar with this significant new technique.

30. Strategy of product quality

ALFRED A. KUEHN and RALPH L. DAY

If marketing executives are truly "consumer-oriented," they know that their marketing efforts face an uphill climb when the physical attributes of their product do not fit the preferences of a substantial group of consumers better than competing brands do. Certainly the physical product is not the only important factor. The consumer purchases a "bundle of satisfactions" that includes a variety of other considerations, such as convenience of purchase, design of the package, manufacturer's reputation, and style of advertising. But it is nevertheless a bad mistake to become so preoccupied with packaging, distribution, and promotional activities as to forget the importance of the *contents* of the package. The marketing manager cannot afford to think that his responsibility for the nature of the product is fulfilled when he has ascertained that his product is "just as good" as competing products are.

In all fairness, it must be recognized that the problem of determining exactly what the attributes of a product ought to be is extremely difficult. We believe, however, that the approach to the measurement and evaluation of consumer preferences presented in this article will make the task much easier for many products. After making some general observations about product quality we shall outline new procedures for (a) matching product features to consumer preferences, and (b) developing measures of the consumer's ability to recognize differences in products. These procedures should help management to—

Recognize what levels of product quality and other characteristics appeal to what proportions of the market.

Reprinted by permission of the publishers from Edward C. Bursk and John F. Chapman, *Modern Marketing Strategy*. Cambridge, Mass., Harvard University Press. Copyright, 1964, by the President and Fellows of Harvard College.

Decide whether or not it is desirable to aim for parts of the market *not* covered by the "most popular" brands.

Ascertain the most promising directions for new products or improvements in existing products.

WHAT IS "PRODUCT QUALITY"?

When considering the physical product apart from the additional attributes, real or fancied, bestowed on it by an effective marketing program, the manufacturer's attention is usually centered on "product quality." In this context, product quality is often measured in terms of the purity or grade of materials used, the technical perfection of design, and exacting standards of production. The *level* of quality is usually set in terms of either meeting or beating competition. Once a level of product quality, in this sense, has been determined, most firms carry out rigorous programs of quality control and product testing to ensure that technical standards of product quality are upheld.

Illusions and Pitfalls

The quest for this kind of product quality on the part of technically trained and oriented people is understandable and, within limits, highly laudable. However, thinking of product quality simply as a function of the commercial grade of materials used or the technical perfection of design and manufacture is a denial of "consumer orientation." Consumers do not make chemical or physical analyses of the goods they buy. They use a product and react to its ability to satisfy their wants. They have little knowledge of, or concern for, the technical standards established by chemists, physicists, and engineers in its manufacture. In fact, they may prefer products made with certain lower cost ingredients while management is equating higher cost with higher quality.

This is not to say that product quality in the technical sense is unimportant. Consumers generally wish to be reassured that they are not getting inferior materials or shoddy workmanship. They can be alienated by lack of consistency in the product characteristics which they regard as important. And they are not as gullible and manipulatable as they are apparently believed to be by some critics of advertising. To be sure, given only minor product differences, or differences in unimportant attributes, advertising can precondition the consumer's feelings and attitudes toward a particular manufacturer or brand and thereby influence his evaluation of and reactions to a product. Thus, preferences *can* be established largely through marketing efforts. The job is much simpler, however, if actual perceivable differences (preferably important differences) can be demonstrated to the consumer.

The manufacturer should also realize that consumer preferences for physical aspects of the product may or may not be closely related to currently established technical measures of product quality. Consumers, for example, may judge such a quality as "softness" of paper products on different grounds than laboratory testing devices do. Laboratory test values, in such a case, may even misdirect research efforts aimed at developing products with greater consumer appeal. In the final analysis of the marketplace, the "quality" of a product depends on how well it fits patterns of consumer preferences.

Unfortunately, giving the consumer what he wants is easier in the saying than in the doing. Standards for measuring certain technical aspects of product quality may be well established in most companies, but how does one establish measures of consumer preferences across the broad ranges of possible product characteristics? That is the question we shall turn to now. The approach we shall describe is not a "drawing board" idea. It is finding acceptance by manufacturers of consumer nondurables and seems to hold promise for an even broader spectrum of products.

PREFERENCE TESTING

Especially in the period since World War II, manufacturers have become increasingly aware of the need to learn more about what consumers like and dislike in the products they buy. Consequently, large sums of money have been spent on consumer research. Many methods have been used to gather information. In addition to the traditional "nose counting" survey, continuous consumer panels have been established on a national basis, a variety of motivational research methods have been used, and extensive field testing of products has been done.

In general, these kinds of research have provided useful information to marketing management, but at times it has been difficult to interpret and apply the results. There have been many cases where the results of costly research have not been used, and also other cases where the results were misinterpreted, leading to ill-advised actions.

The approach to be described was developed in the belief that field research is likely to be worth more than it costs only when it is designed and interpreted within an analytical framework which relates it directly to specific managerial problems. This approach, which might be called "preference distribution analysis," involves no new field research technique. Rather, it provides a meaningful structure for the use and interpretation of an accepted procedure, the "blind," forced-choice, pairedcomparison test, in a way that sheds new light on what consumers want and facilitates development of effective market-segmentation policies.

Elements of Test

The nature of the paired-comparison test is basically simple. Here are the main features:

Samples of two brands of a product, or proposed products which differ in some way, are prepared in identical containers and are given to a representative group of consumers to use.

After they have used the samples, the consumers are asked to pick the one they prefer.

Every effort is made to eliminate any influences other than the features of the products in the packages. For instance, to eliminate "position bias," the order in which they are asked to use the two products is alternated among the members of the test group. Again, the boxes are identified with psychologically neutral symbols, such as three-digit numbers which contain no 7's. It has been found that different colors, single letters, single numbers, or "magic numbers" may introduce biases among those consumers who do not have strong preferences for one of the samples.

Occasionally, the tests are repeated with the same consumers and the same products but with different numbers on the boxes to test the consumers' consistency in choosing between the two products.

After all members of the test group have used the samples and stated their preferences, the results are carefully analyzed to determine the percentages of the test group which preferred each product.

While the paired-comparison test is a very useful method for testing consumer preferences for products, free from any associations created by advertising, its results frequently lead to misinterpretations. That is why we must go several steps further than companies generally do to get the results that we want.

"Majority Fallacy"

The danger of testing in the conventional way can be illustrated by a hypothetical example:

Suppose there is no chocolate cake mix on the market. A company decides to produce a chocolate cake mix and does extensive testing to find the degree of "chocolaty-ness" which consumers prefer. It tests with various levels and finds the degree of chocolaty-ness which the largest number of people prefer —a medium level. It introduces the product with success.

Then another company decides to enter the market and tests various levels of chocolaty-ness against the first company's product. When it tries any other level, either a lighter or darker chocolate, it finds that any such level is less preferred than the medium level.

As more companies enter the industry and test proposed products, the medium level always is preferred by a higher percentage of consumers. So each company enters the market with a medium-level chocolate cake mix, and the consumer has no choice between the brands in terms of physical characteristics. Consumers who like light chocolate and who like dark chocolate are out of luck.

If there were five companies marketing a chocolate cake mix and all their products were at the same level of chocolaty-ness, each company might be expected to get 20 percent of the chocolate cake-mix market if all other factors were equal.

Suppose now that a sixth company wants to enter the market. It decides to test two proposed levels of chocolaty-ness against the existing brands. It tests a considerably lighter chocolate cake mix against each of the established brands and finds that 65 percent of consumers prefer the other brand in each test. It tests a considerably darker chocolate against the established brands and again finds that 65 percent of all consumers prefer the brands against which it is tested. Both proposed products have failed in the preference tests.

This company then tests a product at the medium level and finds that 50 percent of all consumers prefer it when it is tested against any of the present brands. Now the comparison tests indicate that the new company has a product "just as good" as any of the competing brands. This product will be indistinguishable from the established brands and, if it can overcome the disadvantage of being a latecomer in the market, it might eventually be expected to attain a 17 percent share of the market.

This situation illustrates what is sometimes called the "majority fallacy," i.e., assuming that every product must be acceptable to a majority of all consumers if it is to be successful. A little reflection suggests that a substantial number of consumers might strongly prefer a considerably lighter chocolate cake, and another segment of the market might strongly prefer a much darker chocolate. It is certainly conceivable that each of these groups would amount to a larger segment of the entire market than the one-sixth share that our hypothetical new company might eventually expect to attain with a cake mix just like all the others (if it can overcome the handicap of being last in entering the market).

For a picture of the majority fallacy, see Exhibit 1.

Unfortunately, conventional product testing sheds little light on the existence of such submarkets. *However, this failure does not imply that the two-product comparison test is worthless.* Rather, it suggests the need for a more meaningful way of planning product tests and interpreting the results. Preference-distribution analysis fills this need when the important characteristics of a product can be meaningfully "scaled" over a range of values.

STEPS IN ANALYSIS

Just as the cake-mix producers in the foregoing example could vary the level of chocolaty-ness of their products, many manufacturers must

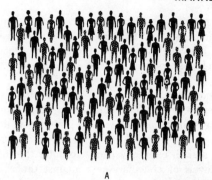

A

Exhibit 1. Illustration of the Majority Fallacy
Here is the market for a product as most companies would view it, i.e., with the
preferences of the majority of consumers appearing to dominate the scene. What
businessmen fail to see under this "majority fallacy" is that there may actually
be a minority or minorities of customers who would prefer a product with quite
different characteristics. Now, for comparison, see Chart B.

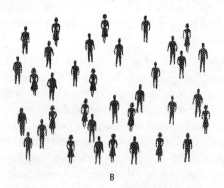

B

Exhibit 1. Illustration of the Majority Fallacy (continued)
In this picture we see just the minority of customers preferring a product with
different characteristics. All of these people are in the preceding chart (A), in
the same positions shown here. If an alert company designs a product to meet
the preferences of these customers, it may "have the market to itself" and profit
more than it would in competition with other firms for the majority of consumers.

choose a product characteristic or feature from a wide range of possible
characteristics. Awareness of the significance of such characteristics and
the ability to vary their levels is not enough, as illustrated in the cake-mix
example. In order to choose the level which will suit the preferences of
the largest segment of the market, management must be able to: (a)
relate the various levels of the characteristic directly to the preferences
of consumers, and (b) determine the proportions of all consumers who

prefer each level. Preference-distribution analysis provides such a means by establishing a scale of feasible values for a product characteristic, estimating the percentage of all consumers who prefer each value on the scale, and providing a probabilistic measure of consumers' ability to distinguish between different values on the scale.

Employing the Scale

The first step is to devise a scale of feasible values for each significant characteristic. The limits of the scale are the lowest value and the highest value preferred by any appreciable number of consumers. Between the extreme values, the scale is divided into a number of equal increments in ascending order. The width of the steps depends primarily on the consumer's ability to perceive differences.

Examples of easily scalable characteristics are the sweetness of cola drinks, the quantity of suds produced by soaps and detergents, and the saltiness of margarine. However, some product characteristics have not as yet been scaled in a way which will permit this form of analysis. For example, no satisfactory techniques have been developed for scaling colors, flavors, and odors in a way amenable to preference analysis. (Although psychologists have developed multidimensional scales for such variables, these scales are not suitable for determining distributions of consumer preferences. For example, orange and red appear close together on most color scales while red and blue are far apart. Yet, in terms of consumer preferences, red and blue might be more interchangeable, or "closer together," than red and orange. Undoubtedly, further research into the nature of human behavior will yield methods for scaling currently intractable characteristics.)

Once a "product attribute scale" is established, otherwise identical samples of the product are made up with each level of the particular characteristic. Each of the values on the scale is then tested in paired-comparison tests against every other value on the scale, using a representative sample of consumers for each test. The results of all these tests are analyzed simultaneously using a computer program which estimates the percentage of consumers who prefer each level, weights these percentages according to rates of use of the product, and provides a measure of the consumer's ability to discriminate among the various levels on the scale. (More will be said about consumer preferences and discrimination presently.)

When the preference distribution for a particular product characteristic has been estimated, a company's existing product or products and all competing products can be analyzed to determine their level on the scale. This will indicate the degree to which existing products match consumer preferences and will reveal any market segments which have been

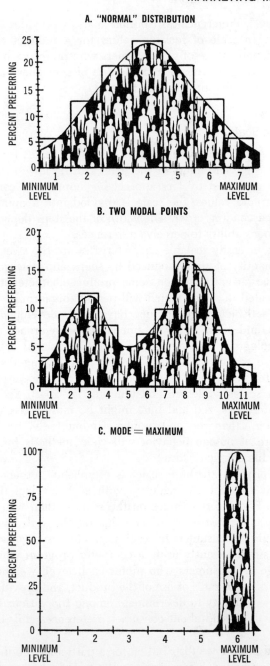

Exhibit 2. Different Patterns of Consumer Preferences over Levels of a Product Characteristic

neglected. Thus, the analysis of the distribution of consumer preferences over a product-attribute scale will provide a highly meaningful frame of reference for the development of product strategies that are truly consumer-oriented.

Analyzing Preferences

The patterns of consumer preferences over a scale may take a variety of forms. Several types of distributions are shown in Exhibit 2. Although the scales must be divided into discrete steps for testing purposes, actual preferences probably follow a smooth curve, as indicated by the dotted lines.

"*Normal Distribution.*" As one might expect, the distribution of preferences over many product characteristics is roughly similar to the "normal" probability distribution, as in Chart A. Preferences are distributed around a more-or-less central value on the scale, tapering off to a low level at both ends of the scale. If preferences for levels of a particular characteristic fit this pattern, would the key question for a firm be the exact level which is the central point of the distribution? It is not clear that this would be the optimal value, even if the company markets only one brand of the product. If several competitors are marketing products with the characteristic at the most popular level (4 in Chart A) or at higher levels, then the optimum point for our firm would most likely be well below the peak point—say, at Level 2. The product would then be better suited to the tastes of a sizable segment of the market than is any competing product.

As we saw in the hypothetical chocolate cake-mix example used earlier, traditional methods of interpreting the results of preference testing lead to the "majority fallacy" whereby all companies tend to introduce products at a "medium" level of a significant product characteristic. Let us assume that the preference distribution for chocolaty-ness looks much like Chart A. Then, if the original five brands in the cake-mix example were at Level 4 on the scale shown in that chart, it seems clear that a new brand at Level 2 would be preferred by a considerably larger portion of the market than it would at Level 4, where all the competing brands are clustered. It could expect to be strongly preferred over all the old brands by consumers with preferences at Levels 1 and 2, and would be equally as attractive as the old brands to consumers at Level 3. A new product at Level 6 would enjoy a similar "preference share" without detracting to any significant degree from the market for the product at Level 2.

Thus, an alert company which knew the preference distribution could bring out two new products which would be preferred over other brands by perhaps 40 percent of consumers (and maybe more), leaving the other five brands each with "preference shares" of about 12 percent (maybe less) of the market.

Even if a new brand could not be expected to obtain a preference share greater than the average for existing brands, it might still be advantageous to introduce it at a level of the characteristic appealing to a submarket neglected by other brands. It would appear to be much easier to attract consumers to a new product which better matches their preferences than to shift consumers from existing brands to another brand which has the same characteristics. In this way, a similar share of market probably could be obtained with much lower promotional costs.

Other Preference Distributions. Chart B in Exhibit 2 illustrates another fairly common pattern of preferences. Preferences tend to cluster around more than one modal point. An example might be preferences for the level of sweetness of a beverage with the peaks representing those who prefer a dry beverage and those who prefer a sweet drink. This kind of distribution will be discussed more fully later.

Chart C shows a concentration of preferences at the highest level on the scale. That is, all consumers prefer a level as high or higher than the highest level now available. This may indicate that there is a technical limitation on the achievement of the characteristic, assuming that Level 6 is the highest commercially available level. (For example, almost every housewife would probably like the lightest possible vacuum cleaner, without loss of power or efficiency.) If consumers would prefer an even higher level of the characteristic, an opportunity for further technical development is suggested.

Changing Preference Patterns. Distribution of consumer preferences may change over time as the result of changes in patterns of end use and shifts in consumer attitudes. The existence of such trends can be established by periodic retesting of consumer preferences.

To what extent can a manufacturer *alter* basic patterns of consumer preferences for product characteristics through its advertising efforts? This is a more complicated problem. In general, it would appear less difficult for manufacturers to adapt their products to consumer preferences than to alter those preferences—but this depends on one's view of advertising effectiveness as well as on the role of fashions, fads, and changing tastes in the particular market being served.

Identification of Desires

How does management obtain a measure of the consumer's ability to recognize the level of a product characteristic that he actually prefers? This step is an important part of consumer-preference analysis. Marketing researchers have long recognized that consumers are not perfectly consistent in their behavior. The consumer will not appear to "prefer" the same value on a product-characteristic scale every time in repeated trials.

It is not at all uncommon for a housewife to choose one of two products in a paired-comparison test only to choose the other if the test is repeated. Yet extensive testing suggests that *most of the time* an individual will choose the product which is on, or is closest to, a particular value on the preference scale.

It is useful to think of the particular value of a product characteristic which a person would choose most often if exposed to repeated trials as his or her "true" preference. Of course, ability to recognize this preferred value when compared with neighboring values varies with the nature of the characteristic, the width of the steps in the scale, the stability of the conditions under which the product is used, and the importance of the characteristic with respect to the use being made of the product. Nevertheless, when choosing between his preferred level and an adjacent value on the scale, the individual will be likely to choose the preferred level more than one-half of the time. The greater the distance of the alternative from the preferred value, the more likely he is to recognize his true preference. For instance, if the alternative product is two steps away on the scale, he will choose his preferred product a greater portion of the time than if it is one step away.

The foregoing observations suggest that it is appropriate to think of consumer choice as a probabilistic process. It is obviously a mistake to assume that consumers are perfectly consistent in their behavior. But it would also be a mistake to assume that it is useless to attempt to analyze consumer behavior because of this inconsistency. The approach used in preference-distribution analysis is to estimate the probability that a consumer will recognize his or her "true" preference, or the product closest to it, when faced with a choice. A "discrimination parameter," developed in the analysis of the results of forced-choice, paired-comparison tests for all possible combinations of values on a preference scale, provides a probability measure of the ability of consumers to discriminate among values on a perference scale.

Once a company knows the distribution of consumer preferences over a product-characteristic scale and has a measure of the consumer's ability to discriminate among levels of the characteristic, it can approximate the preference share for any product, existing or proposed, with regard to that characteristic. When all significant characteristics are studied in this way, the company is provided with valuable new information on which to base its product strategy. The implications are great for the design of new products, improvements in existing products, and the development of marketing strategies to exploit preference advantages.

USING THE NEW METHOD

In recent years, several manufacturers of consumer nondurables have attempted to devise techniques for establishing the distributions of consumer preferences for individual characteristics of products. The method outlined in this article is one such approach which, although still in a development stage, is now in use. Practical results have been obtained from it and are being applied by management in product evaluation and planning.

Although the results obtained in specific applications cannot be disclosed, we can give the essence of the approach by referring to a fictitious example. Let us take a product for which consumer preferences have been extensively studied by many firms—detergents for household use. For purposes of illustration we can draw on knowledge previously reported in the marketing and advertising trade press.

Test and Findings

To begin, how do we ascertain what consumers' preferences are? We could proceed along the following lines:

Extensive consumer research of all types, ranging from traditional interviewing techniques to complex motivational studies, has revealed that there are several basic attributes of the contents of a detergent package which are significant in determining consumer preferences. These include the "washing power" of the detergent, the quantity of suds it produces, and how gentle it is to human skin.

The extent to which a particular detergent formula possesses these properties can be measured in the laboratory. The levels of these properties can be related to the chemical composition of detergents so that a formula can be developed to have any desired level of a given characteristic within the limits of technical feasibility. Thus, the significant product characteristics can be "scaled" over the total range of values which are both technically feasible and within the limits of consumer acceptability. For example—

A "sudsy-ness" scale can be developed to cover the range from completely sudsless detergents up to the maximum amount of suds compatible with ordinary usage. Since the quantity of sudsing agents added to detergents is readily controllable, it is possible to consider a large number of levels, or "steps," in sudsy-ness. However, on any preference scale the steps should be large enough to enable the consumers to distinguish between products at adjacent levels on the scale with better than a 50–50 "pure chance" probability.

Once a preference scale is established, the next task is to estimate the distribution of consumer preferences over the various values on the scale. The usual approach is to prepare product samples with otherwise uniform features for each level of the pertinent characteristic. Then forced-choice, paired-comparison tests are made for each possible pair of samples possessing different levels of the characteristic, using a representative sample of housewives for each combination. That is, the housewives in each of the groups are given samples of detergents with differing sudsy-ness values in identical plain packages. After they have used both packages of the detergent, the subjects are asked to choose the one they prefer.

When the results of the tests are formally analyzed, using a computer program which requires only a few minutes for computation on a high-speed machine, the distribution of consumers' preferences over the various levels of sudsy-ness can be estimated and a measure of the housewife's ability to discriminate between levels of sudsy-ness is obtained.

When the distribution of preferences is obtained, the pattern might be very much like that shown in Chart B of Exhibit 2 (where Level 1 is no suds and Level 2 is maximum suds). A substantial proportion of detergent usage centers about low sudsing products, but the heaviest concentration of usage is around a much higher level of sudsy-ness.

Analysis of Results

The next step is to look for an explanation of the observed pattern of preferences. Often it can be explained by different end uses for the product; that is, those who use detergents in one way want such-and-such a level of "washing power," suds, and so forth, while women using detergents in another manner have different preferences. In other cases the pattern of preferences can be explained in terms of cultural and climatic differences. At times, "there is no accounting for tastes." But, even in the latter situation, knowing the pattern of tastes is of great value in developing product strategies.

In the case of sudsy-ness, the preferred level is clearly related to the end use of the product. Extensive consumer research has shown that housewives tend to prefer a somewhat sudsy detergent in spite of the fact that suds have little to do with cleaning ability. But to the housewife the presence of suds seems to provide reassurance that the product is doing its job. *However,* high sudsy-ness interferes with the operation of automatic washing machines, especially the front-loading type.

With this information about the major end uses of detergents, we can relate observed preferences to the purpose for which the product is used:

Housewives who use automatic washers account for most of the peak toward the lower end of the sudsy-ness scale. (See the left section of the top line in Exhibit 3.)

The higher and broader peak at a considerably higher level of sudsy-ness (right-hand section of the top line) represents the level of suds desired for several other end uses:

One of these uses is dishwashing, which is sufficiently unique to be considered separately.

Other end uses include wringer washers, hand laundry, car washing, household cleaning, and some top-loading automatic washers. Since sudsy-ness preferences for these uses are relatively similar, they can be conveniently considered together as a "general purpose" group.

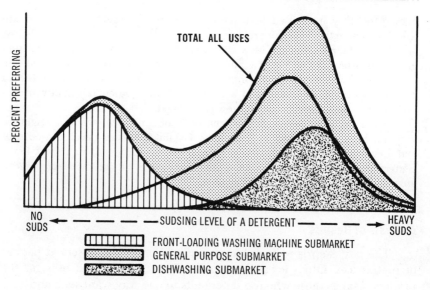

Exhibit 3. Preferences for the Sudsing Level of a Household Detergent

By relating patterns of preferences to the end use of the product, analytically convenient "submarkets" are defined. A company's own products and those of its competitors can then be evaluated in terms of how well their sudsy-ness levels fit the pattern of preferences in each such submarket. Changes in the sudsing level of existing products or opportunities for new products can be considered, and possibilities may be seen for improving advertising, promotion, package design, and so forth.

The preference distributions for other product characteristics such as washing power and gentleness can also be related to the end-use submarkets. This step can provide the basis for the development of an optimal "portfolio" of product features to conform with consumer preferences while taking advantage of any failures by competitors to gear their product characteristics to market needs.

CONCLUSION

To summarize the major steps in consumer-preference-distribution analysis:

1. Determine the physical characteristics of a product that appear to be significant to consumers.
2. Establish a scale of values, in equal increments, from a minimum level up to a maximum level for each characteristic.
3. Test consumer preferences for products located at approximately equal-

increment levels on the scale in a series of paired-comparison tests, using representative samples of consumers.

4. Analyze the results of all the tests for each product characteristic simultaneously, so as to estimate the percentages of consumers who prefer each level and the ability of consumers to recognize their true preferences.

5. Relate preference levels to patterns of end use or other significant actions of consumers.

6. Locate the value on the preference scale possessed by each product already on the market.

7. Estimate the preference shares of existing products and evaluate opportunities for product changes or new product entries in all "neglected" segments of the market.

Other Factors

The physical characteristics of products are not, of course, the only determinants of consumer demand. A product with ideal characteristics for a particular submarket may not obtain as large a share of the submarket as a product of poorer "quality," if the superior product has inadequate distribution and promotion. On the other hand, the job of selling a product will certainly be easier if it matches the preferences of large numbers of consumers more closely than competing products do, and if its promotional efforts are directed to the proper submarket.

The approach to product testing outlined here does not attempt to estimate directly the effects of price on consumer choice. The products being compared are presented to the consumers participating in the test as being identical in price. Price has not been incorporated into this approach to consumer product testing because of the difficulties encountered in obtaining realistic price responses from subjects in the test environment. If a method of product testing capable of eliciting realistic price responses could be devised, however, a simple extension to the technique outlined here would make it possible to estimate the interbrand price elasticities directly from such data.[1]

New Dimensions

The preference-scale approach to consumer-preference analysis adds new dimensions to the manufacturer's concept of product quality. Product-development decisions can be consumer-oriented in a highly meaningful way for the first time with respect to many types of products. Better knowledge of preferences and of how they are related to end uses

---

[1] Another approach to evaluating the influences of price on consumer brand choice has been outlined in an earlier article: Alfred A. Kuehn, "A Model for Budgeting Advertising," in *Mathematical Models and Methods in Marketing*, edited by Frank M. Bass et al. (Homewood, Illinois, Richard D. Irwin, Inc., 1961).

of the product can provide the basis for better marketing planning and more effective utilization of marketing resources. For the consumer, preference analysis promises a more satisfactory range of product choices as the significant characteristics of products are more closely adjusted to preferences.

The distribution of product-preferences approach has not actually been applied to products other than frequently purchased consumer nondurables. Insofar as paired-comparison tests can be used to ascertain consumer preferences for other types of products, however, the methods outlined would be applicable to the analysis of such test data. For example, it might be possible to conduct similar tests to determine the distribution of consumer preferences with respect to the size of freezer compartments in refrigerators, of portable camp stoves, and of electric wall clocks, the width of lawnmowers and men's belts, and the weight of kitchen utensils and fabrics used in clothing.

While the basic concept of the preference-scale approach is quite simple, its implementation is both difficult and expensive. It requires extensive consumer testing, and a proper analysis of the results is too complex to be done without a high-speed computer. This is because the approach calls for testing of consumer preferences for an entire product class rather than a mere comparison of two existing brands (in the latter case, the majority fallacy is a likely result). Making the adjustments in products indicated by new knowledge of consumer preferences can also lead to costly changes in product design and methods of manufacture.

Nevertheless, preference-distribution analysis is a most promising new approach for companies that want to give more than lip service to the concept of consumer orientation. Handsome rewards await the company which offers products that fit the preferences of sizable segments of the market better than competing products do, and then supports these products with promotional efforts directed to the proper target.

APPENDIX. ANALYTICAL PROCEDURE FOR ESTIMATING THE DISTRIBUTION OF CONSUMER PREFERENCES USING PAIRED-COMPARISON TESTS

Let us consider the most simple case, that of estimating the distribution of consumer preferences for a single product characteristic (C). All other product characteristics of the test products will be identical (controlled at some arbitrary value). The analytical procedure outlined below * will then provide an estimate of the distribution of consumer preferences for the product characteristic being studied if we can assume

---

* The authors wish to acknowledge the contribution of Bruce Becker, Yuji Ijiri, and Jon Zoler to the development and programing of the parameter estimation procedures required for the analysis of consumer preference distributions.

that there is no interaction between consumer preferences for product characteristic C and the other characteristics being held constant at some arbitrary value. (If interactions do exist, the problem becomes much more complicated as separate distributions of preferences for characteristic C would be required at the various levels of the other characteristics.)

We first divide the likely or possible range of consumer preference, with respect to the product characteristic under study, into n segments. Associated with each segment is an unknown, w_i, the proportion of consumers (weighted by volume of the product they are likely to consume) having a preference for the product characteristic value specified by the segment i. Table A illustrates how a distribution of consumer preferences for a product characteristic might be represented within the framework of this model.

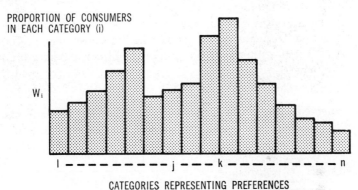

CATEGORIES REPRESENTING PREFERENCES
FOR DIFFERENT VALUES OF PRODUCT CHARACTERISTIC (C)

Table A

Let p_{jk} be the probability that a consumer whose preference falls into the category specified by segment i would prefer Brand A to Brand B, where the product characteristics of Brands A and B fall into the categories specified by segments j and k, respectively. Then, p^i_{kj} represents the probability that consumers in the ith category would choose Brand B in preference to Brand A on a "blind," forced-choice, paired-comparison test.

The consumer's ability to choose (i.e., discriminate) "correctly" between pairs of products depends on a number of factors including the variability of conditions under which the product is used, the importance of the differences to the consumer, and the difference between the two products with respect to how well they match the true preference of the consumer. These factors are taken into account in the following formula representing the probability of a consumer with true preference i preferring a product with characteristic value j to a second product with characteristic value k in a paired-comparison test:

$$p_{jk}^{i} = \frac{(1 - d_c)^{|j - i|}}{(1 - d_c)^{|j - i|} + (1 - d_c)^{|k - i|}} \tag{1}$$

The parameter d is a measure of the consumer's ability to discriminate with respect to the product attribute in question, reflecting both variability in test conditions and the importance of the characteristic to the consumer. If consumers cannot discriminate between products with different values of a characteristic, $d_C = 0$. If consumers can discriminate between very minor differences, d_C approaches 1. The exponents $|j - i|$ and $|k - i|$ represent the degree to which each of the two test products is consistent with the true preference of the consumer.

The $n + 1$ parameters to be estimated in this model are a set of w_i ($i = 1, 2, \ldots, n$) to establish the over-all distribution of preferences and the discrimination parameter d_C.

By a single forced-choice, paired-comparison test of two brands, A and B, we get an estimate of the proportion of consumers preferring Brand A (P_{jk}) and an estimate of the proportion of consumers preferring Brand B (P_{kj}), where

$$P_{jk} + P_{kj} = 1$$

The expected value of P_{jk} is given by the following formula, assuming that the consumers participating in the test were chosen randomly:

$$E(P_{jk}) = \sum_{i=1}^{n} w_i p_{jk}^{i} = \sum_{i=1}^{n} w_i \frac{(1 - d_c)^{|j - i|}}{(1 - d_c)^{|j - i|} + (1 - d_c)^{|k - i|}} \tag{2}$$

Each single comparison test provides one equation. In addition, we obtain one equation from the fact that

$$\sum_{i=1}^{n} w_i = 1 \tag{3}$$

Therefore, given n single comparison tests, the parameters w_i($i = 1, 2, \ldots, n$) and d_C can be estimated. The actual P_{jk} obtained from comparison tests (observed proportions) are used as estimates of the $E(P_{jk})$ in the second equation.

To establish the full range of the distribution of consumer preferences, we need one brand whose characteristic falls into segment 1 and one which falls into segment n, the two extremes, since for all i less than j, p_{jk}^{i} is a constant given by

$$p_{jk}^{i} = \frac{1}{1 + (1 - d_c)^{|j - k|}} \quad \text{where } i < j < k \tag{4}$$

Similarly, for all i greater than k, p^i_{jk} is a constant given by

$$p^i_{jk} = \frac{(1 - d_c)^{|j - k|}}{1 + (1 - d_c)^{|j - k|}} \text{ where } i < k < j \qquad (5)$$

To minimize the effects of sampling variation on the estimates of d_C and the w_i, the products tested should be spaced at equal intervals. The number of segments (w_i) into which the consumer population can be subdivided is then equal to the number of independent, single, paired-comparison tests performed. The maximum number of subdivisions possible

with single paired-comparison testing of N brands is then $\frac{N!}{(N - 2)! \, 2!}$,

the maximum number of pairs which can be formed from N brands each having a different characteristic value.

B. Place

31. Consumer purchase-costs—do retailers recognize them?

WESLEY C. BENDER

As the competition of shopping centers diverted business away from the central business district, concern with barriers to downtown shopping emerged. The parking problem downtown is a difficult barrier to overcome. Other barriers, perhaps less difficult, but nonetheless important, have brought forth various antidotes, some of them merely "gimmicks" to attract customers downtown. But since similar devices were used to attract customers to the suburbs, the flow of the competitive tide was not turned. Thus it may help to view the barriers to shopping in a particular place, or in a particular store, by understanding these in terms of consumer purchase-costs.

The business firm has long recognized that there is a "cost of purchasing" beyond payment of "the price" for a commodity. The price of an item and the cost of obtaining it are not necessarily, or even often, the same thing. When the question is asked, "What did a particular purchase cost the firm?," it is clear that attendant prices such as "freight-in" or the buyer's trip to market are elements of purchase-cost although accounting practice may treat these dissimilarly.

By contrast, the ultimate consumer, some assume, is a purchaser who does not incur purchase-costs beyond the price paid for a commodity. With relatively few exceptions, however, such an assumption is not based on fact.[1] Thus we will explore the concept of consumer purchase-cost as it relates to the consumer's choice among competing stores or shopping

Reprinted from the *Journal of Retailing*, Volume 40 (Spring, 1964); pp. 1–8ff by permission of the author and publisher.

[1] E. B. Weiss, *Planning Merchandise Strategy for 1961–65* (Doyle-Dane-Bernback, Inc., 1960), pp. 6–8. Also, Baumol and Ide, "Variety in Retailing," *Mathematical Models and Methods in Marketing* (Homewood, Illinois: Richard D. Irwin, Inc., 1960), pp. 129–30.

centers *vs.* downtown, and indicate how this concept ought to affect decisions of retail-store executives.

WHAT ARE THE CONSUMER'S PURCHASE-COSTS?

In a purchase and sales transaction the parties to the exchange obtain something from each other with a cost to each. Manifestly, the retailer making a sale does so at a cost. So does the consumer who pays the retailer's price for a commodity. The price of the commodity is a "prime" cost but not the sole cost. A number of "secondary" purchase-costs are necessary to achieve the purchase of the prime or target commodity. Together, prime and secondary purchase-costs comprise total purchase-costs.

Secondary purchase-costs may be defined as all the costs, both monetary and nonmonetary, exclusive of the price directly paid for the target commodity or service, required to effect the purchaser's acquisition of the target commodity or service.

The nature of secondary purchase-costs can be illustrated by the events surrounding the purchase of a lawn sweeper in a downtown store. In order to emphasize the secondary cost elements, we shall rule out the kind of customer who enjoys shopping and who gets a "kick" out of demonstrating his mechanical ability by assembling "knocked-down" gadgets. Some people may enjoy the drive to town but not the potential buyer in this illustration! In the normal order of events, he must bear the costs of time and travel from home to downtown, and if the family car is used he will pay a parking fee. On the down town streets, this shopper will expend time and effort in searching. Even after the purchase decision is made there are secondary costs: waiting time—waiting for a salesclerk, waiting while payment is arranged, and waiting to receive the merchandise. Since the box containing the lawn sweeper is a large one, the buyer's time, effort, and aggravation will accompany the box to the parked car—and perhaps all the way home. In any case, travel time from downtown to home, the additional time and frustration costs of unpacking the sweeper, locating the "Instructions for Assembly" sheet, and the attempt to assemble the sweeper—all these are costs incurred before the buyer can use the lawn sweeper in his yard.

Any particular purchase situation, such as a lawn sweeper purchase, is unlikely to involve *all* possible types of secondary costs. Consequently the retailer need not be concerned with an exhaustive list of them. A more meaningful approach—one which relates categories of secondary purchase-costs to consumer behavior—is suggested.

CONSUMER BEHAVIOR: CHOICE OF STORE OR STORE GROUP

Studies of shopping practices indicate that purchase costs, both prime and secondary, affect consumer choices among competitive stores or store groups. This is not to imply that the choices are made with scientific precision!

But presupposed are at least two important behavioral activities: one, that secondary purchase-costs related to one store or store group are compared with those related to competing stores or store groups— allowing the consumer, if she so desires, to optimize her purchase-cost position. Two, that consumers make decisions involving these comparisons. For were the position taken that consumers cannot compare purchase-costs and that even were they able to do so, their choice of store would not be influenced, there would be no point in carrying forward this discussion.

Few will argue that consumers are unable to compare the prices of identical "prime" or target items (or that sometimes these comparisons involve merely similar but not really *identical* items!). By contrast, however, when the whole range of secondary purchase-costs is considered there *appears* to be no common denominator upon which comparisons can be based. This does not deter the consumer. She simply groups together those secondary purchase-costs that *are* comparable. Thus the whole gamut of these costs can be arranged into three groups and comparisons are made within each of them.

THREE TYPES OF SECONDARY CONSUMER COSTS

In one group containing all *"price"* type secondary purchase-costs, such as parking fees, installation charges, credit charges, sales taxes, and the like, there is easy comparison on a store-by-store basis or a shopping center versus downtown basis in the same way as for the prices of "target" items. In a second category are the *"time"* type secondary purchase-costs, such as waiting time, travel time, or searching time. These may be compared as time units, or they can be converted to money units by using some money value per unit of time.

The third group of secondary purchase-costs is comprised largely of *"psychological"* type factors, such as inner conflict, frustration, depression, anxiety, tension, annoyance, and the like because of human relations, store temperature and humidity, store layout, and physical features of stores, or these in combination with human relations. Within this latter group there is comparability, but this area is more complex than the other two groups.

Consumers who make comparisons among the psychic factors related to purchases appear to do so in many ways. Some ignore purchase-costs of this type, particularly when they are relatively small. At the other extreme, some consumers indicate that they weigh heavily these psychological costs. They are considered more significant than substantial money type secondary purchase-costs.

PSYCHOLOGICAL COSTS VERSUS SATISFACTIONS

Psychological costs can be offset by psychological satisfactions. Moreover, the psychological satisfactions may overcome some or all of the monetary costs. For undoubtedly some consumers do derive pleasure from "searching," from shopping in a store with an "upper crust" image, from "recognition" by the store personnel, or even from assembly of a knocked down appliance. Yet what is pleasurable for one person may be distasteful to another, and what is pleasurable at one time may be distasteful for that person another time. As the psychologists put it, "the cognitive behavior of an individual is a reaction to stimuli as he apperceives them." Thus, although secondary purchase-costs may be balanced out, perhaps, on occasion, leaving a surplus of satisfaction, studies of shopping practices indicate consumer emphasis on the cost elements rather than on the satisfactions when a choice is made of store or shopping center.

As a matter of fact, not all secondary purchase-costs are potentially able to engender satisfactions in ordinary persons. Here a different classification of secondary purchase-costs is helpful. Most individuals are rarely susceptible to the joys, if any, of paying out money. In general, price type secondary-costs such as charges for auxiliary services, taxes, fees, and even "tie-in" deals are in the positive cost category. Along with these are noncompensated losses to property due to risks associated with the buying trip, such as damage to one's automobile, theft of one's purse, and the like. Also included are some psychological costs like frustration, discomfort, depression, anxiety, annoyance, and mental fatigue. Plain physical fatigue should also be added. These constitute a category unlikely to produce satisfaction for *anyone*.

On the other hand, some secondary purchase-costs belong in the category of "sometime" producers of satisfaction. Such buying activities as searching, shopping, looking at displays, travel, assembly of gadgets, meeting people, talking to friends, or even jostling in crowds—all ordinarily secondary purchase-costs—can be enjoyable experiences for some people on some occasions.

This dichotomy of the various secondary purchase-costs is significant for the retailer action that we shall examine later.

PURCHASE-COST DECISIONS

The consumer is neither solely a creature of habit nor does he make scientifically precise decisions. In considering him, therefore, we assume neither total "naiveté" nor total "rationality." And while research on "choice of commodity" indicates that habit is important,[2] it is not so im-

[2] George Katona, *The Powerful Consumer* (New York: McGraw-Hill Book Company, Inc., 1960), p. 159 *et. seq.*

portant for "choice of store."[3] Moreover, wherever found, habit is not unchangeable. Consumers, sooner or later, will examine their shopping practices in response to some stimuli or other and act to adjust these practices so as to minimize subjectively perceived costs. Lack of precision and individual sluggishness may make measurement difficult, but this does not deny the existence of the phenomenon, nor make it less important.

Prime Cost vs. Secondary Purchase-Cost. The decision process—choosing among competing stores—involves some "weighing" of the various elements of purchase-cost. This implies the existence of a hierarchy of these elements and asks, *initially,* which is more important to the consumer: prime cost or secondary cost?

That consumers are influenced strongly by reductions in prime prices in their store choice is not to be denied without vitiating much local advertising. However, prime price comparisons per se are fraught with difficulty. And, except where the consumer is comparing equal "commodity packages" or branded merchandise, errors are likely to be made. Where, for example, major gasoline stations in a particular market quote identical prices per gallon for the "same" grade of gasoline and give equal service, motorists may assume that those dealers giving trading stamps do so without increasing the motorist's prime purchase-cost.

Unfortunately, few purchase events enable the consumer to make as neat a comparison of prime prices as does the gasoline situation. Differences in the "commodity package," the multiplicity of commodities in any one store, each commodity with its own price, the use of loss-leaders where legal and the like, reduce the opportunity for consumers to buy efficiently on the sole basis of prime price comparison. Often in choosing among alternative purchase sites consumers can more easily compare secondary purchase-costs than prime prices.

Some consumers, however, are not strongly influenced by secondary purchase-costs. The "do-it-yourself" customer, whose attention seems to focus upon prime price comparisons, whose income is low, and whose evaluation of his marginal time is low, may prefer to bear secondary purchase-costs when he thinks their shifting to him relieves the retailer of this cost—thereby causing a lower prime price. The rise of self-service stores in the 1930's is some evidence of this view. Under conditions of rising family incomes and ample employment opportunities, a contrary situation tends to prevail.

RELATIVE IMPORTANCE TO CONSUMERS

It is logical to assume that the consumer attaches more or less importance to the monetary type secondary purchase-cost depending upon

[3] Russell S. Tate, "The Supermarket Battle for Store Loyalty," *Journal of Marketing,* XXV, No. 6 (October 1961), pp. 8–13.

the size of the prime expenditure. The larger the prime expenditure, compared to the secondary purchase-cost, the less the importance of monetary type secondary purchase-costs. A consumer seeking to purchase a commodity whose prime price is $100 or more is not likely to be dissuaded by a few dollars of secondary purchase-cost. In a similar situation is the purchaser of a number of articles, each with a small prime price (e.g., grocery items), the aggregate of which is a relatively large sum, say $20. The marginal purchase-cost of adding another item to the group already selected in a particular store is not much more than the prime price of the additional item, since the secondary purchase-costs at the margin are likely to be negligible. Thus the "one stop shopping" appeal has considerable merit.

Within the secondary group, the hierarchy of individual purchase-costs of purely monetary type depends upon the amount of money involved. The larger the amount of money, generally, the more significant to the payer. This seems rather obvious!

More research is needed before much can be concluded about the relative importance of psychological-secondary costs. The impact of a psychological cost depends upon the individual paying it. As mentioned above, "the cognative behavior of any individual is a reaction to stimuli as he apperceives them."

On the other hand, an assay of the relative importance to consumers of psychological cost compared with monetary cost leads to agreement with Katona, who, though writing in a different context, remarks, "The psychological factors do not alone determine the final decision, but under certain conditions they are powerful enough to alter individual as well as mass reactions and thereby influence the entire economy." [4] One observes that some types of consumers put particular emphasis on psychological purchase-cost. Persons in high income brackets, those beyond middle age, those whose sensibility is rather delicately balanced and for whom marginal tensions and frustrations cause more than ordinary distress, are customers to whom shifts of psychological costs should be avoided if practical.

RETAILER ACTION

The retailer who understands his customer, the nature of consumer purchase-costs, and some marketing principles should have no difficulty—if he has a modicum of ingenuity—in devising appropriate action. A retailer's approach to the kind of consumer behavior in his market should not be generalized on the assumption that it is appropriate for any and every market. Here the utmost care must be exercised. Thus it may be imprudent to attempt specific recommendation of particular devices. Yet, the retailer may find useful some evidence that consumers—perhaps

[4] George Katona, *op. cit.*, p. 6.

in other markets—do react to efforts to cut their secondary purchase-costs. Consider, for example, the appeal of the "one stop" buying trip of shopping centers, as well as the increase in automatic vending machine sales and telephone selling.[5] Noticeable, too, is the increase in branch banking and auto-banks. Surveys show that congested shopping centers are losing business to less congested shopping centers where parking is easier and dress more casual.[6]

REDUCING CONSUMER PURCHASE-COST

In general, there are four approaches to a reduction in consumer purchase-cost: (1) lower the prices of prime or target commodities; (2) shift secondary purchase-costs away from the customer; (3) a combination of (1) and (2); and (4) provide offsets to secondary purchase-cost.

Lower Prime Prices. Since as a basic principle, retailer action should aim at minimizing customer total purchase-cost, manipulation of prices on target commodities can be effective where secondary purchase-costs are about equal among competing stores. The dangers of this kind of price competition are well known. The advantages lie in the store-traffic building aspects and in the lower marginal secondary purchase-cost where it is normal to purchase a number of target commodities. Also, the additive effect may produce a relatively large prime purchase dwarfing the total secondary purchase-cost, a point mentioned earlier.

Shifting Secondary Purchase-Costs. Every exchange, every purchase and sale, involves a relationship between the parties to the exchange that may conveniently be called a buyer-seller relation. Within this relation, at the retail level, are performed a number of marketing functions and customer services. It is clear that the cost of performing a function or service can be eliminated only when the function or service is eliminated. By definition, marketing functions cannot be eliminated. When they are not retained by the retail vendor, they are shifted—sometimes back to the wholesaler, sometimes forward to the customer. Customer services are difficult to eliminate; they too are shifted between the retailer and the customer. Customer delivery service, for example, when discontinued by the retailer vendor, is shifted to the customer along with its cost.

Both from a social and an individual point of view, costs tend to be optimized when a function is performed by the most efficient performer. An obvious example relates to retailer-paid store air conditioning. The customer is not likely to perform efficiently within the store the task of keeping his body comfortable during the summer heat! An interesting

---

[5] "Supermarkets Where the Customers Stay Home," *Business Week*, November 22, 1957, pp. 66–68.

[6] Charles Hindersman, "The Evolving Downtown-Suburban Retail Pattern," *Journal of Marketing*, XXV (October 1960), pp. 59–62. Also, same reference, Samuel Pratt and Lois Pratt, "The Impact of Some Regional Shopping Centers," pp. 44–50.

and less obvious illustration relates to shifting the task of assembly of the customer's order from retail clerk to the customer, as self-service stores do. Perhaps few customers really believe that this decreases total waiting time when they must wait at the check-out queue!

COMBINATION OF LOWER PRICES AND SHIFT OF SECONDARY PURCHASE-COSTS

Emphasis here is on total purchase-cost manipulation, so that "on balance" customer purchase-costs are reduced. Suppose, for instance, both prime price and parking expense are lowered for the consumer but searching time is increased because of lack of assortment (other costs unchanged). If for the consumer the increase in the cost of searching time more than offsets the decrease in the cost of parking and prime price, purchase-cost is increased. Contrariwise, if the customer's cost of searching is increased less than the decrease in the cost of parking and prime price, her total purchase-cost is decreased. *What the customer thinks about this is crucial*, and it should be clear that the retailer must know his customer.

Offsets. Inasmuch as shopping "satisfactions" provide offsets to secondary purchase-costs for some people, retailers may succeed in reducing purchase-costs for their customers by employing satisfaction-giving devices. Many stores and shopping centers have done this, using trading stamps, premiums, give-a-ways, entertainment, and other so-called "attractions" and special promotions. Some of these, like most "one-shot" efforts, have fleeting results. Some others, like trading stamps, have their effect dimmed by competitors' similar action.

No retailer should assume he will retain his present customers from habit alone. Just as competitors are actively soliciting each other's customers, there is a continuing requirement that each retailer provide the stimuli necessary to retain present customers as well as to attract others.

SOME OTHER CONSIDERATIONS FOR RETAILERS

Several important factors related to consumer purchase-costs are worthy of retailer consideration. One such factor concerns priority; *i.e.*, to which secondary purchase-costs should the retailer first give attention? The effect of shifting a secondary purchase-cost from the consumer also should be analyzed.

Priority. It would be most helpful to retail executives to have at hand a continually updated checklist of secondary purchase-cost elements arrange on the basis of some certain knowledge of the importance of each purchase-cost element to each customer. Such a list is not available. But where certain costs are known to be heavily weighted by the customer, early action is demanded.

Secondary purchase-costs, however, can be classified on the basis of the frequency with which they are likely to be encountered by the customer. Those of high frequency should get priority in action to shift them away from the consumer. In the high occurrence group are parking fees, travel time and expense, in-store waiting time, searching time, a host of psychological costs due to store personnel, store layout, lack of assortment of goods, store temperatures, humidity, and the like. But other secondary purchase-costs—such as correspondence costs related to ordering, paying and such, credit charges, installation charges, even delivery charges—are not likely to occur with every shopping trip or purchase event. Action on these can be deferred until those with high priority are dealt with.

SOME EFFECTS OF SHIFTING SECONDARY PURCHASE-COSTS

When a cost, ordinarily a consumer secondary purchase-cost of the purely monetary type, like parking expense, is assumed by a retailer, the cost to the customer may be more or less than what is was prior to the shift—again depending upon the efficiency with which it is performed. When the retailer performs a service, like customer parking, its cost might be included in "prime" prices. But an increase in sales volume may so spread the cost per customer that the impact upon the customer of an increase in prime price, if any, is negligible. Then this type of retailer action, in terms of customer purchase-cost effects, has much to recommend it.

On the other hand, retail vendors may be well advised to proceed cautiously when a shift of function or service—previously a dollar cost to the retailer—becomes a psychological cost to the customer. Suppose a store were to curtail its check-out cashier personnel, causing an increase in customer aggravation and tension. Such augmenting of customer's psychological cost, even with a simultaneous decrease in prime prices, may be shortsighted on the retailer's part, for many customers weigh heavily their psychological purchase-cost. Notable, also, is the increased impact on the consumer of additional increments of psychological cost owing to the cumulative effect associated with pyramiding psychological factors.

CONCLUSION

Sellers, long ago, recognized and reacted to consumer's purchase-cost problems then associated with certain types of goods, such as convenience goods, shopping goods, and specialty goods. "Consumers," writes Aspinwall, "cannot easily be forced to expend an amount of time and energy that is disproportionate to the satisfaction they expect to receive from the goods in question." [7] In other words, unless the want is more than normally urgent, a consumer is unlikely to make a sole purchase of a pack of cigarettes if this entails a 35 cent parking fee! Contrariwise, a consumer may be willing to devote considerable time and energy along with other secondary purchase-costs when he is buying a $3,000 automobile.

The concern of retailers about consumer reaction to purchase-events requiring higher purchase-cost is particularly noticeable in store location research efforts, in participation in outlying shopping centers, in financing parking surveys, in downtown rehabilitation, and in attempts to improve store services. Retailers have sought help from experts ranging from psychologists to economic geographers. Obviously, it is believed that shoppers find no satisfaction in paying parking fees, traveling long rather than short distances to a store, or in fact, incurring any avoidable purchase-cost. It is no accident that retail trading area maps indicate that segments close to a shopping center contain a larger percentage of the center's customers than do segments more distant from the center. Nor is the apprehension and alarm of downtown retailers decreased by loss of customers to shopping centers with more ample parking areas. In the final analysis, retailers cannot disassociate themselves from consumer decisions designed to minimize their secondary purchase-costs. Nor can these be completely offset by sole attention to offering slight concessions in prime cost.

Alternative purchase events continuously present themselves for consumer choice. The logical basis for making a choice consistent with consumer goals requires purchase-cost consideration. The manner in which consumers may be expected to approach the choice is a function of three elements: (1) the importance attached to minimizing purchase-costs; (2) individual perception of stimuli suggesting an opportunity to decrease purchase-costs; and (3) the consumer's propensity to make decisions.

The retailer's considerable familiarity with cost analysis and the flexibility of the purchase-cost approach should commend it to the executive who sees the need to target his activity for the consumers in his market.

[7] Leo Aspinwall, "The Characteristics of Goods and Parallel Systems Theories," *Managerial Marketing: Perspectives and Viewpoints*, Kelley and Lazer, ed. (Homewood, Illinois: Richard D. Irwin, Inc., 1958), p. 440.

32. Retail strategy and the classification of consumer goods

LOUIS P. BUCKLIN

When Melvin T. Copeland published his famous discussion of the classification of consumer goods, shopping, convenience, and specialty goods, his intent was clearly to create a guide for the development of marketing strategies by manufacturers.[1] Although his discussion involved retailers and retailing, his purpose was to show how consumer buying habits affected the type of channel of distribution and promotional strategy that a manufacturer should adopt. Despite the controversy which still surrounds his classification, his success in creating such a guide may be judged by the fact that through the years few marketing texts have failed to make use of his ideas.

The purpose of this article is to attempt to clarify some of the issues that exist with respect to the classification, and to extend the concept to include the retailer and the study of retail strategy.

CONTROVERSY OVER THE CLASSIFICATION SYSTEM

The starting point for the discussion lies with the definitions adopted by the American Marketing Association's Committee on Definitions for the classification system in 1948.[2] These are:

Convenience Goods: Those consumers' goods which the customer purchases frequently, immediately, and with the minimum of effort.

Reprinted from *Journal of Marketing*, Volume 27 (January, 1963), pp. 50–55, National Quarterly publication of the American Marketing Association.

[1] Melvin T. Copeland, "Relation of Consumers' Buying Habits of Marketing Methods," *Harvard Business Review*, Vol. 1 (April, 1923), pp. 282–289.

[2] Definitions Committee, American Marketing Association, "Report of the Definitions Committee," *Journal of Marketing*, Vol. 13 (October, 1948), pp. 202–217, at p. 206, p. 215.

Shopping Goods: Those consumers' goods which the customer in the process of selection and purchase characteristically compares on such bases as suitability, quality, price and style.

Specialty Goods: Those consumers' goods on which a significant group of buyers are habitually willing to make a special purchasing effort.

This set of definitions was retained in virtually the same form by the Committee on Definitions in its latest publication.[3]

Opposing these accepted definitions stands a critique by Richard H. Holton.[4] Finding the Committee's definitions too imprecise to be able to measure consumer buying behavior, he suggested that the following definitions not only would represent the essence of Copeland's original idea, but be operationally more useful as well.

Convenience Goods: Those goods for which the consumer regards the probable gain from making price and quality comparisons as small compared to the cost of making such comparisons.

Shopping Goods: Those goods for which the consumer regards the probable gain from making price and quality comparisons as large relative to the cost of making such comparisons.

Specialty Goods: Those convenience or shopping goods which have such a limited market as to require the consumer to make a special effort to purchase them.

Holton's definitions have particular merit because they make explicit the underlying conditions that control the extent of a consumer's shopping activities. They show that a consumer's buying behavior will be determined not only by the strength of his desire to secure some good, but by his perception of the cost of shopping to obtain it. In other words, the consumer continues to shop *for all goods* so long as he feels that the additional satisfactions from further comparisons are at least equal to the cost of making the additional effort. The distinction between shopping and convenience goods lies principally in the degree of satisfaction to be secured from further comparisons.

The Specialty Good Issue

While Holton's conceptualization makes an important contribution, he has sacrificed some of the richness of Copeland's original ideas. This is essentially David J. Luck's complaint in a criticism of Holton's proposal.[5] Luck objected to the abandonment of the *willingness* of consumers to make a special effort to buy as the rationale for the concept of

[3] Definitions Committee, American Marketing Association, *Marketing Definitions,* (Chicago: American Marketing Association, 1960), pp. 11, 21, 22.

[4] Richard H. Holton, "The Distinction Between Convenience Goods, Shopping Goods, and Specialty Goods," *Journal of Marketing,* Vol. 23 (July, 1958), pp. 53–56.

[5] David J. Luck, "On the Nature of Specialty Goods," *Journal of Marketing,* Vol. 24 (July, 1959), pp. 61–64.

specialty goods. He regarded this type of consumer behavior as based upon unique consumer attitudes toward certain goods and not the density of distribution of those goods. Holton, in a reply, rejected Luck's point; he remained convinced that the real meaning of specialty goods could be derived from his convenience goods, shopping goods continuum, and market conditions.[6]

The root of the matter appears to be that insufficient attention has been paid to the fact that the consumer, once embarked upon some buying expedition, may have only one of two possible objectives in mind. A discussion of this aspect of consumer behavior will make possible a closer synthesis of Holton's contribution with the more traditional point of view.

A Forgotten Idea

The basis for this discussion is afforded by certain statements, which the marketing profession has largely ignored over the years, in Copeland's original presentation of his ideas. These have regard to the extent of the consumer's awareness of the precise nature of the item he wishes to buy, *before* he starts his shopping trip. Copeland stated that the consumer, in both the case of convenience goods and specialty goods, has full knowledge of the particular good, or its acceptable substitutes, that he will buy before he commences his buying trip. The consumer, however, lacks this knowledge in the case of a shopping good.[7] This means that the buying trip must not only serve the objective of purchasing the good, but must enable the consumer to discover which item he wants to buy.

The behavior of the consumer during any shopping expedition may, as a result, be regarded as heavily dependent upon the state of his decision as to what he wants to buy. If the consumer knows precisely what he wants, he needs only to undertake communication activities sufficient to take title to the desired product. He may also undertake ancillary physical activities involving the handling of the product and delivery. If the consumer is uncertain as to what he wants to buy, then an additional activity will have to be performed. This involves the work of making comparisons between possible alternative purchases, or simply search.

There would be little point, with respect to the problem of classifying consumer goods, in distinguishing between the activity of search and that of making a commitment to buy, if a consumer always performed both before purchasing a good. The crucial point is that he does not. While most of the items that a consumer buys have probably been subjected to comparison at some point in his life, he does not make a search

    [6] Richard H. Holton, "What is Really Meant by 'Specialty' Goods?" *Journal of Marketing*, Vol. 24 (July, 1959), pp. 64–67.
    [7] Melvin T. Copeland, same reference as footnote 1, pp. 283–284.

before each purchase. Instead, a past solution to the need is frequently remembered and, if satisfactory, is implemented.[8] Use of these past decisions for many products quickly moves the consumer past any perceived necessity of undertaking new comparisons and leaves only the task of exchange to be discharged.

REDEFINITION OF THE SYSTEM

Use of this concept of problem solving permits one to classify consumer buying efforts into two broad categories which may be called shopping and nonshopping goods.

Shopping Goods

Shopping goods are those for which the consumer *regularly* formulates a new solution to his need each time it is aroused. They are goods whose suitability is determined through search before the consumer commits himself to each purchase.

The motivation behind this behavior stems from circumstances which tend to perpetuate a lack of complete consumer knowledge about the nature of the product that he would like to buy.[9] Frequent changes in price, style, or product technology cause consumer information to become obsolete. The greater the time lapse between purchases, the more obsolete will his information be. The consumer's needs are also subject to change, or he may seek variety in his purchases as an actual goal. These forces will tend to make past information inappropriate. New search, due to forces internal and external to the consumer, is continuously required for products with purchase determinants which the consumer regards as both important and subject to change.[10]

The number of comparisons that the consumer will make in purchasing a shopping good may be determined by use of Holton's hypothesis on effort. The consumer, in other words, will undertake search for a product until the perceived value to be secured through additional comparisons is less than the estimated cost of making those comparisons. Thus, shopping effort will vary according to the intensity of the desire of the consumer to find the right product, the type of product and the availability of retail facilities. Whether the consumer searches diligently, superficially, or even buys at the first opportunity, however, does not alter the shopping nature of the product.

[8] George Katona, *Psychological Analysis of Economic Behavior* (New York: McGraw-Hill Book Co., Inc., 1951), p. 47.

[9] Same reference, pp. 67–68.

[10] George Katona and Eva Mueller, "A Study of Purchase Decisions in Consumer Behavior," Lincoln Clark, editor, *Consumer Behavior* (New York: University Press, 1954), pp. 30–87.

Nonshopping Goods

Turning now to nonshopping goods, one may define these as products for which the consumer is both willing and able to use stored solutions to the problem of finding a product to answer a need. From the remarks on shopping goods it may be generalized that nonshopping goods have purchase determinants which do not change, or which are perceived as changing inconsequentially, between purchases.[11] The consumer, for example, may assume that price for some product never changes or that price is unimportant. It may be unimportant because either the price is low, or the consumer is very wealthy.

Nonshopping goods may be divided into convenience and specialty goods by means of the concept of a preference map. Bayton introduces this concept as the means to show how the consumer stores information about products.[12] It is a rough ranking of the relative desirability of the different kinds of products that the consumer sees as possible satisfiers for his needs. For present purposes, two basic types of preference maps may be envisaged. One type ranks all known product alternatives equally in terms of desirability. The other ranks one particular product as so superior to all others that the consumer, in effect, believes this product is the only answer to his need.

Distinguishing the Specialty Good

This distinction in preference maps creates the basis for discriminating between a convenience good and a specialty good. Clearly, where the consumer is indifferent to the precise item among a number of substitutes which he could buy, he will purchase the most accessible one and look no further. This is a convenience good. On the other hand, where the consumer recognizes only one brand of a product as capable of satisfying his needs, he will be willing to bypass more readily accessible substitutes in order to secure the wanted item. This is a specialty good.

However, most nonshopping goods will probably fall in between these two polar extremes. Preference maps will exist where the difference between the relative desirability of substitutes may range from the slim to the well marked. In order to distinguish between convenience goods and specialty goods in these cases, Holton's hypothesis regarding consumer effort may be employed again. A convenience good, in these terms, becomes one for which the consumer has such little preference among his perceived choices that he buys the item which is most readily available. A specialty good is one for which consumer preference is so strong

[11] Katona, same reference as footnote 8, p. 68.
[12] James A. Bayton, "Motivation, Cognition, Learning—Basic Factors in Consumer Behavior," *Journal of Marketing*, Vol. 22 (January, 1958), pp. 282–289, at p. 287.

that he bypasses, or would be willing to bypass, the purchase of more accessible substitutes in order to secure his most wanted item.

It should be noted that this decision on the part of the consumer as to how much effort he should expend takes place under somewhat different conditions than the one for shopping goods. In the nonshopping good instance the consumer has a reasonably good estimate of the additional value to be achieved by purchasing his preferred item. The estimate of the additional cost required to make this purchase may also be made fairly accurately. Consequently, the consumer will be in a much better position to justify the expenditure of additional effort here than in the case of shopping goods where much uncertainty must exist with regard to both of these factors.

The New Classification

The classification of consumer goods that results from the analysis is as follows:

Convenience Goods: Those goods for which the consumer, before his need arises, possesses a preference map that indicates a willingness to purchase any of a number of known substitutes rather than to make the additional effort required to buy a particular item.

Shopping Goods: Those goods for which the consumer has not developed a complete preference map before the need arises, requiring him to undertake search to construct such a map before purchase.

Specialty Goods: Those goods for which the consumer, before his need arises, possesses a preference map that indicates a willingness to expend the additional effort required to purchase the most preferred item rather than to buy a more readily accessible substitute.

EXTENSION TO RETAILING

The classification of the goods concept developed above may now be extended to retailing. As the concept now stands, it is derived from consumer attitudes or motives toward a *product*. These attitudes, or product motives, are based upon the consumer's interpretation of a product's styling, special features, quality, and social status of its brand name, if any. Occasionally the price may also be closely associated with the product by the consumer.

Classification of Patronage Motives

The extension of the concept to retailing may be made through the notion of patronage motives, a term long used in marketing. Patronage motives are derived from consumer attitudes concerning the retail establishment. They are related to factors which the consumer is likely to regard as controlled by the retailer. These will include assortment, credit, service, guarantee, shopping ease and enjoyment, and usually price. Patronage motives, however, have never been systematically categorized. It is proposed that the procedure developed above to discriminate among product motives be used to classify consumer buying motives with respect to retail stores as well.

This will provide the basis for the consideration of retail marketing strategy and will aid in clearing up certain ambiguities that would otherwise exist if consumer buying motives were solely classified by product factors. These ambiguities appear, for example, when the consumer has a strong affinity for some particular brand of a product, but little interest in where he buys it. The manufacturer of the product, as a result, would be correct in defining the product as a specialty item if the consumer's preferences were so strong as to cause him to eschew more readily available substitutes. The retailer may regard it as a convenience good, however, since the consumer will make no special effort to purchase the good from any particular store. This problem is clearly avoided by separately classifying product and patronage motives.

The categorization of patronage motives by the above procedure results in the following three definitions. These are:

Convenience Stores: Those stores for which the consumer, before his need for some product arises, possesses a preference map that indicates a willingness to buy from the most accessible store.

Shopping Stores: Those stores for which the consumer has not developed a complete preference map relative to the product he wishes to buy, requiring him to undertake a search to construct such a map before purchase.

Specialty Stores: These stores for which the consumer, before his need for some product arises, possesses a preference map that indicates a willingness to buy the item from a particular establishment even though it may not be the most accessible.

The Product-Patronage Matrix

Although this basis will now afford the retailer a means to consider alternative strategies, a finer classification system may be obtained by relating consumer product motives to consumer patronage motives. By cross-classifying each product motive with each patronage motive, one creates a three by three matrix, representing nine possible types of consumer buying behavior. Each of the nine cells in the matrix may be described as follows:

1. *Convenience Store—Convenience Good:* The consumer, represented by this category, prefers to buy the most readily available brand of product at the most accessible store.
2. *Convenience Store—Shopping Good:* The consumer selects his purchase from among the assortment carried by the most accessible store.

3. *Convenience Store–Specialty Good:* The consumer purchases his favored brand from the most accessible store which has the item in stock.
4. *Shopping Store–Convenience Good:* The consumer is indifferent to the brand of product he buys, but shops among different stores in order to secure better retail service and/or lower retail price.
5. *Shopping Store–Shopping Good:* The consumer makes comparisons among both retail controlled factors and factors associated with the product (brand).
6. *Shopping Store–Specialty Good:* The consumer has a strong preference with respect to the brand of the product, but shops among a number of stores in order to secure the best retail service and/or price for this brand.
7. *Specialty Store–Convenience Good:* The consumer prefers to trade at a specific store, but is indifferent to the brand of product purchased.
8. *Specialty Store–Shopping Good:* The consumer prefers to trade at a certain store, but is uncertain as to which product he wishes to buy and examines the store's assortment for the best purchase.
9. *Specialty Store–Specialty Good:* The consumer has both a preference for a particular store and a specific brand.

Conceivably, each of these nine types of behavior might characterize the buying patterns of some consumers for a given product. It seems more likely, however, that the behavior of consumers toward a product could be represented by only three or four of the categories. The remaining cells would be empty, indicating that no consumers bought the product by these methods. Different cells, of course, would be empty for different products.

THE FORMATION OF RETAIL STRATEGY

The extended classification system developed above clearly provides additional information important to the manufacturer in the planning of his marketing strategy. Of principal interest here, however, is the means by which the retailer might use the classification system in planning his marketing strategy.

Three Basic Steps

The procedure involves three steps. The first is the classification of the retailer's potential customers for some product by market segment, using the nine categories in the consumer buying habit matrix to define the principal segments. The second requires the retailer to determine the nature of the marketing strategies necessary to appeal to each market segment. The final step is the retailer's selection of the market segment, and the strategy associated with it, to which he will sell. A simplified, hypothetical example may help to clarify this process.

A former buyer of dresses for a department store decided to open her own dress shop. She rented a small store in the downtown area of a city of 50,000, ten miles distant from a metropolitan center of several

Table 1

Proportion of Potential Dress Market in Each Matrix Cell

Buying Habit	% of Market
Convenience store—Convenience good	0
Convenience store—Shopping good	3
Convenience store—Specialty good	20
Shopping store—Convenience good	0
Shopping store—Shopping good	35
Shopping store—Specialty good	2
Specialty store—Convenience good	0
Specialty store—Shopping good	25
Specialty store—Specialty good	15
	100

hundred thousand population. In contemplating her marketing strategy, she was certain that the different incomes, educational backgrounds, and tastes of the potential customers in her city meant that various groups of these women were using sharply different buying methods for dresses. Her initial problem was to determine, by use of the consumer buying habit matrix, what proportion of her potential market bought dresses in what manner.

By drawing on her own experience, discussions with other retailers in the area, census and other market data, the former buyer estimated that her potential market was divided, according to the matrix, in the following proportions.

This analysis revealed four market segments that she believed were worth further consideration. (In an actual situation, each of these four should be further divided into submarket segments according to other possible factors such as age, incomes, dress size required, location of residence, etc.) Her next task was to determine the type of marketing mix which would most effectively appeal to each of these segments. The information for these decisions was derived from the characteristics of consumer behavior associated with each of the defined segments. The following is a brief description of her assessment of how elements of the marketing mix ought to be weighted in order to formulate a strategy for each segment.

A Strategy for Each Segment

To appeal to the convenience store-specialty good segment she felt that the two most important elements in the mix should be a highly accessible location and a selection of widely-accepted brand merchandise. Of somewhat lesser importance, she found, were depth of assortment, personal selling, and price. Minimal emphasis should be given to store promotion and facilities.

She reasoned that the shopping store-shopping good requires a good central location, emphasis on price, and a broad assortment. She ranked store promotion, accepted brand names and personal selling as secondary. Store facilities would, once again, receive minor emphasis.

The specialty store-shopping good market would, she believed, have to be catered to with an exceptionally strong assortment, a high level of personal selling and more elaborate store facilities. Less emphasis would be needed upon prominent brand names, store promotions, and price. Location was of minor importance.

The specialty store-specialty good category, she thought, would require a marketing mix heavily emphasizing personal selling and highly elaborate store facilities and services. She also felt that prominent brand names would be required, but that these would probably have to include the top names in fashion, including labels from Paris. Depth of assortment would be secondary, while least emphasis would be placed upon store promotion, price, and location.

Evaluation of Alternatives

The final step in the analysis required the former dress buyer to assess her abilities to implement any one of these strategies, given the degree of competition existing in each segment. Her considerations were as follows. With regard to the specialty store-specialty good market, she was unprepared to make the investment in store facilities and services that she felt would be necessary. She also thought, since a considerable period of time would probably be required for her to build up the necessary reputation, that this strategy involved substantial risk. Lastly, she believed that her experience in buying high fashion was somewhat limited and that trips to European fashion centers would prove burdensome.

She also doubted her ability to cater to the specialty store-shopping good market, principally because she knew that her store would not be large enough to carry the necessary assortment depth. She felt that this same factor would limit her in attempting to sell to the shopping store-shopping good market as well. Despite the presence of the large market in this segment, she believed that she would not be able to create sufficient volume in her proposed quarters to enable her to compete effectively with the local department store and several large department stores in the neighboring city.

The former buyer believed her best opportunity was in selling to the convenience store-specialty good segment. While there were already two other stores in her city which were serving this segment, she believed that a number of important brands were still not represented. Her past contacts with resources led her to believe that she would stand an excellent chance of securing a number of these lines. By stocking these brands, she thought that she could capture a considerable number of local customers who currently were purchasing them in the large city. In this way, she believed, she would avoid the full force of local competition.

Decision

The conclusion of the former buyer to use her store to appeal to the convenience store-specialty good segment represents the culmination to the process of analysis suggested here. It shows how the use of the three-by-three matrix of consumer buying habits may aid the retailer in developing his marketing strategy. It is a device which can isolate the important market segments. It provides further help in enabling the retailer to associate the various types of consumer behavior with those elements of the marketing mix to which they are sensitive. Finally, the analysis forces the retailer to assess the probability of his success in attempting to use the necessary strategy in order to sell each possible market.

33. Social pressures and retail competition

STANLEY C. HOLLANDER

The most ambiguous, the most accommodating and changeable, and yet the most pervasive and potent forces that control retail competition are custom, consumer expectations, and social pressure. Suppliers frequently try to direct their dealers' behavior. Retail unions and other worker groups have sought, sometimes successfully, to influence store hours, services, and operating methods. The market in many ways limits what retailers can do. The wares that merchants offer must be adjusted to customer needs and tastes: the sale of antifreeze at the equator and of bathing suits at the Arctic Circle usually are not viable merchandising alternatives. Similarly, price policies must be adapted to the incomes and spending habits of the market. But in some sense even more fundamental than the market is the set of ideas that both merchants and the public share as to what is the proper way for a retail business to be conducted.

In some cases the public's concept of what is appropriate retail action becomes crystallized in legislation. Legislative action may result when the behavior of some retailers differs substantially from what an influential segment of the public believes to be fitting and proper conduct. Aside and apart from formal legislative codes, however, custom and expectations create very real, even if somewhat vague, limits on the competitive alternatives that the retailers can successfully adopt.

The relationship between retailing and its environment is complex. It is difficult for us to perceive that relationship as it operates within our own culture, since our questions and expectations of retailing are very largely determined by that same culture. A sort of cross-cultural anthro-

Reprinted from *Business Topics*, Winter, 1965, pp. 7–14, by permission of the publisher.

pological economic analysis is needed to discover the social determinants of retailing. In the past few years marketing specialists and anthropologists alike have become increasingly interested in that sort of analysis; and so we have recently had, for example, some fascinating studies of the social forces that determine trading relationships, the use of credit, and merchandising practices in Indonesian villages. British economists have tried to establish statistical relationships between socio-economic variables, on one hand, and, on the other, the number and kind of stores that will operate within a given community. Many other interesting studies are becoming available,[1] and while they still are exploratory rather than definitive, they do much to suggest society's role in shaping the limits of competition.

SOCIETAL CONTROLS

Most merchants are even unlikely to conceive or consider alternatives outside those limits, a fact that in turn reinforces the original impact of the social controls. Few merchants in America today, for example, would consider as a competitive tool the use of a "puller-in," that is, a man stationed at the doorway to coax window shoppers into the store. The use of these men was once a common competitive tactic, yet today it is simply outside the average merchant's frame of reference.

The August fur sale illustrates the self-reinforcing nature of many retail customs. At one time very few furs were sold in August, which is what one would expect to have been the case in the days before air-conditioning. Apparently some furriers tried offering drastic price inducements to offset this normal seasonal slump in business. Their competitors followed suit, and eventually a large, price-conscious segment of the market began to do its fur shopping in August. Consequently, the merchants who wanted to attract this segment had to offer their more attractive specials that month, before the customers purchased elsewhere. The concentration of specials, in turn, tended to strengthen the consumers' belief that August was the time to buy, and so on in circular fashion.

A similar illustration of self-reinforcement appears in the recommendations that the American Newspaper Publishers' Association offered to the retail trade for many years. Although the Association's Bureau of Advertising has recently modified its position somewhat, it used to suggest that retailers concentrate their advertising of each type of merchan-

---

[1] See the sources cited in Stanley C. Hollander, "Retailing: Cause or Effect," in William S. Decker (ed.), *Emerging Concepts in Marketing* (Chicago: American Marketing Association, 1962), pp. 220–32. Also see Robert Bartels, *Comparative Marketing* (Homewood, Illinois: Richard D. Irwin, Inc., for the American Marketing Association, 1963), pp. 1–6, 283–308, for a discussion of comparative analysis in wholesaling.

dise in those months when the consumer purchases of that merchandise were greatest.

Of course, societal forces shape all businesses, not merely retailing alone. As one economist has put it:

No less important is the unconscious influence provided by the mores, folklore, customs, institutions, social ideals, and myths of a society which lay the foundation for formal organization. More immediately relevant to any one firm's behavior are the standards and values of the groups with which it comes into contact as an organization, as well as the groups, communities and organizations to which its members belong. It should be clear that the preference system of the firm, as well as the attitudes of the participants in the firm's organization toward such things as co-operation, efficiency, innovation, etc. must be profoundly affected by the broader community within which the firm operates.[2]

The totally public nature of retailing and of some of the service trades does nevertheless create some special problems for businessmen in those fields. Often a factory or a wholesale establishment in an isolated or unfrequented location, for example, may operate at full force on Sunday subject to possible resentment only among its own employees and their families. The storekeeper who opens on Sunday, however, is more likely to come to the attention of, and to irritate, segments of the general public that may include both voters and potential customers. Local sentiments, which vary from place to place, determine whether clothing merchants must cover their windows when changing the garments on the display dummies.

In an entirely different sense as well, dealing with the ultimate consumer probably leaves the retailer more susceptible to the influence of custom and tradition than most other businessmen. For over two hundred years economists, marketing specialists, and psychologists have debated whether habit and past practice are more important in guiding the purchases of consumer buyers than those of the supposedly more rational industrial and commercial buyers. This debate has often centered around the supposedly more crucial role of customary prices in consumer markets than in commercial ones. The argument is by no means settled, but the only question in all the debate has been whether consumer dependence on tradition is greater than or only equal to that of business buyers. No one has ever seriously urged that it is less. The retailer's problem is that his public is indeed *the* public.

Caplow has argued that the prevailing customs and expectations influence the retailer's entire relationship to his customers and, to a considerable extent, even his behavior outside the store. In contrasting the occupation of shopkeeper with that of factory worker, he says:

[2] Andreas G. Papandreou, "Some Basic Problems in the Theory of the Firm," in Bernard F. Haley (ed.), *A Survey of Contemporary Economics* (Homewood, Illinois: Richard D. Irwin, Inc., 1952), II, 192.

the control of occupational behavior is entirely different, being at once much wider and much more diffuse. Indeed, it is the popular belief that self employment in a small business carries with it freedom from personal coercion which constitutes the principal appeal of retail trade, just as it is often the impact of impersonal coercion which subsequently disillusions the neophyte proprietor.

He describes the coercion as originating with suppliers, creditors, and customers. Then he goes on to say:

[Compared to the rigid system of control exercised by suppliers and other creditors], the control which the customer exerts upon the occupational comportment of the merchants is very informal. It is none the less important. Particularly since the restrictions of price and quality competition, personal relations with customers are often the decisive factor in the history of a retail business.

The "rules" are essentially these:

1. The merchant is expected to minimize his status and exaggerate that of the customer by exaggerated forms of deference, by yielding in minor arguments, by expressing more interest in the customer's personal affairs than the customer is expected to show in his, and by small personal services.

2. Under this ritual, it becomes essential that the habits of the customer be identified and protected. A strain is thus produced on the merchant to maintain nearly absolute consistency in his manners, his purchasing routines, and his hours of work. . . .

The norms of deference imposed on the shopkeeper prevent him from displaying a distinctly higher status than his customers [in life style], while his aspirations toward the role of businessman impel him to do so.[3]

This picture is somewhat overdrawn, particularly if it is used to depict all retailer-customer relations. Certainly many of the most successful mass-retailers exhibit little of the deference suggested by the first "rule" cited above. And the smaller merchants who have succeeded without much servility are also numerous. But in spite of these and other criticisms of Caplow's picture, we must grant that a retailer in the typical American community today cannot long behave like the operator of a trading post on the Navaho reservation who says: "The important thing is to show the Indians who is boss."[4] Nor can he expect to take on the general role of social, economic, financial, and technical advisor to the community, as did so many pioneer merchants of the Western frontier.

---

[3] Theodore Caplow, *The Sociology of Work* (Minneapolis: University of Minnesota Press, 1954), pp. 118–19, 128–29. Caplow, it should be made clear, directs his remarks specifically to small shopkeepers.

[4] William Y. Adams, *Shonto: A Study of the Role of the Trader in a Modern Navaho Community*, Smithsonian Institution, Bureau of American Ethnology, Bulletin 188 (Washington: U.S. Government Printing Office, 1963), pp. 210–12, 287–90. The traders cited by Adams reverse every one of the rules of deference indicated above, and in order to discourage automobile ownership among the Indians, go so far as to deliberately create disorder and uncertainty in the marketing of gasoline.

In short, society has dictated the general limits of the retailer's role. It also dictates many of the details of his operation.

PRICING

As any one retailer faces his world, he finds that it tells him a number of things about what it considers appropriate pricing policies. Our society, for example, regards haggling and bargaining as permissible in some retail situations and improper in others. Automobile dealers are expected to bargain, haberdashers are not. Of course, the explanation can be offered that the size of the automobile transaction and the unstandardized condition of the trade-in are conducive to bargaining in the car dealership, while different conditions obtain in the haberdashery. This is perfectly reasonable, and true. But the point is that in other times, and at other places, haberdashers have been expected to bargain, while in our society they definitely are not expected to do so. Also, we generally feel that such professional men as architects and physicians, whose output is also unstandardized and sometimes of substantial size, should not bargain, although under some conditions they may discriminate between patrons.

Some patterns of discriminatory prices have become so widely accepted in the sale of some, *but not all*, goods and services that it requires a conscious effort of mind to appreciate that these patterns do, in fact, discriminate between customers. These conventional discriminations are often based upon age, and occasionally upon sex. Children's rates, lower than those for adults, are frequently offered in the sale of transportation, amusement, and other services. In cases such as the provision of restaurant meals and haircuts, it can properly be argued that the child receives a different, albeit perhaps more troublesome, service than the adult. This is not so in the case of many amusement and transportation services in which the child, charged the lower rate, receives exactly the same privileges as the higher rated adult. Some aspects of family-plan airline and railroad fares, and the free admission of women to baseball parks on Ladies' Day are examples of similar discriminations based upon sex.

Some discriminatory practices based on the patronage status of the purchaser seem to be of general acceptability. Special introductory rates for new subscribers are very frequently used in building magazine subscription lists. Department store private sales for the benefit of old customers cast the discriminatory advantage in the opposite direction. While magazine introductory rates usually are actually restricted to new subscribers, many so-called private sales are much less impregnable. In many stores the term is used to describe the practice of giving charge customers notice of approaching sales before the advertisements appear in the newspaper. Rational justifications can be offered for each of these discriminations. But again the point is that each of these sets of price differentials seems to be regarded as acceptable only within a particular context. Clothing merchants usually find that extra alteration charges are more readily accepted in the sale of women's clothing than in menswear. Generally however, commodity retailers, unlike service trade operators usually do not think in terms of age or sex-based price differentials and the public doesn't seem to expect them to do so, although there is as much social justification for a child's discount on toothpaste as on movie admissions. A department store sale that was confined to noncustomers would engender waves of ill will, and no department store executive would dream of such a sale. Yet magazine publishers do it every day, with apparently very little criticism.

Another curious way in which public expectations, reinforced by retail practice, limit the retailer's freedom to select among competitive pricing alternatives is in the matter of "customary prices." This is the popular belief that only certain prices or price endings are appropriate for certain types of goods. The use of these prices has been condemned as a mechanism that forces price increases into unnecessarily large steps, and praised as a device that facilitates consumer comparisons. Whether desirable or not, most retailers feel that the public's expectation that these traditional price endings should be used is a very real force that must be considered in setting prices. Very few studies attempting to measure the strength of consumer attachment to customary prices have been reported. The best known one started with a hypothesis on the part of the researcher and his mail-order house sponsors that the whole thing was a myth. The only conclusion was that the dangers of testing out-weighed the possible benefits of the test.[5] And finally the public often seems to have some vague sense of what it considers as unfair or fair prices. An experienced retailer puts it this way:

It is generally accepted as poor policy to charge what the traffic will bear. Whenever an article is priced higher than eye-value would seem to justify, the retailer is at pains to explain that the fault is not his, but the high price of the manufacturer. Indeed, he may often shade his mark-on in order to avoid criticism.[6]

MERCHANDISE

The public also has some expectations as to the type and nature of the merchandise that each type of retailer will carry. Such expectations

[5] Eli Ginzberg, "Customary Prices," *American Economic Review*, XXVI (June 1936), 296.
[6] *Oswald Knauth*, "Considerations in the Setting of Retail Prices," *Journal of Marketing*, XIV (July 1949), 7.

are in fact necessary, if shopping is not to be a matter of haphazard searching. The importance of these traditional expectations about merchandise offerings is denied to some extent by recent developments of "scrambled merchandising," i.e., the sale of many types of goods in nontraditional outlets—for example, the introduction of non-foods into grocery supermarkets. Yet it is interesting to note that some commodity lines, which the public apparently considers too different from the usual grocery stock, such as clothing accessories, have encountered considerable customer resistance in many supermarkets. On the other hand, soap is considered so traditional a grocery line that no one ever refers to it as a "non-food," even though it is hardly edible; and consequently, no grocer would dare exclude it from his stocks.

A very different sort of public pressure arises if the retailer handles goods that come from sources that are objectionable to some portion of his public. The reaction may take the form of picketing, boycotts, or attempts to secure some type of controlling legislation. Most recently this sort of reaction has occurred in connection with the sale of goods originating in the communist-bloc countries. At various times, similar responses have been evoked by the sale of low-priced Japanese textiles, products made by firms that practice racial discrimination, prison-made and non-union-made goods, and items from Nazi Germany and elsewhere.

And, of course, the public or a segment may protest if it considers the merchandise itself objectionable. Again, apparently, the reaction will often be directed with different strength against different types of retailers. At least one book distributor reports that the public seems to tolerate more lurid paperbacks in drugstores than it will in supermarkets.

SERVICES

When the Twentieth Century Fund sponsored its classic study of distribution costs a number of years ago, it also asked a distinguished panel to prepare recommendations on ways of reducing those costs. Among other things, the panel recommended that retailers separate the charge for each service rendered the customer from the basic price of the merchandise itself.[7] This suggestion was based upon the belief that the general practice of quoting a single price for the item and the attendant services leads many consumers to use more services than they really want or would be willing to pay for in a free market. The panel felt that many consumers would like the option of choosing between service and price savings. Also charging for services in proportion to use would be more equitable than the prevailing practice. The idea seems thoroughly reasonable. Yet many merchants, and especially the ones to whom this sug-

[7] Paul W. Stewart and J. Frederick Dewhurst, *Does Distribution Cost Too Much?* (New York: Twentieth Century Fund, 1939), pp. 351–52.

gestion was particularly addressed, were, and to a great extent still are, extremely reluctant to adopt it.

Their reluctance has been based upon a strong feeling that the public associates a particular bundle of services with each type of store, and that any attempt to reduce those bundles will create a sense of outrage. Again, the public expectations seem to have a differential impact. As a very perceptive analyst points out, what is considered appropriate will vary with the store's price-policy and with the socio-economic class it seeks to attract.[8] Department store operators claim that their comparatively long history as operators of full service institutions makes them subject to consumer expectations of expensive delivery, credit, exchange, return, and miscellaneous other privileges. Yet, they allege, the same consumers will patronize such competitive outlets as discount houses, chain stores, and mail-order house retail shops without demanding any of the services whose discontinuance by department stores would be vigorously resented. Undoubtedly the harshness of the situation is sometimes exaggerated by department store people as an excuse for poor profit performance, but nevertheless the problem does exist.

One aspect of retail services about which many people, including both customers and non-customers, have strong feelings is the matter of store hours, and particularly the question of Sunday openings. In many areas local pharmacists' associations have detected some public dissatisfaction with the hours observed by drug stores and have formulated plans under which there will always be at least one pharmacy open in the community at any hour to handle emergency needs. In contrast, an increasing trend toward Sunday sales on the part of roadside clothing, hardware, furniture, general merchandise stores, and automobile dealers has induced a call for some type of control in many parts of the country. The issue is complicated by the varying economic interests of the retailers and the communities involved, the diverse desires of retail workers, and the thorny question of the proper position of government in matters that have religious overtones. But it is clear that a number of people in this country do believe that at least some types of stores should close on Sunday.

IMPACT OF SOCIAL PRESSURE

The strength of the social forces that we have just looked at can easily be overestimated. The merchants who are affected by these forces may be particularly likely to see more power than is actually there. Customs may persist, not because of any inherent vitality, but because of inertia and the absence of any strong incentive for change. Department

---

[8] W. T. Tucker, *The Social Context of Economic Behavior* (New York: Holt, Rinehart & Winston, Inc., 1964), pp. 73–81.

store merchants who have been beset by discount house competition have found that they could, in many cases, move to self-service, to the elimination of some frills, and to separation of commodity and service charges. Possibly this increased freedom to compete has been due to changes in the consumer between 1935 and 1950 and 1964. Some of it probably is. But at least some of the change probably is a correction of an erroneous impression as to the amount of service the consumer really wanted. Katona mentions another instance of failure to judge what was permissible among the many apparel merchants who offered totally unnecessary seasonal reductions during the wartime shortage years of 1942 and early 1943.[9] Other such examples could be cited.

Yet in spite of all such instances, the fact remains that the retailer is in the business of dealing with the public, and so he must be responsive to the public's demands upon him. Frequently, as in the case of the mail-order firm that wanted to question the strength of customary pricing, attempts to test those demands involve risks of lost sales or of customer alienation. The risks are greatest, although sometimes the rewards also may be greatest, when an individual retailer tries to move independently, counter to the practices of his competitors. Thus, for example, two authors who generally favor independence and competitiveness in retailing, urge group action to reduce the returned goods rate:

Although the individual store can do much to reduce its returns, group action of the retailers within a given shopping area is often necessary for best results. The group can afford to do many things which the individual store cannot do. Also, some of the steps the individual retailer might take would merely drive his customers to competitors, where they would still return as much merchandise, so that the returned-goods problem of the community would be as important as before. Group action, therefore, has the major advantage of making it easier to establish a sound educational program on the costliness of returns and of making it less difficult for individual stores to refuse returns because of the established "law" in the community governing such matters.

Realizing the advantages of group action, merchants in such cities as Dallas, Los Angeles, Kansas City and Milwaukee have joined together to reduce returns. Such action usually involves agreement on one or more of the following points: establishing uniform time limits, setting up a standard policy of refusing to pick up certain merchandise for return, standardizing extra charges for return pickups, framing sanitary provisions and obtaining local ordinances involving sanitary considerations, activating educational campaigns and providing material for publicity drives, exchanging information about customers with records of excessive returns, and exchanging return-ratio data.[10]

[9] George Katona, *Psychological Analysis of Economic Behavior* (New York: McGraw-Hill Book Company, Inc., 1951), p. 51. See also John K. Galbraith, *The Theory of Price Control* (Cambridge: Harvard University Press, 1952), p. 12.

[10] Delbert J. Duncan and Charles F. Phillips, *Retailing: Principles and Methods* (6th ed.; Homewood, Illinois: Richard D. Irwin, Inc., 1963), pp. 591–92.

Anyone who is dedicated to a classical "hard-core" antitrust position might question the propriety of some of the actions outlined above, although several of them are similar to recommendations of the Twentieth Century Fund's distribution cost panel. But they do also illustrate the difficulty of making individual changes in the established way of dealing with the public.

34. Linear programming for merchandising decisions

E. LAWRENCE SALKIN

The maturation of the computer as a standard tool for use in business has resulted in the concomitant growth of a new technique for management decision-making known as management science. Management science, in the main, is based upon the application of mathematical theories that before the development of the computer were regarded as mere mathematical curiosities. This was true because of the vast number of calculations required to solve the problems. With a computer, the application of these mathematical theories becomes practical and a tremendous aid to the decision-maker. Such problems as inventory control, allocation of personnel, capital and expense budgeting, marketing plans, can be solved more logically through the use of the various techniques of management science.

Retailing is a highly complicated business operation, and retailing executives can profitably make use of many of the techniques mentioned above to chart a course through the complex maze of decisions required to cut costs and increase profits. At this point, most computer installations in retail companies are being used as workhorses, processing accounts receivable, accounts payable, payrolls, and merchandise information. As the problems arising from putting these functions on a computer are solved, it is conceivable that computer time will be made available for the scientific applications required for the mathematical analyses of management science. Looking forward to this development, the enlightened retail executive should familiarize himself with the techniques for scientific decision-making.

It is the purpose of this paper to illustrate just one of the many ways

Reprinted from the *Journal of Retailing*, Volume 40 (Winter 1964/1965), pp. 37–41ff. By permission of the author and publisher.

a scientific approach to decision-making can be implemented. The case cited herein is hypothetical and simplified, since no computer was available for calculations required for a more expanded situation; however, it is felt that the problem stated is a valid one, and, by expanding the mathematical model herein presented, can be effectively used in real situations with the aid of a computer. The mathematics used is based upon linear programming theory, and the approach and techniques used have been adapted from *Executive Decisions and Operations Research*, by Miller and Starr.

THE PROBLEM

Let us imagine a buyer of a budget skirt department with the bulk of his volume achieved by two price lines: $4.00 and $7.00. The buyer, contemplating no change in his current price lines, wishes to maximize gross margin for these two price lines combined for the coming season within the framework of certain predetermined goals. To do this, the buyer must plan to have sold a certain number of units of the $4.00 and $7.00 skirts by the end of the season. Though he has past unit sales records to guide him, he does not wish to rely on his empirical judgment alone to make the decision. The buyer decides that with the data available he can use a linear programming model to help determine the optimum number of skirts in each of the two price lines that should move through his department during the season. The data to be used is shown in Table 1, including the algebraic symbols that will be used for the formulas.

Four factors have been selected: Cost of Sales, Turnover, Average Age, and Average Income of Customers. Cost of Sales have been selected since it is reduced from initial markon to arrive at gross margin. The gross margin is the figure arrived at after accounting for markdowns, shortages, etc. Turnover is selected since it determines the amount of average inventory investment required to attain the desired volume. As turnover is increased the investment required is correspondingly lowered. Customer Age and Income are selected since these factors are basic in determining the character of the department.

Other factors, such as sales per square foot, average gross sales, mark on, etc., could have been selected. However, care should be taken to use those factors that are most relevant to the problem. The use of too many factors complicates considerably the computations required for a solution.

COMPILATION OF DATA

The buyer has compiled the data used from various sources: *Gross Margin, Cost of Sales, and Turnover,* listed in columns A and

B, are estimated from past figures attained by the department for each classification.

Family Income and Age Level, listed in columns A and B, are supplied by the Market Research Department from a recent research study of customer habits.

Average Planned Goals per unit for both skirts combined are listed in column C. In effect, these figures are the quantification of management's merchandising policy for this department. For example, management desires to concentrate most of its promotional activity toward the $7,000-and-over income level, with an age level of 27 years and over; therefore these goals are listed as averages per unit to be attained for the coming season.

Gross Margin, Cost of Sales, Turnover, Income and Age Level form the boundaries within which the optimal number of skirts to be carried will be found. Any combination of skirts carried that does not equal or surpass the planned goals listed in Table 1 are not acceptable as a solution. The problem is to select the combination of skirts that achieves all the planned goals and, at the same time, maximizes gross margin. In this

Table 1
Planned Goals for Season Sales of $4.00 and $7.00 Skirts

	A $4.00 Skirt* Symbol	A $4.00 Skirt*	B $7.00 Skirt* Symbol	B $7.00 Skirt*	C Planned Goals
Gross Margin Per Unit (in dollars) . .	P_1	$1.50	P_2	$2.70	Maximum
Cost of Sales Per Unit.	C_1	$ .45	C_2	$ .65	$ .60
Turnover for the Season.	T_1	4.0	T_2	3.0	3.2
Average Family Income (in thousands) Purchasing Each Type Skirt.	I_1	$5.5	I_2	$7.8	$7.0
Average Age Level Purchasing Each Type Skirt	A_1	22	A_2	30	27

*The symbol for the $4.00 skirt is S_1 and the symbol for the $7.00 skirt is S_2.

problem, the combination that maximizes gross margin with cost of sales equal to or less than $.60, turnover equal to or better than 3.2, income equal to or better than $7,000, and age equal to or better than 27 years is the best solution to be found. It is this solution that the buyer will use to plan for the coming season.

THE FORMULAS

The formulas for this particular linear programming model are shown in Table 2, with the customary use of such symbols as $\geq$ and $\leq$ meaning "equal to or greater than" and "equal to or less than," respectively. This form is used because, as explained previously, the buyer wishes to equal or improve on the planned goals, not *merely* equal them. Inequations 1., 2., 3., 4., 5., 6., and 7. form boundaries comprising all the goals desired. In technical terms, these are called the "constraints" or "restraints" of the linear programming problem. Inequations 6. and 7. are included as constraints since the solution to the problem must result in a zero or positive value for each skirt in order to be implemented. It is impossible to merchandise a negative number of skirts. Equation 5. is known as the objective function, which, in this case, means that gross margin is to be maximized within the boundaries desired.

The right hand side of the inequations ($\leq \overline{C} \geq C$ Minimum; $\geq \overline{T} \leq T$ Maximum, etc.) are written in this form to further delineate the area within which the optimal solutions must be found. To illustrate, when we substitute the values found in Table 1 into inequation No. 1. of Table 2 we have the following:

$$.45S_1 + .65S_2 \leq .60 \geq .45$$

This means that the average cost of sales in the final or optimal solution must be equal to or less than .65 and equal to or greater than .45. It is obvious that it would be impossible to have an average cost of sales of less than the minimum of .45, and any average cost of sales over .60 is unacceptable as it exceeds the boundaries for this factor. This is true for the remaining inequations, except that the maximum values would be considered impossible.

Table 2
Inequations for the Linear Programming Solution

1. $C_1S_1 + C_2S_2 \leq \overline{C} \geq C$ Minimum

2. $T_1S_1 + T_2S_2 \geq \overline{T} \leq T$ Maximum

3. $I_1S_1 + I_2S_2 \geq \overline{I} \leq I$ Maximum

4. $A_1S_1 + A_2S_2 \geq \overline{A} \leq A$ Maximum

5. $P_1S_1 + P_2S_2 =$ Maximum

6. $S_1 \geq 0$

7. $S_2 \geq 0$

Note: $\overline{C}, \overline{T}, \overline{I},$ and $\overline{A}$ indicate planned figures, as shown in Column C, Table 1.

COMPUTATION OF THE OPTIMAL SOLUTION

The computations required for arriving at a solution to this problem involve no more than simple algebra. It is the large number of computations required that complicates matters. The number of computations in the method presented here increase considerably as the number of variables and constraints are increased. Other computational methods, such as the Simplex Method, can be used for expanded problems but are too unwieldy for this comparatively simple algebraic approach.

As for the solution itself, the data listed in Table 1 is substituted into the inequations listed in Table 2. The inequations with the values substituted are shown in Table 3.

Each combination of two of the above inequations are solved simultaneously as linear equations.[1] If there were three skirt classifications considered, each combination of three inequations would be solved simultaneously as equations, etc. The values obtained for each skirt classification from each solution is substituted back into inequations 1 through 5 to find a total value for each factor. In order to determine the optimal solution, all that do not fall within the values listed on the right hand side of the inequations are eliminated from consideration.

After eliminating all the combined solutions that do not satisfy all the constraints, we then look for the solution that satisfies all constraints and will yield the highest gross margin. All solutions with factors that fall outside the boundaries are italicized in Table 4. As can be seen, the values computed from equations 1–2 yielding an average gross margin of $2.41 is the optimal solution.

All other values, except for those of equations 2–3, fall outside the boundary. For example, equation number six yields a gross margin of 2.49, but one of the tabulations is outside of our boundary limits. In this table all figures listed in italics represent figures outside our boundary limits.

Table 3
Inequations to be Solved for the Optimal Solution

1. $.45S_1 + .65S_2 \leq .60 \geq .45$ 5. $1.50S_1 + 2.70S_2 = $ Maximum

2. $4.00S_1 + 3.00S_2 \geq 3.20 \leq 4.00$ 6. $S_1 \geq 0$

3. $5.50S_1 + 7.80S_2 \geq 7.00 \leq 7.80$ 7. $S_2 \geq 0$

4. $22.00S_1 + 30.00S_2 \geq 27.00 \leq 30.00$

The S_1 and S_2 values for equation 1–2 are converted into percentages of 22.6 percent and 77.4 percent respectively. These percentages are applied to the planned sales for the season, in this case $100,000. Thus the optimum sales that would maximize gross margin for both skirts would be $22,600 for the $4.00 skirt and $77,400 for the $7.00 skirt. These

---

[1] For example, equations 1–2 would be solved as follows:
$$.45S_1 + .65S_2 = .60$$
$$4.00S_1 + 3.00S_2 = 3.20$$
with the solution resulting in $S_1 = .224$ and $S_2 = .768$. This, by coincidence, is the optimal solution.

Table 4

Solutions for Combined Equations

Equations	Values S_1	S_2	Equation 1	Equation 2	Equation 3	Equation 4	Average Gross Margin Per Unit*
1-2	.224	.768	$.60	3.20	7.30	28.00	$2.41
1-3	-2.000	2.308	.60	—	7.00	—	—
1-4	-.563	1.313	.60	—	—	27.00	—
1-6	0	.923	.60	2.77	7.20	27.70	2.49
1-7	1.333	0	.60	5.32	7.30	29.30	2.00
2-3	.269	.708	.58	3.20	7.00	27.20	2.32
2-4	.278	.697	.58	3.20	6.97	27.00	2.30
2-6	0	1.067	.69	3.20	8.32	32.00	2.88
2-7	.800	0	.36	3.20	4.40	17.60	1.20
3-4	.091	.833	.58	2.86	7.00	27.00	2.39
3-6	0	.897	.58	2.69	7.00	26.90	2.42
3-7	1.272	0	.57	5.10	7.00	28.00	3.43
4-6	0	.900	.59	2.70	7.02	27.00	2.43
4-7	1.227	0	.55	4.90	6.75	27.00	1.84

*All figures listed in italics are outside our boundary limits. That is why the figure $2.41 is considered the largest gross margin per unit.

sales are converted to 5,650 and 11,057 units respectively with a resulting total gross margin of $38,328.90.

No other combination of $4.00 and $7.00 skirts within the constraints set up would yield a greater gross margin.

Table 4(A)

Optimal Solution Converted to Total Units
Based on $100,000 Planned Sales

	$4.00 Skirt	$7.00 Skirt
Value from Equation 1-2	.224	.768
Proportional Percent	22.6%	77.4%
Proportional Sales	$22,600	$77,400
Number of Units to Order	5,650	11,057
Gross Margin	(for both skirts)	$38,328.90

CONCLUSION

At first reading, this approach to decision-making might seem ponderous and complicated. In reality, the theory and implementation are fairly simple. The data to be used for the solution are usually easy to obtain and the availability of a computer makes the large number of computations involved in expanded applications of the linear programming model a routine matter.

Analyses of this nature can be used for any period of time desired, and, in conjunction with the open-to-buy, are useful in developing merchandising plans as the season progresses.

The advantages of this mathematical approach to decision-making over empirical judgments are considerable:

1. The decision-maker is required to approach the problem in an orderly, logical manner, and remove all extraneous factors from consideration.
2. The ultimate goal in the problem is the maximization of profit, which is the ultimate goal of any business endeavor.
3. The merchandising policies of the department are more clearly defined, and help to pinpoint those merchandise lines that contribute most to the department's merchandising image with the greatest profit.

In closing, this scientific approach to solving retailing problems in no way impinges upon the artistic aspects of merchandising; taste and fashion sense are still required in selecting the best sellers within each price range. The day-to-day operational problems within each department would still have to be solved without recourse to mathematics. However, the scientific approach is most useful in reducing the number of decisions to be made, and allows the merchant to concentrate on those problems that require his most creative attention.

C. Promotion

35. New study tells TV advertisers how advertising builds sales and share of market

ALLEN R. DODD, JR.

Somewhere in the U.S. today, a management group is mapping an ad campaign. It will cause some movement in the firm's future share of sales; the planners know this, and they hope it will be upward. They may or may not realize that nearly three-quarters of the elements that will affect that future movement are directly or indirectly under their control right now.

"Well, the budget's a major factor, of course." That could be one of their assumptions and if it is, recent research indicates that they may be in trouble before they've even spent a cent. This research, conducted over the past five years by the Schwerin Research Corp., holds that the planners can actually predict the probable change in their share of sales within reasonable limits if they give priority to:

The quality of their commercials, an element which far outweighs variations in expenditures. After studying 67 television campaigns (actually "measurement periods") totaling nearly $82-million, the Schwerin people decided that "dollars spent on advertising provide only a comparatively small part of the explanation for sales changes."

THE IMPORTANCE OF QUALITY

The influence of quality of the campaign was far more important. On the average, whether the advertising was superior or inferior was more than twice as weighty as variations in spending in accounting for

Reprinted from *Printer's Ink*, May 8, 1964, pp. 27–29.

whether sales went up or down. The quality element is under the direct control of management, and if the planners follow the researcher's guidance, they'll take steps to find out how effective their commercials are in shifting brand preferences before they commit themselves to a campaign.

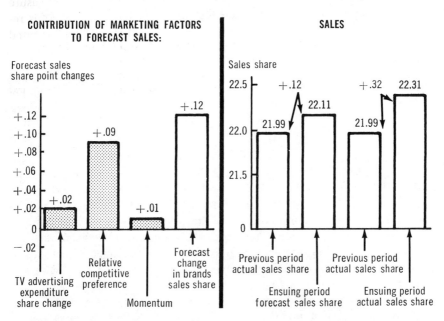

CONTRIBUTION OF MARKETING FACTORS TO FORECAST SALES:

Forecast sales share point changes

TV advertising expenditure share change

Relative competitive preference

Momentum

Forecast change in brands sales share

SALES

Sales share

Previous period actual sales share

Ensuing period forecast sales share

Previous period actual sales share

Ensuing period actual sales share

Forecast for period of June–September 1963: Brand Z—light duty liquid detergent
Here is a typical case of predicting sales-share change for a product in the light duty detergent field. Schwerin measurements determined the value of the momentum variable to be +0.05—a negligible, but still positive momentum. Relative competitive preference was measured at +0.42—this is a small, but again positive force, which is the dominant variable in this campaign. TV-advertising-expenditure-share change was established at −0.96, indicating a small decrease in Brand Z's share of total TV expenditure for the product class in the study period. From historical observations, the importance of each of these variables in affecting sales-share change has been established. When the values of the variables (given above) are multiplied by their coefficients, we get a measure of the amount each contributes to sales-share change in the ensuing period. The total of these individual contributions gives the forecast change in sales-share—in this case +0.12 sales-share points. Brand Z controlled 21.99 percent of the market. The mathematical model said that in the ensuing period the sales share would increase to 22.11 per cent. In actuality, sales-share increased 0.32 points, resulting in an actual share of 22.31 percent of the market. This prediction indicated relatively little change in the brand's market share during the coming period, which is actually what took place. The average movement in the product field from period to period is almost a share point (±0.91). The .20 difference between the predicted and actual change is 78 percent less than average movement in the product field.

The brand's "momentum"—positive or negative—in the market; an element which might be described as the carry-over of a brand name, previous advertising or consumer experience with the product. "Momentum," in Schwerin's terms, is the difference between the market share of a product and its share of consumer preference when they are measured simultaneously. It obviously is not under the direct control of those who are planning a campaign today, but they can note its existence, measure it and plan their expenditures accordingly. In a speech outlining this research last fall, Henry Schachte of J. Walter Thompson, who participated in the project when he was a Unilever executive, declared,

This discovery of the factor of . . . momentum has made a very basic and important contribution to the correlation of specific brand advertising. For when we add statistically the factor of momentum to advertising effectiveness and advertising dollars we get an extremely high and accurate explanation of total sales-change results . . .

Expenditure. This, too, is under the direct control of the planners, who can decide whether their expenditure should be increased or decreased after checking the effectiveness of their commercials against those of the competition and determining the influence of "momentum." In extreme cases, a situation, perhaps, where there is a predicted loss but no satisfactory substitute campaign available, the management can avoid wasting money and exerting negative pressure on the market. Instead, it can hold the line for a few months, keep the brand name before the public with short reminder commercials and shape a new campaign.

What it cannot do, the researchers warn, is buy its way out of trouble. Their study of TV campaigns, the Schwerin people reported, showed that dollars spent affected sales far less than campaign quality or momentum. In some cases, share of sales actually went down when expenditure increased.

Schachte commented as follows on the implication of these findings to management:

This being so, you would probably be concerned with imposing a discipline on your organization that would:

First, provide for a supply of alternative advertising ideas so that there would be a range of commercial ideas for testing.

Second, provide for a testing procedure that would identify the most effective of these and then rate them against the messages of your competitors, since we see that advertising quality, like other parts of the marketing cycle, is truly a competitive marketing function.

Third, check on the competitive quality of the commercials actually being used on the air by you and your competitors and do it on some periodic scheduled basis to make sure of just what your standing is.

Schachte added:

I must say that when I was studying these data in detail there were times when I was distressed by what I saw. There were instances where momentum was negative and advertising effectiveness inferior and yet . . . someone full of hope and courage opened up the money bags. And there, just a short time later, was the unhappy and highly predictable sales decline. If only they could have known!

Then, too, there were the lost opportunities where, with positive momentum and effective advertising, a small dollar increase would have paid sizable rewards—and yet the reverse decision about spending was taken.

The Schwerin research covered major television campaigns in seven product fields—margarines, light-duty liquid detergents, laundry detergents, hair tonics, stomach remedies, headache remedies and toilet soaps. The end product was a mathematical model—a multiple linear correlation equation—based on three independant variables: effectiveness, momentum and expenditure, and the dependent variable, sales. The three independent variables, the research firm says, account for about 73 percent of all movement in share of sales.

Said board chairman Horace Schwerin:

The analysis made it clear that large amounts of money are being spent on advertising messages that are inferior and are associated with losses in share of sales with the inevitable translation into a negative influence on the earnings picture. It has demonstrated that we can tell which expenditures are being wasted and which can get the most return for the dollar. It also showed that momentum—which often isn't recognized as a factor by many advertisers—is far more important than had previously been believed. There is every reason to suspect that negative momentum can be corrected, provided management recognizes that it exists. My impression from the advertisers we serve is that attention to these matters is increasing and that, more and more, the reconciliation of these factors is becoming the concern of someone on the top management team, whatever his title and his other roles.

RECONCILING THE INQUIRIES

The research was launched five years ago by the late Benjamin Potter, onetime Borden and A. C. Nielsen executive. He sought to reconcile two lines of inquiry that were going on at the same time.

In the case of advertising expenditures, management consultants were feeding these and other data into the new computers in an effort to make better budget predictions. The term "operations research" got a big and perhaps somewhat premature play.

Meanwhile, researchers such as Schwerin, who measured the effectiveness of the advertising itself, had to rely on the case-history method. The advertiser-client pre-tested his commercials and then checked their sales results on the air, ideally in a carefully controlled test-market situation.

For example, Potter dug up such studies as one conducted in 1959 by Alberto-Culver and Wade Advertising to assess the relative strength of two commercials for a hair product. The two commercials had been pretested by Schwerin's competitive preference test, one showing a 6.9 percent effectiveness in shifting consumer preferences and the other, apparently stronger, chalking up a 10.8 effectiveness. Two midwestern cities were picked in which the product held similar market positions and a commercial was aired in each one through a four-month period. Sales figures were then audited and they showed that the brand's share of market had jumped in each city, but considerably more in the community that had been exposed to the commercial that scored highest in the pre-testing.

Potter spent the next three years searching out all available examples in which expenditure and effectiveness data could be matched against the actual sales results. To establish the proper yardsticks, he specified nationally distributed products that had been established for more than three years, annual expenditures of at least $1-million and the use of television as the dominant medium.

Schwerin vice-president Malcolm Murphy took over the project in 1962 and added further data. He was puzzled by a few "maverick cases" where there seemed to be inconsistencies between the brand preference shifts and the shifts in actual share of sales. In one instance (it involved a detergent) the advertising was inferior in effectiveness to that of the competition, but the share of sales increased. The researchers identified this as the result of "positive momentum" provided by an old and respected brand name and advertising that had been effective in the past. This positive momentum was reflected in the fact that the percentage of customers preferring the brand before exposure to the advertising was greater than its market share.

Its momentum was so strongly positive that the downward shift in preference caused by the inferior commercial still left a larger proportion of people preferring the brand than the percentage buying it. This balance of favorable attitudes brought about the sales-share gain.

The present four-variable model can be made more comprehensive. Murphy explained,

We have three independent variables now, but we know that others exist and some of them may be important. There's no reason why any company with a sophisticated marketing department couldn't follow the matter up and apply additional variables, such as other advertising in addition to the dominant medium.

Theorists of the past, holding that advertising and sales could not be directly related, have urged management to define its intermediate goals and then evaluated each one separately in terms of that definition.

If the lesser goals are achieved, they reasoned, the sales goal will be achieved, too.

The theory, however, in addition to the problems created by its cumbersome, step-by-step nature, overlooks such elements as momentum, which can cause sales to move downward when all other indications point to an upward shift. The premise that emerges from the Schwerin study is that the management complex's components can be analyzed both separately and interdependently, that some of these have a more marked effect on the movement of sales share than others and that all of them can be either directly controlled or recognized and taken into account by management. In this framework, it's the campaign and what the brand name already has going for or against it that counts. The promise for the future is that, as knowledge of how to treat these elements increases, advertisers will determine sales results with greater accuracy than has hitherto been possible.

36. The Schwerin model:
How you can use it to build your
share of market

PATRICK J. KELLY

Product fields were chosen for this study according to four basic criteria. After seven fields were found that satisfied these criteria, all measurement periods during the past three years for which Schwerin had scores on the qualitive effectiveness of TV commercials became a part of the analysis. The only exceptions were periods when brands had been on the market less than one year. Other marketing factors, as well as those introduced in this study were recognized as being of great importance during the "launch period" of a new brand. The four basic criteria for product field selection were:

(1) that a product field of directly competing brands could be defined; (2) that effectiveness measurements for a minimum of six periods were available; (3) that most of the brands constituting the field were distributed nationally; and (4) that the brands in a field were major, national advertisers, with television as their principal advertising medium.

Within the seven product fields that met the four basic criteria, Schwerin effectiveness measures—for other than newly introduced brands —were available during a total of 67 periods. Each of these 67 periods were included in the study.

All of the seven product fields chosen may be generally classified as consumer packaged goods. The numbers of periods for which data were available varied somewhat from field to field, ranging from six to 12 periods.

Reprinted from *Printer's Ink*, May 8, 1964, pp. 30–38.

Scope

Product Field	Brand Measurement Periods
Margarines	11
Light Duty Liquid Detergents	12
Laundry Detergents	7
Hair Tonics	6
Upset Stomach Remedies	12
Headache Remedies	11
Toilet Soaps	8
	67

The study took the form of a mathematical model, which can formally be described as a linear multiple correlation of four variables. It demonstrates mathematically the relationship between three marketing factors, which statistically are termed independent variables, and sales movement, which statistically is called the dependent variable.

Measures for one of the independent variables, the relative effectiveness of the commercials televised, were made during research sessions in the Schwerin theaters. Full-time theaters are operated in New York, London, Montreal and Toronto and sessions are often conducted in theaters in St. Louis, Chicago, San Francisco, Los Angeles and New Orleans.

Using the New York operation as an example (tests in other cities are conducted on the same basis), the theater audience—the population sample—is drawn from the ten metropolitan New York counties. Each sample is constructed through random selections from residential telephone listings. The average sample size used is 350 respondents.

This audience participates in simulations of real buying situations. The simulations are conducted both prior to the introduction of an advertising stimulus and following the stimulus. In the case of this study, all the advertising stimuli were in the form of television commercials.

At the beginning of a session, the respondents are led through a questionnaire that covers the usual facts on their demographic characteristics. At this time they are told that their prime purpose in attending is to express opinions on pilot films of possible future TV programs, on television commercials and also on the medium of television as a whole.

Before being exposed to any stimuli, the respondents are given an opportunity to win some prizes. They are told that there will be a drawing and the winner's prize will be a large supply of whichever brand was checked on a list of competing brands. Three such check lists are used. Since the possible prize is related to the brands selected, it inspires a truthful answer on the checklist. These checklists provide data for what is called a *pre-choice* measurement, indicating the proportionate predisposition of these respondents toward brands in certain product fields at the time they enter the theater.

APPRAISING COMMERCIALS

Next the audience watches a half-hour television show that has never been aired. Inserted in the customary fashion are commercials for one brand on each of the three checklists. Except when a client requests an appraisal of a specific program, the same show is repeated session after session, thus eliminating the possibility of a commercial having more compatibility with one show than another.

After viewing the show and the included commercials, and using identical checklists, brand choices are again elicited from the audience. The results this time are termed *post-choice* measurements.

These two measurements, *pre-choice* and *post-choice*, constitute the basis of the advertising variables that pertain to consumer preference, which have been introduced into the model.

Since every checklist encompasses brands within a homogeneous product field, and since a brand's pre-choice and post-choice measurements are expressed as a percentage of the selections of all brands on a given list, these two values may be recognized as measuring movements in *secondary demand*. They do not reflect increases or decreases in consumer demand for the product category as a whole—or what would be called change in *primary demand*.

The difference between these two measurements is termed *competitive preference*. It may be regarded as a predicted shift in a brand's share of favorable consumer attitudes under circumstances of no competitive advertising, which have been assumed for measuring purposes.

Obviously, it is unrealistic to assume that all advertising will be dropped by competitors, so the competitive-preference measurement has to be modified by the aggregate impact from advertising by other brands in the field.

Through the introduction of another value, the *product field norm*, the effect of competitive brands may be taken into account. The value of the product field norm is the arithmetical average of recent competitive preference scores of all brands in the field.

Subtracting the value of the "norm" from the competitive-preference score of the subject brand, the shift in a brand's share of consumer preference under actual market conditions may be forecast. This change in a brand's share of favorable consumer attitudes, which would be brought about by airing the test commercial, is termed *relative competitive preference*. Relative competitive preference is the first independent variable in the model.

The impact of relative competitive preference is on the proportion of consumers currently predisposed to a specific brand and not on the proportion of consumers that are now buying it. In order to demonstrate the sales outcome of different advertising creative strategies, a connection must by made between attitude and purchasing levels. Such a link has been devised through the differential between a brand's pre-choice percentage and its actual market share just prior to the research session. The difference between these two is called *momentum,* and this is the second independent variable in the model. A brand's momentum may be either negative or positive, depending on whether its sales share is above or below its pre-choice percentage.

Since relative competitive preference represents predicted movements in a brand's share of consumer predilections within a homogeneous product field, it is a measurement of the effect on secondary consumer demand. Because large portions of the advertising efforts of most companies are directed toward capturing as big a piece of a market as possible, rather than to expanding a market as a whole, this is the kind of demand most advertisers are especially interested in influencing.

At Schwerin it was decided that any reflection in sales of the effectiveness of secondary-demand advertising would most logically be in the form of sales-share movements between consecutive time periods. Arranging sales data in four-month time spans, market shares of individual brands, as well as changes in their shares, were derived. These period-to-period changes in each brand's market share have been adopted as the model's dependent variable.

The number of times that consumers have been exposed to any advertising message—whether it be powerful or weak—is another factor that should be considered when the influence of advertising on marketplace behavior is being assessed. Lacking complete statistics in terms of viewers, dollar expenditures for television advertising were used as the basis for an exposure measure. Each brand's share of the total spent on TV advertising by brands in its product field was determined, and changes in these shares for individual brands between measurement periods were calculated. Changes in TV-advertising expenditure shares have been introduced as the third independent variable, and it is the final one in this model at its present stage of development.

In order to understand the relationships among the four variables in detail, it is necessary initially to examine the dependent variables of sales-share change. Among the 67 measurement periods the range of sales-share is from a gain of 1.7 share points to a loss of 2.1 share points. There is a fairly even dispersion of individual sales-share changes through the array of 67 periods, with more than half a share point movement occurring during about 50 percent of the periods, while each of those periods in the remaining 50 percent have less than half a share point movement. One standard deviation of the sales-share changes has been computed as plus, or minus, 0.85 of a share point.

MEASURING VARIABLES

The first independent variable, relative competitive preference, measures the persuasive powers of one brand's commercials during a specific measurement period in comparison with the persuasive powers of its competitors' commercials. Among the 67 measurement periods, relative competitive preference has a range from plus 14 to minus 6.5, with about two-thirds of its values falling between plus two and minus two.

Plotting all 67 relative-competitive-preference measures on a graph opposite their respective sales-share-change values, it may be observed that a pattern of relationship exists between the two variables. In the upper right-hand quadrant there are 20 positive relative-competitive-preference values that are associated with increases in sales shares, while in the lower right-hand quadrant there are just ten positive relative-competitive-preference values that are associated with decreases in sales shares. Similarly, in the lower left-hand quadrant there are 25 negative relative-competitive-preference values for periods with losses in sales shares, but in the upper left-hand quadrant there are only 12 negative relative-competitive-preference values for periods experiencing gains in sales shares.

Computing a regression line of sales-share change on relative competitive preference, and the dispersion of sales-share changes around that line, it is found that the standard deviation of sales-share change from the regression line is plus, or minus, 0.78 of a share point. Since this standard deviation is less than the standard deviation of the sales-share change variable alone, which is 0.85 of a share point, a degree of mathematical correlation between these two variables has been shown across all seven product fields.

Higher degrees of correlation have been computed in separate analyses confined within each product field, and the final results are based on individual product field correlations. For illustrative purposes, the values for all seven fields have been shown here in one combined field graph.

When simple correlations between these two variables are computed separately in each of the seven fields, it is found that on the average 33 percent of all sales-share changes have been explained by their corresponding relative-competitive-preference values. Statisticians would recognize this as an average of the coefficients of determination (or r^2) for each product field.

The second independent variable, momentum, describes the extent that a brand's market share is lagging behind its share of favorable consumer attitudes. When its share of favorable consumer attitudes within its product field—as measured by its pre-choice percentage—is above its market share, there is a tendency for the brand to gain in share of market.

Conversely, when its share of favorable consumer attitudes is below its market share, there is a tendency for the brand to experience a loss in share of market. Among the 67 measurement periods, momentum has a range from plus 11.3 to minus 9.8. About 40 percent of the momentum values lie between plus two and minus two.

Plotting all 67 momentum measures on a graph opposite their respective sales-share-change values, a relationship between these two variables becomes apparent visually. In the upper right-hand quadrant there are 22 positive momentum values that are associated with increases in sales shares, in contrast to 11 positive momentum values in the lower right-hand quadrant that are associated with decreases in sales shares. In the lower left-hand quadrant there are 24 negative momentum values for periods with losses in sales shares, but in the upper left-hand quadrant there are only ten negative momentum values for periods during which a brand's sales-share increased.

Computing a regression line of sales-share change on momentum, and the dispersion of sales-share changes around that line, it is found that the standard deviation of sales-share change from the regression line is plus, or minus, 0.77 of a share point. As in the case of the combined-field correlation of relative competitive preference with sales-share change, the standard deviation about the regression line is less than the standard deviation of the sales-share-change variable alone. Again, a significant degree of mathematical correlation has been shown across all seven product fields between these two variables, and the degree of correlation happens to be quite close to that discovered for relative competitive preference.

COMPUTING THE CHANGES

When correlations are computed separately within each product field, 34 percent of the sales-share changes are found on the average to be explained by the corresponding momentum values. In statistical terms, this percentage is an average of the coefficients of determination (r^2) that have been computed within each product field.

The third independent variable, TV-advertising-expenditure-share change, is an approximate measure of the period-to-period variation in the exposure on television of one brand's commercials in comparison with the exposure of commercials by other brands in its field. Among the 67 measurement periods, it has a range from plus 15.7 share points to minus 7.3. Forty percent of the expenditure-share-change values lie between plus two and minus two.

When all of the 67 expenditure-share-change values are placed on a graph opposite their respective sales-share-change values, a mild relationship may be noticed, but it depends entirely on the sizes of the changes in the expenditure proportions. Merely counting the numbers of plotted points in the four quadrants, there appears to be a lack of relationship between the two variables. In the upper right-hand quadrant, where expenditure shares were increased, there were 17 periods experiencing a sales-share gain. In the lower right-hand quadrant, where expenditure shares were also increased, there were 20 periods having a decrease in sales shares. Similarly, there were 15 plotted points in each of the two left-hand quadrants, indicating that as many periods had sales-share gains as declines when expenditure shares were decreased.

When a regression line of sales-share change on TV-expenditure-share change is computed, it is found that the dispersion of sales-share change around that line is plus, or minus, 0.83 of a share point. This is only very slightly less than the standard deviation of the sales-share variable alone, so a high degree of correlation has not been discovered across all seven fields.

An average of separate correlations within each product field between TV-expenditure-share change and sales-share change was computed at 18 percent. This percentage in statistical terms is an average of the coefficients of determination (r^2) that were computed within each product field.

When the three independent variables are taken together in a multiple regression formula, they offer in combination an astonishing average explanation of sales-share movements in the seven product fields of 73 percent (R^2). Momentum and relative competitive preference still remain as the most important of the three variables, contributing 34 percent and 31 percent, respectively. The contribution of TV-advertising expenditure-share change was relatively minor at 8 percent.

The goal of this study was to provide management with a system for estimating the probable sales effect of two variables directly controlled by management—TV-advertising expenditures and relative competitive preference—and a third variable, which is in part a derivative of them—momentum.

Having established the relative importance of these three variables from historical observations, values for these variables can now be multiplied by their derived weights. When the products are added together with a small statistical constant for the product field, they yield an estimate of sales-share change. This estimate has a known degree of probability of being within certain tolerances. Knowing the values of the variables for a brand at any point in time, it is possible to forecast its sales movement into the ensuing sales period.

To illustrate the relationship that has been found, pick a point in the past for which the values are known, then estimate sales behavior for the following period and match the estimate to actual sales results. Here is how it worked out in the margarine field, where observations were available for five brands during 11 four-month periods.

The historical examination of the 11 campaigns showed that TV expenditures explained 7 percent of the sales change in a simple correlation. Another 26 percent explanation was added by relative competitive preference, and momentum added 42 percent.

When these variables were analyzed together, they remained in the same rank order, but the contributions of each were: momentum, plus 41 percent; relative competitive preference, plus 27 percent; and expenditures, minus 2 percent. In this particular field the advertisers tended to increase their expenditures when they had ineffective commercials and/or negative momentum, so the expenditure contribution became negative.

The model faithfully estimated the correct direction of the sales-share change in ten of the 11 periods. In campaign E1, the model computed a slight loss of 0.2 points, and it actually had a gain of 0.3 points.

But more important is the degree of accuracy of the estimates. The average sales-share change in this field was plus, or minus, 0.64 sales-share points. Since this is average movement, about half of the cases should fall outside this, if it were used as an estimating method. However, when 0.64 is used as a tolerance around these estimates, nine of the cases were within and only two were outside of it. On the average, the model deviated from the actual sales share change by 0.42, or less than half a sales-share point.

In summary, the model predicted the right direction in 91 percent of the cases, and 82 percent of the predictions fell within the average sales-share movement of the margarine-product field.

FINAL RESULTS

Following the same procedure for the other six product fields, the results were as follows:

In the light-duty-detergent field, all of the estimates fell within the estimating tolerance (the average sales-share change in that field), with an average difference between estimated and actual sales-share change of 0.4 of a share point.

In the seven cases from the laundry detergent field, six out of the seven fell within the tolerance, with an average difference of 0.2 of a share point.

For the six cases in the hair-tonic field, all fell within the tolerance. The average difference was about 0.2 of a point.

Eleven of the 12 stomach-remedy cases were within the estimating tolerance, showing an average difference between the forecast and actual sales-share change of 0.2 of a share point.

In the headache-remedy field, where actual sales-share change was only plus or minus 0.32 of a point, eight of the 11 cases fell within the tolerance, the average difference being 0.26 of a share point.

In the toilet-soap field, where the average sales-share change was more than one point, eight cases fell within the tolerance, with an average difference of about 0.4 of a share point.

In total, 60 of the 67 cases (90 percent) of the forecasts fell within the estimating tolerance. Using average sales movement alone, approximately 50 percent should be expected to be within this range. In 61 out of the 67 cases (91 percent), the direction was correctly predicted. These 90 percent results, when by average movement alone about 50 percent would be the case, means that the formula increased the accuracy of estimating by 80 percent.

SCHWERIN RESEARCH TERMS—AND WHAT THEY MEAN

Pre-Choice

The proportion of consumers predisposed to a specific brand at the time a test is being conducted in one of the Schwerin theaters. It is affected by the cumulative pressures of all previous marketing influences exerted for, or against, a particular brand. Included are such factors as promotional activities, packaging, product quality image, extent of distribution, personal salesmanship and the advertising strategies pursued up to that time.

Post-Choice

The proportion of consumers who would prefer a certain brand at some time in the future. This measure is also determined in the test theater after the audience has been exposed to a test commercial. It assumes for testing purposes that all competitive advertising has been discontinued.

Competitive Preference

This is the difference between the pre-choice and post-choice percentages. It is a prediction of the shift in a brand's share of consumer attitudes, either up or down, under the assumed condition of no competitive advertising.

Product Field Norm

This value indicates the average size of competitive preference for all brands in a homogenous product group. It is the mean average of recent competitive preference scores of all brands in a specific field, as determined by Schwerin Research in test theaters.

Relative Competitive Preference

This value is the difference between the competitive preference score for a specific brand and the product field norm. It measures the shift in a brand's share of consumer preferences under market-place conditions. It reflects the proportion of those currently predisposed to a specific brand and not those currently buying that brand. When negative, the brand's share of favorable consumer attitudes will shrink if the subject commercial is used, indicating a rather ineffective commercial. When positive, the reverse is true. This is the first independent variable in this mathematical model.

Momentum

This measure is a link between those predisposed to a brand and those who are buying it. The value is the difference between the brand's pre-choice percentage and the brand's share of the total market just prior to the research session. When its pre-choice is greater than its market share, the momentum is positive, and there is a tendency for the brand to achieve a sales-share gain. When its pre-choice is below its market share, momentum is negative, and there is a tendency for the brand's sales share to decline. This is the second independent variable in this model.

Advertising Share Movements

Television advertising investments by brand are arranged in four-month time periods. Each brand's share of the total expenditure and period-to-period movements are determined. This is introduced into the mathematical model as the final independent variable.

Sales-Share Movements

Sales data within a homogenous field are arranged by brand in four- or six-month time spans. Each brand's share of the total market and the changes in share of market between sales period are calculated. This is the dependent variable in the model.

Primary Demand

This term concerns the total demand for all brands in a product field. When primary demand is increased, the total number of users of a product is increased.

Secondary Demand

This term refers to the demand for one brand over another within a product field. A shift in secondary demand alone will result in a change in one brand's share of the market, but it will not change the total demand for the particular kind of product.

37. Practical media models—what must they look like?

WILLIAM T. MORAN

What is a practical media model? That's easy. It's one that works!

What must practical media models *look* like? . . . There we start running into trouble. Suddenly nobody's talking . . . suddenly there are secrets worth keeping.

Let's try to take a look anyway . . . a look at this semi-secretive development which seems to have materialized, full-grown, on the advertising scene.

What's happened? How can we account for this burst of progress? Is it due to the high speed of computers? Is it because mathematicians have invaded the sanctum of the social statisticians?

No, it's something else.

PRINCIPLE VS. FACT

Advertising research has broken out of its fact-finding prison. It's on the loose and it's threatening . . . looking right down the throat of the business process. It's getting inside, describing how business decisions are made—and how they *should* be made.

Fact-finding is not enough. Facts must be fitted together by the development of principles . . . models . . . in this case, models of profitable decision-making, models about how does advertising work, anyway?

Why isn't fact-finding enough in itself? Einstein had a word on this subject. "As long as the principles capable of serving as starting points for the deduction remain undiscovered," he said, "the individual fact is of

Reprinted from *Proceedings,* 8th Annual Conference, Advertising Research Foundation. © Advertising Research Foundation, 1962.

no use to the theorist." To us it means: without a governing theory or concept the analysis of data is doomed to sterility. *Here* is the explanation for what has begun to emancipate advertising research. *Here* is a reason why some media decision models are practical and others are not. Keep this point in mind as our story unfolds.

To illustrate, a few years ago a scientist at Los Alamos designed a model of the game of chess and programmed it on a large computer, enabling the computer to compete with human opponents. The computer was given the rules of play and some fairly straightforward points of strategy. Due to its speed and memory capacity it was able to scan all possible combinations of moves two moves ahead, and to assess the likely consequences of each possible move—a prodigious feat which no human could approach, as there are 360,000 possible combinations. Yet, although it played a pretty mean game, top-flight chess players could beat it fairly regularly.

Another model of chess was readied on another computer. This model allowed the computer to consider only a random 2,500 out of the 360,000 combinations, but it incorporated a more complex and sophisticated set of decision rules or playing strategy. When pitted against each other, machine versus machine, the second chess model with fewer facts and more sophisticated rules wins hands down!

Today we are studying the marketing process, describing it, and building models of it. These models, the decision rules by which business operates, provide us with a mathematical fluoroscope. With this dynamic fluoroscope advertising research need no longer study still pictures of outside symptoms. It can look right inside and see the system working and moving.

But this inner vision is not all there is to our fluoroscope. Because it is dynamic it can look ahead (or behind) in time. And better yet, it permits us to play the creative game of "What if . . . ?" "What would happen if we changed the rate of heart beat; or fed the system more sugar; or circulated more blood to the brain; or cut out the fat in the front office? . . . What if . . . ?"

And the fluoroscope provides answers at no risk to the real corporate body. What an opportunity to try out creative ideas! What an advantage to the creative mind! What a threat to the rigid, formula thinker!

THE SEARCH FOR THE UNDERLYING PRINCIPLE

When will the computer successfully invade media planning? Not until there are practical media models . . . not until we have models which reproduce those subtle considerations which occur to top-flight media planners. The issue has nothing to do with "what computer d'ya buy?" In business even more than in chess it is not enough merely to scan a million facts in an instant. Successful enterprise is not the proliferation of a thousand tireless clerks. (Perhaps those other great chess players on the steppes to the east of us have known that principle all along, while we have been admiring the encyclopedia and the quiz show.) Successful enterprise—and successful models—are built on sound and imaginative judgment . . . in other words, on good decision principles.

So step number one in building a practical media model is to find the underlying allocation principle . . . the keystone decision rule . . . upon which to build the great structure of the model. It cannot be a rigid rule-of-thumb. It must be broad and all-inclusive.

For example, consider this simple illustration.

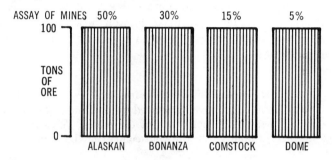

Greedy Goldmine Company—Cost of Mining Ore $100 Ton—Operating Capital $15,000
© Research Department, Young & Rubicam, Inc.

Here we have the Greedy Gold Mining Company. It owns four gold mine claims (Alaskan, Bonanza, Comstock and Dome) . . . and limited capital resources: $15,000 operating capital. At $100 per ton for digging ore, it had a problem deciding how best to allocate its resources. One

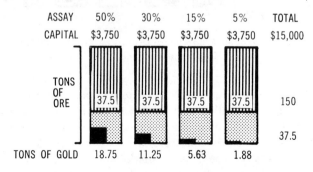

Allocation Decision Model—Broad Dispersion Principle
© Research Department, Young & Rubicam, Inc.

of the officers of the company had been in the business a long time and cherished the firm belief, based on his experienced judgment, that "gold is where you find it." On those grounds, he quickly advocated the *Broad Dispersion* allocation principle.

By spending at an equal rate against all mines, $3,750 per mine, he would get 37.5 tons of ore out of each mine. As it later turns out, the ore in the Alaskan mine is 50 percent gold, so he would have gotten almost 19 tons of gold. The other mines, having less rich ore would produce less gold; and his total return would have come to 37.5 tons of gold. (At $35 per ounce for gold he wouldn't have to care about the efficiency of his operation. Too bad it's only a hypothetical case!)

Now, there was another fellow in the company of a more painstaking turn of mind. He had no experience out in the field, but he was a pretty fair bookkeeper. When he could make himself heard, he suggested another way of doing it, one which appealed to him as having a great sense of orderliness about it.

He said,

First, let's do some research. Let's draw a sample of ore from each consumer segment—I mean, mine—and have it assayed to determine the proportion of prospects—oops, I mean *gold*—from each of the mines. Then we can expend our money in direct proportion to the gold content of the mines and increase our payoff.

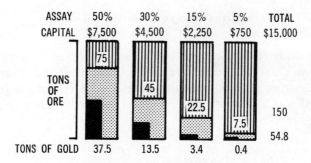

Allocation Decision Model—Proportional Dispersion Principle (Profit-Matching)
© Research Department, Young & Rubicam, Inc.

He called his decision system the *Proportional Dispersion Principle.*

As you can see, by allocating capital in proportion to the gold content of the mines—that is, by profile matching—he would increase the payoff substantially . . . to 54 tons of gold! You may think that on these grounds the company would have made him Research Director, but they didn't. As a matter of fact, he went on to become the financial officer, for very good reason, too. Because whatever his system lacked in aggressive, competitive exploitation it made up in conservative caution.

A third fellow came up with yet another decision model which has a lot more to do with the real world of gold mining. Making use of the very same facts as the previous fellow, he suggested that they spend *as much money as they could* exploiting the mine with the highest assay; then, with the remaining capital, on to the one with the next highest assay, and so forth, until they ran out of operating capital.

You can see from the payoff (65 tons of gold) that the HIGH ASSAY PRINCIPLE * is the one we have been looking for! Here we have the foundation principle for more profitable enterprise. And, by substituting consumer segments (and media audiences) for the mines, we have the basis of the decision rules for practical media models.

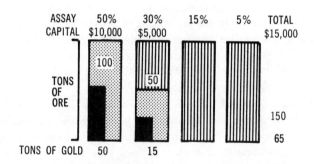

Allocation Decision Model—*High Assay Principle—*TM
© Research Department, Young & Rubicam, Inc.

This principle is familiar to all of us. After all, when introducing a new product, we are pretty careful to gain distribution in the high volume outlets before we move on to the Mom 'n Pops. And, similarly, industrial advertisers who use specialized media are utilizing the HIGH ASSAY PRINCIPLE * in part.

So far, this sounds like a ready-made problem for a linear programming model. What are we waiting for? Let's get our electronic shovels and start digging! . . . but wait a minute. Is it really as easy as all that? I wish it were. As soon as we start rushing out to do it, we bump right into some real world considerations which we failed to mention in the gold mining example. How do we know ahead of time how much money can profitably be spent in the highest assay mine? In reality, mines are not all of the same depth. We have to know how deep each mine is, the rates at which the cost of mining increases and how the assay declines as the mine is increasingly exploited. Unless we know these factors we cannot determine how much money should be allocated to the richest mine

* Trademark

and how much applied against the next mine. There is the danger of not spending enough to exploit the mine (or to make the sale) and there is also the danger of allocating too much and wasting money which could better be spent elsewhere.

A practical media model *must* be founded on the HIGH ASSAY PRINCIPLE.* It, therefore, must make provision for handling information about the depth of potential, the effectiveness of an advertising exposure, the change in effect with changes in frequency, and those other dynamic functions of the advertising process which critically influence the selection of an optimum media schedule.

For example, two brands, one with a 25 percent share of market and the other with a 65 percent share—even if everything else about their markets and copy performance were identical to each other—should not allocate their advertising dollars in the same way, now should they? It won't work the same way for each . . . a difference between two products in the length of the *purchase cycles* has logical and demonstrable consequences in the way their advertising dollars should be spent. And different *brand switching rates* call for different media strategies; this is the familiar "leaky bucket" analogy.

Our idealized, sophisticated media planner takes these dynamic functions into account . . . so must a practical media model. There must be, so to speak, a dial on the computer, representing each one of these critical functions so that their values can be set and their logical interrelationships given to the computer as part of its decision rules.

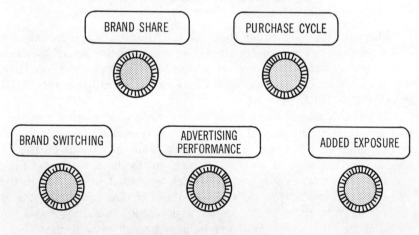

BORROWING A MODEL

Because we like to avoid hard work as much as anyone, when we took our first cut at the problem early in 1959, we hunted through the

* Trademark

handbook of ready-made models for one that could be adapted to the media allocation decision rules. Among the existing techniques, linear programming seemed to be the one which best fit our decision problem. The Y&R adaptation of linear programming to media allocation appeared in Miller and Starr's book, *Executive Decisions and Operations Research*, written in 1959 and published by Prentice-Hall in 1960.

While this model qualified at the time as an interesting technical achievement, we soon had to face the realities of practical application. Linear programming was designed to reflect the decision rules of production and transportation scheduling. The analogy to media scheduling, as a consequence, is more apparent than real. For example, there is no way linear programming can incorporate the critical dynamic functions mentioned earlier or cope satisfactorily with audience duplication between media.

DESIGNING A MODEL

Obviously, we gave up the search for ready-mix models. Models designed for the decision problems of factory production scheduling or transportation scheduling *sound* like close analogies to media scheduling, but they are not. So, two years ago it was "back to the old drawing board" . . . we were going to have to do it the hard way. As you can imagine, this was a very difficult decision. Nonetheless, we felt we had no choice.

We deliberately set ourselves back two years and set about building a media model from scratch, one which faithfully reflects our best understanding of real world decision rules. The result of these efforts is what we call our HIGH ASSAY MEDIA MODEL.*

This chart schematically portrays what goes on. As you can see, the process is comprised of the usual major components: the Data Input and the Decision System. The Data Input consists of three categories: Consumer-Product Behavior, Consumer-Media Behavior and Consumer-Advertising Behavior. These are familiar categories, but within them you will notice that there is provision for those critical factors, *the dynamic brand functions*, without which the HIGH ASSAY PRINCIPLE * cannot be applied . . . brand share, switching probabilities, purchase rate, audience duplication, effect of multiple exposures, etc. . . . *dynamic data*. Each of these factors is like a dial on the computer which can be set to the appropriate value. The dynamic data tell us how deep the various consumer mines are, what it costs us to keep digging, and how much gold we will be able to get.

Now, given these data, our Decision System can go to work and

* Trademark

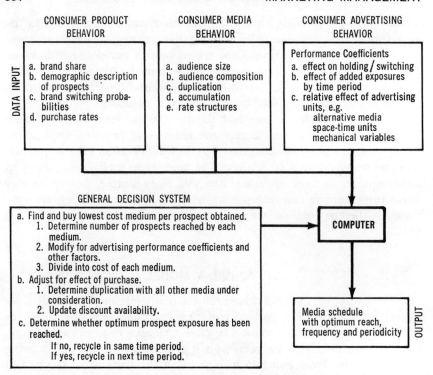

CONSUMER PRODUCT BEHAVIOR

DATA INPUT

a. brand share
b. demographic description of prospects
c. brand switching probabilities
d. purchase rates

CONSUMER MEDIA BEHAVIOR

a. audience size
b. audience composition
c. duplication
d. accumulation
e. rate structures

CONSUMER ADVERTISING BEHAVIOR

Performance Coefficients
a. effect on holding / switching
b. effect of added exposures by time period
c. relative effect of advertising units, e.g.
   alternative media
   space-time units
   mechanical variables

GENERAL DECISION SYSTEM

a. Find and buy lowest cost medium per prospect obtained.
   1. Determine number of prospects reached by each medium.
   2. Modify for advertising performance coefficients and other factors.
   3. Divide into cost of each medium.
b. Adjust for effect of purchase.
   1. Determine duplication with all other media under consideration.
   2. Update discount availability.
c. Determine whether optimum prospect exposure has been reached.
      If no, recycle in same time period.
      If yes, recycle in next time period.

COMPUTER

Media schedule with optimum reach, frequency and periodicity

OUTPUT

Y & R's High Assay Media Model

invest our capital for maximum payoff. Let's take a close look at how the heart or, better yet, the mind of the model works.

The model buys periodically; the periods can be of any duration—we generally use one week. First, all the data are scanned to find and buy the lowest cost medium per prospect obtained. To find this medium the computer scans the prospect and audience data to determine the number of prospects reached by each medium. The computer then modifies these data to incorporate intuitive judgments (or facts, where we have them) on the influence of editorial climate, mechanical features such as color or motion, different space or time units and on copy effectiveness. The result of this computation is then divided into the cost of each medium.

The computer then purchases one unit of the best medium. It then must adjust the facts about all the media in order to reflect the effect of having made a purchase. Duplication of audiences between the one purchased and all the others is determined, and discount availabilities are updated.

Having adjusted for the effect of that purchase, the computer then determines the extent to which that buy has crept up on the optimum advertising exposure rate for that brand. Quite a number of factors are involved in this computation: the number of customers and non-customer prospects in the population, the switching rates, the purchase cycle, the copy effectiveness . . . in effect, all the dynamic marketing and advertising functions . . . and, of course, any budgetary limitations.

These are the functions which enable us to tell when to stop digging in one mine and move on to the next. If optimum prospect exposure has not been reached, the computer recycles in the same time period to make another buy. If it has, it moves on to the next time period, always minimizing the average cost per customer obtained (our criterion function).

The end product is a recommended media schedule which the computer prints out . . . what an intricate path from problem to schedule! Our ideal media planner is quite a guy, isn't he? In effect, we have carefully recorded the thinking processes and considerations of this tireless genius.

The capability of practical media allocation by computer exists today. We all know, however, that this model is no less dependent upon good data than is any human decision maker. And much necessary data are lacking. Let's digress a moment to look at the condition of the data problem.

THE DATA PROBLEM

Consumer-Product and Media Behavior data have long been accumulated. But even in these areas there is much more missing than available. For that reason we were forced to build a second model—one that is peripheral to the Decision Model—to supply estimates of missing data, to stretch the balance in our data banks.

This DATA BREEDER MODEL * is an 18,000 sample simulation of consumer behavior which has been developed by Y&R. It has been programmed on our general purpose Remington Rand Univac computer because it has a memory capacity of over 25 million digits. It was accomplished with the active cooperation and generous programming assistance of the professional staff of the Remington Rand System Design and Application Group in Philadelphia. And this Y&R DATA BREEDER MODEL * will be made available by Remington Rand to those who wish to make use of it with their own data banks.

Although not itself a decision model, this is a very useful type of model for providing data input to a decision model or for analyzing certain aspects of existing media schedules. (At another panel session we will see a case history demonstration of how such a data model can be used directly to perform certain kinds of comparisons of existing media schedules.)

And, of course, virtually nothing is known about our third category

* Trademark

of data input, Consumer-Advertising Behavior . . . e.g., the effect on advertising performance of one medium *versus* another; different time and space units, varying frequency patterns and, most important, the effect of your competitor's schedule.

Much will be done in this area as advanced decision models erase the false line of demarcation between media and copy research. Meanwhile, there are some tricks as imaginative as the DATA BREEDER * for estimating these values. We will get to them in a few minutes, but first, let us get back to operating the decision model itself.

PUTTING THE MODEL TO WORK

In order to put the DYNAMIC HIGH ASSAY MODEL * into actual day-to-day use, Y&R has obtained a second electronic computer. This one is a special purpose scientific computer for the Research Department to use in the further development of our media model and our other models (e.g., our NATURAL SALES PROJECTION MODEL * and a model for new product development decisions). This second computer is an IBM 1620 and, I want to say, the IBM people were of great help in getting our program de-bugged and operational in record time. Possession of the Univac and the 1620 gives us both enormous capacity and great flexibility. Of course, the important issue is never the computer itself . . . it is the mathematical models which we design for it.

There is enormous capacity for growth in this sophisticated HIGH ASSAY MODEL * due to its provision for the relevant dynamic functions. In fact, few advertisers know enough about the dynamic marketing and advertising characteristics of their brands to take immediate advantage of all the model's capabilities. No matter . . . the dials are there to be used when data or worthwhile judgments are available. Meanwhile, all that has to be done is to set the unused dials on "Neutral" and the model will produce the best recommendation possible under conditions of limited information. The important fact is that the relevant conditions can and *must* be specified.

It is surprising, and sometimes embarrassing, how important an unspecified condition can be. During World War II a major shipbuilder in one of our southern ports built a dozen ships of a new design. They were special-purpose ships, to perform under *certain specified conditions*. By working on the ships simultaneously, they were able to float them all at about the same time.

One day, as the vessels rode at anchor, the Bureau of Ships came to inspect them. You know how those desk sailors conducted formal inspections—sort of like a car buyer kicking the tires. They went through the first ship looking for dust and trying out the light switches. Then they

* Trademark

went below to inspect the "head." Naturally, our tire kicker had to try out the flushing . . . fortunately, they all made it to the launch just in time to see our ship go to the bottom. A critical but unspecified condition had been overlooked and someone built the "heads" below the waterline!

Many conditions—less well understood than they should be—are critical to practical media decisions. Since in reality they are critical, we cannot make them disappear by designing models which ignore them. To demonstrate the influence of some of these conditions, let's get away from the abstract and look at an actual case study which we conducted on a product about which we have quite a bit of information.

Brand "Y" Case Study

LIST OF MEDIA   • AUDIENCE   (AGE, SEX, INCOME, RESIDENCE)
                        • RATE STRUCTURE
                        • MEDIUM PERFORMANCE INDEX
                        • UNIT PERFORMANCE INDEX

American Home	Saturday Evening Post	General Drama	1 hr.
Better Homes & Gardens	Reader's Digest	Western	$\frac{1}{2}$ hr.
House Beautiful	TV Guide	Western	1 hr.
Family Circle	American Weekly	Western	1 hr.
Woman's Day	Parade	Western	1 hr.
Good Housekeeping	This Week	Suspense Drama	$\frac{1}{2}$ hr.
Ladies' Home Journal	Family Weekly	Situation Comedy	$\frac{1}{2}$ hr.
McCall's	Sunday	Situation Comedy	$\frac{1}{2}$ hr.
Cosmopolitan	Catholic Digest	Situation Comedy	$\frac{1}{2}$ hr.
Parents'	Presbyterian Life	Situation Comedy	$\frac{1}{2}$ hr.
Redbook	Together	Children's	$\frac{1}{2}$ hr.
True Story	Newsweek	Children's	$\frac{1}{2}$ hr.
Life	Time	Quiz Panel	$\frac{1}{2}$ hr.
Look	Holiday	Comedy Variety	1 hr.
		Mystery Drama	1 hr.
		Adventure	1 hr.
		General Variety	1 hr.

Source: © Research Department, Young & Rubicam, Inc.

Here is the list of media which was given to the computer to consider, along with the rate structures, the audiences, and advertising performance characteristics of the media (details of which are omitted in the interest of public safety).

Naturally, the product also is masquerading today as the relatively unknown Brand "Y." In this case the only media units under consideration were four-color pages for print and one-minute commercials.

This next chart contains a condensed version of the performance characteristics of the brand.

Brand "Y" Case Study

PERFORMANCE CHARACTERISTICS

	AGE	SEX	INCOME	RESIDENCE
	Under 30 : 19-45	Male : 0	Upper : 13-50	Metro : 13-58
	30-54 : 26-46	Female : 13-58	Middle : 22-31	Non-Metro : 24-50
	55 & over : 13-58		Low : 31-46	

Prospect Probability

Purchase Cycle : 6 Weeks

Over-All Brand Share : 20%

Repeat Purchase Probability : 68%

ADVERTISING

Probable "Switch Froms" Who Are Held : 1.2-2.3%

"Switch To's" (Proportion of exposed Non-Customers) : 0.8-3.0%

Multiple Exposure Coefficient : 0.5

Source: © Research Department, Young & Rubicam, Inc.

The prospect probability information was obtained in this case from the Y&R Consumer Poll. Similar information could be obtained, of course, from a number of research sources. The probabilities are shown here as ranges, e.g., 19 percent to 45 percent for people under 30 years of age. The reason for the ranges is to keep from filling up the chart with all the specific combinations which were given the computer, e.g., under 30, female, middle income, living in a metropolitan area, etc. for every one of the possibilities.

The average purchase cycle is six weeks. If seasonality were a factor, it could have been introduced. The brand share information was actually given individually for each demographic segment, not just the national average. Then we gave the computer the repeat purchase and switching dynamics of the brand and its advertising. Now let's look at the next chart and see what the computer bought.

BRAND "Y" SCHEDULE #1

DYNAMIC CONDITIONS
ACTUAL

MEDIA	1	2	3	4	5	6	7	8	9	10	11	12	13	TOTAL	Insertions/Minutes
					TIME PERIOD (Weeks)										
LIFE	■		■				■			■					4
READER'S DIGEST					■				■						2
PARADE	■		■				■			■					4
THIS WEEK	■		■	■		■		■		■		■			7
HALF-HOUR SITUATION COMEDY #1			■	■			■	■			■	■			6
ONE HOUR WESTERN				■	■				■						3
Total Audience Index	108	36	93	142	101	79	101	81	153	79	101	142	81		100
Cost/customer Obtained Index	67	71	52	75	98	84	126	146	140	87	125	146	82		100

Annual Budget $4,000,000

High Assay Allocation*—*Trademark
© Research Department, Young & Rubicam, Inc.

To keep things a little easier to see we are showing only a thirteen-week segment of the year's schedule. The $4 million figure at the bottom right is the budget for the entire year.

You will notice that the right hand column indicates the total insertions bought in each medium. If we were doing this thirteen-week period with a linear programming model, it would have picked different media and, in addition, it would only have given the total insertions. It would not have indicated how these insertions should be spaced from week to week.

The HIGH ASSAY MODEL,* on the other hand, indicates that the four insertions in *Life Magazine* should occur in the first, fourth, ninth and twelfth weeks in order to maximize the effect of the advertising. Insertion periods for all the other buys are similarly indicated. (I need not mention that it is corporate television properties which permit the spacing of broadcast insertions shown.)

The effect is not the result of artificial and arbitrary constraints placed on the operation of the model. It is the result of the computer's own computations involving the dynamics of this particular brand.

The bottom two rows indicate additional information. Although we show them here as indices, the absolute numbers are actually obtained. The Total Audience and the Cost per Customer Obtained enable us to compare alternative schedules in terms of dollar cost efficiency.

But what would happen if the specified dynamic conditions changed? Our sophisticated media planner would take these changes into account. Will the HIGH ASSAY MODEL? * The next chart shows what would happen if Brand Y had a shorter purchase cycle.

First of all, you notice a change in the media selected. I should caution you that the particular media selected as a result of the change reflect the composition and behavior of the prospects for this particular brand. The same change might produce the opposite result for another brand.

But the most significant result of the change in the dynamic conditions is in the spacing of the insertions from week to week. If you look at the next-to-bottom row, you can see how the total audience reached varies. As you can see, there is a pulsing effect which builds up to a peak in the tenth week. This is due to the complex interaction of all the dynamic functions and the efforts of the model to maximize the effective use of the advertising resources.

This tactical weapon—pulsing the advertising—depicts a planning concept beyond simple advertising frequency. We call it *periodicity*. It is called for under certain dynamic conditions. A simple example of one of them would be in the case of a brand whose budget is of a size that if it

* Trademark

DYNAMIC CONDITIONS

SHORTER PURCHASE CYCLE

BRAND "Y" SCHEDULE #2

MEDIA	TIME PERIOD (Weeks)													TOTAL Insertions/Minutes
	1	2	3	4	5	6	7	8	9	10	11	12	13	
LIFE			■							■				2
READER'S DIGEST	□			■				■					■	4
HALF-HOUR SITUATION COMEDY #1		■	■		■	■		■		■	■			9
ONE HOUR WESTERN	■			■				■		■	■			5
Total Audience Index	155	52	124	116	92	52	52	116	92	187	116	52	92	100
Cost/customer Obtained Index	74	63	103	92	63	91	88	102	84	190	182	82	87	100

Annual Budget $4,000,000

were spread like butter—evenly across the year—it would always fall just short of tripping sales. In such an extreme case the entire budget would largely go to waste. By pulsing the advertising, it periodically gets up over the lip and into the range of optimum effectiveness. Purchase cycle, copy performance, the value of added exposures . . . all affect optimum periodicity.

And a change in Brand Y's copy strategy also might alter the most efficient media schedule. For example, if the copy were changed to be more effective at holding present customers at the expense of its *aggressive* effectiveness, the following change would occur in the recommended schedule.

These examples dramatize the importance of the dynamic functions.

DYNAMIC CONDITIONS
COPY PERFORMANCE
CHANGED:
MORE DEFENSIVE

BRAND "Y" SCHEDULE #3

MEDIA	TIME PERIOD (Weeks)													TOTAL Insertions/ Minutes
	1	2	3	4	5	6	7	8	9	10	11	12	13	
FAMILY CIRCLE				■				■				■		3
GOOD HOUSEKPG.				■				■				■		3
LIFE	■				■	■				■		■	■	6
HALF-HOUR SITUATION COMEDY #1	■	■	■			■	■	■	■	■		■		10
HALF-HOUR SITUATION COMEDY #2		■			■				■	■		■		5
Total Audience Index	109	93	46	70	109	109	46	123	93	155	46	185	109	100
Cost/customer Obtained Index	79	75	71	96	101	109	79	142	73	152	89	123	107	100

Annual Budget $4,000,000

High Assay Allocation*—*Trademark
© Research Department, Young & Rubicam, Inc.

And they show that a sophisticated model such as the HIGH ASSAY MODEL * can be used to teach *us* a thing or two about advertising.

In advertising, as in gold mining, some planners try to make one rule-of-thumb fit all cases. It won't work . . . at least not if you want maximum profits. If the mines are shallow and if every additional shovelful costs quite a bit more than the one before, then the Broad Dispersion Principle is appropriate. If the opposite is true, then the most profitable course of action is to concentrate entirely on the first mine.

According to the particular *dynamics* of the individual case, our sophisticated HIGH ASSAY MODEL * will adopt either course of action . . . or, as is most often the case, one somewhere between these extremes.

* Trademark

Proportional Dispersion or "profile-matching," of course, is one possible in-between allocation which has been a popular system. As a rule-of-thumb, it can be demonstrated that profile-matching makes sense only under conditions of a *no-information* strategy contest. Thus, it can properly be labeled the "ignorance" system. Its only virtue is that in addition to minimizing possible gains it also minimizes possible losses. It is the "safe play" for contented brands . . . safe, that is, *unless* your competitor is *not* competing under conditions of equal ignorance. That may have been a safe assumption in the past (although it really hasn't, as we have all seen the insurgent brand which employed an outrageous formula and swept over entrenched competition).

Today, in an age of HIGH ASSAY ALLOCATION * it is no longer safe to assume equal ignorance on the part of your competitor. Some fantastic things are going to happen!

UNMASKING INTUITIVE VALUES

Even with limited input data the HIGH ASSAY MODEL * provides us with a great tool for experimentation. It can be used, for example, to determine what is worth arguing about in the case of any given brand. By changing the dial settings, in effect, on each of the dynamic functions and observing whether or not there is any substantial change in the recommended schedule, we can quickly establish what is and what isn't important to that brand. By eliminating the *insensitive* functions from further argument, we concentrate professional judgment and product group debate where it counts.

Thus, "sensitivity testing" can save needless argument. With it the computer can enlighten us on aspects of the advertising process which are too complex to think through alone.

It will be some time yet before we use the computer to make complete recommendations as standard practice. We have a great deal of learning to do, and so does the model. But it can learn awesomely fast, especially the way we are using it.

Consider this exciting use of our model . . . look back at this schematic chart for a moment.

Instead of using the model in the standard fashion—that is, putting the Input Data and the Decision System through the computer to generate the Output (a recommended media schedule)—we run it *backward.* We take two recommended schedules for a brand—one *you* suggest and one *he* suggests—put them in at the Output end, run the model backward . . . and solve for the intuitive values which underlie your recommendations.

Thus, we can unmask the hidden intuitions which lie behind *your* recommendations and *his.* This use of such a sophisticated model has

* Trademark

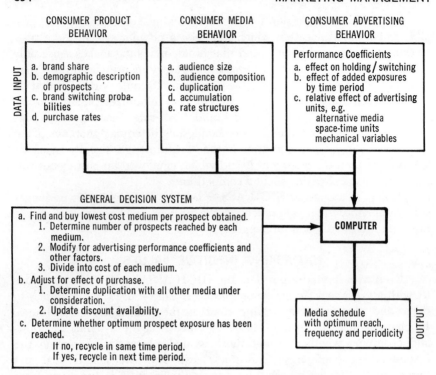

Y & R's High Assay Media Model

frightening implications, as you can see. But it will serve us well until the day we have good objective data on the dynamic advertising functions.

In this fashion, the HIGH ASSAY MEDIA MODEL * can be used to study and learn from the top media minds in the country, identify their intuitive feelings about the most subtle aspects of advertising, and then turn around and use this knowledge on the next problem. In a sense, the HIGH ASSAY MEDIA MODEL * studies the minds of men, teaches itself, and grows increasingly in sophistication. Shades of 1984!

IMPLICATIONS FOR ADVERTISING

We have a new era of competition—for media and for brands. To the media salesman—as this researcher sees it—it means back to selling editorial values and the dynamics of media use . . . as the numbers game is taken over by computers. It will also mean the strengthening of the *editor* as the guiding hand on the destinies of media. (I'm pretty sure it will pay more to have distinctive character than simply circulation.)

* Trademark

To brands it means an era when competition can be more purposeful and devastating. Possession of practical models, designed to reflect the organic processes of the advertising business, will encourage more daring and imaginative media strategies—strategies which otherwise would appear too speculative to contemplate.

And your competition can study *your* media allocation on *their* computers and strike where you are most vulnerable. Information on the consumer dynamics of product use, such as brand switching, and of advertising performance will provide your competitors with shattering power if they have it all to themselves. And we believe, perhaps immodestly, that those who have the HIGH ASSAY MODEL * available to them will have important lead time advantage over their competitors.

What, then, is a practical media model? A model built from principle, responsive to relevant functions, Janus-like in its ability to look backward *and* forward, ever-increasing in sophistication. It is in this sense, we believe, we *have* in our HIGH ASSAY MODEL * a practical media model today.

* Trademark

38. Seven principles in image formation

BARDIN H. NELSON

The creation of markets for products is as necessary as the creation of products for the market. And modern management, through costly experience, has become aware of the significance of consumer attitudes or expectancies. Most executives now realize that the decision makers in industry are so remote from their customers that they do not know what customers really want. This awareness has created a desire for sounder evidence about consumer patterns of response or resistance to products, to help guide management decision making.

The needs of people with respect to physiological necessities in the United States have by and large been fulfilled, and are taken for granted by most people. Discriminative buying of items from the viewpoint of satisfying other motives has allowed consumers to play a more significant role in marketing decisions and product development.

A psychological break occurred after World War II. Buying sentiments were no longer characterized by the pessimism of depression years. The increasing psychological acceptance of credit buying enabled consumers to make greater annual expenditures than their current incomes and cash reserves formerly warranted.

Management, realizing that it must have predictive information to adjust to the consumer's optimism or pessimism, began to turn to the behavioral sciences for further help. After reviewing research concerning consumer attitudes and the group actions of consumers, some heads of businesses became enamored with the possibility of attitude measurement as an indicator for necessary future adjustments by business. Although the instruments used were imperfect in many respects, they provided the kinds of information which enabled business to have greater ability to

Reprinted from the *Journal of Marketing*, Volume 26 (January, 1962) pp. 67–71, National Quarterly Publication of the American Marketing Association.

anticipate changing market situations and to make necessary adjustments.

Individuals in a mass society have difficulty in maintaining a strong sense of personal identity because of competing reference groups, conflicting social norms, and various other cultural influences. Increasingly, businessmen became aware that an important factor in group influence is the impact of uniform stimuli reaching people in similar situations with similar attitudes, needs, and aspirations. This awareness opened the eyes of management to the feasibility of giving direction to such stimuli in order to maintain optimum sales volume of their products.

Thus, psychological and sociological principles to some extent have become important business principles. In their attempts to forecast business trends, research economists at Michigan State University, Texas A. & M., and other institutions now study "consumer sentiments" as well as levels of income, prices, liquid assets, and debts.

Although they represent oversimplifications, the following ideas have emerged:

1. *An attitude is preparation for behavior.* A composite of the attitudes which a group of people hold toward a product constitutes an image. Influence their images, and you influence their behavior.
2. *People have hidden urges or desires* which have been repressed or buried in the subconscious areas of the mind. Build an image around a product that satisfies these needs, and people will buy the product. Satisfy the hidden motives.

As early as 1918, Thomas and Znaniecki demonstrated that the effect of a phenomenon upon an individual depended not only on the objective content, but more specifically on the subjective standpoint taken by an individual toward the phenomenon.[1] What the individual's mind defines as reality is real in its consequences for that individual. Thomas and Znaniecki revealed that a product was not just a *physical* object, but that it was what people *thought* it was.

Physical attributes of a product act only as stimuli capable of developing certain associations in the minds of individuals. Such associations may be pleasant or unpleasant. The image makers strive to translate these stimuli into images favorable to their product.

Although there are numerous complex psychological processes relevant to image formation, only a limited number of steps involved in creating an image will be dealt with here.

REFERENCE POINTS

Human beings in a complex society are constantly making choices or judgments. Perhaps it is a judgment concerning financial affairs, or the

---

[1] W. I. Thomas and F. Znaniecki, *The Polish Peasant in Europe and America* (Boston: Richard G. Badger, 1918–1920), 5 vols.

proper degree of control to exercise over children. In making such judgments they utilize standards derived from many sources. To judge anything, they must have something as a basis for comparison.

If no objects or experiences are available as reference points, it becomes virtually impossible for individuals to orient to their surroundings or circumstances. Captain Charles Yeager tells of his experiences when he flew the first plane to reach and maintain supersonic speed:

I had a hard time judging my speed. The little Mach needle and other instruments kept telling me that no one had ever gone faster, but I was so high and so remote, and the airplane was so very quiet that I might almost have been motionless. You sense speed in terms of something stationary, something outside yourself.[2]

In social life, individuals frequently make immediate on-the-spot judgments of persons or of performance and achievement of other people. The anchorages or reference points involved in making such judgments stem from past experience, from a positive or negative stand on an issue, or from positive or negative relationships with the persons in question. What is distinct or significant in experience depends upon our "anchorages" which may be external, internal, or both.

External factors include social influences such as instruction, suggestion, group pressures, or group participation. Intensity, size, novelty, repetition, contrast, and movement are also external factors that may determine what stands out in experience.

Internal factors include: personal interest; state of the organism, such as emotional state or physical state; motives, such as hunger or thirst; and attitudes, prejudices, or other feelings concerning individuals or groups.

PRINCIPLES INVOLVED IN IMAGE FORMATION

Following are seven principles:

Principle No. 1: People are not "exclusively" rational creatures. Their behavior is usually determined, not entirely by knowledge and reason, but also by feelings and unconscious drives. At best, behavior or thought of the average individual represents a combination of emotional and rational elements. We must always recognize the obvious impossibility of any individual's capability of recognizing and tracing back all the influences upon his behavior, some of which may have originated in early childhood.

A group of Swazi tribesmen from South Africa visited London. After they returned home, it was noted that the thing which remained most vividly fixed in the tribesmen's minds was their image of the English

[2] M. Sherif and C. Sherif, *An Outline of Social Psychology,* revised edition (New York: Harper and Bros., 1956), p. 47.

policeman regulating traffic with uplifted hand. The Swazi greets his fellowman or visitor with uplifted hand. Here was the familiar gesture, warm with friendliness, in a foreign country. It was one of the few things they saw that fitted immediately into their own well-established social framework and thus produced an enduring effect.[3] From a rational standpoint, one might point to thousands of objects in London that possess more significance than the raised hand of a policeman.

Housewives seemingly influenced by the color factor in certain selections readily admitted that color did not affect the utility of particular products. They had difficulty in explaining the bases for their particular color preferences. The following excerpts from an interview show this response pattern:

Mrs. B:

The three major grocery stores where I buy my groceries carry three brands which I've used. There's really not enough difference to tell between ———, ———, and ———. I think ——— is real nice because of its rich yellow color. I like the yellow wrapper on ———. It's a pretty yellow. I'm like a child. If you fix things up pretty, I'll buy them. I didn't see any way it was put in the can or any way it was different from the others.

Interviewer X:

Do you have any ideas about what causes frying failures?

Mrs. B:

As I told you, any one of the three good shortenings I've used is all right for frying or baking. They probably weren't watching what they were doing.

Principle No. 2: People respond to situations in ways which appear to them to protect their self-images.

Human beings have emotional foundations which undergird their behavior and which are as much a part of them as their arms or legs. For one to attack or threaten an individual's psychological being is almost as bad as hacking at his hands or legs with a knife. Whenever an individual faces activity or events which produce disequilibrium, the mind seeks ways and means for restoring the equilibrium. Such attempts explain why individuals will give socially acceptable answers or even completely erroneous answers concerning their behavior.

For example, respondents were asked the direct question: "Why don't you serve chicken and dumplings more often?" Only 20 percent answered either "hard to make" or "can't make good ones." Respondents were shown a picture frustration question in which a little boy was saying to his mother, "Tommy's having chicken and dumplings for supper. Why don't we ever have them?" When asked to give their ideas as to

---

[3] Same reference as footnote 2, p. 82.

what the mother's answer was, 54 percent said, "She told him she didn't know how to make good dumplings." [4]

Principle No. 3: We need to determine the various images and reference points or anchorages which already exist in the minds of a particular group or society. Seldom are there revolutionary changes in people's images.

The weight of evidence indicates that actually very little change occurs during college in the essential standards by which students govern their lives. The values with which they arrive and which are integral elements of their personality, are still there when most students leave.[5]

Messages received may clarify the image—make something which was less certain, more certain. However, messages or stimuli may have the reverse effect. They may introduce doubt or uncertainty concerning the image. In either case, the significance of the stimuli usually depends on the reinforcement received from other like stimuli or messages. To tear down a conflicting image or to build upon one that is compatible, the image maker must first know the images that already exist in the minds of people. The necessity for such knowledge has given social-psychological research new status, particularly in the eyes of management. Projective tests are being more widely used. "Depth interview" has become a frequently used phrase among corporate heads.

The image that people held of a certain chain store operation could best be described as "high priced." Considerable probing revealed, however, that the interviewees felt that numerous items in specific departments were priced well in line or even cheaper than at other chains in the same locality. A word-association test revealed that interviewees associated good food with the advertised products of a certain company. Comparison shopping revealed that these products were priced higher at the chain operation being studied than at other chain stores.

A revision of prices of a nationally advertised brand of canned goods, plus the promotion of brand-name specials, gradually produced a significant change in the image which people held of these stores. There are key factors which appear on the surface to be incidental, but which exert tremendous influence in the formation of images. Shop-worn vegetables in the vegetable bins of a food store may establish a negative image concerning cleanliness in a store which is otherwise spotless.

Principle No. 4: If an image appears stable and if reference groups surrounding the individual continue to support the image, both internal and external forces opposing the image will be resisted.

[4] Henry V. Courtenay, *An Analysis of Response Variation Encountered With Selected Interviewing Techniques in Consumer Marketing Research,* unpublished Master's Thesis, College Station, Texas, May, 1960, pp. 13–14.

[5] Philip E. Jacob, *Changing Values in College* (New York: Harper and Bros., 1957), p. 53.

At the A. & M. College of Texas a very stable image exists concerning the role of a freshman. Organizational structures strongly support the image. A freshman's father told him, "Explain to your Commanding Officer that you didn't clean up your room because you weren't feeling well."

The father did not fully understand when he was told, "Sir, there is only one response I can make to my C. O. and that is 'No excuse, Sir.'" The freshman's image of his role was important to him.

Excerpts taken from an interview are typical of responses obtained in a survey conducted in a large residential area surrounding an industrial section.

Interviewer X:

———— has a supermarket in ———— Shopping Center. Do you ordinarily buy some of your groceries at that unit?

Mr. S:

My wife and I buy most of our groceries on Friday afternoon. That's my afternoon off from the plant. I guess we bought the bulk of our groceries from ———— until last year. They have good stuff and it's real convenient—close and the parking and all. But we quit them last year. They had always been a real friendly place, but last year they ordered me over to a little window to get my check cashed. They'd built this little room off the office. I let them belittle me, standing there in that line. I talked to several of my buddies at the plant. They felt just like I did. We decided somebody new must have come in. Some of them still go there, but me and most of my buddies don't like this new management.

The initial purpose of the survey was to determine why particular units of the chain operation had suffered a loss in volume of business the preceding year.

Principle No. 5: If an image is marked by doubt, uncertainty, or insecurity, utilize additional means for creating further doubts. Present the new image in a form whereby it will dispel anxiety or doubts.

The Chinese Communists were aware of considerable resistance among U.S. citizens to our entry into the Korean War. Newspapers carried headlines, "Is This War Necessary?" Some disgruntlement also existed because of a mild economic recession prior to our involvement in Korea. Furthermore, the Chinese Communists knew that the image which the average American soldier held of them was a type of Dr. Fu Manchu who had all kinds of exquisite Oriental tortures, including that of burning bamboo splinters under one's fingernails. They also knew that many soldiers thought of themselves as peacetime boys who could hardly wait to get back to their families, wives, sweethearts, and the comforts of home.

Based upon this and other knowledge of the image held by U.S.

soldiers, the Communists developed an approach to creating new images. This procedure began when a soldier was captured. It began first of all with a speech of welcome and introduction. A young English-speaking Chinese officer appeared, often a graduate of an American university, in civilian clothes and affecting a friendly and conciliatory attitude:

We welcome you to the ranks of the people. We are happy and privileged to have liberated you from the Imperialist Wall Street warmongers who started this war. We have nothing against you personally. We are not going to abuse you. We are going instead to offer you a fair shake. Let us present to you our side of the picture, and in return we promise you there'll be no slave camps, no work groups, no road crews. We ask only that you hear us out, which is only American fair play, and make up your minds about what is true.

How much better this plan sounded as compared to one involving burning bamboo splinters; it was a reprieve from almost certain death. This procedure was the first step in a plan which followed well-known psychological principles.

The president and founder of an old, reliable, well-established business in the downtown area of a major city experienced feelings of doubt and anxiety when lower management suggested that three new units be established in shopping centers. The president was so fearful that the reputation of the business would be endangered that he suggested there be no further discussion of the matter.

Lower management began to emphasize in subtle fashion various problems and negative forces confronting the business. The research department included as a part of their field studies an investigation which revealed: (1) that the average customer of the business came to the downtown area of the city only twice a year; (2) that generally interviewees thought that a business which did not have some units in the new shopping centers was either extremely limited in scope of operation, was failing, or would be failing shortly; and (3) that interviewees thought that the effect of additional units upon the prestige of an old established downtown business would depend largely on design, styling, type of operation, and particular location of the new units.

The president's increasing uncertainty concerning the future was replaced with a degree of certainty, based upon his confidence in the research department. He gave leadership to the development of two new units in shopping centers. The information which influenced his actions was used as promotional material for the general public to remove their doubts about the company's plans for the future. The campaign utilized the selection of particular centers, the styling of the units, and various other special features to create a new and stronger image of a business that could adjust to social, economic, and technological change and still maintain an exclusive personality.

Principle No. 6: Place the desired image in the most favorable set-

ting. If at all possible, clothe the new image in the already accepted values of the people.

In the 1960 political campaign, President Kennedy made widespread use of the names, Woodrow Wilson and Franklin Delano Roosevelt—identified as men of action who moved America out of the doldrums.

Restaurant managers are aware that most people prefer the traditional items offered on the menu. Consumer research indicates, however, that preference for new or "exotic" dishes varies according to educational levels. Customers with a college education may choose "exotic" dishes twice as frequently as customers with junior high-school education. Significant differences are also observed between selections of customers with junior high-school education and customers with high-school education.

Thus, a restaurant operator should consider carefully the educational level of his potential clientele as he seeks to determine the most appropriate image for his business.

Principle No. 7: To stimulate development of a new image, one must attract the attention of large numbers of potential consumers.

Based on consumer research conducted in Texas, the housewife's image of chicken with respect to method of preparation focuses on one method—frying. Since use of chicken tends to be confined to frying, it is used mostly for variety among other meats rather than being used as a dish frequently served but varied by preparation in several different ways. Little effort has been expended by the poultry industry to establish a broader image by promotional campaigns emphasizing the ease of preparation and the tastes of other chicken dishes, such as Chicken Tetrazzini or Coq au Vin. In areas where favorable images already exist concerning the economy and flavor of chicken dishes, the probabilities of projecting a broader and increasingly favorable image of chicken seem excellent; but such a change in image would require the transfer of new ideas and information to broad cultural groups.

The more striking the attraction used to gain attention, the better. Reinforce an image by clearcut, simple imagery such as catch phrases or slogans. Fairly continuous repetition of slogans or catch words is necessary for a long period of time.

Enable individuals through the imagery to escape the known and to conquer the unknown. Allow them to experience the magnificent, and thus escape the small perimeters of their daily lives. Ernest Dichter tells his clients: "Sell emotional security or go under." [6]

However, where images are stable, any techniques designed to replace them will be resisted. It is true that a change which might take a generation to accomplish in a slow-moving, nonliterate society may be

[6] Ernest Dichter, *The Strategy of Desire* (Garden City: Doubleday and Co., 1960), pp. 112, 169.

accomplished in months or even days in a society with mass communications. Nevertheless, the message is not always as important as the kind of image that it produces.

The success of any method of influencing people depends upon a favorable climate or environment for its use. The question then arises as to what is the most favorable environment. It is one where the people experience (1) painful uneasiness or anxiety; (2) a feeling of separation from the group or isolation from group standards; and (3) a feeling of pointlessness or that no certain goals exist.[7]

Can we defend the use of the social sciences in influencing people? As Dichter says:

People have tried to influence each other since the origins of intelligent behavior in mankind. The real issue is one of determination of goals. A butcher knife can be used to murder or to cut meat.[8]

Perhaps a more appropriate illustration might be, "It's a good fire that warms you and a bad fire that burns you."

[7] Sebastian De Grazia, *The Political Community* (Chicago: The University of Chicago Press, 1948), pp. 105–106.
[8] Dichter, same reference as footnote 6.

39. Advertising repetition put to the test

Not always does it pay to repeat advertising, researchers have learned in an unusual 20-weeks' marketing experiment with two new products.

Advertising, the study found, may give rise to a "negative awareness" on the part of the consumer that destroys his "spirit of self-discovery." Under these conditions, the more money spent to advertise a new product, the fewer the steady customers to cover the expense.

But for another new product in the same market at the same time, advertising may be just the thing to ensure success.

This seeming anomaly was among several conclusions drawn by Dr. John B. Stewart, professor of business administration, from a newspaper experiment in Fort Wayne, Ind. Dr. Stewart sought the answers to such questions as these:

What happens when an identical advertisement for a new product is repeated as often as 20 times in 20 weeks in one newspaper? Does the ad become more effective or less as time goes on? Are sales helped or hindered?

To try to find out, the Newsprint Information Committee, composed of Canadian newsprint producers, sponsored Dr. Stewart's study. It was conducted under the auspices of the Harvard Graduate School of Business Administration in collaboration with the Bureau of Advertising of the American Newspaper Publishers' Association.

EXPERIMENT IN FT. WAYNE, IND.

Two new products—Lestare, a dry laundry bleach, and Chicken Sara Lee, a frozen prepared dinner—were placed on the market in Fort Wayne. Split-run display advertising in the *News-Sentinel,* an afternoon newspaper, provided three different controlled exposures in three matching areas of the city. The ads ran once a week—for four weeks in one area,

Reprinted from *Media/Scope,* April, 1964, pp. 62–66.

eight weeks in another, and 20 weeks in a third. In a fourth matching zone the ads were not circulated; it became a control area.

The same advertisements were used throughout the experiment to avoid any side effects of varying creative treatment. No other advertising was used.

More than 6,000 personal interviews with housewives were conducted over a 23-weeks' period. The measures of effects included brand awareness, accuracy of knowledge about the products, attitudes toward the products, purchase intentions, claimed purchases and brand preferences.

Here are some of the key general findings by Dr. Stewart:

Advertising caused a rapid initial rise in awareness which then leveled off. Repeated advertising maintained the level of awareness but did not increase it appreciably. When the advertising stopped, awareness tended to fall.

The quality of awareness was essentially the same in areas exposed to advertising and in the area not exposed to it.

Substantial repetition of advertising was needed to achieve efficient buying results; there was a time lag before awareness was transformed into purchase behavior.

The lowest advertising costs per "extra" purchase did not occur until the 15th consecutive ad had appeared. A short campaign of only three or four insertions proved inefficient.

Though the campaigns for the two products were apparently similar, widely differing results were achieved. The introduction of Chicken Sara Lee was deemed an advertising success, that of Lestare an advertising failure. But Lestare's poor showing was linked to some unknown negative factor in the ad itself rather than to the duration of the campaign.

MEASURABLE EFFECTS SMALL

In some respects, Dr. Stewart found the results disappointing. Overall, the measurable effects of the advertising were small. The conclusions were not always the stark black-and-whites one might have hoped for in a controlled experiment.

From the businessman's viewpoint, Dr. Stewart reports, there is only one clear major conclusion:

Getting a new product such as Lestare or Chicken Sara Lee established in the minds of consumers is a tough job when the competing brands are well known and well distributed.

A "surprising" finding was that large differences in advertising effects exist among various demographic types of consumers. The study isolated, for example, housewives who were 26 times as likely to be aware of Chicken Sara Lee as other housewives were. Some differences had been expected, but not such big ones.

Dr. Stewart recommends that advertisers give thought to viewing their programs as capital investments rather than current expenditures. He suggests,

The ideal approach might be to test market a new product without advertising for a period of one or two months on a small scale. After several hundred customers have bought the product, they should be contacted and interviewed to bring out their reactions to the product.

By sorting out the triers who preferred the new product over competing brands and learning what their knowledge of the product was and attitudes toward it, copywriters could then create a copy and layout which then would expect to attract similar types of people and create a product image similar to that held by the satisfied buyers. Several logical media could then be used for test periods of three to four months and the genuine selling power of the programs measured at numerous points in time.

Each proven program developed in this way would probably cost between $50,000 and $100,000. Once developed, however, they could easily pay for themselves by higher sales results and by establishing a profitable theme around which supplementary programs could later be developed.

Without benefit of test-marketing, the advertising in the Fort Wayne study produced some perplexing results. For Chicken Sara Lee, the outcome was positive:

In the area where no advertising was used, few persons (only about 1 percent of *News-Sentinel* subscribers) tried the product.

Four weekly insertions of the ad encouraged a few more to buy sooner than they would have.

Eight weekly insertions doubled the customers, but business fell off abruptly when the advertising stopped.

"CONTINUOUS AND EXTENDED REPETITION"

Fifteen insertions rolled up the greatest total of additional buyers per ad dollar.

Twenty weekly insertions attracted even more customers—four times as many as in the zone where no advertising was done—but the ad-dollar cost was up slightly over the 15-weeks' level.

Dr. Stewart concluded,

The pattern of Chicken Sara Lee triers makes a perfect case for the virtues of continuous and extended repetition [of advertising] . . . .

But for Lestare, the story was curiously different. Advertising caused an initial rapid rise in brand-name awareness. After a while, however, awareness in the no advertising zone was just as high. Moreover continuous exposure to advertising not only did not produce more customers, it might indirectly have driven some away. By the 20th week, 3.5 percent of housewives in the area without advertising were buying Lestare, as against only 3 percent in the areas exposed to the ad.

Dr. Stewart reports,

The end result for Lestare was that advertising obtained no additional purchasers and in fact did damage by attracting a type of prospect less likely to prefer the brand than if no advertising had been done.

Why the inverse effect with advertising? Dr. Stewart suggests that in this case

the advertising was destroying a natural force that would otherwise have promoted purchase.

There might be, he speculates,

a particular type of innovator whose tendency to try a new product was inversely related to the amount of advertising done for that new product.

Presumably, a large fraction of these evanescent prospects would try the product if no advertising were done. If advertising were started, it would squelch the spirit of self-discovery among these prospects and thereby destroy a major portion of their motivation to risk trial.

There are times, Dr. Stewart postulates, when

some advertising is not necessarily better than no advertising.

He notes,

The problem was not with the product itself. Lestare went on to become the nation's largest selling dry bleach.

Even when successful, advertising should not be used indiscriminately, the professor cautions. With Chicken Sara Lee, the study found, the advertising efficiency

was just barely high enough to justify the expenditure.

Dr. Stewart says,

If we had known originally what we now know in retrospect, we would have run the advertisements weekly for the first four weeks, every other week from week 5 through 12, and monthly from week 13 through 24. We believe this frequency of scheduling would have been nearly optimum.

D. Price

40. A note on the relationship of price and imputed quality

D. S. TULL, R. A. BORING and M. H. GONSIOR

Conventional demand theory endows the consumer with a vast amount of information. The consumer is held knowledgeable of the configuration of attributes that comprise a product or service. Further, he is aware of the product-price alternatives available to him, has well-defined tastes and preferences, and can determine his marginal rate of substitution for each product for the other possible alternative products involved in a particular purchase decision.

The real-world consumer is not so fortunate. Many of his purchase decisions are made with a lack of information concerning some of the options available to him and a considerable amount of uncertainty about the attributes of the products or services of which he is aware. He does not have all the information provided his theoretical brother, and search costs are frequently such as to make it uneconomic for him to obtain it.

The consumer's perception of the quality of a product is an admixture of a variety of informational inputs concerning a set of criteria he has established for judging the product. The uncertainties associated with assessing the quality of a particular product stem from (1) uncertainty concerning the criteria that should be used, (2) uncertainty as to the degrees of completeness and reliability of the information held on each criterion, and (3) uncertainty about the predictive value of each criterion.

How does the consumer judge quality when he does not have much of the information he requires in each of these areas? Reference to our own experiences as consumers suggests an answer: he tends to judge in part by the level of the price.

Reprinted from the *Journal of Business*, April, 1964, pp. 186–191, by permission of The University of Chicago Press.

An earlier investigation, carried out by Harold J. Leavitt indicates that, when there is considerable uncertainty concerning the quality level between brands of the same product class, some consumers will choose a higher-priced rather than a low-priced brand.[1] This suggests that these consumers imputed quality on the basis of price.

The Leavitt experiments consisted essentially of the following steps.

1. A convenience sample of adults was asked to select two classes of products whose brands they believed to be "pretty much alike" and two classes they believed to have "big quality differences" between brands. The selection was made from a list of fifteen convenience items.

    Cooking sherry and moth flakes were selected as being the most similar and razor blades and floor wax as being the least similar among brands.

2. A different convenience sample was asked to make simulated purchases of one of two hypothetical brands of each of the four product classes. The only information given the respondent by which to differentiate the two brands of each class was an assignment of different prices. The subjects in this sample were also asked to go through the procedure described in step 1, and the same results were obtained.

3. A measure of the degree of confidence the respondent felt in making his choice between the brands of each product class was obtained.

The results showed that a larger percentage of subjects selected the higher-priced brands of the "big quality difference" product classes (razor blades and floor wax) than they did for the "pretty much alike" classes (cooking sherry and moth flakes).[2] However, the differences in these percentages are convincing only in the case of floor wax; the differences in the percentages for the other three products would not be significant if the sample had been randomly selected and the same results obtained.

Some of Leavitt's conclusions are that "these findings suggest that demand curves may not invariably be negatively sloped, that price itself may have more than one meaning to a customer, and that a higher price may sometimes increase, rather than decrease, his readiness to buy." He also adds that "in any case, the area seems deserving of further exploration."

This note reports some further exploration in the area.

THE PRESENT INVESTIGATION

Our experiments were conducted along somewhat the same lines as Leavitt's, with some modifications and additions. Their purpose was to

---

[1] "A Note on Some Experimental Findings about the Meanings of Price," *Journal of Business*, XXVII (July, 1954), 205–10.

[2] "When faced with choices between two brands of floor wax, 57 percent of our subjects selected the higher-priced brand; 30 percent of the subjects chose the higher-priced razor blades; 24 percent, the higher-priced moth flakes; and 21 percent, the higher-priced cooking sherry" (*ibid.*, p. 208).

determine if his findings on the imputation of quality based on price could be duplicated with an added assumption given the respondent concerning the price of the brand of the product class "you usually buy." We were also curious as to whether any substantial differences in simulated purchase behavior could be found between classes of consumers. For example, is there any seeming difference in behavior in imputing quality based on price between men and women? Between different age groups? Between groups with differing levels of education?

Determination of brand similarity and dissimilarity. A questionnaire was prepared listing twenty toilet articles, household, and food items. The items selected were ones with which, it was believed, all respondents would be familiar and would have had some actual purchase experience. Included were such items as toothbrushes, aspirin, table salt, margarine, light bulbs, floor wax, liquid shampoo, and liquid shoe polish. A judgment sample of 110 respondents was selected, and each respondent was asked to indicate whether he believed the brands of each of these product classes are "essentially similar," "vary substantially," or whether he was "uncertain concerning similarity."

The results of the interviews were that brands of table salt and aspirin were found to be considered the most similar and brands of floor wax and liquid shampoos the least similar. These product classes were used for the simulated purchase experiments.

Simulated purchase experiments. A questionnaire was constructed using these four product classes and three alphabetically lettered brands of each. The questionnaire asked the respondent to assume the role of the family shopper and set up the hypothetical situation that "while shopping for the products listed below you find that the brand you usually buy of each is out of stock." He was further told that "you have no information on the available brands other than that given below" and asked to check the one brand of each product class he would buy.

Identical quantities by varying prices were shown on the questionnaire for the three brands of each product class. The aspirin brands were priced at $0.49, $0.59, and $0.69 for 50 tablets; table salt at $0.11, $0.15, and $0.19 for 1 pound; floor wax at $0.99, $1.19, and $1.39 per quart; and liquid shampoo at $0.42, $0.45, and $0.48 for 4 ounces. These prices were ordered on the questionnaires to prevent bias; each price for each brand was used an equal number of times.

A departure from the procedure used by Leavitt was to give the respondents a reference price, the assumed price of the brand "you usually buy." It was hypothesized that, if the respondents were told that the price of the brand of each product class they normally buy was equal to the *lowest*-priced hypothetical brand they could buy in the experiment, two desirable features would be introduced into the experimental design. Provision of a reference price would give each respondent a similar point of reference and thus tend to reduce one source of variability in the experiment. Further, providing a *low* reference price should tend to inhibit the degree of imputation of quality based on price. If significant differences still appeared in the simulated purchasing behavior between the "similar-brand" and "dissimilar-brand" products, the evidence would be the more convincing that price is frequently used as a predictor of quality in purchase decisions with a high degree of uncertainty. Finally, to test the inhibiting effect of the low reference price, a questionnaire was constructed giving the median price and another the highest price as a reference.

Three separate judgment samples of more than sixty subjects each were selected and interviewed, one sample for each reference price. Information on sex, age, and educational level was obtained from each respondent.

THE FINDINGS

Low reference-price experiment. The results of the simulated purchase decisions with the lowest price given as the reference in each product class is shown in the left-hand column of Figure 1. About one-quarter of the respondents indicated they would buy one of the two higher-priced brands of the "similar-brand" products (26 percent for aspirin and 28 percent for table salt). Almost one-half of the respondents chose the higher-priced brands of the "dissimilar-brand" products (46 percent for floor wax and 49 percent for liquid shampoos). These results show a high degree of consistency and, had the sample been randomly selected and the same results obtained, would be significant at the 1 percent level.

The similarity of the appearance of these curves to what we normally consider a demand curve to look like is so striking that there is a tendency to consider them as *being* experimentally derived demand curves. They are not. Some reflection will indicate that three different brands of the product are conceptually involved and, even though the subject had no information on which to differentiate the brands other than price, those subjects who indicated they would purchase the higher-priced brands most have imputed quality differences. For those "consumers" at least, the three brands were conceptualized as being three different products. In the framework of conventional demand theory, therefore, these curves cannot be considered to be demand curves. It is for this reason that they have been designated "price-purchase preference" curves.

Median and high reference-price experiments. The results of the median and high reference-price experiments are shown in the right-hand columns of Figure 1. It is evident that the higher reference prices substantially increased the proportion of respondents selecting the higher-

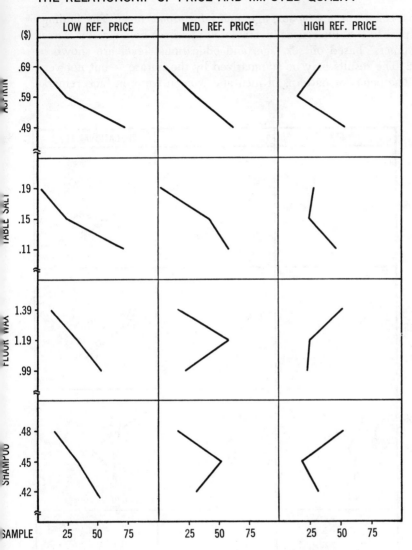

Figure 1. Price-purchase preference curves
Sample size: low reference price, N=65, median reference price, N=61; high reference price, N=72

priced brands. As shown there, increases in "purchases" were registered in all cases at the reference price. These findings suggest that the low reference price did in fact have an inhibiting effect on the selection of the higher-priced brands. This tends to lend additional credence to the conclusions reached from the findings of the low reference price experiment.

Cross-classifications by sex, age, and educational level. The findings with respect to the differences in simulated purchase behavior by classes of "consumers" based on sex, age, and educational level are shown in Figure 2. The results may be summarized by the phrase "—but not very much." The behavior patterns of men and women were, in fact, remark-

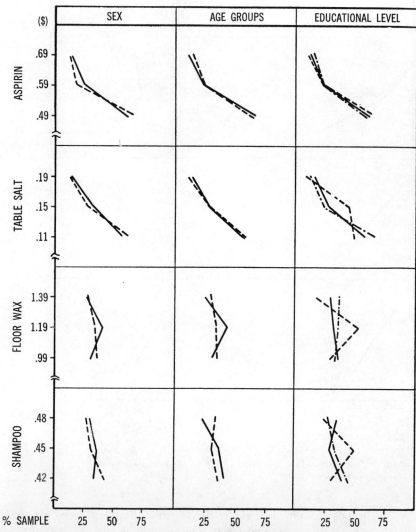

Figure 2. Price-purchase preference curves, by classes of consumers

Sex: men (dashed line), N = 72; women (solid line), N = 126. **Age groups:** less than 35 years (dashed line), N = 118; 35 years or more (solid line), N = 80. **Educational level:** 12 or fewer years (dashed line), N = 49; some college (solid line), N = 88; college graduate (dash-dot line), N = 61

ably similar. The patterns by age group also showed negligible differences. The educational level groups examined showed a tendency for those subjects having no more than twelve years of formal schooling to "pay" the median price more frequently than their better educated counterparts, particularly for the "dissimilar-brand" products. Additional evidence is needed, however, to provide firm support for the inference that this is a characteristic trait.

CONCLUSIONS

The findings of these experiments closely support those of the earlier investigation. The findings, in conjunction with those of the earlier study, strongly suggest that consumers rely heavily upon price as a predictor of quality when there is a substantial degree of uncertainty involved in the purchase decision.

These findings have some interesting implications for price theory and pricing practice. They suggest that, for some products, the price-quantity-sold relationship may indeed be kinked (even to the point of bending backward), but for quite a different reason than that usually proposed in discussions of the kinked demand curve.

The findings also lend support to the use of "skimming" pricing for those products whose quality is difficult to judge by other criteria. In these cases the term "skimming" may be a misnomer; instead of the higher price limiting the market it may actually expand it.

41. Bayesian decision theory in pricing strategy

PAUL E. GREEN

Since the publication of Robert Schlaifer's pioneering work, *Probability and Statistics for Business Decisions*,[1] The Bayesian approach to decision making under uncertainty has received much comment, pro and con, by theoretical and applied statisticians alike.

However, in contrast to the large number of theoretical contributions being made to decision theory in general and Bayesian statistics in particular, reported applications of these procedures to real-world problem situations have been rather meager. Applications appear especially lacking in the marketing field.

In highly oversimplified terms, the Bayesian approach to decision making under uncertainty provides a framework for explicitly working with the economic costs of alternative courses of action, the prior knowledge or judgments of the decision maker, and formal modification of these judgments as additional data are introduced into the problem.

In the Du Pont Company, the decision theory approach, often augmented by computer simulation, has been used experimentally over the past few years in a variety of market planning applications, ranging from capacity expansion problems to questions concerning the introduction of new products and long-range price and promotional strategy. The

Reprinted from the *Journal of Marketing,* Volume 27 (January, 1963), pp. 5–14, National Quarterly Publication of the American Marketing Association.

[1] Robert Schlaifer, *Probability and Statistics for Business Decisions* (New York; McGraw-Hill Book Co., Inc., 1959). In addition, two excellent general articles dealing with the Bayesian approach are: Harry V. Roberts, "The New Business Statistics," *Journal of Business,* Vol. 33 (January, 1960) pp. 21–30, and Jack Hirshleifer, "The Bayesian Approach to Statistical Decision—An Exposition," *Journal of Business,* Vol. 34 (October, 1961) pp. 471–489.

application to follow concerns the use of Bayesian decision theory in the selection of a "best" pricing policy for a firm in an oligopolistic industry where such factors as demand elasticity, competitive retaliation, threat of future price weakness, and potential entry of new competitors influence the effectiveness of the firm's courses of action. Although the content of this case is aprocryphal, its structure has been compounded from actual situations.

No attempt will be made to describe even superficially all of the many facets of the Bayesian approach to decision making under uncertainty. The content of this article is focused on only two main considerations.

First, in dealing with actual marketing situations, for example, pricing problems, the opportunity to obtain field information may be nonexistent. Second, in dealing with actual marketing problems, the complexity of the situation may force the analyst to develop a problem structure in much greater detail than has been described in the literature.

AN ILLUSTRATIVE APPLICATION

Since early 1955, the Everclear Plastics Company had been producing a resin called Kromel, basically designed for certain industrial markets. In addition to Everclear, three other firms were producing Kromel resin. Prices among all four suppliers (called here the Kromel industry) were identical; and product quality and service among producers were comparable. Everclear's current share of Kromel industry sales amounted to 40 percent.

Four industrial end uses comprised the principal marketing area for the Kromel industry. These market segments will be labeled A, B, C, and D. Three of the four segments (B, C, and D) were functionally dependent on segment A in the sense that Kromel's *ultimate* market position and rate of approach to this level in each of these three segments was predicated on the resin's making substantial inroads in segment A.

The Kromel industry's only competition in these four segments consisted of another resin called Verlon, which was produced by six other firms. Shares of the total Verlon-Kromel market (weighted sums over all four segments) currently stood at 70 percent Verlon industry, and 30 percent Kromel industry. Since its introduction in 1955, the superior functional characteristics per dollar cost of Kromel had enabled this newer product to displace fairly large poundages of Verlon in market segments B, C, and D.

On the other hand, the functional superiority per dollar cost of Kromel had not been sufficiently high to interest segment A consumers. While past price decreases in Kromel had been made, the cumulative effect of these reductions had still been insufficient to accomplish Kromel sales penetration in segment A. (Sales penetration is defined as a market share exceeding zero).

In the early fall of 1960, it appeared to Everclear's management that future weakness in Kromel price might be in the offing. The anticipated capacity increases on the part of the firm's Kromel competitors suggested that in the next year or two potential industry supply of this resin might significantly exceed demand, if no substantial market participation for the Kromel industry were established in segment A. In addition, it appeared likely that potential Kromel competitors might enter the business, thus adding to the threat of oversupply in later years.

Segment A, of course, constituted the key factor. If substantial inroads could be made in this segment, it appeared likely that Kromel industry sales growth in the other segments not only could be speeded up, but that ultimate market share levels for this resin could be markedly increased from those anticipated in the absence of segment A penetration. To Everclear's sales management, a price reduction in Kromel still appeared to represent a feasible means to achieve this objective, and (even assuming similar price reductions on the part of Kromel competitors) perhaps could still be profitable to Everclear.

However, a large degree of uncertainty surrounded both the overall attractiveness of this alternative, and under this alternative the amount of the price reduction which would enable Kromel to penetrate market segment A.

PROBLEM STRUCTURING AND DEVELOPMENT OF THE MODEL

Formulation of the problem required a certain amount of artistry and compromise toward achieving a reasonably adequate description of the problem. But it was also necessary to keep the structure simple enough so that the nature of each input would be comprehensible to the personnel responsible for supplying data for the study.

Problem components had to be formulated, such as: (a) length of planning period; (b) number and nature of courses of action; (c) payoff functions; and (d) states of nature covering future growth of the total Verlon-Kromel market, interindustry (Kromel vs. Verlon) and intra-Kromel industry effects of a Kromel price change, implications on Everclear's share of the total Kromel industry, and Everclear's production costs.

Initial discussions with sales management indicated that a planning period of five years should be considered in the study. While the selection of five years was somewhat arbitrary, sales personnel believed that some repercussions of a current price reduction might well extend over several years into the future.

A search for possible courses of action indicated that four pricing alternatives covered the range of actions under consideration:

1. Maintenance of status quo on Kromel price, which was $1.00/lb.
2. A price reduction to $.93/lb. within the next three months.
3. A price reduction to $.85/lb. within the next three months.
4. A price reduction to $.80/lb. within the next three months.

Inasmuch as each price action would be expected to produce a different time pattern in the flow of revenues and costs, and since no added investment in production facilities was contemplated, it was agreed that cumulative, compounded net profits over the 5-year planning period would constitute a relevant payoff function. In the absence of any unanimity as to the "correct" opportunity cost of capital, it was decided to use two interest rates of 6 and 10 percent annually in order to test the sensitivity of outcomes to the cost of capital variable.

Another consideration came to light during initial problem discussions. Total market growth (for the Kromel or Verlon industry) over the next five years in each market segment constituted a "state of nature" which could impinge on the Everclear's profit position. Accordingly, it was agreed to consider three separate forecasts of total market growth, a "most probable, optimistic, and pessimistic" forecast.

From these assumptions a base case was then formulated. This main case would first consider the pricing problem under the most probable forecast of total Verlon-Kromel year-by-year sales potential in each segment, using an opportunity cost of capital of 6 percent annually. The two other total market forecasts and the other cost of capital were then to be treated as sub-cases, in order to test the sensitivity of the base case outcomes to variations in these particular states of nature.

However, inter- and intra-industry alternative states of nature literally abounded in the Kromel resin problem. Sales management at Everclear had to consider such factors as:

1. The possibility that Kromel resin could effect penetration of market segment A if no price decrease were made.
2. If a price decrease were made, the extent of Verlon retaliation to be anticipated.
3. Given a particular type of Verlon price retaliation, its possible impact on Kromel's penetration of segment A.
4. If segment A were penetrated, the possible market share which the Kromel industry could gain in segment A.
5. If segment A were penetrated, the possible side effects of this event on speeding up Kromel's participation in market segments B, C, and D.
6. If segment A were not penetrated, the impact which the price reduction could still have on speeding up Kromel's participation in segments B, C, and D.
7. If segment A were not penetrated, the possibility that existing Kromel competitors would initiate price reductions a year hence.
8. The possible impact of a current Kromel price reduction on the decisions of existing or potential Kromel producers to increase capacity or enter the industry.

Table 1
Subjective Probabilities and Data Estimates Associated
with Everclear's Pricing Problem

1. If Kromel price remained at $1.00/pound and market segment A were not penetrated, what market share pattern for Kromel industry sales pounds would obtain in segments B, C, and D?

Base Assumption—Kromel Industry Share

	Segment B	Segment C	Segment D
1961	57.0%	40.0%	42.0%
1962	65.0	50.0	44.0
1963	75.0	80.0	46.0
1964	76.0	84.0	48.0
1965	76.0	84.0	50.0

2. If Kromel price remained at $1.00/pound, what is the probability that Kromel would still penetrate market segment A?

Probability of Penetration—Segment A

1961	.05
1962	.10
1963	.20
1964	.25
1965	.40

3. Under price strategies $.93/pound, $.85/pound, and $.80/pound, what is the probability of Verlon industry price retaliation; and given the particular retaliation (shown below), what is the probability that Kromel would still penetrate market segment A?

Pricing Case (entries are probabilities)

Verlon Industry Retaliation	$.93 Case	$.85 Case	$.80 Case
Full match of Kromel price reduction	.05	.15	.38
Half match of Kromel price reduction	.60	.75	.60
Stand pat on price	.35	.10	.02

Given a Particular Verlon Retaliatory Action, the Probability that Kromel Would Still Penetrate Segment A

	$.93 Case			$.85 Case			$.80 Case		
	Full Match	Half Match	Stand Pat	Full Match	Half Match	Stand Pat	Full Match	Half Match	Stand Pat
1961	.15	.20	.35	.20	.40	.80	.75	.80	.90
1962	.25	.30	.60	.30	.60	.90	.80	.85	.95
1963	.35	.40	.65	.40	.65	.95	.85	.90	1.00
1964	.60	.65	.75	.70	.75	.98	.90	.95	1.00
1965	.65	.70	.80	.75	.80	.98	.95	.98	1.00

Table 1 (continued)

4. If penetration in market segment A were effected, what is the probability that Kromel would obtain the specific share of this segment (a) during the first year of penetration, and (b) during the second year of participation?

Share	First year	Second year
25%	.15	.00
50	.35	.00
75	.40	.00
100	.10	1.00

5. If Kromel penetration of market segment A were effected, what impact would this event have on speeding up Kromel industry participation in segments B, C, and D?

Segment B—Would speed up market participation one year from base assumption shown under point 1 of this Table.

Segment C—Would speed up market participation one year from base assumption shown under point 1 of this Table.

Segment D—Kromel would move up to 85% of the market in the following year, and would obtain 100% of the market in the second year following penetration of segment A.

6. Under the price reduction strategies, if Kromel penetration of market segment A were not accomplished, what is the probability that Kromel industry participation in segments B, C, and D (considered as a group) would still be speeded up one year from the base assumption shown under point 1 of this Table?

	Probability of Speedup
$.93 Case	.45
$.85 Case	.60
$.80 Case	.80

7. If Kromel price at the end of any given year were $1.00/pound, $.93/pound, $.85/pound, or $.80/pound respectively, and if market segment A were not penetrated, what is the probability that present competitive Kromel producers would take the specific price action shown below?

If Kromel price	Action	Probability
@ $1.00/pound	$1.00/pound	.15
	.93	.80
	.85	.05
	.80	.00
@ $ .93/pound	.93	.80
	.85	.20
	.80	.00
@ $ .85/pound	.85	1.00
	.80	.00
@ $ .80/pound	.80	1.00

Table 1 (continued)

8. Under each of the four price strategies, what is the probability that competitive (present or potential) Kromel producers would add to or initiate capacity (as related to the price prevailing in mid-1961) in the years 1963 and 1964? (No capacity changes were assumed in 1965.)

Competitor	$1.00/pound	$.93/pound	$.85/pound	$.80/pound
R	.50	.20	.05	.00
S	.90	.75	.50	.20
T	.40	.10	.05	.00
U	.70	.50	.25	.00
V	.70	.50	.25	.00

Timing and amount available beginning of year

Competitor	1963	1964
R	10 million pounds	20 million pounds
S	12	20
T	12	20
U	6	12
V	6	6

While courses of action, length of planning period, and the payoff measure (cumulative, compounded net profits) for the base case had been fairly quickly agreed upon, the large number of inter- and intra-Kromel industry states of nature deemed relevant to the problem would require rather lengthy discussion with Everclear's sales personnel.

Accordingly, introductory sessions were held with Everclear's sales management, in order to develop a set of states of nature large enough to represent an adequate description of the real problem, yet small enough to be comprehended by the participating sales personnel. Next, separate interview sessions were held with two groups of Everclear's sales personnel; subjective probabilities regarding the occurrence of alternative states of nature under each course of action were developed in these sessions. A final session was held with all contributing personnel in attendance; each projection and/or subjective probability was gone over in detail, and final set of ground rules for the study was agreed upon. A description of these ground rules appears in Table 1.

USE OF TREE DIAGRAMS

The large number of alternative states of nature which were associated with inter- and intra-industry factors necessitated the construction of "tree diagrams" for each pricing alternative. These diagrams enabled sales management to trace the implications of their assumptions. Figure 1 shows a portion of one such tree diagram.

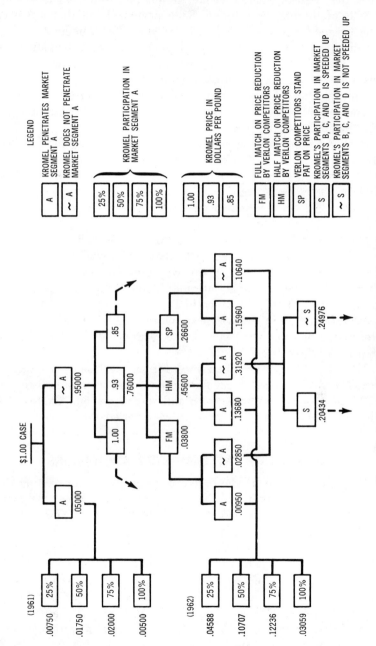

Figure 1. Portion of a "tree diagram"; Kromel price simulation

LEGEND

| A | KROMEL PENETRATES MARKET SEGMENT A |
| ~ A | KROMEL DOES NOT PENETRATE MARKET SEGMENT A |

25%	
50%	KROMEL PARTICIPATION IN
75%	MARKET SEGMENT A
100%	

1.00	
.93	KROMEL PRICE IN DOLLARS PER POUND
.85	

FM	FULL MATCH ON PRICE REDUCTION BY VERLON COMPETITORS
HM	HALF MATCH ON PRICE REDUCTION BY VERLON COMPETITORS
SP	VERLON COMPETITORS STAND PAT ON PRICE
S	KROMEL'S PARTICIPATION IN MARKET SEGMENTS B, C, AND D IS SPEEDED UP
~ S	KROMEL'S PARTICIPATION IN MARKET SEGMENTS B, C, AND D IS NOT SPEEDED UP

423

A word of explanation concerning interpretation of the probability tree is in order. The two principal branches underneath the $1.00 case refer to the event of whether or not Kromel penetrates segment A in the first year of the planning period. Sales personnel felt that a 5 percent chance existed for penetration, hence the figure .05000 under A.

However, if A were penetrated, four market participations were deemed possible: 25, 50, 75 and 100 percent carrying the conditional probabilities of .15, .35, .40 and .10 respectively.

Multiplication of each conditional probability, in turn, by the .05 marginal probability leads to the four joint probabilities noted in the upper left portion of the chart.

Next, if Kromel did not penetrate segment A during the first year, a probability of .80 was attached to the event that competitive Kromel producers would reduce price to $.93/lb. Multiplying the conditional probability of .80 by .95 results in the .76000 probability assigned to the joint event, "did not penetrate segment A and Kromel price was reduced to $.93/lb."

However, if Kromel price were reduced to $.93/lb., Verlon retaliation had to be considered, leading to the joint probabilities assigned to the next set of tree branches. In this way probabilities were built up for each of the over-400 possible outcomes of the study by appropriate application of the ground rules noted in Table 1.

A mathematical model was next constructed for determining the expected value of Everclear's cumulative, compounded net profits under each price strategy. See Table 2.

This model was then programed for an electronic computer. The simulation was first carried out for the base case assumptions regarding total Verlon-Kromel market growth and cost of capital. Additional runs were made in which these assumptions were varied.

RESULTS OF THE COMPUTER SIMULATIONS

The computer run for the base case showed some interesting results for the relevant variables affecting Everclear's cumulative, compounded net profits position at the end of the planning period. These results are portrayed in Figures 2 through 4.

Figure 2 summarizes the cumulative probability of Kromel's penetration of market segment A (the critical factor in the study) as a function of time, under each pricing strategy. As would be expected, the lowest price strategy, the $.80 case, carried the highest probability of market penetration. However, the cumulative probability approached 1, that *all* price strategies would eventually effect penetration of market segment A by the end of the simulation period. This behavior stems from the impact of price decreases assumed to be initiated by Kromel *competi-*

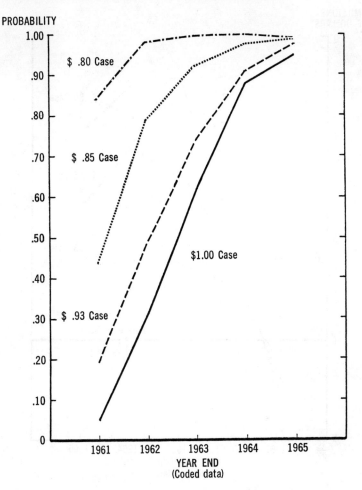

Figure 2. Cumulative probability of Kromel's penetration of market segment A (as a function of time and initial price)

tors (if penetration were not initially effected under the original price strategies) which in turn changed the probability of Kromel's penetration of segment A in later years, since this probability was related to price.

Figure 3 shows the expected incremental sales dollars (obtained by subtracting the expected outcomes of the $1.00 case, used as a reference base, from the expected outcomes of each of the other three cases respectively) generated for Everclear under each price strategy. While some tapering off in average sales dollars generated from the price reduction cases compared to the $1.00 case can be noted near the end of the simulation period, this tapering off is less pronounced than that which would be experienced by the total Kromel industry.

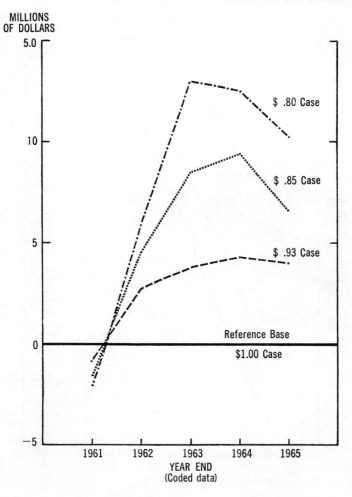

Figure 3. Kromel sales volume—Everclear Plastics Co. (incremental sales dollars generated over $1.00 case)

The reason for this different pattern is that the price reduction strategies (by reducing the probability of future capacity expansion on the part of existing and potential Kromel competitors) led to gains in Everclear's market share, relative to market share under the $1.00 case. These increases in Everclear's market share, under the price reduction strategies, partially offset the decline in incremental sales dollar gains (experienced by the Kromel industry near the end of the period) and thus explain the difference in sales patterns that would be observed between Everclear and the Kromel industry.

Figure 4 summarizes the behavior of Everclear's average, year-by-

Table 2

Kromel Model — Expected Value of Cumulative, Compounded Net Profits

The mathematical model used to determine the expected values of Everclear's cumulative, compounded net profits was as follows:

$$CCN\ (X_k) = \sum_{j=1}^{n} p_j \cdot \sum_{i=1}^{m} [(1 + r)^{m-i}\ T\{(D_{ij} - Z_{ij})(K_{ij}M_{ij})\}]$$

$$Z_{ij} = \emptyset\ (K_{ij}M_{ij})$$

$CCN\ (X_k)$ = Expected value of Everclear's cumulative, compounded net profits under each X_k price strategy $(k = 1, \ldots, 4)$.

p_j = Probability assigned to the j th outcome $(j = 1, 2, \ldots, n)$.

r = Interest rate per annum, expressed decimally.

T = Ratio of net to gross profits of Everclear's Kromel operation (assumed constant in the study).

D_{ij} = Kromel price in \$/pound in the i th year $(i = 1, 2, \ldots, m)$ for the j th outcome.

Z_{ij} = Cost in \$/pound of Everclear's Kromel resin in the i th year for the j th outcome. (This cost is a function of the amount of Kromel pounds sold by Everclear.)

$\emptyset$ = Function of.

K_{ij} = Everclear's over-all market share of Kromel Industry sales (in pounds) in the i th year for the j th outcome (expressed decimally).

M_{ij} = Kromel Industry poundage (summed over all four market segments) in the i th year for the j th outcome.

year (compounded) net profits performance again on an incremental basis compared to the *\$1.00 case*. As would be expected, time lags in the penetration of segment A, under the price reduction strategies, result in an early profit penalty compared to the *\$1.00 case*. This penalty is later overbalanced by the additional sales dollars accruing from earlier (on the average) penetration of segment A under the price reduction strategies versus the status quo price case.

The overall performance of each pricing strategy on Everclear's cumulative, compounded net profits position (expected value basis) at the *end* of the 5-year planning period is shown in Table 3. These values were obtained by application of the formula shown in Table 2.

Table 3 shows that all of the price reduction strategies yield expected payoffs which exceed the *\$1.00 case*. These additional profits stem from two principal sources: (a) the higher profits generated in the middle portion of the planning period, as a function of the increased probability of effecting penetration of market segment A, and its associated effect on Kromel industry sales in market segments B, C, and D; and (b) the higher market share for Everclear, resulting from the influence of the price reduction strategies on lowering the probability of capacity expansion and/or entry by Kromel competitors (existing or potential). These combined factors

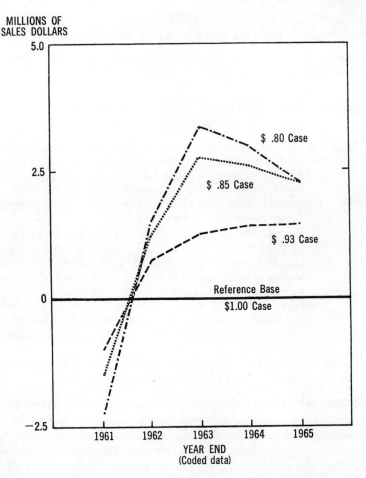

Figure 4. Compounded year-by-year net profits of Everclear Plastics Co. (compound rate equals 6% annually)

overbalance the lower profit margins per pound associated with the price reduction strategies compared to the *$1.00 case*.

However, a relevant question arose concerning the influence of the more favorable market share factor (under the price reduction cases) on the outcomes of these strategies vs. the *$1.00 case*. Suppose that no favorable difference in market share were obtained under the price reduction strategies compared to the no-price reduction case. That is, suppose the probability that lower Kromel price would discourage future competitive expansion of Kromel industry capacity in the 1963–64 period were zero. How would this affect Everclear's profit position?

In order to test the impact of this variable on Everclear's cumulative, compounded net profits, the market share factor was held constant at the trend level estimated under the no-price reduction, or $1.00 case, over the simulation period. This analysis resulted in the formation given in Table 4.

It is clear from Table 4 that the market share factor is important in producing Everclear's higher profit position as associated with the price reduction alternatives noted in Table 3. If increased share for Everclear were *not* obtained in the 1963–65 period (relative to the share expected under the $1.00 case), all strategies would yield close to equal payoffs. That is, over the planning period, the increased sales volume resulting from earlier (on the average) penetration of segment A under the price reduction strategies just about balances the less favorable profit margins associated with these strategies.

However, beyond the planning period, all strategies have for all practical purposes accomplished penetration of segment A. The impact of *higher market share* for Everclear thus assumes an important role toward maintaining higher payoffs for the price reduction cases versus the $1.00 case.

When computer run results were analyzed for the sub-cases (varying the total market forecast and cost of capital variables), it was found that the study outcomes were not sensitive to these factors. Although the absolute levels of all payoffs changed, no appreciable change was noted in their relative standing.

In Summary

This illustration has shown two principal findings regarding the expected payoffs associated with the alternative courses of action formulated by Everclear: (a) all price reduction strategies result in higher expected payoffs than that associated with the status quo pricing case and of these, the $.80 case leads to the largest expected value; (b) the higher payoffs associated with the price reduction strategies are quite sensitive to the assumption that Everclear's future market share would be favorably influenced by reductions in Kromel price.

Everclear's management is now at least in a position to appraise the *financial implications* of its marketing assumptions in order to arrive at a reasoned selection among alternative choices.

IMPLICATIONS

The preceding illustration indicates the extent of problem detail which can be (and frequently must be) introduced to reflect adequately the characteristics of real market situations. Nevertheless, this illustration omits some important features of Bayesian decision theory.

Table 3
Cumulative, Compounded Net Profits — Everclear Plastics Co.
(1961-65)

Price strategy	End of period profit position
$1.00 case	$26.5 million
.93 case	30.3 million
.85 case	33.9 million
.80 case	34.9 million

Table 4
Profit Position — Market Share Held Constant
(Everclear's Cumulative, Compounded Net Profits; 1961–65)

Price strategy	End of period profit position
$1.00 case	$26.5 million
.93 case	26.9 million
.85 case	27.4 million
.80 case	25.2 million

First, payoffs were expressed in monetary terms (cumulative, compounded net profits) rather than utility, in the von Neumann-Morgenstern sense, as discussed by Schlaifer. One assumes implicitly, then, that utility is linear with money. As tempting as this assumption may be, some small-scale studies at Du Pont in which attempts were made to construct empirical utility functions raise some questions regarding the assumption of linearity. However, this feature of the Bayesian approach may well take many years of further education and development before it may find regular application on the industrial scene.

Second, while a plethora of Bayesian prior probabilities were used in this problem, no mention was made of analyzing sample data and calculating *posterior* probabilities. How does one investigate states of nature in problems of this type? Certainly the problems of conducting meaningful experiments are hardly trivial in pricing problems, or the general area of market planning.

Third, just how detailed a structure can be warranted, particularly when the imputs to the problem are largely subjective in character? One may obviously over-structure as well as under-structure a problem. This *caveat*, however, applies to all model building. While sensitivity analysis may be used to shed light on which variables "make a difference," the fact remains that the model-building process is still based largely on the builder's intuitive grasp of problem essentials and the interplay between analyst and decision maker. The structure of the problem discussed in this article turned out to be complex precisely because the variables included *were* deemed important by the decision maker(s). And part of the analyst's job is thus to examine the impact of supposedly important variables on the relevant payoff junction and then feed back his findings to the decision maker.

Finally, in conducting this study, realistic problems have a way of generating quite a lot of arithmetic detail, for example, a multi-stage set of alternative states of nature and payoffs. Implementation of the Bayesian approach must, therefore, frequently be aided by recourse to a high-speed computing device. Moreover, a computer model also facilitates the task of running sensitivity analyses concerning either changes in probabilities originally assigned to states of nature or changes in the payoff values related to any particular combination of state of nature and course of action.

Our experience has indicated that the Bayesian approach, even coupled with the ancillary techniques of computer simulation and sensitivity analysis, does not offer any foolproof procedure for "solving" market planning problems. Still, it would seem that this method *does* offer definite advantage over the more traditional techniques usually associated with market planning. Traditional techniques rarely consider *alternative* states of nature, let alone assigning prior probabilities to their occurrence. Moreover, traditional market planning techniques seldom provide for testing the sensitivity of the study's outcomes to departures in the basic assumptions.

At the very least, the Bayesian model forces a more rigorous approach to market planning problems and offers a useful device for quickly finding the financial implications of assumptions about the occurrence of alternative states of nature. In time, this procedure coupled with a more sophisticated approach to the design, collection, and interpretation of field data appears capable of providing an up-to-date and flexible means to meet the more stringent demands of dynamic decision situations, so typical in the problems faced by the marketing manager.

V. Marketing Tomorrow

INTRODUCTION

Marketing must inevitably change, either voluntarily or involuntarily. Voluntary change and improvement will occur within marketing as a profession and an academic pursuit if those involved take appropriate action when the need arises.

The areas of change include research methods, applications of this research, and, in general, the acceptance of a never-ending need for change resulting from growth outside the firm and the possibilities of improvement from within.

Involuntarily change will occur when a market grows or declines in quantity or, more importantly, in its qualitative aspects. In addition, political and economic environments can change in complexity to such a degree that a company's existence can be threatened if the marketing manager is not capable of adjusting to such changes. Competitive innovation may cease in some firms, but rarely can it be expected that competition in today's markets, which feature development of precisely differentiated and better products and improved management practices, will disappear.

Many of the earlier readings emphasized the positive, voluntary changes that have occurred and which easily can be predicted to continue. The computer, for example, has been recognized voluntarily for its positive values in certain aspects of marketing. Since its usefulness in the future holds even greater promise, other firms will be forced to adopt similar computer systems simply because they cannot allow more efficient competitors to gain the profit and sales edge indefinitely.

The student is invited to speculate openly concerning the eventual value that certain lines of research may achieve for marketing. This type of thinking need not be limited to the two articles here. Instead, a creative search of prior readings and other materials reviewed by the student should ultimately prove to his satisfaction that marketing is only beginning to move toward its destination as a discipline that can efficiently serve society, the firm, and thus, the marketing manager.

42. The future challenges marketing

ROBERT C. GARRETSON and FERDINAND F. MAUSER

Since the end of the 1929–1933 depression, the gross national product of the United States has increased from $127 billion to $550 billion. Over the span of 30 years a total of more than $6 trillion worth of production has been added to what would have been produced at the 1933 rate. This astonishing increment was accomplished largely as a result of improved production methods and facilities.

As Leonard Silk, author of *The Research Revolution,* put it, "In our own time some economists have reached the conclusion that technological advance has accounted for about 90 percent of the rise in productivity—output per man-hour—in the United States since the latter part of the 19th century." [1] Progress toward the complete mechanization of industry and the development of electronic controls and automation has made it possible to produce more and more goods each year. And until recently it has been relatively easy to find markets for everything that could be produced.

It is only in the last few years that the lack of profitable markets has seriously limited the rate of growth of the U.S. economy. To put the matter bluntly, industrialists and economists agree that it would be easy enough to increase total production at a much faster rate, if it could be demonstrated that profitable markets for the increased production would be available.

What is our gross national product? If present trends in population, hours worked, and productivity should continue, a gross national product of $1,000 billion annually—or $1 trillion—would be reached in 30 years. As Exhibit 1 shows, by 1933 another $450 billion per year would be

Reprinted from the *Harvard Business Review* (November/December 1963), pp. 168ff.

[1] New York, McGraw-Hill Book Company, Inc., 1960.

	1933	1963	1993
Population (in millions)	125	185	250
Work force (in millions)	51	80	105
Employed (in millions)	42	75	100
GNP (in billions)	$127	$550	$1,000
Household Consumption (in billions)	$103	$375	$700
Investment (in billions)	$4	$75	$150
Other (in billions)	$20	$100	$150
Per capita GNP (in billions)	$1,015	$3,000	$4,000
Household consumption (in billions)	$820	$2,040	$2,800

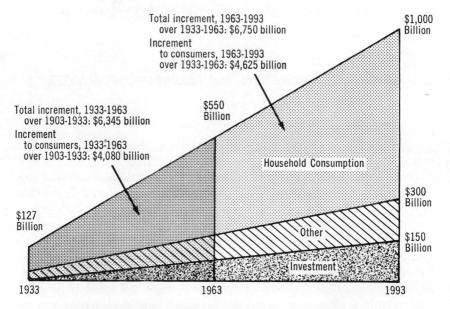

Exhibit 1. U.S.A. Projected Gross National Product by Final Use

added to what would have been produced at the 1963 rate—making a total over the 30 years of nearly $5 trillion worth of additional goods and services to be marketed to consumers at a profit (shown as "increment to consumers, 1963–1993 over 1933–1963").

Of course, the figures would vary according to changes in the trends of population, productivity, and hours worked; Exhibit 2 shows some of the alternatives for GNP. But the important point is that, whatever the assumptions, the marketing task is enormous—anywhere from $3 trillion to $7 trillion more goods and services to be moved to consumers than at present (the figures shown for increment to consumers).

None of these projections should be taken literally. Their purpose is simply to get a bearing on the size and kind of job marketing should be prepared to handle.

Can we do it? The lowest two-fifths of our population still have basic, unsatisfied needs and, according to some distinguished economists,

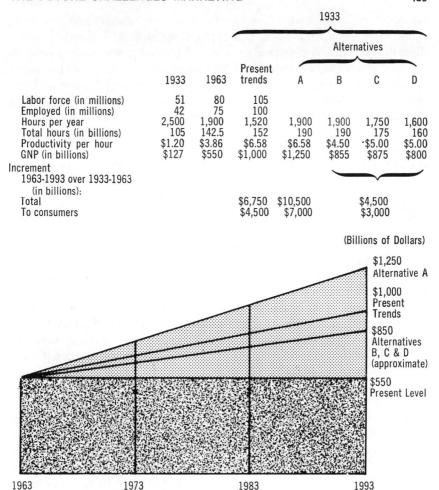

	1933	1963	Present trends	A	B	C	D
Labor force (in millions)	51	80	105				
Employed (in millions)	42	75	100				
Hours per year	2,500	1,900	1,520	1,900	1,900	1,750	1,600
Total hours (in billions)	105	142.5	152	190	190	175	160
Productivity per hour	$1.20	$3.86	$6.58	$6.58	$4.50	·$5.00	$5.00
GNP (in billions)	$127	$550	$1,000	$1,250	$855	$875	$800
Increment 1963-1993 over 1933-1963 (in billions):							
Total				$6,750	$10,500	$4,500	
To consumers				$4,500	$7,000	$3,000	

Exhibit 2. U.S.A. Alternative Projections of Gross National Production, 1963–1993

had less than a decent standard of living in 1960. But needs exist elsewhere that, while less basic, are nearly as urgent—better housing, better education for the children, new appliances, a trip to Florida, or a new lawn mower. Everyone wants to improve his standard of living, his way of life, his interests, his understanding, and his culture. It would seem to be logical and even moral for an economy like that of the United States to have as its objective the satisfaction of as many of these needs as possible.

With the statistics that are now available, and the easily obtainable information about patterns of consumption by various income groups and segments of the population (broken down by ethnic characteristics, education, age, occupation, and geographical situation), it should not be difficult for marketing to predict what additional goods and services of the kind *now being produced* will be wanted and purchased as the economy continues to expand and people acquire additional income and the chance to purchase more goods. The paths of progress are clearly marked by what has happened in the past; people have taken the same steps up toward better standards of living and have left a record of what things they desired and purchased.

But what will *not* be obtainable from the statistics and the records will be the effect of new products, new promotion, and new processes on the patterns of consumption. Nor will it be possible to measure in advance the changes in buying habits that accompany new cultural interests, broader education, and new techniques of communication.

The problem of finding what will be needed in the future is more than just a problem of adding up the figures for what is lacking today. It includes the exciting task of conceiving what it is that would be wanted if only it were invented or could be imagined. What is needed is not just more of the same, in different sizes and shapes. What is needed is solace, and comfort, and beauty, and a new way to live that is constructive and satisfying and always changing. What is lacking may not be things, but may be ideas and dreams that can be captured with the help of better schools and roads, and subsidized security as well as color TV and world travel.

In the last few years marketing has become fascinated by and engrossed with the potential it has discovered for doing a more efficient job of distributing available production. It has made great strides in the fields of goods handling, packaging, and communication, and has inevitably been led to concentrate much of its attention on the mechanics of getting the goods produced to market. It has learned to use computers for controlling inventories, measuring sales, and allocating production, and it has developed new mechanized systems for warehousing and moving goods from factories to retail stores. Retailing itself has changed dramatically with the advent of shopping plazas and discount houses.

What marketing has not done is to recognize the size of its future job and the extent of its responsibility for finding out *in advance* the quantities of additional goods and services that will be needed and can be distributed at a profit in an economy that could expand at a continuing rate of 3 percent or 4 percent per year. Production knows how to design the needed tools and machines, but marketing does not seem to understand that it must begin to find new markets to absorb the increased production. (In fact, much of the recent decline in the rate of growth of the GNP and today's continuing high level of unemployment may be due already to marketing's failure to do this fast enough.)

What is needed, essentially, is a shift in emphasis from selling to consumption. This may seem to involve a small and perhaps inconsequential difference in attitude. But it is the difference between (a) looking at the marketing problem from the viewpoint of the consumer, and (b) considering the same problem from the narrower viewpoint of the producer, who would much prefer to satisfy present needs with the kind of goods he already knows how to turn out and distribute efficiently.

It may also be the difference between (a) planning in advance to produce all the goods that the economy has the resources to produce, and (b) lagging a year or two behind until in the end the real needs of consumers are recognized and production is expanded to satisfy those needs. It may even be the difference of one or two percentage points in the growth rate of the economy.

Robert C. Garretson

Since the Garden of Eden, civilization's institutions and precepts have been based on two assumptions: that there is always a scarcity of material things, and that for the masses of people work is inevitable. But today these two assumptions are becoming less and less valid. For, as man comes to emphasize consumption, many of the precepts at the very base of his society must change. One key change lies in the attitudes he takes toward ownership. Such changes are already taking place. In the new world of technological affluence, the principle of ownership of material possessions by individuals is fast becoming an anachronism.

Through the ages, people placed value on ownership because there were not enough goods to go around. They were willing to accept ownership responsibilities to assure themselves of supplies of scarcities.

Reflect for a moment. How many people actually want to own an automobile, take home a "handy six-bottle carrying case" of soft drinks, or have a drawer full of shirts they can call their own? In the final analysis, not many.

In reality, what they want is a car in the model of their choice, well-maintained, kept in excellent mechanical condition, and at their disposal when they want it. Cars get bumps and scratches, brakes need relining, and all must be pampered into running and retaining their resale value. As for soft drinks, a person wants to have a cold drink in his hand when he wants it. "Handy" carrying cases imply returning bottles, lugging, and storing.

A man holds little affection for shirts as such. What he wants is a freshly laundered shirt with all buttons in place, in a weight and style to meet the seasonal and social situation he intends to face. Thus, people in a busy, rapidly moving, affluent society increasingly realize that they are not interested in things per se, but rather in their use in a convenient and worry-free manner.

The implication is clear. The affluent citizen of the next century will be oriented to *buying time rather than product*. He will take the myriad of sophisticated products at his disposal for granted. His chief concern will be to provide himself with free time in which he can conveniently use products that function to conserve time for leisure and pleasure. It is scarcity which creates value. Hence, *as scarcity of product disappears, the scarcity of time ascends the value scale*.

Since time grows more valuable as people grow in affluence, service expenditures increase proportionally as incomes rise. In the past, when domestic and service personnel were available, wealthy segments of society spent large proportions of income for service manpower (for housemaids, butlers, grooms, gardeners, game keepers, and so on). These helpers made time available for convenient and pleasant use of owned properties and possessions.

The affluent masses of today seek to free time in a similar manner. However, because the personal service of domestics and service staffs is not available, the factory is expected to produce the wherewithal for freeing time. Throw-away goods; leasing communally owned facilities (where maintenance and servicing responsibilities are assumed at centrally located places that are staffed by experts); highly processed goods such as frozen foods, instant coffee, and the like (which provide a sort of built-in maid service)—all of these developments help to free time. In essence, citizens provide themselves with time by shedding themselves of ownership responsibilities.

The realization by consumers that they prefer to spend their incomes for *time-oriented use values* rather than *product-oriented asset ownership* has enormous implications that are largely unrecognized. An enticing aspect of this switch in attitudes is that it holds a key to solving one of capitalism's basic problems, namely, the instability of employment.

Unemployment is a perpetual erosion which undermines the foundations of capitalism. During the first part of the twentieth century the idea emerged that modern capitalism's survival depended on its ability to provide continual production expansion. In the later part of the twentieth century, two essential corollaries must be added to the goal of production expansion: (1) production must be steady, and (2) increased convenience must regularly be provided for the products in order to facilitate their consumption. Most hopefully, the use-value doctrine can contribute to achieving these goals for stabilizing capitalistic economies. It is ironic that automation, which is roundly accused of causing unemployment, provides the affluence which will in the long run stabilize and expand employment.

Stabilization involves getting at one symptom of business cycles, namely, fluctuation in the rates at which individuals, industry, and government spend money. Fluctuations in spending reflect directly on production scheduling. Production must be steady, for this is the only means of assuring steady incomes for those who produce. Furthermore, efficiencies of automated production can only be fully realized when output is even and regular. Expansion or curtailment of automated manufacturing is so costly that its advantages are quickly lost when production fluctuates.

Stabilized production is also a necessary adjunct to introducing a still shorter workweek. The shorter workweek compounds problems in manufacturing and selling in feast-or-famine industries.

Elimination of fluctuations in spending requires that businessmen must increasingly apply their marketing ingenuity to secure regularly committed amounts from each individual's income.

The privilege of individuals doling out their incomes at any rate of speed or schedule they please will be a luxury which will have to be curtailed (not by fiat, but by persuasion) if we are to fully reap the material benefits of an automated world. The question is: Can we take advantage of the time-oriented use value to secure this effect?

If the goals of economic stability and full employment are to be achieved, marketing must be viewed as a social force. The public in general, and business leaders in particular, must better understand the place of marketing in the new society, for it is the force which will shape economic destiny by expanding and stabilizing consumption.

Methods for forcing consumption must be expanded and widely accepted as a permanent part of our social convention. The tempo of continuous consumption must be accelerated. Puritanical attitudes (mothered all these centuries by scarcity) that view excessive consumption as immoral must be discarded. For example, the question of whether we basically need or even wish the goods that are produced is beside the point. Thinking in terms of conservation of replaceable resources will not solve the problems of the Age of Consumption.

The complexity of the problems involved in the social and economic adjustments which will be necessary to stabilize and increase the rate at which the private citizen spends his money staggers the imagination. However, the problems must and can be grasped with purposeful vigor. The largest roles in overcoming this Gargantuan challenge will be played by marketing men. In their hands lie the keys to selling merchandise so the family income is doled out in committed amounts, without interruption, and at accelerating rates. How this can be done is not so farfetched as to evade the imagination.

One of the more promising approaches to spending family income in committed amounts is either to lease merchandise or to sell it on a replenishment contract basis.

Many steps in the direction of contractual selling and leasing are already in evidence. As instances:

A large appliance manufacturer has announced that it will rent home appliances to apartment-house owners. Not only will refrigerators, air conditioners, dishwashers, freezers, washers, and dryers be rented, but they will also be serviced and replaced by newer models.

Auto rental companies are already among the fastest expanding in our economy. One of the largest auto rental companies plans to extend a New York experiment with cars garaged directly in luxury apartments.

Department stores are promoting their own rental services. A leading store in Washington advertises availability of hundreds of items for rent, among them dishwashers, public address systems, linens, china, power tools, baby bassinettes, and wheelchairs.

Even further steps are possible. Under a contract selling plan, which is a method for getting people used to leasing what they traditionally owned, automobile contracts could stipulate, for example, that a manufacturer will provide the family with a new automobile every three years. The amount paid each month would be fixed and the all-important delivery date would be left to the discretion of the manufacturer.

Let us look at a hypothetical sales contract embellished with merchandising gimmicks. For customers entering into a contract for two, three, or four cars delivered at three-, six-, and nine-year intervals, the inducement might be a completed-contract "dividend" at the end of each three-year period which would make the next car 10 percent to 15 percent cheaper than one bought in the present manner.

Indeed, such savings dividends would be wholly practical since renewal sales costs would be small. Costs also would be reduced because the buyer under contract would be asked to indicate the model of car he wants perhaps six months in advance of delivery date. The buyer would choose his car by visiting a centrally located showroom where a complete range of the latest models would be displayed.

This method of advance ordering would create the ideal situation manufacturers have dreamed about since the beginning of mass production, for it enables the manufacturer to plan production on a long-range basis. Certainly greater facility in planning ahead would lead to cost reductions that could be passed on to consumers. The promise-to-buy provision in the contract might be for a minimum of two cars with a right to cancel at the end of any three-year period, the penalty for canceling a contract being the loss of the 10 percent to 15 percent renewal dividend.

The selling format of the Book-of-the-Month Club, which has been widely adapted for selling things other than books, provides us with a precedent for this kind of selling. The method has already demonstrated that such contracts force sales, for it has sold many books that would otherwise never have been sold. It is also able to sell books the year round, doing much to compensate for Christmas and vacation sales peaks. Use of contractual selling means that competition would be as vigorous as ever, just as it is now among the book and record clubs.

Variations of contractual arrangements, such as those mentioned for automobiles, could be worked out for many lines of goods. For example, shoes could be provided at the rate of four pairs each year, for $5 per month; three suits a year, at $10 a month; and so on. This is actually not a far cry from the monthly payment of installment selling which is already well entrenched. Indeed, it seems that the British may have intuitively seen sales contracts and leasing coming, for they use the term "hire-purchase plan" when referring to selling on the installment basis.

Another convincing piece of evidence that contract selling is on the way is the extension by the automobile companies of service warranties, which have increased from 10,000 to 100,000 miles in a short time. The warranty, in essence, is recognition that the customer prefers buying use-value and is not interested in ownership responsibility. Long warranties serve to stabilize the repair business, which illustrates in part how contractual selling serves to stabilize the economy as a whole. When a customer has a warranty, he brings his car in for repairs at the time the repair is needed. He is less inclined to postpone a repair for seasonal reasons, nor does he wait until the economic climate is right. Manufacturers benefit by being able to forecast parts and service requirements more accurately. Long-range planning can be entered into, the benefits of which can be passed along from supplier to supplier for end benefits to the economy as a whole.

Two additional areas for expanding and stabilizing expenditures hold attractive potential. One area may be called throw-away consumption. This is the new world of disposable tableware such as plates, cups, tablecloths; single-use medical supplies such as needles, sheets, and dabbers; and portable and switchable building décor items such as curtains, partitions, and lighting fixtures. Expansion possibilities for disposables are unlimited. Consumer purchases of disposable items are continuous and regular and relate closely to use patterns.

The other area for steadying spending lies in the provision of centralized facilities for communal living. People living in apartment houses and suburban areas increasingly provide themselves with communal recreational and service facilities. Swimming pools and tennis courts, guest and reading rooms, and laundry and hobbyshop facilities will be increasingly provided privately for smaller and smaller groups of people. Payment for such facilities becomes an adjunct to the monthly rent, a steady claim on income which is economically desirable.

By all these means, the increasing inclination of consumers to spend income for use-value instead of asset ownership can be capitalized on. This will help stabilize the economy to the extent that people thus are involved in long-term commitments that are paid for at regular intervals. In addition, people also tend to use up what they lease or contract for quicker since they do not take care of things as well. In this way, consumption also would be stepped up. Furthermore, requests for replacements for worn-out, obsolete, or otherwise unsuitable merchandise would be made as the need occurs; thus, the psychology of needing to make a decision to buy that upsets economic stability is bypassed.

A review of emerging consumption-forcing methods which seek to expand and stabilize spending makes it clear that most of them (leasing, contract selling, consumption of disposables, communal facilities) do indeed relieve the citizen of property ownership responsibilities. Use-value rather than individual ownership implications dominate.

This silent revolution—which substitutes use-value for asset-ownership and raises the relative importance of time desirability over product desirability on the consumer's scale of values—has fantastically important implications for the business leader. Businessmen must be counted on to provide the leadership which will gain the silent revolution victories in the marketplace.

The challenge for awareness by the businessman is two-dimensional. First, there is the social and economic dimension and the preservation and strengthening of capitalism. The business leader has to be aware of the magnitude of the silent revolution and understand the significance of how his role as the marketing leader and policy-maker is tied to production expansion and stabilized spending. Second, there is the business operational dimension. Here the silent revolution must be understood so that management decisions are geared to seizing the real business opportunities the Age of Consumption presents.

The change from a production- to a consumption-oriented society implies that enlightened business leadership must increasingly understand and cater to the many needs and desires of a society in transition. Consumers, on the one hand, must be given to feel that their property-owning standards of the past are not violated. On the other hand, they must be made to feel comfortable about a future which will be more rootless, yet will have the modern advantages of providing free time for leisure, pleasure, convenience, mobility.

Correct business decisions will be made most frequently by leaders who understand these conflicting needs on the part of the consumer of the future. Furthermore, tomorrow's executives will have to be fast on their feet. Use-value emphasis will most certainly produce a market which reacts more quickly to various influences. An economy with no ownership can more rapidly embrace change and improvements, for there are no property franchises to disentrench or dispose of.

"Buy use, not ownership" is the rallying cry of the Age of Consumption. The idea is not so radical as a first-blush consideration of it may suggest. As has been shown, installment selling, extended warranties, and growth of leasing have already led us far along the road to divorcing the U.S. public from ownership. Further evidence that indicates trends leading to contractual spending are found in growth of prepaid medical service, payment of utilities and heating costs in 12 identical payments spread over a year, and rental of works of art by local museums.

Provision for steady spending of the major portion of all incomes is the last link in the chain after mechanization, mass selling, mass credit, and automation. Provision for steady spending will forge the greatest material well-being the world has ever seen. By promoting the goals of stabilized and expanded spending of incomes, the marketer's ingenuity can reduce business-cycle fluctuations and ensure prosperity. Theirs is the moral obligation to do this even if in the process they may be damned and misunderstood.

Ferdinand F. Mauser

43. Computers begin to solve the marketing puzzle

Routinely, every evening at J. C. Penney stores across the country, a chain of events begins that reflects the changing nature not only of retailing but of every other marketing practice.

The small, punched tickets that have been taken off merchandise sold during the day are dispatched to either New York City or Los Angeles. There the tickets, coded to describe the merchandise to which they were attached until it was sold, are fed into machines that transfer the information to punched cards. From cards, the data can be put on magnetic tape or fed directly into electronic digital computers.

The computers have been programmed to know what each store should stock of so-called "staples"—men's shirts, socks, ladies' hose, lingerie, and similar goods.

Every two weeks, a computer will match a store's planned stock level against merchandise sold in that store; and, when a store needs merchandise, the computer will send out an order to buy, along with shipping instructions.

Theory into fact. A retail store doesn't have to be as large as Penney —1,700 stores and $2-billion annual sales—to use computers in this way to control its stock level and ordering procedures. A score or so of stores around the country are using some variant of the system. In fact, some local chains, such as Woodward & Lothrop in Washington and Goldblatt Bros. in Chicago, use more complex and sophisticated systems to give them daily reports of stocks and sales.

In theory, it has always been true that a store's buyers could give management a daily report of stock conditions and what was sold the preceding day—just as in theory someone in almost any business gets the pertinent marketing figures every day. But as a matter of hard, cruel fact —as opposed to theory—this just hasn't been so.

The importance of what Penney and other companies are doing is

Reprinted from *Business Week*, April 17, 1965. Pp. 114–138.

simply this: They are turning the computer with its fantastic computational speed into a new marketing tool. It may be just a big adding machine, as is often said, but it adds at a speed that hardly gives a man a chance to have a second thought.

Legerdemain. A customer of Owens-Illinois Glass Co. had that brought home to him recently. He had ordered some containers from O-I's Libbey Products Div., changed his mind, and called to cancel the order. He couldn't cancel; the shipment was already at his plant.

This disconcerting legerdemain was possible because Owens-Illinois is one of the hundreds of U.S. companies that are managing production, finished inventory, and distribution with a mathematical system controlled by computers.

O-I's data processing headquarters in Toledo (10 computers and 100 people) is connected by wire to 100 different sales and manufacturing locations. An order comes in, the computer determines whether the product ordered is in stock, indicates where it is, and sends a release and shipping order to the warehouse, or orders to a plant to make it.

What the customer who couldn't cancel was relying on is an order-shipping-billing procedure that is passing from the industrial scene. Normally, weeks elapsed between the time a salesman took your order and you got the shipment and the invoice. At Owens-Illinois, says Thomas H. Browning, manager of data processing, electronic data processing cuts the time to no more than 35 hours.

Over the wire. Helping to reduce the order-shipping-billing time is a system tying the computer that manages inventory to a data transmission network employing any one of a group of devices known as a Data-Phone. It is an adaptation of a normal telephone, and is used with what the trade calls a "terminal" (the exact designation varies according to who makes it).

Together they transmit voice and numeric signals. Instead of a salesman dropping around to fill out an order pad, orders are filed by punched card or tape over wires direct to the supplier's receiving equipment, where they are put into form to go into the computer.

At Beals, McCarthy & Rogers, Inc., a large Buffalo industrial distributor, the combination of computer-managed inventory and Data-Phone ordering in the past four years has meant a reduction of inventory of $200,000 and a sales increase of more than $2-million, according to Frederick L. Davis, the company's marketing manager. When you can know faster, and fill quicker, what your customers are ordering, you can carry a smaller stock.

It works if you're the customer, too. When you can get faster delivery you can carry a smaller inventory. Davis reports it is common now for his customers to do without general stores and tool cribs entirely. Normally, placing an order costs $15 and up; a BM&R customer has reduced this by 17 percent.

Taking over. The computer is flashing with dazzling speed across the panorama of marketing—which takes in the entire relationship between the designer of a product, the manufacturer, seller, buyer, and user.

Electronic data processing not only is managing inventory in nation-wide chains of retail stores; it is telling large department stores which customers are the best prospects for certain merchandise, is "advising" a food company when to offer special "deals," is giving rifle-accuracy to the calls of an apparel manufacturer's salesmen, is forecasting crop yields for a canner, giving greater precision to the selection of media by advertising agencies.

There are still plenty of skeptics. A computer guided by programmers unfamiliar with the specific industry so thoroughly fouled up one heavy equipment maker's replacement parts production that it took two years to untangle. Most retailers, particularly supermarkets, are loath to use computers as anything but bookkeepers.

Too late? Strictly marketing uses of EDP, going beyond inventory management, are still uncommon in U.S. business. But those who have sampled its magic are convinced the hour is late for the laggards. In a shockingly matter-of-fact way, a department store man in an Eastern metropolis says: "Our competition is finished; they can't compete with us any more. They started too late with their [EDP] systems and now we are getting so much of the business they'll never be able to afford the system to do the job."

His competition is about as old, as well-established, and as outwardly prosperous as his own store. But in the age of the computer, the hands on marketing's clock are at half-past eleven—30 minutes before the witching hour. The use of EDP is about to become routine in many marketing operations which until now have defied systemization.

Only a year ago, Richard F. Neuschel, a director of McKinsey & Co., wrote in *Marketing and the Computer:* "In none of the major functions of American business has the impact of the computer been so lightly felt as in marketing. Yet, in none of the major functions is its potential so great."

I. THE DATA COLLECTORS GO TO WORK

The potential of EDP in marketing is great simply because of a pervading belief that there are not enough good, hard numbers in marketing to make a fair-sized computer work up a mild sweat.

In the book, *Decision Exercises in Marketing,* Dr. Arnold Corbin, professor of marketing at New York University, Dr. George Blagowidow, and Dr. Claire Corbin, write: "To many people, marketing . . . is regarded as a business function in which most decisions are highly qualitative in nature and strongly rooted in intangible factors. . . . Hence marketing decisions are often made on the basis of hunch, guess, or intuition, rather than on a rational analysis of the measurable relationships among the principal variables involved."

John F. Stolle, a Booz, Allen & Hamilton vice-president and specialist in operations research, comments that "marketing is the most difficult area to get quantification in."

You hear that strain throughout business: EDP, to do any good, needs hard data, tons of them, needs them fast—and there is a lack of data all through the marketing stream.

The automobile industry is about the only one that really knows who buys each of its products, where the customers live, and other useful bits of information about them. In contrast, another consumer goods manufacturer refuses to advertise in Indianapolis because his records show no sales there; actually, his Chicago distributor serves Indianapolis retailers, but the manufacturer's own positive information about sales stops at the distributor level.

Bridging the gap. Yet, it simply isn't true that data do not exist in marketing; they exist in probably greater quantities than in any other business function. Until now there has never been a means to collect the information or to analyze it fast enough for it to be useful.

With the "peripheral" equipment associated with the computer— input-output devices such as the Data-Phone, tape, ticket and card readers, and high-speed printers, for feeding information to the computer and getting it out—the vast gap between collection of information and its analysis has been bridged.

Archibald J. McGill, an industry manager for the Data Processing Div. of International Business Machines Corp., figures that only 5 percent of the solution of what he calls the distribution problem is the computer, and 95 percent is the system. "Input-output devices are of more significance in distribution than the computer itself," he says.

There are computers whirring and blinking throughout U.S. business —for the accounting department. Now, with the input and output devices, the marketing department also is finding ways to get information for the computer to work on.

The Machine Knows What's in Stock

While the retailer is by no means in the van in the use of EDP, what's being done in stores around the country is exciting because it shows how much can be done.

You can see the future best, perhaps, at Woodward & Lothrop, Inc., in Washington, D.C. There, C. Robert McBrier, vice-president, finance, has installed what many authorities think is the most advanced EDP system in the country. Soon, Woodward & Lothrop executives every morning will get an 81-page report that, for each of the company's nine stores, will give the previous day's sales by store, by department, by dollar amounts, and a comparison with the previous year-to-date and the trend of sales. A record of sales for selected items will also be available.

The key to this astonishing flood of figures is a special cash register, for which McBrier designed the keyboard. There are eight keys across and nine from top to bottom, in addition to 13 control keys. The salesperson can punch in everything store management needs to know; every detail of every transaction is recorded on optical tape.

Each evening the information on the tape is read by an optical scanner and "exploded" into separate pieces for accounts receivable, accounts payable, inventory management, reordering and other store functions.

More and more. When additional equipment is received later this year and next, Woodward & Lothrop's system will include a direct connection from cash register to computer, a voice response from the computer when a clerk checks the credit standing of a customer, and even a daily report on the sales performance of each person on the selling floor.

Other big department store operations have many elements of what Woodward & Lothrop is doing; Joseph Horne Co., in Pittsburgh, is one step away from a voice response on credit authorization—the computer keeps up to date a list of accounts that, for one reason or another, should not be honored. Bullock's-Magnin Co. on the West Coast has its charge accounts so well organized they can be used for imaginative merchandising.

Goldblatt Bros., Inc., in Chicago, one of the most sophisticated EDP users in the country, even has a Data-Phone system to transmit daily sales reports of tapes from its 29 stores in the area to its State Street headquarters store.

Buyers' new role. Management's daily report of stock condition is already changing one hallowed role in department stores: the preeminence of the buyer. Since retailing began, buyers have been the leading figures, responsible for keeping their stores stocked with salable merchandise. But because of the enormous increase in the number of items a store now carries, the buyer has become too busy with a physical count of stock to try to know what the customer wants and when.

At EDP-equipped stores, management knows before the buyer does what's moving and what isn't. Some buyers find this disconcerting indeed. In the words of Jack Jacobson, Goldblatt's director of electronic data processing, they "don't trust computers and are not analytically inclined."

But others use the freedom EDP has given them to get out on the floor once more to see what customers are like. Jack Hanson, senior vice-president of Macy's New York, says buyers now have a chance to "get back into the market where they were 30 years ago, to get better prices and better merchandise."

Penney's merchandise planning and control manager, Emerson Tolle, sees another advantage to the end of physical stock-taking (Penney's counts stock only every quarter): "Instead of being under the counter counting stock, the sales clerk can be standing up taking care of customers."

Precise weapon. Putting accounts receivable—customers' charge account records—on the computer might seem to be only another accounting procedure. But it can be a merchandising weapon of profitable precision. Macy's has more than 1.3-million charge accounts on magnetic tape. Depending on what it is told to do, the computer will break up those accounts any way the store wants them—by alphabet, by house number, by size of average charge.

Not long ago Macy's had its computer print out a list of all charge customers of the Herald Square store who lived in four counties, and invite them to a special after-hours sale of furniture and furnishings.

The results can't be measured precisely because nothing like it had been done before; but compared with other special sales using radio and direct mail, the computer-based effort cost less and sold more.

Smaller Stock, but More Stores

In food retailing, the problems are different from those in a department store, and EDP has scarcely penetrated the retail end of food distribution.

For one thing, food retailing is about the most hidebound of all businesses dealing with the consumer. For another, a food store's after-tax profit is normally less than 2 percent on sales—so operators look at the cost of EDP and blanch. Yet, their low rate of return is in itself a reason to get involved with EDP; it offers opportunities for cutting costs and raising profits.

In food processing and warehousing, though, EDP has cut deep, mostly by use of an IBM-developed system known as Impact (Inventory Management Program and Control Technique). All major food manufacturers, as well as other companies that sell through supermarkets—Scott Paper Co. and Procter & Gamble Co., for example—have data links between sales offices, plants, distribution and shipping points, and are managing production, warehousing, and shipping by computer-programmed economics.

Latest link. The newest trend is a data link between a manufacturer and a distributor for the automatic ordering of staple items.

This has barely started. Kellogg Co. warehouses are linked with warehouses of Safeway Stores, Inc., on the West Coast and of Wakefern

Food Corp., a distributor for a group of New Jersey supermarkets. Pillsbury Co. has a similar hookup with Spartan Stores, Inc., a small chain in the Grand Rapids (Mich.) area—after having proved the procedure in experiments with Kroger Co. and Super Valu Stores, Inc.

Savings with this sort of system can be sensational; James Rude, Pillsbury director of information services and systems, quotes a Spartan official as saying the chain can save enough in lead time and storage to build another store.

There is no longer any question about the marketing power of a data link between supplier and customer. The clincher is what has happened in industrial selling.

Save Customers and Prepare for Systems

The data link between supplier and customer originated on the West Coast with Ducommun, Inc., an industrial distributor, about three years ago.[1] It is now in use all over the country, but has reached perhaps its most influential and precedent-setting level in the Houston area.

"Ordermation"—a very well-suited term coined by *Industrial Distribution,* a McGraw-Hill magazine—was just beginning to be known in Houston when J. K. Bevel, purchasing agent at Hughes Tool Co., took a worry to Jack P. Cunningham, whose Cunningham Bearing Co., does an annual volume of about $1.5-million. Bevel wanted to cut down on the time his buyers were spending in placing repetitive orders, and thought an automatic ordering system would do it.

But he was aware of one danger: When you have a number of distributors in an area, each may use a different system; so a customer dealing with more than one distributor could wind up with a roomful of incompatible systems. Bevel warned Cunningham that, as a customer, he would use one data transmission system and expect his suppliers to conform. But that way, he pointed out, a single distributor could wind up with as many as 18 different systems.

Taking off. From this came the Houston Industrial Distributors Assn. With an IBM salesman coordinating the effects—the IBM 1001 in conjunction with the Data-Phone is the common transmission device—the association now has 30 distributors "on line" to 10 customers. It will take 40 to 50 customers for the system to remain economically feasible. Cunningham hopes the idea "will really take off once the results begin coming in from the customers already participating."

Although the Houston operation is being studied by groups of industrial distributors in other parts of the country—and is bound to be a pattern—ordermation has not aroused universal enthusiasm. Distributors' reservations come mainly from unfamiliarity with EDP; some fear the system will make them lose contact with customers.

[1]*Business Week,* July 21, 1962, p. 64.

That fear is not shared by Owens-Illinois Glass Co.'s Thomas Browning. He asks: "How much does it mean, for example, if we can cut delivery time for a good customer from six days to one day? It may not mean much in one case; in another, it may mean that we have retained business that might have gone elsewhere. How do you measure that?"

Goal. The data link alone, of course, cannot make a radical cut in delivery time. It is an essential input, though, to a procedure that goes a long way toward the goal of building a "total information system." And that is the goal at Owens-Illinois, at General Mills, Scott Paper, Procter & Gamble, Hotpoint Div. of General Electric, and other long-time EDP users. Westinghouse Electric Corp. is one of the very few companies that already has a total system.

To such companies, inventory management, sales analysis, a rapid order-shipping-billing cycle, though rewarding in themselves, eventually become as routine as the coffee break. But they are a necessary preliminary to more complicated and challenging EDP work—getting the information to use in making the decisions that bring higher profits.

The ultimate question. There's an example of where this is heading in the Carborundum Co., which has been using computers for about 10 years and, says Group Vice-President Robert W. Lear, is "still experimenting." Carborundum, with more than 1,000 programs on computers, is ready for the next plateau, which is defined best by a series of questions Lear asked in a recent speech:

"Which of our districts, salesmen, distributors, customers, markets, and products are the real profit producers? How much does it cost to make a sales call? What does it cost to process an order item? If it's four bucks, can we afford to continue accepting five-buck or even twenty-five-buck orders without some kind of a surcharge or premium?

"What was the return on investment from our last promotion? Did we even try to calculate it? Which is more profitable—a direct sale, or one through a distributor? Did our last price adjustment take into consideration the distribution cost for each item, or did we just study our factory gross margins and assume an arbitrary average for everything below the line?"

Those questions get to the heart of the reason for using computers in marketing, for you can't answer them without getting data. Then, for the first time in marketing, management can ask the question: "What if . . . ?"

II. MARKETING BY MATHEMATICS

Dr. Wendell R. Smith, president of the Marketing Science Institute, tells of a former business associate who constantly used computers to ask the question: "What if . . . ?" He explained to Smith: "I can ask the computer without starting a rumor. If I went to the controller and asked him what would happen to our profits if we dropped a certain product line, it would be all over the plant before lunch that we were getting ready to go out of that particular business."

Storage in a computer of mathematical models that simulate a market or that duplicate a marketing situation is perhaps the ultimate contribution EDP can make to marketing.

C. A. Swanson, manager of P&G's Data Processing Systems Dept., lists four things his company expects from EDP: savings of money, accuracy, speed, and "doing things not otherwise possible."

There is wide agreement that model-building and simulation is perhaps the most significant of those things not otherwise possible without a computer. As of now, an electronic digital computer is the only device that can handle variable on top of variable and give management a choice of alternatives while there's still time to make a decision.

Changing management. In a masterful little book, *Mathematical Models and Marketing Management,* published by the Harvard Business School last year, Prof. Robert D. Buzzell wrote: "The model-builder offers a general, systematic approach to the analysis of management problems. To the extent that this approach is accepted and implemented, fundamental changes may take place in the practice of marketing management."

The biggest change that model-building is bringing about in marketing management is almost defamatory to mention: It is forcing management to plan, and to define its goals. To John Stolle, of Booz, Allen & Hamilton, one of the things that has slowed down the use of EDP and model-building in marketing is simply the fact that "it exposes the non-planners."

As Buzzell brings out, few developments in marketing have churned up so much skepticism and down-right suspicion among marketing executives as model-building and simulation. The man who rose through the ranks from salesman to vice-president for marketing usually has little sympathy for the "fellow who's never met a payroll"—and into that category fall most of the mathematicians who are skilled at model-building and simulation.

But already models are regulating some marketing programs.

It's Better Than a Crystal Ball

Just about a year ago, Chrysler Corp.'s top management asked its planners the sort of question with which all marketing efforts must begin, for it was about the future.

"Can you tell us what the market for heavy trucks will be in 1970?"

The market analysts broke out the significant components of the heavy truck market for every year back to World War II. They determined the relationship of truck sales, by weight class, to population, national income, industrial production, and so on.

In about a month, they had a mathematical model—a simulation—of the heavy truck market. They found that of 36 variables in the model only about a dozen had substantial significance. Applying these variables in different combinations, they plotted the range for heavy truck sales in 1970.

Shortly afterward, Chrysler made an effort to merge with Mack Trucks, Inc., but was restrained by the Justice Dept.

What's new? There was nothing new in the Chrysler people's approach to the problem. Examination of past relationships—multiple regression analysis—is a standard statistical technique, and mathematical models are ancient.

The new thing was the speed with which the analysts were able to process an enormous amount of data and in only a month or so give management the information needed for a decision. That speed was due to the electronic computer.

Light on lamps. General Electric Co. (one of its divisions was the very first to put the computer to work on business problems, in 1954) has at least two models routinely assisting marketing management. One is in the Photo Lamp Dept. This division has 2,000 distributors, who customarily order in September (Christmas is the peak selling time for photo lamps) and pay in January.

The model is constructed on the assumption that each distributor has an interest problem; it takes into account 25 different types of distributors and interest rates and arrangements. It is designed to give answers to the question. What will happen if we let distributors delay payment—will they order more lamps?

At one of GE's heavy apparatus operations, a model is producing results that you'd expect only from a ouija board. This division sells on a bid basis, and the computer model is programmed to propose bids on the likelihood of what competitive bids will be. Says a GE man: "They have been amazingly accurate."

Routine. Simulation with computer models also is routine at all of the big package goods companies such as P&G, Pillsbury, General Foods, Libby, McNeill & Libby, and General Mills. Usually, companies such as these test in models the presumed results of price changes and promotions and what the probabilities are of competitive responses.

Producers of consumer durables use models to forecast sales. International Minerals & Chemical Corp. has a model of its complete agricultural chemical business (65 percent of the company's total volume), which has a strange cycle: Its year begins in July, but no fertilizer sales are made until the following spring.

Surprised admen. Models were at the root of all the hoopla in advertising agency circles a year or so ago about using computers to select media. The intention was to simulate a market area, then test the exposure gained by differing combinations of media buys. The problem, to a large extent, was proper data. The agencies didn't have it. Now they are collecting it—and are finding some strange byproducts.

At Leo Burnett Co., Inc., accumulation of demographic and economic data for one account showed a wide open area for a new product. At another agency, the collection of data showed that the agency's principal client should have very high on its magazine schedule one of the "confession" books. The magazine has never made a presentation to the agency—and the client is not yet ready to concede that his customers have such reading tastes.

The agencies are still far from satisfied with the data that can be obtained. The biggest hole is pointed out by Seymour Banks, a vice-president at Burnett: "What happens when people are exposed to an ad?" The agencies, meanwhile, are doing the best they can with what they have.

The top agencies all have simulation models; Norman Sondak, data processing director at J. Walter Thompson Co., says: "We continue to build models closer and closer to reality." And at several agencies, work is beginning on models that simulate test markets.

Bringing Marketing into Management

Advertising practitioners have always presumed that what they do is more art than science. So it may seem strange that all of the larger agencies now have people practicing operations research, which is presumed to be a science—the science of management. In reality it is not strange at all, for part of operations research deals with the weighing of alternatives—and the advertising man may have more numeric alternatives to deal with than anybody.

A media man with one ad and 30 media where he can spot it can be confronted with more than one billion combinations. The computer—that big adding machine—is the only way to run quickly through those combinations and weed out the obviously worthless.

What combinations remain are subject to management decision. The example used is in advertising, but it could just as well be in other marketing functions. Throughout marketing these days you are finding the computer used to weed out the obviously worthless things to do, leaving management with only a few alternatives to consider—sometimes, even, alternatives leading to a go or no-go decision:

What would be the returns now, compared to 60 days from now, on a cents-off promotion? Would it be more efficient to ship to Point A from Plant 1, or build a new distribution location to serve Point A and a potential future Point B? Would it be more economic to double our order for fast-moving baby food and receive shipments every other week rather than every week, even though it ties up more capital? Would it be more profitable to kill immediately Old Product, the life cycle of which is ending, and use the resources to push New Product harder?

Total. Decisions such as these involve determining the proper allocation of a company's total resources—in other words, operations research. Only now are the numbers so necessary for operations research being assembled for the marketing function, for only now is there a way to work with them: the computer. The more EDP sophistication pervades marketing, the closer a company moves toward a total management information system, toward true operations research. Says John Stolle, the OR man at Booz, Allen & Hamilton: "When we add marketing to our collection of trophies, we will be able to build models of total business systems."

It will still be some years before marketing's scalp hangs from the belt of the OR man, but the way marketing data already are being used indicates some changes the future may bring.

III. BIG BROTHER WILL ALWAYS WATCH

What's ahead for marketing because of EDP is summed up pithily by Michael H. Halbert, technical director of the Marketing Science Institute: "A man can no longer get away with the excuse 'We've thought about it, but we don't know how to get it.' "

Today, if "it" exists in numbers, or can be assigned numerical values, "it" can be used in an EDP system. What this means, explains Robert G. Dee, vice-president, marketing, at RCA Electronic Data Processing Div., is that in the future "marketing staffs are going to get a greater amount of direction, and get a better hit value for the money spent."

One of the first groups to feel the effects of this will be the salesmen —no matter what they sell.

Bobbie Brooks Inc., Cleveland-based manufacturer of ladies' sportswear, presents a fairly common example of what is on the way. Each week, the salesman gets a report showing the current orders and past activity of the stores in his area. This tells him where he should be spending his time.

Bobbie Brooks also prints out a report of each salesman's results by style, color, and frequency of order. "By looking at the report," says Burton L. Kamberg, vice-president, "our supervisors can tell if a man has perhaps prejudged a garment and left it in his car rather than taking it into the stores." If he's taking Thursdays off, or avoiding certain stores, that shows up, too.

"The salesman gets used to living in a goldfish bowl," Kamberg says, "and we don't stress the Big Brother side of the computer, but the helpful side. It gives the salesman an excellent selling tool. He can, for example, tell his customers what styles are going best across the country, and help them in their purchasing."

Death of a Salesman, Birth of a Consultant

The computer not only is changing the selling function; it is going to change the salesman. He will have to know far more about merchandising than he does now; he will have to know far more about his customer's business and how it fits into an EDP system—already, some food companies report that their salesmen have had to show distributors how to fit new products into the IBM Impact system, which began with food distributors. In short, the salesman will have to be more of a consultant than ever.

Salesman's week. Herbert M. Cleaves, senior vice-president of General Foods Corp., describes the week of a food salesman in the computer age—but it could just as well be any salesman:

Monday, the salesman calls on a major food chain, passes right by the buyer and goes to the chain's home economist to ask her support for a new recipe that will be used in a regional promotion. Next, he discusses details of the promotion's advertising program with the chain's advertising manager, and of store displays with the merchandising manager.

Tuesday, the salesman goes from store to store explaining the promotion to the managers and making suggestions for tie-ins and displays. Wednesday, he is in the chain's warehouse to learn how his company can pack a product differently to save the customer money.

Thursday, the salesman is back in the stores to explain a new shelving arrangement his own company's market planners had worked out to solve a particular problem. The salesman spends all day Friday in his home office working with his district sales analyst on a presentation to a chain that does not carry his products.

The week has passed, Cleaves emphasizes, and the salesman "hasn't personally made a traditional sales pitch or taken an order." The orders have been transmitted electronically, "and his supervisor knows before he does how well his various marketing efforts are being translated into orders."

Eyes and ears. Data transmission devices cast a long shadow, blotting out the routine calls that salesmen have been accustomed to make. So in the future the salesman who now spends a good part of his time writing orders is going to have to spend more time digging out new accounts, and ideas for new products.

He will have one other, potentially enormously valuable function. He will be his company's eyes and ears, its intelligence agent, in his territory, compiling information on market growth and development, competitive efforts, and everything his company needs to know.

Lots of Products and Plans for Retailers

In perhaps no area of marketing is EDP going to make as many changes as in retailing—which lags not only in use of EDP, but frequently in modern business thinking.

In a study of department store control systems, Douglas J. Dalrymple, assistant professor of business administration at the University of California at Los Angeles, found "that a small minority of the merchandising executives . . . believed that stock turnover was an important control factor, but to most executives it was only a vague concept of secondary importance." Yet, fast stock turnover was the weapon the discounters turned loose on department stores 15 years ago. The higher the turnover, the higher the profit on a constant amount of money used in the business.

But the computer is forcing retailers to become aware of the importance of stock turnover.

The EDP way. Stock turnover is usually about four times a year for general merchandise and about twenty times for dry groceries. There's a traditional way to turn it faster: Simply sell more without carrying a higher inventory. But it's a rare merchant who can do that.

The EDP way to get a higher turnover is by keeping such fresh data on sales that you know what's moving fast and what isn't, and by having a data hookup that will give you automatic replenishment of the fast-moving or high-profit items. In food retailing, one estimate is that a 24-hour replenishment cycle will reduce inventory by 30 percent, without creating out-of-stock situations that hurt sales.

In general merchandising, Seymour Helfant, head of the Small Stores Div. of the National Retail Merchants Assn., says he has reports of stores using EDP that lower their inventory by 25 percent and increase profits by 25 percent. And a specialty store that formerly turned its stock six times a year has added one full turn.

Analysis of information handled by a store's EDP system can also guide store executives in when, what, and how to promote.

Big and small. The benefits of EDP are not reserved for the big stores and chains. "Any retailer, regardless of size, will be able to be on-line to a big processing center," says James Hotchkiss, assistant director of product planning of National Cash Register Co., which probably has more experience than any other computer manufacturer with the problems of small retailers. NCR, of course, has data processing centers throughout the country,[2] as do GE, IBM, and other computer manufacturers. NRMA is sponsoring a cooperative processing center for small retailers.

An example of what a data processing center can do for small retailers is found at Santoro Management Consultants, Inc., in Houston.

[2] *Business Week,* August 8, 1964, p. 66.

Santoro has 60 clients—whose volumes range from $50,000 to $500,000—
for whom it provides a full package: budgets, advertising, merchandising,
sales analysis and projection, inventory records. Says Mrs. Daisy Strother,
of Fort Worth: "The service took the butterflies out of my stomach. We
know which department is making money . . . our buying is controlled,
dead merchandise eliminated and we have reorder money."

At present, most of the small stores mail or deliver tapes to the
processing centers. But when Hotchkiss says small stores can be "on-line,"
he means a direct data link to some establishment using a computer.
Once such a link is created, it will drive right through a barrier that
(excepting, again, only the automobile business) still separates a manufacturer from sure knowledge of what's happening on the retail level.

A few months ago, B. S. Durant, president of RCA Sales Corp., did a
little dreaming for a group of marketing executives. RCA, in common
with other consumer electronics producers, is always in doubt as to how
much of its product is in distributors' warehouses and how much is moving out of retailers' doors.

Durant began by conceding that a small retailer will probably never
be able to afford a computer, "but he could afford a low-cost transactor
of some type. . . . Before the dealer goes home at night, he would put
the transactor device on standby. Somewhere along about a quarter after
two, a central computer would interrogate the transactor and take from
it the data covering the dealer's daily business transactions." Durant
offered a new, and provocative thought: The independent distributor
might have that central computer and be the retailer's data processing
center.

If the distributor's computer could interrogate the retailer's transactor, then each night the manufacturer's computer could interrogate the
distributor's computer. The next morning, the manufacturer's executives
would have—for the first time in their experience—actual records of their
product sales at retail the day before.

Gleaming vistas. This opens vistas that gleam so brightly that any
marketing man has to shield his eyes to avoid snow blindness. New product performance could be gauged day-by-day and promotion money
deployed for maximum effectiveness. A product that isn't going to make
it could be withdrawn from the market before it hurt either profits or
reputation significantly. When you know precisely what is selling where,
and when, you can identify your customers, plan future promotions intelligently, simulate all sorts of situations.

You would even know enough to advertise in Indianapolis.

EB 315
20